HONOR THY GODS

JON D. MIKALSON

Honor Thy Gods

Popular Religion in Greek Tragedy

The University of North Carolina Press / Chapel Hill and London

© 1991 The University of North Carolina Press
All rights reserved
Manufactured in the United States of America

The paper in this book meets the guidelines for permanence and durability of the Committee on Production Guidelines for Book Longevity of the Council on Library Resources.

95 94 93 92 91   5 4 3 2 1

Library of Congress Cataloging-in-Publication Data
Mikalson, Jon D., 1943–
   Honor thy gods : popular religion in Greek tragedy / Jon D. Mikalson.
     p. cm.
   Includes bibliographical references and index.
   ISBN 0-8078-2005-9 (alk. paper).
— ISBN 0-8078-4348-2 (pbk. : alk. paper)
   1. Greek drama (Tragedy)—History and criticism.
2. Gods, Greek, in literature. 3. Religion in literature. I. Title.
PA3136.M54 1991   91-50282
                                                  CIP

τὸ πλῆθος ὅ τι
τὸ φαυλότερον ἐνόμισε χρῆ-
ταί τε, τόδ' ἂν δεχοίμαν

Euripides *Bacchae* 430–432

Contents

Preface ix

Abbreviations xiii

ONE

Introduction 1

Mythology and Popular Religion 3
The Fragments of Greek Tragedy 5
Irony and Interpretation 8
The Need to Particularize 9
Tragedy and Cult Prehistory 13

TWO

The Deities 17

The Presence of a God 17
Gods and *Daimones* 22
Gods and Heroes 29
Divine Intervention 45

THREE

Challenges to Popular Religious Beliefs 69

Asylum 69
Xenia 77
Oaths and Perjury 80
Divination 87

Death, Burial, and Afterlife   114
Conclusion   129

FOUR

The Pious and the Impious   133

Creon and Antigone   139
Ajax and Odysseus   142
Hippolytus   144
Pentheus, Teiresias, and Cadmus   147
Troy and Athens   152
Polyphemus   157
Conclusion   158

FIVE

Piety and Honor   165

Pieties and Impieties   166
Piety and Justice   178
Piety, Folly, *Sophrosyne*, and *Hybris*   179
Piety and Τιμή   183

SIX

The Tragedians and Popular Religion   203

Aeschylus   210
Sophocles   217
Euripides   225
Exodos   236

Notes   237

Bibliography   307

Index of Passages Cited from Tragedy   319

General Index   355

Preface

The religion found in Greek tragedy is, like the language of Homer, a complex hybrid, a hothouse plant which never did and probably never could exist or survive in real life. Although the components of the hybrid are heterogeneous, they have been fused so expertly by the genius of the poets that the original distinctions between them are seldom apparent. At the risk of considerable oversimplification, we may designate as major components of religion in tragedy (1) the anthropomorphic deities of the Homeric pantheon; (2) beliefs and deities once part of popular religion but in the classical period virtually extinct; (3) deities, beliefs, practices, and cults of contemporary fifth-century society; (4) a concern with the morality and justice of the gods; and, finally, (5) contemporary or recent philosophical conceptions of deity. In varying degrees each element has itself influenced or been influenced by others, and traces of one can usually be found in another. Despite this, each has, for purposes of analysis, a fairly distinct character, and taken together they provide a context for understanding religion in tragedy in relation both to the beliefs and practices of the audience and to its uses as a vehicle of literary expression.

To further complicate the situation, this potpourri of beliefs, cults, deities, and myths is set in a legendary period, within a generation or two of the Trojan War, a "dramatic" time when gods and rituals are often in the process of becoming what was familiar to the fifth-century audience. Often the gods themselves are changing and new cults are being introduced. Several tragedies dramatize the very moments when gods, heroes, cults, and rituals are transformed from what the poet imagined them to be in a legendary past to the form that was familiar to the audience of the fifth century.

Attention to religion in tragedies has centered almost entirely upon the behavior of gods and upon the poet's and modern critic's evaluation of that behavior. On stage and off, gods do or do not speak or intervene in certain situations, and modern critics discuss at great length whether such behavior is moral or immoral by the standards of the critic, of the playwright, and of the fifth-century audience. The poet is judged to be religious and pious if he represents his deities as just and moral. Some deities of tragedy behave in ways which are, to say the least, problematic for a moralizing critic, and as a result their creator is, depending on the preferences of the critic, praised or damned for being a godless detractor of traditional religion. The underlying premises of such discussions of "religion" in tragedy are (1) that Olympian deities like Zeus, Apollo, Aphrodite, and Poseidon, *as they are depicted in tragedy,* were "believed in" and "worshiped by" fifth-century Athenians, and (2) that ordinary Athenians of the time included among their religious concerns the expectation that gods be "just" with a justice similar or identical to that expected among men. Both assumptions are open to grave doubt and require, at the least, examination in terms of what we know of fifth-century religion.

There are, however, many more elements of religion, and many elements perhaps more religious in Greek tragedy than the anthropomorphized Olympian deities whose virtues and vices the critics have meticulously weighed. My interest is the religious beliefs and attitudes of ordinary Athenians of the classical period. These are the beliefs about which they spoke and upon which they acted in daily life. In *Athenian Popular Religion* I collected a corpus of these beliefs as they were expressed in orators, historians, and inscriptions of the late fifth and fourth centuries B.C. The result was a set of beliefs, usually expressed casually, briefly, and starkly, beliefs for which an Athenian speaker or writer expected general acceptance among his audience. When we find similar beliefs expressed in the tragedies, we are now able to identify them, with some justification and confidence, as beliefs commonly held by the audience of tragedy. From the orators, inscriptions, and Xenophon we have the skeletal structure of this system of beliefs. Tragedies afford the possibility of adding flesh to this skeleton, because there characters in lifelike situations express these beliefs, talk of the reasons behind them, and act upon or against them.

In the plays many characters act with what would be, by the criteria of popular religion, exemplary piety or impiety. Occasionally these matters are the focus of an entire play; more often they arise only incidentally to the main action. But even short scenes allow us to discover considerably more about the nature of popular beliefs and the rationale behind them. We may know, for example, from the offhand comment of an orator or historian that it was impious to violate the rights of asylum, but when a dramatist places on stage suppliants pleading with a king to protect such rights, the abstract belief is brought to life. We hear arguments and issues, religious and other, that may be involved in such a situation. The belief, *mise en scène,* is given flesh and blood.

In addition, since we have knowledge of these beliefs independently from the poetic tradition, we can often isolate instances in which tragedians, individually or as a group, refashioned popular elements so as to make them something different from that commonly believed and practised by their audiences. It is at this point that we must return to the hybrid character of religion in Greek tragedy, because when a popular belief is remodeled or recast, it is usually done so under the influence of one of the other elements of that hybrid.

I consistently speak of religion *in* Greek tragedy and not of the religion *of* tragedy, because the individual dramatists employ religion in such very different ways. Aeschylus, Sophocles, and Euripides put different emphases and interpretations on religious aspects of, for example, perjury and asylum, matters which we know were of religious concern to their audiences. Often the three tragedians present beliefs and practices in just the form and context in which we find them in popular religion. When, however, they vary or refashion these popular beliefs, they may be drawing from quite different elements of the hybrid of tragic religion.

There has been an enduring interest, since antiquity, to rank the tragedians, to find the "most religious," the "least religious," and so forth. This quest, focusing as it has on only the treatment of the deities, has been, in terms of the practised religion of the period, misleading. Should we grant that such ranking has merit, the scores will vary considerably depending on whether we look at the behavior of the anthropomorphic gods, the presentation of the myths, the philosophical and theological theories introduced, or the popular religious beliefs expressed. For this last, my primary interest, we now are able to investigate whether a poet, in assigning rewards and punishments to characters who act, by contemporary standards, piously or impiously, is in accord with the beliefs of his audience. Consistent accord would suggest that the poet accepted, supported, and even promoted conventional religious beliefs, whereas frequent disagreement would indicate dissatisfaction and attempts at reform.

My focus and emphasis throughout are on the religious beliefs and practices which can be shown to be those of the audience of the fifth and fourth centuries. I do not propose to describe synoptically the religion of tragedy, a task which may well be impossible given the differences between the tragedians and even between plays by the same poet. I hope to delineate better the religion of the Athenian people of the classical period, both as that religion was practised and as it was represented in their theater. Tragedy often allows us to get beyond the simple statement of a belief to ideas lying behind it and to actions resulting from it. We also have in tragedies the opportunity to examine how the poets manipulated popular beliefs for particular literary and dramatic purposes. Despite their presentation in religious festivals, most tragedies are not, fundamentally, about religion. They are about exceptional men and women in exceptional situations. There is to most of these situations a religious dimension; it is only one of several dimensions, but the one, I think, least understood and explicated by modern critics. It is upon this and upon fifth-century Athenian popular religion that I would hope to shed a little light.

This study is the product of several years' work, the most pleasant and profitable of which I owe to Glen Bowersock, Christian Habicht, and their colleagues at the Institute for Advanced Study in Princeton. P. David Kovacs, Richard Hunter, Robert Garland, and Mary Lefkowitz have, in an encouraging and gentle way, offered many criticisms and suggestions, and where I have been sufficiently wise to accept them, the book has been considerably improved. I express my gratitude to them, and to Gail Moore and her staff, who have provided much valuable assistance and expertise in the modern-day mechanics of manuscript preparation. I thank Mary and Meli Mikalson for their careful and patient help with the proof and indexes.

A Note on Spelling

The names of ancient authors and their works and the spellings of the names of characters of the tragedies are, with a few exceptions, those of the second edition of the *Oxford Classical Dictionary* (1970). The epithets of deities and some place names are, however, in the Greek, not Latinized, style.

Abbreviations

Full references for all works cited appear in the Bibliography. Textual editions are commonly indicated in citations by author's last name only (see Editions Cited in the Bibliography). Journals, major reference works, and ancient works are cited in the general style of abbreviations in *L'année philologique* and the second edition of the *Oxford Classical Dictionary*.

The Tragedies

A. *Ag.*   Aeschylus *Agamemnon*
    Ch.   *Choephoroi*
    Eum.   *Eumenides*
    Pers.   *Persae (The Persian Women)*
    Pr.   *Prometheus Bound*
    Suppl.   *Supplices (The Suppliants)*
    Th.   *Septem contra Thebas (Seven against Thebes)*

E. *Alc.*   Euripides *Alcestis*
    Andr.   *Andromache*
    Ba.   *Bacchae*
    Beller.   *Bellerophon*
    Cycl.   *Cyclops*
    El.   *Electra*
    Erech.   *Erechtheus*
    Hec.   *Hecuba*
    Hel.   *Helen*
    Heraclid. *Heraclidae*
    HF   *Hercules Furens (Heracles)*

	Hipp.	Hippolytus
	Hyp.	Hypsipyle
	IA	Iphigeneia Aulidensis (Iphigeneia in Aulis)
	Ion	Ion
	IT	Iphigeneia Taurica (Iphigenia among the Taurians)
	Med.	Medea
	Or.	Orestes
	Ph.	Phoenissae (The Phoenician Women)
	Sthen.	Stheneboea
	Suppl.	Supplices (The Suppliants)
	Tr.	Troades (The Trojan Women)
	Rh.	Rhesus
S.	Aj.	Sophocles Ajax
	Ant.	Antigone
	El.	Electra
	OC	Oedipus Coloneus (Oedipus at Colonus)
	OT	Oedipus Tyrannus
	Ph.	Philoctetes
	Tr.	Trachiniae (The Trachinian Women)

Modern Works

A	Austin, *Nova Fragmenta Euripidea*
APR	Mikalson, *Athenian Popular Religion*
Burkert, GR	Burkert, *Greek Religion*
DK	Diehls and Kranz, *Die Fragmente der Vorsokratiker*
IG	*Inscriptiones Graecae*
Jacoby, FGrHist	Jacoby, *Die Fragmente der griechischen Historiker*
K	Kannicht and Snell, *Tragicorum Graecorum Fragmenta*, vol. 2
N	Nauck, *Tragicorum Graecorum Fragmenta*^{2} (with supplement by B. Snell)
P	Page, *Greek Literary Papyri*
R	Radt, *Tragicorum Graecorum Fragmenta*, vol. 3 (Aeschylus) and 4 (Sophocles)

RAC	*Reallexikon für Antike und Christentum*
RE	*Realencyklopädie der classischen Altertumswissenschaft*

Journals

ABSA	*Annual of the British School at Athens*
AJAH	*American Journal of Ancient History*
AJP	*American Journal of Philology*
BICS	*Bulletin of the Institute of Classical Studies*
CJ	*Classical Journal*
CP	*Classical Philology*
CQ	*Classical Quarterly*
GR	*Greece and Rome*
GRBS	*Greek, Roman and Byzantine Studies*
HSCP	*Harvard Studies in Classical Philology*
HThR	*Harvard Theological Review*
JHS	*Journal of Hellenic Studies*
REG	*Revue des études grecques*
RhM	*Rheinische Museum*
SIFC	*Studi italiani di filogia classica*
TAPA	*Transactions of the American Philological Association*
YCS	*Yale Classical Studies*
ZPE	*Zeitschrift für Papyrologie und Epigraphie*

ONE

Introduction

In *Athenian Popular Religion* I collected and described religious beliefs of ordinary Athenians of the late fifth and fourth centuries B.C. as they appeared in the writings of contemporary orators and historians and in dedications, epitaphs, sacred laws, and cult regulations. My attention centered not on poets and philosophers but on the townspeople of Athens, average Athenian citizens, those who, no doubt, constituted the majority of the audience of fifth-century Greek tragedy and comedy. A corpus emerged, not surely of all religious beliefs of the time, but of a good number which Athenians expressed publicly and for which they expected to find widespread acceptance.

At that time I excluded tragedy and comedy as reliable sources of information for popular belief, not because they had little to offer,[1] but because I found it impossible to isolate elements of popular religion in these poetic genres until I had developed a rather precise notion of what was—and what was not—popular religion. When a character in a play expresses an opinion on a religious topic such as divination, oaths, or prayer, there had been little, apart from the instincts of the scholar, to determine whether this character's view was one widely held by members of the audience or was somehow at variance with the usual view. Too often the procedure, especially among Euripidean scholars, was simply to dismiss statements of belief in the gods or in their justice and benevolence as "popular" or "traditional" and to label criticisms of myths, affirmations of atheism, or statements even faintly resembling current philosophical theories as "enlightened."[2] Crudely put, what appealed to the scholar's conception of what religion should be was praised as "enlightened." The rest, often the object of disdain, was merely "traditional" or "popular."

Statements about gods and religion abound in tragedy and comedy, and it would have been relatively easy to list or describe in *Athenian Popular Religion* poetic passages which parallel, to some degree, what is to be found in the prose sources. I chose not to do this, because even a cursory examination of the material warned me that the examination of popular religion in drama was no simple matter. The poets have interwoven these elements into the fabrics of their plays and, for the most part, they cannot simply be torn from their contexts for citation. A religious belief or concept may be expressed or even challenged in a play, but its full import or a response to the challenge may appear only hundreds of lines later. Often too the personal character, good, bad, or indifferent, of the individual expressing the belief is important in our evaluation. But it is not simply that evil characters speak irreligiously and good characters piously. Occasionally wicked characters use, in distorted ways, widely held religious beliefs to justify evil actions. The context—both the immediate context of the passage and the play as a whole—must be taken into consideration in interpreting and judging the import and significance of statements of a religious as well as of a moral nature.

Also, in contrast to orators, historians, legislators, and common citizens, tragic poets present religious views and topics in the framework of a legendary, largely mythical past. These are the days of kings, of Agamemnon, Oedipus, and Theseus. The resulting social and religious order is, in several ways, more akin to that of Homer than to that of fifth-century Athens. Into this legendary past are fit moral, political, and religious concepts and values of the fifth century,[3] but in the time shift they too can be transmuted in subtle and significant ways, and we must take cognizance of this.

But perhaps the most significant difference, and one that most seemed to recommend two separate studies, is that in the Greek tradition poets, unlike orators, historians, and governmental and religious authorities, had the inclination and license to alter, transform, and challenge current and traditional religious views and practices. Here we must be alert to how, and for what purposes, a poet is presenting or manipulating a religious datum known from other less inventive or polemic sources.

In understanding this process of poetic adaptation of current religious beliefs, we must give some preliminary attention to (1) the relationship of poetic gods, mythology, and popular religion, (2) the appropriate use of fragments from lost plays, (3) ironical interpretations of plays and scenes, (4) the tendency of Greek religion to particularize deities by locale and function, and (5) the depiction of cultic prehistory in tragedy.

Mythology and Popular Religion

Scholarly discussions of religion in Greek tragedy have treated almost exclusively the morality and the justice of individual gods. Is Zeus just or unjust, moral or immoral, in his neglect of his son Heracles in Sophocles' *Trachiniae*? What are we to think of Athena, who punishes mercilessly her former favorites in Sophocles' *Ajax* and Euripides' *Troades*? Is Aphrodite justified and is she wise in her vengeance on Hippolytus in Euripides' play of the same name? What of Apollo in the *Ion,* a god who raped a mortal woman, seemingly abandoned her and his child, gave a false oracle, and then lacked the courage to face the music as *deus ex machina*? How much responsibility and guilt should be assigned this same Apollo in the versions the dramatists give of Orestes' murder of his mother? Almost universally, real or presumed moral censures of gods in the plays are viewed as attacks by the poets on religion and on contemporary religious beliefs. This, however, is true if, and only if, these gods with their human personalities and passions formed part of the religious beliefs of the fifth-century Athenian public.

What most surprised and in fact disappointed me as I gathered the sources for *Athenian Popular Religion* was how very separate from these gods of poetry were the everyday beliefs, practices, and religious concerns of fifth- and fourth-century Athenians.[4] "The gods" and individual gods were often spoken of, but *never* in those terms familiar to us from Homer and other poetry. The relationship of the deities of poetry to the deities of cult and worship is ill-defined and problematic, largely because it has not been systematically investigated in either theoretical or practical terms. Students of Greek religious cults occasionally note the differences between the gods of cult and those of myth and literature, whereas most literary critics presume that, for example, an Athena of a Sophoclean play is to be identified, at some level, with the Athena whom Athenians worshiped in their city. But what is this level? The gods of cult and poetry shared names, and this of course suggests some identification, but, to put it simply, they shared first names only. We do not know whether an Athenian, as he made his morning offering at the little shrine of Zeus Ktesios in his house, thought of Homer's thunder-bearing, cloud-gathering Zeus. There is no evidence that he did, and the two deities, both named Zeus, are very different in both appearance and function.[5] Athena Polias was the namesake and mistress of Athens, with two major sanctuaries, the Erechtheum and the Parthenon, on the Acropolis,[6] but one is hard put to demonstrate that in cult she was assigned any of those features which most characterize the Athena of Sophocles' *Ajax* or Euripides' *Troades*. Likewise the Aphrodite of Euripides' *Hippolytus* appears quite unlike the Aphrodite worshiped in Athens.[7] And, conversely, there are among the major divine actors of tragedy no deities similar to Zeus Ktesios, Zeus Herkeios, Demeter, Athena Hygieia, Asclepios, and most other deities central to Athenian worship.

Because of the limited evidence available, it is unlikely that we shall ever satisfactorily understand the relationship of cult deities to those of poetry, but the most promising avenues of approach are iconography and aetiological myths. Cult statues, dedications, and vase paintings often do represent cult deities in the manner and garb we know from the poetic literature, and we may expect that worshipers visualized some of their gods in this form. But whether this visual image carried over to the attribution of the functions and virtues and vices that these deities are given in poetry is by no means certain. Here we may turn to aetiological myths, myths which provide an explanation of a local deity, cult, institution, or practice. Localized aetiological myths are the point at which worship and mythology intersect, and the myth, we may assume, reveals something of what local people thought about the deity, ritual, or cult.[8] Some such aetiological myths were dramatized, as, for example, that of Athena in Aeschylus' *Eumenides* and of Apollo in Euripides' *Ion,* and we shall consider these in turn. But aetiological myths form, if not in origin then at least by the fifth century, a group quite distinct from the myths taken from the epic cycles with their Panhellenic, anthropomorphic, and free-spirited Olympian gods and goddesses. My work in Athenian cult and belief inclines me to see the differences between these deities of the Panhellenic poetic tradition and the deities worshiped in Athens. The deities of poetry were well known, they were loved and hated in the literary context, and they were praised or criticized by poets and philosophers for ethical and theological reasons, but they were not worshiped as cult deities were. In the form that Homer and the tragedians present them, they did not have temples, sanctuaries, or altars in Greek cities. They did not receive dedications, sacrifices, or prayers. The gods of poetry are, I would claim, the products of literary fantasy and genius, not of the Greek religious spirit. Criticisms of these gods and of the myths encompassing them need not be criticisms of contemporary religion and of its beliefs and practices.[9]

Others may understandably judge differently the gods of poetry and their relationship to the deities of cult and may be reluctant to deny the deities they know to the religious beliefs of the Athenians. But all will agree, I trust, that in the wealth of tragedy there are many elements of religious belief apart from these anthropomorphic gods, elements which have been overlooked in our concentration on the actions and morality of the individual deities. We know, for example, that piety consisted of belief in and reverence for the gods of the city, maintenance of oaths, respect for the rights of asylum and hospitality, observance of tradition and law in cult sacrifices and in tendance of the dead, loyalty to one's country, and proper care of one's living parents. The person who violated oaths, maltreated those having asylum, violated traditional practices in sacrifice or the rites of the dead, betrayed his country, neglected his parents, or committed murder or other similar acts was impious and incurred the hostility of the gods, a hostility which might manifest itself in the suffering and misfortune of him, of his family, or even of his country.[10] It is this complex of ideas—the corpus of Athenian popular religious beliefs—and its presentation in tragedy to which I wish to direct attention. Apollo, Athena, and Zeus will appear now and then, but this is not a study of "the gods of Greek tragedy." That is more properly a topic of mythography, literary criticism, and intellectual history.

The Fragments of Greek Tragedy

Whether they refer to religious beliefs or anything else, two or three lines of a play require a context in order to be interpreted. Even with that context, the interpretation is sometimes problematical. Interpretation becomes virtually impossible when those two or three lines are all that we possess of a play. Well over three thousand fragments of lost plays by Aeschylus, Sophocles, and Euripides have survived, discovered on papyri or quoted by grammarians, scholiasts, anthologists, and other late sources. Some of these consist of only a single word, others of single lines, short passages, whole speeches, or even entire scenes. Many were copied out by anthologists just because they contain a complete, pointed, and epigrammatic statement of a moral or religious idea. The following examples, from Euripides, are characteristic of this latter kind:

> The gods turn the errors of parents upon their children.
> (980[N])
> Even if someone laughs at the story, Zeus and the gods exist, looking upon human sufferings.
> (991[N])
> The gods, who are more powerful than we, trip us up with many forms of clever tricks.
> (972[N])
> The prophet who guesses well is best.
> (973[N])
> The Mind (Nous) is a god in each of us.
> (1018[N])

Such fragments have played, vis-à-vis the complete plays, a disproportionately large role in discussions of religion in tragedy, particularly of Euripides' own religious beliefs and his criticisms of mythology and contemporary religion. Wilhelm Nestle, for example, in his highly influential study of the *Theologie* of Euripides regularly argues from these fragments to his conclusion that Euripides, strongly influenced by Heraclitus and contemporary philosophy, rejected popular and traditional religion, developed his own consistent theology, and himself became the poet of the Greek enlightenment.[11] Nestle then fits, sometimes with considerable difficulty, complete plays into a scheme which he has constructed from the fragments. This he sometimes is able to do only by invoking Verrallian irony, assuming that, to those few in the audience as sophisticated as the poet and the critic, the play meant something different from or opposite to its apparent meaning. In their emphasis on the fragments many other scholars who have written on Euripides are little more circumspect and judicious than Nestle.[12]

To scholars, as to anthologists, these fragments are attractive as precise and elegant statements of religious principle or belief. They also offer the engaging prospect of composing, from them and the myth cycle, one's own Greek play. But—and for our purposes this is the critical flaw—these fragments lack context. We are never able to know what motivated the statement, whether, for example, it is a momentary doubt expressed by a basically pious character or a reasoned argument by a blatantly impious individual, or whether, if it is a challenge to conventional belief, it was ultimately justified or refuted.[13] We may guess, of course, but in a study of religion in Greek tragedy there is little need for such guesswork when we have at hand thirty complete or nearly complete plays.

A brief but telling example of the unreliability of fragments is Hippolytus' famous line, spoken when he recognizes the nature of the secret (his stepmother's passion for him) which he had sworn not to reveal: "My tongue has sworn the oath, my mind has not" (E. *Hipp.* 612). Maintenance of one's oath was considered an important, perhaps the key, element of personal piety.[14] Had the play been lost and only this line, quoted by Aristotle (*Rh.* 1416a32), survived, it would be touted as an example of Euripides' cynical treatment of contemporary religion and morality. In fact it has been treated just this way by critics from Aristophanes to the present day,[15] despite the fact that the whole play survives and we learn that Hippolytus never acts upon these words. Quite the contrary. Four hundred lines later he says expressly that for religious and practical reasons he will *not* violate his oath (1060–1063; cf. 657–658).[16] When a line like this, standing in the midst of a complete play, can be so misused by critics, we can hardly put our trust in lines or short passages where the context is altogether lacking or, at best, can be only hypothetically restored.[17]

My own experience in epigraphy suggests that it is a mistake to argue from restorations of fragmentary sources to or against complete texts. We must begin with the whole plays, for there we learn the character of the individual speaking the lines, the circumstances in which he spoke them, and, if that is made an issue, their ultimate resolution. What the Euripidean fragments best illustrate is something we can also see clearly from complete plays: that Euripides was willing, somewhat more willing than either Aeschylus or Sophocles, to put into the mouths of characters statements that were blasphemous, impious, or otherwise somehow unconventional. As George Grube warned us years ago, the occurrence of a religious statement in a fragment indicates only that such a view could be expressed by some character or chorus in some setting in tragedy.[18] That and little more we have to learn from the fragments. This study has been based on complete or nearly complete plays, and fragments are introduced only as parallels, in thought and language, to passages about which we are better informed.

Irony and Interpretation

Since the end of the nineteenth century a major concern of literary critics, particularly those of Euripides, has been the detection of irony.[19] This is not the "dramatic irony" so characteristic of Sophocles, whereby the audience has been told explicitly something of which a major character is unaware and whereby that character's words take on, unbeknownst to him, double or treble meanings. This broader irony, "deep" irony, so important to modern criticism but unknown to theoreticians of antiquity, consists of, to give Dr. Johnson's definition, "Saying one and giving to understand the contrarye."[20] Apparently straightforward statements and claims in the plays are belied by the use of subtly undercutting words, by allusions to other plays, to philosophical theories, or to variant forms of the myth, by deliberate but often slight contradictions within or between scenes, by the use of images and symbols opposed to words or actions of characters, or in the expectation that members of the audience assumed, to give pertinent examples, that all prophets are corrupt and lie, or that "on the Euripidean stage whatever is said by a divinity is to be regarded, in general, as *ipso facto,* discredited."[21] Modern ironologists call into question the apparent meaning of virtually every scene and every play, and since Verrall's day much of the irony they have detected has been directed against gods, mythology, and conventional morality and religion.

The discovery of this "deep" irony requires an exceptionally close reading of the text (or, in some cases, of the "subtext") of the play, and for those less devoted to literary theory and more interested in the Greeks as a people the question naturally arises, to whom in antiquity was this irony apparent? The critics who concern themselves with this question seem to agree that only a small group (in addition to the poet, of course) of "enlightened," "sophisticated," and "intelligent" spectators would grasp the ironic or full meaning of the play.[22] The rest, "the great mass of the Athenian public," as Nestle puts it, would have to content themselves with the play's apparent meaning.[23]

My interest happens to be with this large group of average Athenians, "the great mass of the Athenian public," and I am most concerned to understand how they saw their own religious beliefs dramatized upon the stage. They may have lacked sufficient literary training and imagination to follow the ironic "subtext" of, say, Euripides' *Suppliants,* but they did have their own religious beliefs and every year saw these represented, in various and sundry ways, in their theater. Since my topic is the average Athenian citizen, his religious beliefs, and their presentation on the Athenian stage, I may perhaps be forgiven for not embracing or even repeating interpretations of plays, passages, and characters which even their proponents consider intelligible to only a handful of the audience. Those few enlightened Athenians, if they existed, would themselves be a fascinating subject of inquiry, but they have little to contribute to the subject of Athenian popular religion.

The Need to Particularize

The Helen of Euripides' *Helen,* produced in 412, spent the years of the war chastely in Egypt, while only an image of her was in Troy, sleeping with Paris. The Helen of Euripides' *Troades,* a play produced just three years earlier, was with Paris at Troy and is a real Helen; no thought of an image or of a Helen in Egypt is possible. In Sophocles' *Antigone* Creon defies the laws of the gods and lacks basic human sympathies. In the *Oedipus Tyrannus* he is not heroic, to be sure, but full of respect for the gods and of concern for his fellow man. In the *Oedipus at Colonus* we find him again impious and villainous. The Agamemnon of Sophocles' *Ajax* is as impious and unfeeling as his brother Menelaus in attempting to prevent Ajax' burial, but in Euripides' *Hecuba* an Agamemnon with some moral authority assists Hecuba in her vengeance on the immoral, impious Polymestor. Such variations in conception of the "same" myth cycle and the "same" character between plays could be multiplied manyfold. Tragic poets had the license, within rather broad limits, to choose or create for each play one version of the myth and one conception of their characters. We can expect in this regard to find consistency within a play, but have no right to expect it—without evidence to the contrary—between plays, even between plays by the same poet.

This principle is acknowledged for human characters and myths but is not nearly so well observed when gods, seers, rituals, or other aspects of religion become the topic of discussion or interpretation. A common assumption in critical literature, particularly that concerning Sophocles and Euripides, is that Zeus is Zeus, Apollo is Apollo, Artemis is Artemis, and that's that. Deities are treated as fixtures with stable characters and characteristics, and what ill or good is said of a deity in one play may therefore be applied to the same deity in another play. This, of course, often results in the discovery of irony. But in fact characteristics of deities and often their fundamental natures vary markedly from play to play. The Artemises of Euripides' *Hippolytus* and *Iphigeneia among the Taurians* are each carefully delineated but have almost nothing—apart from their names—in common. So too the Athenas of Aeschylus' *Eumenides* and Sophocles' *Ajax*, or the Zeuses of the *Agamemnon* and *Prometheus*. The tragic poet makes of a god, as of a myth or a human character, what he wants him to be for his purposes in a given play, and in this process he has, for at least two reasons, considerable latitude.

First, the gods of tragedy are, like all gods of Greek literature, hybrids with various and sundry components from poetic (especially epic) and philosophical traditions, from cult, and from the poets' own inventiveness. The gods' myths are much more broad, layered, and variegated than those of individual human characters such as Agamemnon and Creon, and the poet therefore had a far larger pool of material from which to create his god.

The second factor is the audience's own familiarity with significantly different conceptions of the "same" deity in practised religion as well as in literature. Greek popular religion was highly particularized: in a particular place one appealed to a particular deity to fulfill a particular need.[24] As place (even within the same city) or need changed, so did the deity, often in basic nature and function if not in name. To Athenians Athena Polias, Athena Skiras, and Athena Hygieia were separate, for all practical purposes independent deities. They had separate myths, sanctuaries, cult officials, festivals, and rites, and they provided different services. In literature, where the possibilities of portrayal were so much more extensive, it was incumbent upon the poet to define the deity he chose to represent.[25]

The deities of cult also varied significantly from one city-state to another, and dramatists, I think, paid more attention to this than is generally recognized. When Euripides set his *Medea* in Corinth, he adopted basically a Corinthian scheme of deities and cults. In Aeschylus' *Oresteia* different deities become immediately concerned as the scene moves from Argos (in the

Agamemnon) to Delphi and Athens (in the *Eumenides*). From the abundant and often contradictory cult and literary mythology of each god the poet chose what suited the locale and purposes of his play. For the next play he might choose considerably different or even contradictory elements of the "same" god. As a result we must take care not to assume that, for example, every Athena in tragedy is the Athenian Athena Polias, or that the audience would take each Athena in tragedy to be "their" Athena. If the dramatist wants an Athenian Athena, he must make her such, as Aeschylus does in the *Eumenides* and Euripides does in the *Ion*. The Athenas of the *Troades* and *Ajax*, however, are given no Athenian associations, and criticisms of them should not be transferred to the Athenas believed in and worshiped by Athenians.

The economy of Greek drama also affects the portrayal of deities. While an individual in real life might, in a year, turn to forty, fifty, or more deities to satisfy his religious needs, the tragedian had no wish to clutter the stage or diffuse attention by involving fifty, or ten, or even five separate deities in the action of one play. The major deity to play a role in each story was usually determined by the mythological tradition. For a tale of Heracles it must be Zeus and Hera. An Orestes would have his Apollo, an Ajax his Athena. But once the central deity was decided, there was a subtle but detectable tendency to concentrate upon him most or all the religious concerns of the poet and of the characters in the play, concerns which in real life fell into the bailiwick of quite different members of the pantheon. By limiting the number of deities in a given play to one, two, or a handful, the poets often loaded upon the chosen few deities functions and responsibilities which these gods appear not to have borne in practised religion. And, of course, a deity, once created, like a human character was intended to serve only one play. The same poet might, next year, attribute to a deity of the same name significantly different characteristics, functions, and concerns.

A similar variety, not so extensive but arising for many of the same reasons, may be found in the treatment of seers and religious rituals. By convention a seer in a Theban play must be Teiresias, as the Greek seer in a Trojan play must be Calchas. But that does not mean that in each play we have before us the same Teiresias or seer. The Teiresias of Sophocles' *Oedipus Tyrannus* differs sharply from that of Euripides' *Bacchae*, both as a seer and as a person. So too there is not just one prophetess figure. Theonoë of Euripides' *Helen* has little resemblance to the Delphic Pythia of the *Ion* or the Cassandra of the *Troades*. Each of these characters has been particularized, not only in personality but also as prophet and prophetess, and criticisms of one in one play cannot simply be transferred to another in another play. Each was created for particular circumstances in a particular play.

Religious rituals, especially those of burial, death, and sacrifice, also afforded to the poet a rich and varied combination of elements, any one or group of which he could select to describe or emphasize. The rituals become, in each play, what the poet chooses to make them. In Euripides' *Troades* Hecuba, Andromache, and the chorus invoke for help their deceased loved ones. No help comes; the prayers are in vain. In Aeschylus' *Persae* the Persian queen invokes her dead husband Darius, and in response he appears— on the stage. This does not necessarily indicate a change in religious belief in the fifty-seven years between 472 and 415 B.C., or even differing beliefs of the two poets. Aeschylus wanted Darius present; Euripides did not want Priam, Hector, and a swarm of dead Trojan men in his play. Likewise Clytemnestra's killing of Agamemnon in Aeschylus' *Agamemnon,* Aegisthus' sacrifice in Euripides' *Electra,* Heracles' killing of his children in the *Heracles,* and the sacrifice of Iphigeneia in *Iphigeneia at Aulis* are each drawn from the same sacrificial ritual, but the effect of each is very different. For rituals interpretation has become complicated by the modern notion that certain rituals, qua rituals, provoked an automatic response in the audience. If, for example, the Greeks assumed sacrificial ritual was an expression of social solidarity, of the horror of violence, of the cosmic hierarchy of god and man, and of such things, then the ritual, qua ritual, becomes an independent determinant in interpretation of a play, a determinant which critics often find in opposition to words and actions of the characters and thus contributing substantially to the ironic subtext of the play.[26] There is, however, scarcely any evidence that the Greeks recognized consciously or subconsciously in their rituals what modern theoreticians make of them, and even less evidence from the plays themselves that the tragedians then played upon the resultant "feelings" in the composition of their plays. Until these connections are made, this new theoretical movement has little to tell us of popular religion in tragedy.

The gods, religious officials, and rituals are, within rather broad limits, what the poet chose to make them in each play. We must be careful how we argue from one play what they meant in another. We are on safer ground here, I think, to argue from what we know to be widely held religious beliefs, because they would apply equally to all the plays. But if we wish to understand how religion in tragedy is related to the practised religion of its time, we must attempt to see each deity, seer, and ritual in the context of its own play and not generalize overhastily what is in fact particular.

Tragedy and Cult Prehistory

The surviving tragedies, apart from Aeschylus' *Persae,* are set in a legendary, prehistorical past. The dramatic time of most is the Trojan War, give or take a few generations. One, the *Prometheus,* is in much earlier days of mankind. These are the times of heroes past, times when, in several plays, Greek religion is in flux. New cults are being introduced, old cults are being changed, and functions and prerogatives of deities are being established. In most instances of change the movement is from a prior situation to a cult, ritual, or deity familiar to the fifth-century audience. The results of the change are the cult sites Greeks frequented, the rituals they performed, and the deities they worshiped. The "prior situation," however, the status before the change, and the reasons for the change are largely the free invention of the poetic tradition and of the individual dramatists.

The Erinyes and Semnai of Aeschylus' *Oresteia* are a particularly illustrative example. The Erinyes hound Orestes from the end of the *Choephoroi* and, as avengers of the murder of blood kin, intend to suck his blood. If the Athenians do not punish Orestes, the Erinyes will cast a blight on the city. Such Erinyes are nowhere to be found, in this form or this role, in the practised religion of archaic or classical Athens. How are we to explain this major dichotomy between the religion of tragedy and that of real life?

Aeschylus provides one answer, for in the *Eumenides* he describes, at considerable length, the transmutation of these hounds of Hell into the beneficent but still awesome Semnai ("Revered Ones"). He dramatizes the beginnings of their cult at the foot of the Areopagus and the new, positive role they are to play in Athenian life. It was this cult of the Semnai that fifth-century Athenians knew, and this cult was to maintain itself at least into the second century A.D. (Paus. 1.28.6). The original Erinyes, however, did not exist as deities or spirits for fifth-century Athenians and may never have done so. They, or at least the form and role they have in the *Oresteia,* were created by Aeschylus when he imagined to himself from what kinds of powers might have developed the Semnai whose cult was associated with the Areopagus and its court. Just as he imagines through the Pelopid family the vengeful form of justice before the civilizing effect of homicide courts, so he imagines what types of divine forces might have been associated with these processes of vengeance. The Erinyes were hypothetical, imaginary spirits, created in part from bits and pieces of the literary/mythological tradition and in good part from Aeschylus' imagination. In practised religion, at least in the archaic and classical periods, the Erinyes did not exist in Athens. Even in "literary" time, at least since Aeschylus, they had ceased to exist with their metamorphosis into Semnai those few years after the Trojan War. The Semnai did exist in fifth-century Athens and surely long before that. Aeschylus has put his characteristic stamp on their character and role,[27] but to the audience they and their cult were known and familiar.

There are in the tragedies numerous such changes of deities and cult, each moving from a hypothetical prior status to one familiar in the time of the dramatists. They are treated in their proper places later in this book. What is important here for understanding religion of the fifth century, however, is the distinction between these two groups. The deities, cults, and rituals to which the change is made are, for the most part, those of practised religion. Those from whom the change is made are almost purely literary. We need not, indeed should not assign descriptions or criticisms of the first group to Athenian popular belief. When changes occur we should direct our attention not so much to the pre-change status or the reasons for the change as to the results of the change.

Despite the complexities and problems of interpretation, an investigation of popular religion in tragedy is worth the effort. It complements nicely and in valuable ways what we find in prose sources. Orators, historians, and inscriptions reveal in passing, without polemic or introspection, much of the everyday course of religious thought. They give voice to, as Guthrie put it, "the routine of religion which was accepted by most of the citizens of Athens as a matter of course."[28] They represent the conventional, the consensus, and the generally acknowledged, but they scarcely ever rise above this. The tragedians, however, each with his own preoccupations, create from the myth cycles hypothetical situations that put these religious beliefs into conflict, challenge them, or put them to the test in tortuous ways. Ordinary and comfortable beliefs about asylum, *xenoi,* and murder are stretched and strained when they are applied to the stories of the Danaïdae, of Admetus, and of Orestes. The tragedians afford us the opportunity to see these beliefs put into practice, not in ordinary life, but in some of the most difficult circumstances the human mind could imagine.

Tragedy also represents extraordinary individuals functioning within a more or less ordinary society. In every play about a Heracles or Hippolytus there is also a nurse, a paedagogue, a messenger, or a herald, and a chorus. These choruses, nameless characters, and many of the minor characters often express religious views and concerns of the larger society, the ordinary society in the midst of which an Oedipus or a Heracles functions in his idiosyncratic ways. Literary critics look to the heroes and heroines, but in studying popular religion in tragedy we should devote special attention to the various background societies of the plays, the societies represented by these choruses, messengers, heralds, and nurses, because they represent, if anyone does, the collective voice, the *vox populi.*

In the very last chapter I discuss each tragedian's presentation of popular religion. There I am not concerned, nor do I think it even possible, to describe the theology or personal beliefs of the dramatists. In Aeschylus religious beliefs often seem the center of attention in a play, and while many of the beliefs he presents are popular and conventional, the theological scheme and the theodicy into which he places them are not. For Sophocles and Euripides religious beliefs occasionally become objects of major concern, but most often they appear peripheral, introduced primarily to create or develop situations and characterizations. Since they most often serve purposes beyond themselves and are employed to illustrate such a variety of situations and characters, we need not expect—without evidence to the contrary—that they form a consistent pattern or developed theology. Tragedies are dramatizations of human situations and events, not theological tracts. Consistency can be expected and is found within individual plays, but between plays, as with characterizations and versions of myths, there are significant differences. I hope to give due weight to the differences as well as to the similarities.

I leave aside for now, as I did before, Aristophanes, Menander, and other writers of comedy. Like the prose authors their media and their purposes differ so fundamentally from tragedy and raise such very different problems of methodology and interpretation that they require a separate study.

My interest is popular religion, religion as it was practised by Athenians of the classical period. It is from this perspective that I look at the plays and the three tragedians. Although problems of literary interpretation regularly arise and must be dealt with, I do not take up this subject in order to offer new interpretations of the plays. In what interpretations I offer (particularly in chapter 4), I look at the plays from one perspective, that of their relation to popular religious beliefs. A full interpretation of a character or a play would require many other perspectives, and I recognize that my interpretations are one-sided, but it is a "side" of Greek tragedy that has been neglected and misunderstood. I put forward my conclusions not to replace results from other lines of inquiry but to find a place among them and to be put into the balance with them. My prime purpose is better to understand Athenian popular religion. Secondarily I hope to bring attention to the genuinely religious element of Greek tragedy.

I treat religious beliefs in their historical and literary contexts, and, amidst the vast number of books and essays on Greek tragedy, I have concentrated on those which seem to me best to suit the texts of the plays and the literary and historical circumstances of the authors and their audience. In the bibliography and the notes I indicate only that modern scholarship which has contributed substantially to my own understanding of the various topics.

TWO

The Deities

Characters in tragedy address, pray to, and speak of a wide variety of supernatural forces, including gods of the upper world and underworld, heroes, *daimones,* and even fortune and fate. In this chapter we first examine how tragic characters recognize a divine presence, how they distinguish between gods, *daimones,* and heroes, and then what they expect in the way of evil or good from each class of deity. We conclude with the uniquely tragic *deus ex machina.* Throughout, tragic conceptions are compared to those of popular religion.

The Presence of a God

The Athenians, like most peoples, felt the presence of their deities in significant events they found to be mysterious and inexplicable.[1] There are some peculiarly Greek conceptions of this divine presence, and the following two vignettes from the *Orestes* and *Iphigeneia among the Taurians* of Euripides suggest these conceptions and how they themselves differ in tragedy and real life.

In the *Orestes,* as Orestes has Helen in his grip and is about to murder her, she suddenly vanishes. This miraculous disappearance is first described to the audience by one of Helen's attendants, a Phrygian with traits of cowardice, effeminacy, excitability, and fawning which Greeks commonly associated with such foreigners.[2] The Phrygian imagines that Helen must have vanished by means of drugs, by the tricks of the *magoi* (Persian priests),[3] or by a theft of the gods (1493–1498). The first two possibilities he suggests are un-Greek in conception and form part of his characterization as a barbarian. In describing this same incident Orestes, very much the Greek, claims he was "robbed by the gods" (1580),[4] with no thought of drugs or priests' tricks. Greek priests were sacrificers (ἱερεῖς), not magicians (μάγοι), and here Greek and barbarian are clearly and comically differentiated. It is in the Greek tradition, in both poetry and life, to attribute otherwise inexplicable events not obviously in a specific god's domain to a generalized, depersonalized, abstract collective of the gods. This collective is occasionally referred to in the singular, as "the god" or "a god," but most often, as here, in the plural, "the gods."[5] Unless a specific deity has been otherwise indicated, to say "the gods did it," "the god did it," or "a god did it" means virtually the same thing. In each case an unidentifiable divine force has intervened.

What happened was ultimately to be to Orestes' benefit (1625–1665), but here (1580) he thinks he has been cheated of his purpose and lays the blame on "the gods." Characters in tragedy are much more inclined than were ordinary people to impute failures, misfortunes, and other such bad events to "the gods," to this abstract divine collective. There was a marked tendency in popular religion to assign to "the gods" responsibility only for what was, in a person's view, good and desirable. For failure they blamed, if not themselves, then fortune (τύχη), a *daimon,* or fate.[6] Characters in tragedy also regularly fault such agents for their failures and sufferings, but—and this is a fundamental difference between tragedy (poetry, in fact) and life—they also accuse the collective of the gods and, of course, individual gods.

In a public funeral oration of about 440 B.C., Pericles, as reported by Plutarch (*Per.* 8.6), said, "We do not see the gods themselves, but we infer their immortality from the honors which they have and *from the good things they provide us.*" This statement, if genuine,[7] is a precious contemporary summation of abundant evidence from popular sources that points in the same direction. We know the gods "from the good things they provide us," not—for there is no mention of this—from the evils they cause.[8] Herein lies one critical distinction between the religion of the people and that portrayed throughout Greek poetry from its very beginnings with Homer. A religious system which presumes that its deities give to man only what is good and desirable differs in many essentials, in its conceptions of deity and of morality, in its worshipers' feelings towards the deities, and in its tone and substance, from a system in which the gods are thought to dispense misfortunes and evils as well as the good. With certain important qualifications Athenian popular religion represents the former; religion in tragedy, especially that of Sophocles and Euripides, represents the latter.

Orestes holds responsible for Helen's disappearance neither potions nor magician priests, but "the gods," divine forces he cannot at the moment identify. As Pericles says, "We do not see the gods." Poets, however, do see their gods, and Euripides at the end of the *Orestes* has Apollo, *deus ex machina*, reveal that he, under orders from Zeus, had rescued Helen (1633–1634). We are told which deity intervened and why. The ordinary Greek, much like Orestes, would have been unable to ascertain which deity had intervened in most events of his everyday life.[9] But the poet could, if he so chose, provide the deity's name, characterize him, and give precise reasons for his intervention. This too is, of course, a fundamental difference between the two religious systems.

Although Pericles did not see the gods themselves, a pious Taurian cowherd thought he did, and Euripides' dramatization of this scene in *Iphigeneia among the Taurians* illustrates possible reactions, ancient and modern, to a divine presence in tragedy. Some cowherds spot two unknown young men amidst the cliffs of a remote beach on the Black Sea, and they speculate as to their identity. They respond as common people to what might well be a divine epiphany. One of the discovering party reports to Iphigeneia:

> One of our cowherds saw two young men and came back on tiptoe.
> "Don't you see them?" he said. "These are some *daimones* sitting
> here." And one of our group, a god-respecting man,
> when he had looked, held up his hand and prayed, "O master
> Palaimon, son of Leukothea of the sea, guardian of ships,
> be kindly (ἴλεως) to us, if it is the two Dioscuroi
> who sit on our shore or those favorites of Nereus,
> the man who begot the well-born chorus of fifty Nereids."
> But another fellow, rash and bold in his unconventionality,
> laughed at these prayers. He said that
> they were shipwrecked sailors who were sitting in the
> ravine in fear of our custom, because they had heard that
> we sacrifice foreigners here.
>
> (*IT* 264–278)

The three men react quite differently to the sudden and mysterious appearance of the two strangers. The first calls them *daimones,* another common term for deities whom one cannot at the moment identify. The second man, characterized as god-respecting (θεοσεβής, 268), wishes to be more specific and suggests they may be the Dioscuroi or the Nereids. He adds a general, all-purpose prayer, "Do not be angry with us" (271).[10] The third cowherd to speak, the rash, unconventional fellow, laughs at the prayers of his comrade. The narrator, a cowherd himself, disapproves of him, but it turns out that the skeptic is correct. The audience know the mysterious pair are Orestes and Pylades and that they are in fact trying to avoid becoming victims for Artemis (69–75, 106–112).

The scene is conventional: a messenger's report of quarrelsome rustics urgently discussing a mysterious event and deciding on a course of action.[11] Here we have, as they call themselves, "lowly" cowherds on a desolate beach at the frontiers of the known world. They are not Greek, but like many barbarians in tragedy they are considerably Hellenized. Such scenes of disputing ἄγροικοι have an unmistakable touch of humor. Humor here also lies, I think, in the gods whom the "god-respecting" cowherd imagines. The Dioscuroi and the Nereids are each associated with the sea, and to this extent they are appropriate to the situation.[12] The two young men might well resemble the youthful twin Dioscuroi, Castor and Polydeuces, but how could anyone identify them with the *daughters* of Nereus?[13] It is little wonder that the third cowherd laughs at this. The Nereids are an inept suggestion, and it is an ineptness one prefers to attribute to a cowherd rather than to Euripides.

It is, however, significant and highly unusual that a correct view is attributed to a man "rash and bold in his unconventionality,"[14] peasant or not, while the god-respecting man is proven wrong. Some have extrapolated from this a Euripidean view that skepticism and rationality are the proper reactions in confrontations with the mysterious and potentially religious.[15] This is an attractive view, especially since in these very years (ca. 414), if we are to trust Thucydides and Plutarch, overconfidence in favorable oracles, fears aroused by the mutilation of the herms and the parody of the Eleusinian Mysteries, and delays caused by Nicias' "superstition" (θειασμός) all contributed substantially to the disaster suffered at Syracuse.[16] The historians unmistakably describe a brief period of intense religious credulity and fear among both the leaders and the people of Athens. The overtaxed religious sensitivities of Athenians in 415–413, however, involved beliefs about seers, omens, and sacrilege, all major items of practised religion. The implied criticism in *Iphigeneia among the Taurians* 264–278 hits an ignorant, credulous peasant who sees a deity behind each tree and in every cave. His middle-class urban counterpart was to be caricatured in Theophrastus' "Superstitious Man" (*Char.* 16) late in the fourth century, and the effect there, as here, was largely humor. Athenians of the fifth and fourth centuries did not see gods popping up here and there. The last recorded epiphany of an Olympian god in Athens was Athena's appearance in the middle of the sixth century, and that was carefully staged by the tyrant Pisistratus.[17] Fifth-century Athenians, like Pericles himself, did not "see" the gods, and, like Herodotus (1.60.3), would look upon such stories with bemusement. And so too, I expect, in 414 they looked with amusement upon the befuddled ideas and prayer of a Taurian cowherd.[18] We should not make of this charming little scene a rationalistic, "enlightened" criticism cutting to the heart of contemporary religion.

In the *Ajax* of Sophocles, Odysseus, an intimate of Athena very much in the Homeric manner,[19] learns from her directly that she deluded Ajax and caused him to attack not the Atreidae, as he intended, but herd animals (1–70). It is never said how Ajax recognized Athena as the agent of his misfortune (cf. 401–402, 450–453), but here and throughout this study we cannot expect the poet to answer every question which might happen to interest us. The chorus and other characters are unsure which deity caused the madness and for what reason. The chorus suggest Artemis Tauropolos, Ares, and Enyalios.[20] They are wrong, but the reasons they proffer are instructive: the failure to make an offering due after a military or other victory, or the failure to celebrate a festival (172–181).[21] Tecmessa, Ajax' concubine, attributes the situation to "the gods" (950, 970) and Ajax' odd behavior to a *daimon* (243–244), the usual superhuman agents of misfortune and death. The chorus and most characters learn of Athena's role only from the detailed explanation of the whole situation by the prophet Calchas (756–777), and the misguided Menelaus seems to have missed even that. In 1057–1061 and 1128 he continues to refer to "some god" responsible for it all. We have here the full range of human knowledge and understanding of an incident of divine intervention. That the goddess herself revealed the situation directly to her favorite is a feature of Homeric religion which persists throughout the later poetic tradition. The other manners and degrees of knowledge about the divine world are more from life.[22]

Gods and *Daimones*

The term *daimon* (δαίμων), in the singular or plural, may indicate, like θεός ("god") or θεοί ("gods"), the abstract, undifferentiated collective of the gods, but it may also, like θεός, refer to a specific deity.[23] Poseidon can be called a *daimon* (S. *OC* 709; *Rh.* 240–241), even by a fellow deity (E. *Tr.* 49). Similarly Apollo (S. *OT* 244–245, *El.* 658; E. *Ion* 827, 1353), Ares (A. *Th.* 106), Hera (E. *HF* 1311–1312), Aphrodite (E. *Hipp.* 1401, 1406), Dionysus (E. *Ba.* passim, *Cycl.* 524), and even Zeus (S. *Ph.* 1467–1468, *OC* 1480) are termed *daimones*.[24] Much later, under the influence of Platonic philosophy, *daimones* became thought of as inferior deities, intermediates between true divinities and mortals.[25] There are, however, few probable uses of *daimon* in this sense in tragedy of the fifth century.[26] *Daimon* is also widely used by tragedians to represent fortune or an agent dispensing fortune. This fortune may be good but, as already seen, is usually bad.[27] It may be the fortune primarily of one family,[28] or of one individual. The individual then may speak of it as "his *daimon*," just as he would of "his bad fortune."[29] This personal *daimon* is not similar, in religious terms, to the Roman *genius*, a personal spirit or guardian angel which one received at birth and for which one established a household sanctuary and to which one rendered worship. The Greek *daimon*, like fortune in the fifth century, was not a cult deity whom one could influence with sacrifice and prayer. It simply was a cause of what (usually bad) happened, and therein lies its similarity to τύχη. It is a profane, not religious, conception.

Euripides' *Phoenissae* well represents tragedy's tendency to hold *daimones*, fortune, and fate responsible for evils but, unlike in life, also to extend this responsibility to "the gods" as a group, though usually not to one specific god, especially not to one worshiped in Athenian cult. With some exceptions (treated below), individual deities and especially cult deities are introduced as givers only of what is, in the speaker's estimation, desirable. In its wide range the *Phoenissae* treats almost all the sufferings of the immediate family of Oedipus, from his ill-fated birth to his exile. These include (1) the prophecy that, if born, Oedipus will become the murderer of his father, (2) Laius' death at the hands of Oedipus, (3) the appearance and destruction of the Sphinx, (4) Oedipus' marriage to his mother, Jocasta, and the birth of their children, (5) Oedipus' blinding, (6) Oedipus' curses on his sons Polyneices and Eteocles, (7) the mutual slaughter of Polyneices and Eteocles, (8) Jocasta's suicide, and (9) Oedipus' exile. This catalogue of misfortune and suffering is unparalleled, even in tragedy, in the life of one man,[30] and it is most interesting to note how Euripides has various characters and the chorus allot divine responsibility for it all. Though it is not Euripides' concern in this play to examine divine responsibility for human suffering, the chorus and characters in their laments so often raise the subject that patterns emerge.

Apollo in an oracle bade Laius "not to sow the furrow of children against the will of the *daimones*" (μὴ σπεῖρε τέκνων ἄλοκα δαιμόνων βίᾳ, 17–18). The *daimones* are here, as throughout the play, virtually identical to the generalized, undifferentiated group of "the gods," and thus Teiresias can restate this point as "After Laius had children against the will of the gods" (βίᾳ θεῶν, 868). The oracle was that Laius' son, if born, would become the murderer of his father and the family would be destroyed by bloodshed (13–23, 1597–1599). Apollo's oracle defines and brings to light this tragic situation but does not cause it. In this play no character holds Apollo responsible for it. To Oedipus it is Moira (Fate) which bore him, from the beginning, miserable and suffering (1595–1596). Laius, yielding to sexual pleasure, ignored the oracle and begot Oedipus (21–22).[31]

The newborn Oedipus was exposed on Mount Cithaeron, and there is unanimous agreement in the play that in light of later events death there would have been desirable. But Oedipus was saved, and both he and the chorus hold responsible for this miraculous survival not a specific god, but Mount Cithaeron herself (801–805, 1604–1606). A *daimon*, in Oedipus' view, arranged his reception in Polybus' house in Corinth (1606–1607). Oedipus and Laius both journeyed to Delphi, Oedipus to learn of his true parents and Laius of the fate of his exposed son (33–37). In their encounter Laius was killed. Oedipus then went to Thebes after receiving from Delphi an oracle (1042–1046), no doubt the oracle known to us from Sophocles (*OT* 787–793, 994–996) and so familiar to an Athenian audience that Euripides had no need to describe its contents. The chorus mentions this oracle in passing (1042–1046) and again offers no hint that it or Apollo was in any sense responsible for causing the situation which resulted.

At Thebes Oedipus encountered the Sphinx, the monstrous offspring of Ge and a chthonic snake (*Ph.* 1019–1020). In 806–811 the chorus states simply that Hades had sent it against the Cadmeians, but in 1031–1032 it is less sure: "Murderous is that one of the gods who brought these things to pass." Hades is the first specific god to emerge from this chronicle of Oedipus' sufferings, but he was no cult figure of Athens or Thebes.[32] In 806–811 he seems rather to represent death itself, and he is, in the pantheon of myth, an appropriate master of this monster. If Oedipus' victory over the Sphinx had been a conventional story of dragon slaying with a happy ending, we would likely find in literature accounts of a deity who had assisted the hero. But Oedipus' victory introduces only a new series of misfortunes for him, and divine helpers are absent. In Euripides' version, at least, Oedipus in his confrontation with the Sphinx depends entirely upon his own resources while enjoying, perhaps, a bit of good luck (49–50).[33]

In regard to the birth of Oedipus, her marriage to him, and the birth of Polyneices, Jocasta complains of "some god" (θεῶν τις) who is destroying the race of Oedipus (379–381). As is common in popular religion, Jocasta uses "some god" to refer to the generalized collective of the gods, as her next words unmistakably indicate: "One must bear what *the gods* give" (382). Antigone earlier had spoken of the "suffering-causing Fate" by which Polyneices had been born (156–157). Oedipus in this play, interestingly, nowhere holds the gods or fate responsible for his marriage to Jocasta or for the birth of their children. It is otherwise with the deaths of Polyneices and Eteocles. A central feature of the *Phoenissae* is that each brother makes decisions and performs acts that cause his own and his brother's death, but Euripides has introduced numerous causative factors in addition to this. There is "hostile-*daimoned* Strife" (δυσδαίμων Ἔρις, 811) between them, and the chorus personifies this Strife as a deity (θεός) "who has devised these sufferings for the royal family of this land" (798–800). The children of Oedipus are, according to Teiresias, plagued by a *daimon* (δαιμονῶντας, 888). There is, in addition, the curse which Oedipus, sick and dishonored, placed upon his sons (66–68, 874–877, 1354–1355). Oedipus, in retrospect, thinks it impossible that he acted so unintelligently as to destroy his own sons, as well as to blind himself,[34] "without some one of the gods" (ἄνευ θεῶν του, 1612–1614). And, finally, the curses of Oedipus are fulfilled through "a god" (1426) or "the gods" (69–70). It is to fulfill these father's curses against sons that the Erinyes and "avenging spirits" come into play. In this play they are concerned primarily with these curses (253–255, 1556–1558, 1592–1594) and elsewhere in the play appear simply, I think, as paradigms and metaphors of extreme horror and death (1029).[35]

The chorus and each of the characters, in summarizing past events, lay responsibility on *daimones,* fate, or the collective of the gods. Jocasta once lists various possibilities: "May it perish, if a sword, or a quarrel, or your father is responsible for these things, or if 'the *daimonic* element' (τὸ δαιμόνιον has gone into a mad revel against the house of Oedipus" (350–353). Moments later Jocasta speaks of "some god" (θεῶν τις) in this same regard (379). Antigone laments to her father that "the god who brings these things to pass collected together on this one day all griefs for our house" (1579–1581). Creon, in his tense dialogue with Antigone, declares, "The *daimon* has decided not those things which seem right to you" (1662). Oedipus, who justifiably views himself as "ill-*daimoned*" (1615), virtually closes the play by saying, "A human being must endure the necessities that come from the gods" (1763). These many references in the *Phoenissae* are all, despite their varying forms, to the collective of the gods. Although there were numerous opportunities to do so in laments and dialogues, the chorus and characters nowhere assign responsibility for Oedipus' sufferings to well-defined or cult deities. This is equally true, in this play, of the numerous misfortunes of Thebes, of Polyneices and Eteocles, and of the young hero Menoeceus, but the point has been sufficiently documented for our purposes. Euripides and the other tragedians generally followed popular religion in attributing misfortune, suffering, and death to *daimones,* fate, and fortune. They parted ways from popular religion in attributing these evils to "the gods" in general, but they did not go so far as to assign them to specific, worshiped deities.

Death, especially premature death, is usually treated as an evil, and here we find the same cluster of evil-causing divine forces at work. In epitaphs and prose sources "the gods" or a specific god are not held responsible, but rather a *daimon,* fortune, or fate.[36] In tragedy too *daimones* are occasionally given the blame.[37] Fortune and fate, independent of the gods, are also invoked, but infrequently.[38] The poets tend rather to hold gods responsible. There are the well-known instances of individual gods bringing death, usually through human agents, to specific people—Aphrodite and Poseidon to Hippolytus, Apollo to Neoptolemus, Apollo to Clytemnestra, and so forth. But poets also have characters claim, in passing, that death comes from "the gods" or "from Zeus."[39] This difference between popular and tragic religion arises in part because poets are more inclined to attribute evil to their gods, but also because poets, when they have assumed their "superdivine" narrative posture, are in a better position than ordinary people to proffer detailed explanations of individual deaths. They make death not merely a random product of fortune or one's share of the human fate to die, but an event guided by a specific god for a specific purpose. Their gods therefore become much more involved in issues of death than do those of popular religion.

In the *Alcestis* of Euripides death and its supernatural causes are objects of major interest, and there we have the opportunity to examine a poet's treatment of this theme. In this play too death is often attributed to a *daimon,* fortune, or fate.[40] In a lovely ode (962–990) Euripides expands upon this common conception of the impersonal, fated character of death. He makes Anangke (Necessity) rule supreme. No magical[41] or medical drug affects her, and in her case alone one cannot approach an altar or cult statue or expect return for sacrifices.[42] *Daimones,* fortune, and fate share the characteristic that in this period they did not have cults and were not accessible to conventional forms of worship, that is, to prayer and sacrifice. Euripides has, as it were, created a new member of their group, Anangke, and he has made her, like them, a divinity, but one whom humans cannot influence or sway. He has articulated and poeticized a conventional belief of popular religion. Thanatos (Death) himself is a character in the *Alcestis,* and the personality Euripides gives him (28–76) reflects death's inaccessibility (in profane, not religious terms) to all forms of reason, persuasion, and appeasement.[43] He and Hades are the "deities" to whom tragic characters pray for death.[44] Only in Aeschylus is a wish for death, by the Persian king Xerxes, directed to an Olympian god (Zeus) (*Pers.* 915–917). Thanatos is a simple personification, and Hades, though he has an elaborate mythology, shares with *daimones,* fate, fortune, and Thanatos the characteristic that, in classical Athens, he did not receive cult.[45] He, like Euripides' Anangke, is inaccessible to worship.

In the *Alcestis,* however, Alcestis and her husband Admetus are both rescued from death by specific deities, Apollo and Heracles. The helplessness and hopelessness of human beings in the face of death form a leitmotif of the play,[46] but these two people are saved by divine intervention. We have here, in the clearest possible terms, a literary conception juxtaposed to one of contemporary religion. The popular view included the inexorable *daimon,* fate, and fortune with the attendant helplessness and hopelessness. But Admetus and Alcestis are creatures of the literary and mythological tradition. They are royalty in heroic, legendary times when Apollo might lodge with human beings and Heracles dine with them. It is because of the hospitality and favors that Apollo and Heracles personally received in the palace of Admetus that they employ measures (exceptional even for these deities) to rescue these mortals from untimely, premature deaths.[47] Ordinary mortals of the classical period did not enjoy such personal relationships with deities. The rescue of Admetus and Alcestis is an exception possible only in the artificial, mythological world of poetry.[48]

The helplessness and resignation in the face of death expressed by the chorus and others in the play are more characteristic of fifth-century attitudes,[49] whereby their deities—deities to whom they turned for the good things—were remote from, in fact avoided, the circumstances of human death. In cult, death and the dead were forbidden from sanctuaries.[50] In poetry, Apollo and other Olympians withdraw at the approach of death and do so to avoid its pollution (*Alc.* 22–23).[51] One might expect healing deities to intervene at such a time, but in the *Alcestis* Euripides goes out of his way to indicate that Asclepios, the preeminent healing deity, does not operate in this realm, and he gives a mythological reason why he does not. Asclepios had once revived a dead man, and for this extraordinary act he was himself "killed" by Zeus (3–4, 122–130).[52] Thus the Greek deities, even the healing ones, are of no assistance. Sacrifices and prayers bring no relief (112–120, 132–135).[53] At the encounter with death, unless you are a legendary hero or heroine, the deities who have served you in life disappear. The only divine presence—the only superhuman element—is the nameless, characterless, cultless, unapproachable *daimon,* or fortune, or fate, or, as Euripides enriched the concept, inexorable Anangke. The distinctions between good and

28 Honor Thy Gods

evil, between *daimon,* fortune, and fate and the deities of cult and worship are nowhere clearer than in the encounter with death.

In *Oedipus Tyrannus* we can see Sophocles shape the assorted meanings of *daimon* and its complex relationship with θεός into a structure significant for his play as a whole, a structure supporting the general movement from ignorance to understanding on the part of Oedipus.[54] The *daimon* which afflicts Oedipus is increasingly personalized, increasingly recognized as peculiarly Oedipus', and is finally even identified as a specific cult deity. Sophocles does not link Oedipus with *daimones* until the king begins to realize that he may have murdered Laius and, in cursing the murderer to social and political banishment, may have cursed himself: "Who could be more miserable than I, who could be more '*daimon*-hated'?" (815–816). From this moment on, as Oedipus' unhappy past is gradually revealed, he becomes more and more "ill-*daimoned.*" Again in reference to the possibility that he killed Laius, he says, "Wouldn't a man be right in judging that these things come upon me from a savage *daimon*?" (828–829). The chorus, upon learning the full horror of Oedipus' past, refer to "his" *daimon*: "Having your *daimon*, yours, as an example, poor Oedipus, I think men have no blessedness" (1193–1196). When Oedipus rushes into his palace and straightway, "as if with a guide," finds his wife (1260), the messenger disclaims his own and others' responsibility by attributing it to "some one of the *daimones*" (1258–1259).

Up to this point Sophocles' handling of *daimones* and misfortune in the Oedipus story does not differ significantly from that of Euripides in the *Phoenissae*. But as Sophocles' chorus behold the blinded Oedipus, they pepper him with questions: "What madness came upon you? Which *daimon* is it that, on top of your (already) ill-*daimoned* fate, leapt leaps[55] greater than the longest?" (1300–1302). "How did you have the heart to destroy your eyes like that? Who of the *daimones* incited you to it?" (1327–1328). At this moment Sophocles varies a tragic convention and, simultaneously, ties a knot, an interpretive knot which is unsolved and is perhaps insoluble. He moves from one conventional notion of *daimon* as "fortune," "ill-fortune," and "fate" to another of *daimon* as a single but unidentified deity. In response to the chorus's insistent question "Who of the *daimones* incited you to do it?" Oedipus finally cries out, "It was Apollo, Apollo, my friends, the one who is bringing to pass these evil, evil woes of mine" (1329–1330). In Oedipus' mind, at this moment, Apollo is the oft-mentioned *daimon* afflicting his life. It is Pythian Apollo, a cult deity, who is causing his misery and suffering.[56]

In creating this sequence Sophocles delicately merged rather distinct tragic usages of *daimon* one into another. Oedipus first appears as "*daimon*-hated" and afflicted by "a savage *daimon.*" In both expressions the distinction between "that indeterminable force that causes evil" and "a specific deity" is left open, to be explored later. But by lines 1193–1196 Oedipus has his own *daimon,* and this calls into play the concept of one's personal good or (usually) bad fortune.[57] Then the *daimon* is personified by both the chorus and Oedipus ("He leapt," 1300–1302, 1311). Thereupon one can ask his identity ("Which *daimon*? Who of the *daimones*?"), and, in a dramatic twist, an answer can be given ("Apollo"). By using in this sequence the multiple dimensions of the concept *daimon* Sophocles was able to fuse all the responsibilities of fate, of Apollo and his oracles, and of Oedipus himself into one mass, a mass which has not been, and from the way Sophocles has presented it, perhaps cannot be analyzed.

Gods and Heroes

There are in Greek tragedy human beings who when they die receive or are promised cult and worship. They are termed heroes (ἥρωες), and in the classical period and in modern scholarship they are most often distinguished from gods (θεοί) and even *daimones.*[58] The cult of heroes was more an elaboration of the ritual devoted to the ordinary dead than a by-form or development of the cult of Olympian gods. The center of worship was the tomb. Offerings, usually of blood, were poured onto the grave, and worship was local, seldom crossing national boundaries. These heroes were multifarious in origin, ranging from prehistorical Cretan vegetation deities to famous contemporary athletes and generals. Their worship and cults were usually the product of long local development and varied widely, with some in form approximating that of gods.

The functions of these heroes also varied. In the late sixth and fifth centuries the Athenians seem to have turned some preexisting heroes to the democracy's purposes. In 508/507 the Athenians had the Delphic oracle select ten local heroes from a list of one hundred to serve as the eponyms of their newly created ten tribes. The select ten, Erechtheus, Aegeus, Pandion, Leos, Acamas, Oeneus, Cecrops, Hippothoön, Ajax, and Antiochos, then received worship, probably in the form of annual offerings or festivals, from their respective tribes.[59] Before the battle of Salamis in 480 the Greeks summoned for aid Ajax and Telamon from Salamis and Aeacus and the Aeacidae from nearby Aegina (Hdt. 8.64). Aeacus and the Aeacidae then appeared as armored men to some in the heat of the battle (Plut. *Them.* 15).[60] Pausanias (1.36.1) reports that in the same battle a snake appeared amidst the ships, a snake which Apollo of Delphi later identified as the Salaminian hero Cychreus. Theseus had appeared as an armed phantom (φάσμα) during the battle at Marathon,[61] and in 476/475, at Delphi's bidding, the Athenian general Cimon recovered Theseus' bones from Scyros and returned them to Athens. The Athenians delightedly received him, "as if he were coming home," with processions and sacrifices. A sanctuary was established for him in the middle of the city and became a place of asylum for slaves and others who feared their superiors. Theseus thenceforth was "honored" annually with sacrifices (Plut. *Them.* 35.5–36.4, *Cim.* 8.5–6; Paus. 3.3.7).

The legendary heroes Theseus, Ajax, Telamon, and the neighboring Aeacus and Aeacidae all provided military assistance in a time of great crisis, but the Persian Wars apparently marked the end of such appearances, at least for Athenians.[62] Thucydides, Xenophon, and the various other sources report no other epiphany of a hero to Athenians in the numerous but much less glorified battles of the rest of the classical period.

The *oecists* (founders) of colonies form another, very distinct class of heroes.[63] Upon their deaths these normal but prominent mortals received, from the eighth century B.C. on, typical heroic honors from the citizens of their new states: burial within the city, a sanctuary, and, probably, annual offerings. An *oecist* was rewarded as benefactor and came to symbolize the unity and independence of the new state. The Athenians, of course, viewed themselves as autochthonous and hence had no *oecist*. But for them Theseus was, if not an *oecist*, a *synoecist*, and this may in part lie behind the public honors rendered to him after 476/475.

From the late fifth century to the death of Alexander one finds, elsewhere in the Greek world, heroic honors occasionally given to generals and, under special circumstances, even to prominent athletes, but not in Athens.[64] The Athenian heroes with identifiable names remain those of the legendary past. In the Persian Wars these heroes rendered military assistance, but no later. Otherwise their involvement appears to have been primarily political, with Theseus representing unified Athens and the eponymous heroes their individual tribes. It would seem that from such "political" heroes there later developed, in Athens and throughout the Greek world, the cults of living and dead political leaders and kings. But these Hellenistic ruler cults almost immediately assumed attributes of divinity, and the kings were worshiped with "god-like" (not "hero-like") honors for their power and for the benefits they brought to their own states and others.[65] Such cults were a natural result of what I believe to have been a remodeling and politicization of hero cults beginning in the sixth century B.C.

Lesser, often nameless heroes also appear occasionally on local calendars of religious events in the classical period.[66] Generally there is no indication of their function, but some may, like Iatros (Physician) or the Halon whom Sophocles served,[67] have provided healing. The role of such healing heroes may have been diminished with the importation of the cult of Asclepios to Athens in 420/19.[68]

Though the major heroes of classical Athenian cult thus appear benevolent, another, perhaps older view of heroes is also attested.[69] An early medical writer claims that night terrors, fears, and panic attacks are caused by Hecate and heroes ([Hipp.] *De Sacro Morbo* 4). A fragment of Menander (394 [Körte]) says heroes are more ready to cause harm than good. They do not, it says, "possess the beneficial."[70] Even the contemporary athletes who were made heroes elsewhere in Greece in the classical period received cult not for their athletic prowess but for deeds of violence demonstrating their wrath.[71] Hence in addition to the benevolent political and neighboring heroes, there were also present heroes known for their evil deeds, heroes whose worship was based on fear.

How do the heroes, the divinized mortals, of tragedy fit into this varied group of cultic heroes? There are similarities but also significant differences. Let us first treat the heroes of the tragedies on their own, as they emerge from the plays, and then compare the results to what has just been said of Athenian cultic heroes.

Sophocles' *Oedipus at Colonus* dramatizes the heroization of its title character and is a most valuable source for ancient hero cult and hero worship. It must, however, be used with caution. Since there are some superficial similarities between the cult of heroes and that of Christian saints,[72] critics unfamiliar with the intricacies of Greek hero cults tend to interpret the heroization of Oedipus as though it were beatification, that is, a reward to the individual for a good, virtuous, or heroic life. To understand Sophocles' Oedipus, let us first investigate heroes in tragedy apart from the *Oedipus at Colonus* and then look again at Sophocles' hero.

The setting of Euripides' lost *Erechtheus* is the Athenian victory over invading Thracians led by the Eleusinian Eumolpus. The Athenians learned from Delphi that they could repel the Thracians only if Erechtheus sacrificed one of his daughters. The daughters swore among themselves an oath that, if one should be sacrificed, the others would commit suicide. Chthonia was sacrificed, and the others hurled themselves from the Acropolis. In the battle itself Erechtheus was killed by Poseidon's thunderbolt. Of the family only Erechtheus' wife, Praxithea, survived.[73] Much of Athena's speech as *deus ex machina* survives in a papyrus fragment (frag. 65[A]), and here she tells the Athenians how they are to regard the dead and living members of Erechtheus' family. Her instructions illustrate both the divisions and the vagaries in Greek concepts of the divinization of the dead. Praxithea, who survives, is, as a reward for surrendering her daughter for the state's welfare, to become a priestess of Athena (95–97). Erechtheus, "hidden beneath the ground" by Poseidon's thunderbolt (59–60), is given a sanctuary enclosed by a stone wall (σηκός, 90–91). In association with Poseidon, as Poseidon-Erechtheus he is to receive ox sacrifices (92–94), no doubt those described also in the *Iliad* (2.550–551).[74] Chthonia and her sisters will share a tomb at the place Chthonia died, Chthonia honored for her self-sacrifice, her sisters for not abandoning their oath. Their souls are to go not to Hades but, by Athena's intervention, into the sky (*aither*). Athena will make them famous throughout Greece as the Hyacinthid goddesses (θεαί). Athenians are to honor them with annual sacrifices, with offerings of cattle, and with dances of maidens. They will receive also the first fruits of battle, wineless offerings of honey and river water.[75] Their sanctuary is not to be open to the public (ἄβατον), and no enemy is to sacrifice there lest he cause defeat and misery for the Athenians (65–89).

At first glance it looks as though the daughters of Erechtheus are to be honored as goddesses, the king himself as a hero. Their souls go into the sky; his, presumably, to Hades. They are to have a *temenos*, he a σηκός. They are to receive annual sacrifices, and dances, and first fruits of battle. He, in association with Poseidon, receives only annual sacrifices. Their fame is to be international; his is only local. They are expressly termed goddesses (θεαί); his status, as commonly for heroes, is not given. The implication is that the Hyacinthids can provide victory in battle (88–89); Erechtheus is assigned no definite function. But the Hyacinthids also have traits of hero status, as Erechtheus does of divine status. First and foremost, the Hyacinthids are mortal girls who died, and their sanctuary is their tomb. The wineless libation of honey and water they will receive as first fruits from battle is more characteristic of funerary than of Olympian cult. Their souls have gone into the sky, but so did the souls of the fallen warriors at Plataea in 432 and even those, occasionally, of ordinary men.[76] That, by itself, is no sure sign of apotheosis or even heroization,[77] although Euripides seems to make it such here. Erechtheus may originally have been a vegetation deity, of the type of the Spartan Hyacinthus or the Cretan Zeus, and his association with Poseidon and the sacrifices of oxen may be vestiges of his early, prehistoric status as a θεός. The sanctuary he shared with Poseidon and Athena in Athens was the Erechtheum, a temple (ναός) and not a hero shrine. The Panathenaia, the festival with which he was most intimately associated, was for gods, not heroes.[78]

The Hyacinthids and Erechtheus remind us of what Farnell and Nock have taught us, that the distinction between god and hero was blurry and, on occasion, lost. The humans who almost completely broke the barrier and were treated after death primarily as gods (Heracles, Asclepios, and the Dioscuroi) are famous but very few.[79] I think, however, that other criteria emerge for the distinction of god and hero in tragedy. The first is the "function" of the divinity, the second the "atmosphere" surrounding the cult. The daughters of Erechtheus may serve to represent the divine here. For the heroic we may begin with Erechtheus but must soon turn to other heroes of tragedy about whom we are better informed. The Hyacinthids, Athena tells us (frag. 65[A], 65–80), are to be made goddesses expressly as a reward for their virtue, Chthonia for her self-sacrifice, the others for maintaining their oath—both acts of piety. As goddesses they will assist the Athenians in gaining military victories, without specification of the future enemy. The annual sacrifices they receive and the dances in their sanctuary suggest a festive occasion, a *heorte*.⁸⁰ In short, their cult is conceived of in positive terms. Virtue is rewarded, victories are promised, and the ritual is, mostly, festive. To Erechtheus Athena assigns no function; nor, interestingly, do we learn from later sources any specific contribution he made to fifth-century Athenian life.⁸¹ This may be because of his early, prehistoric absorption by Poseidon and then Athena,⁸² but it also may be the result of his fifth-century status as a hero. We also learn nothing of the "atmosphere," negative or positive, that attended his cult, but here again we cannot expect the poet to provide data on all topics that interest us.

For the "function" of heroes and the "atmosphere" that surrounds their cults, we may turn to the Eurystheus of Euripides' *Heraclidae*. This persecutor of Heracles was trapped in Athens after his unsuccessful attempt to steal away and kill Heracles' children. The Athenians rejected the demand of Heracles' wife that they kill the captive Eurystheus, and he, in gratitude, revealed to them an oracle:

> Since this city spared me and was ashamed to kill me,
> I will present it with an old oracle of Apollo Loxias,
> an oracle which, in time, will benefit you more than you expect.⁸³
> When I die, you will bury me where it is fated,
> in front of the divine maiden of Pallene.⁸⁴
> I shall always lie there beneath the ground,
> a foreigner well-intentioned towards you and protecting your city,
> but most hostile to the descendants of Heracles,⁸⁵
> whenever they attack here with a large force,
> betraying the favor you gave them. . . .
>
> But do not allow drink offerings or blood to drip into
> my tomb. In return for this I will give to
> Heracles' descendants an evil return home.
> (*Heraclid.* 1026–1036, 1040–1043)

Eurystheus is, himself, in no sense a good, virtuous, or heroic man. Throughout the play his motives are bad, his character is evil, and in attempting to drive Heracles' family from their place of asylum by force he acts impiously. There is no indication, implicit or explicit, that his heroization is a reward to him or that he in any sense benefits from it. His heroization is, rather, a reward to the Athenians for their respectful and pious treatment of a *xenos*. His tomb, like a talisman, is to protect Athenians from invasion and occupation by the Dorians, Eurystheus' fellow tribesmen. The function of the heroized Eurystheus, while benefiting Athenians, is formulated negatively. He is not bringing Athenians victory, but causing the Dorians defeat. The outcome might be very much the same to Athenians, but the perception of the hero's activity is very different. The prescriptions for his cult are also negative: Athenians are *not* to make drink and blood offerings. If they obey him in this, Eurystheus will cause "an evil return home" for the Dorians. This is far different from the usual scheme of Olympian religion, according to which the gods help bring victory if their worshipers honor them with annual festivals, prebattle sacrifices, and, in gratitude, first-fruit offerings.

Similar differences may be seen in the cult and worship of other divinized dead humans in tragedy. Orestes in Aeschylus' *Eumenides* vows to the Athenians an eternal military alliance with his Argives (762–774). If years later the Argives should violate his oath, he promises that from his tomb he will afflict his countrymen with "unmanageable failures," making their military expeditions "dispirited and ill-omened" (767–771). Like Eurystheus, in his gratitude to the Athenians for their kindly treatment of him he will bring misfortune to his own countrymen. His function as a hero in Argos, though not defined, was perhaps not to be exclusively negative,[86] but Aeschylus only has need to describe the negative side.

The chorus of Euripides' *Alcestis*, in admiration of Alcestis' virtue in voluntarily dying to spare her husband, imagines special honors for her. She is to have place of honor at Persephone's side in Hades (742–746),[87] and she will be a "blessed *daimon*" (1003). But she is also to be honored similarly to the gods (θεοῖσι δ' ὁμοίως τιμάσθω) and is asked, in the language of prayer, "to give good things" (995–1005). The chorus, in their enthusiasm, momentarily conceive of the dead Alcestis as a deity.

The Agamemnon of all three tragedians, the Proteus of Euripides' *Helen*, and the Darius of Aeschylus' *Persae* each represent tragedy's tendency to present deceased kings as heroes worshiped by surviving members of the royal family. These dead kings fall into a middle ground, superior to ordinary dead but inferior to established heroes of state cult. Electra in Euripides'

Electra laments that in the several years since Agamemnon's death his tomb has not received honors of drink offerings, sprigs of myrtle, and adornments of the altar (323–325). Orestes and the trusty nurse of Agamemnon, on their first visits to the tomb, begin to rectify this. The old man pours libations of wine and places branches of myrtle about the tomb (511–512). Orestes, as a son, weeps there, deposits offerings of his own hair, and sacrifices on the altar a black-fleeced sheep (91–92, 513–515).[88] Electra has, despite the advice of her friends (193–197), continued throughout the years the traditional acts of mourning: weeping, uttering laments, tearing the skin of her neck, pulling her hair, and beating her head (58–59, 144–150, 193). Drink offerings, sprigs of myrtle, and hair offerings were all usual rites of burial and tendance of the tomb in the fifth and fourth centuries. Electra's acts of mourning are thus conventional,[89] except that due to the dramatic situation and her own personality they have been continued extraordinarily long. An altar at the tomb and animal sacrifices, however, had no place in the cult of the ordinary dead in the classical period.[90] These are features of hero cult, and it is only as a hero that Agamemnon can be prayed to, conjured up, and expected to provide tangible assistance to the living.[91] There are similar prayers to Agamemnon for assistance in the Electra plays of Aeschylus and Sophocles,[92] but there the details of Agamemnon's cult are not so fully described. But in each he is invoked, by family members, as a hero,[93] not as one of the ordinary dead.

Deceased barbarian kings are treated even more clearly as divine by the tragedians. In the opening of his *Helen* Euripides has Helen take sanctuary at the tomb of Proteus, the Egyptian king to whom Zeus seventeen years earlier had entrusted her for safekeeping. Euripides presents the recently dead Proteus as a hero and his tomb as a *heroön*. The altar for burnt offerings indicates this (547), as well as the tomb's placement not only within the city but adjoining the royal palace.[94] As Proteus' son comes and goes from the palace, he greets his deceased father (1165–1168),[95] who inhabits this tomb (962). It is only as a hero, and not as an ordinary dead person, that Proteus can offer Helen asylum.

The deceased Persian king Darius is, in Aeschylus' *Persae,* "god-equal" (ἰσόθεος, 856; cf. 643, 655), a *daimon* (620–621, 634, 641–642). Darius, as he himself claims, has special power in the underworld, and for this reason he can leave Hades and respond to his wife's invocations (688–692). He receives the usual offerings to the dead (219–223, 607–622, 685), but he is by no means a usual dead person. In creating his Darius Aeschylus brought together three elements: (1) a royal family hero cult like that of Agamemnon, (2) Greek ideas of the divinity of the Persian king,[96] and (3) necromancy, on the model of Odysseus' summoning and consulting the seer Teiresias in *Odyssey* 11. Darius is honored and appealed to with conventional offerings and laments—on a royal scale, of course—much like those of Agamemnon, but unlike Agamemnon he is described as a god. When his ghost does appear from Hades, it is to reveal an oracle and to give a superhumanly foresighted and wise assessment of the current situation (631–632, 739–831). Darius is a hybrid, in part Greek (offerings), in part Persian (god status), and in part purely literary (Teiresias figure).[97] It is as this artificial figure only that Darius can be successfully summoned by his wife and can actually appear on the stage. Agamemnon, Darius, and Proteus are alike in being deceased kings worshiped by their own families, but each has his own distinct characteristics suited to the needs of the play. They are neither usual state heroes nor ordinary dead. Details of their cults and descriptions of their afterlife should not be—as is too often done—introduced willy-nilly into descriptions of popular beliefs about the dead. The cults of these famous dead kings are literary creations and in their essentials do not reflect the beliefs of fifth-century Athenians about their own dead.

The similarity between these deceased kings and real, publicly worshiped heroes may result from two independent but converging developments. The ritual and cult of real heroes, so far as can be determined, were the elaboration and extension of cult and practices rendered to the ordinary dead. For tragedy, however, this is not the starting point. Tragedy tends rather, like epic but not to the same degree, to intensify and magnify the religious practices of its characters beyond the level of those of ordinary members of the audience. Therefore rituals and rites for its dead personages, always royal figures of legendary times, are elaborated and enhanced to attain the nobility of the persons and times. Since real hero cult elaborated ordinary rituals and since the tragedians did the same for their royal characters, the results were very much the same. The rites and beliefs concerning dead royal personages of tragedy became very much like those of genuine heroes.

Achilles in Euripides' *Hecuba* may provide a final example before we turn to Sophocles' *Oedipus*. Achilles, who in fact received hero and divine cult in several locales of Greece,[98] appeared above his tomb to the Greek army as it awaited favorable winds to allow departure for home. He asked, according to Polydorus' ghost, for Polyxena, the daughter of Priam and Hecuba, to be sacrificed at his tomb (37–44). The demand for a victim and for honor would suggest to the fifth-century audience that Achilles was a hero, not one of the common dead.[99] This may even have been an unstated purpose of Achilles' visitation: by receiving a sacrificial victim and by hearing and answering a prayer (527–542), he was, as it were, elevated from the status of an ordinary dead man to that of a hero, a status to which he no doubt thought himself entitled (cf. 114–115).

As a preliminary to the sacrifice of Polyxena, Neoptolemus, who as Achilles' son performs the ritual, invokes Achilles and presents him drink offerings (χοαί, 527–536). In the cult of the ordinary dead such drink offerings seem mere gifts whose purpose is no longer understood or stated.[100] In hero cult, as here, the offerings, like the invocation, are meant to "entice" (κηλητήριοι) and "attract" (ἀγωγοί) the hero (535–536), as were the similar offerings and laments to Darius (A. Pers. 685–688, 697) and to Teiresias (*Odyssey* 11). The cultic purpose of the sacrifice of Polyxena is that Achilles may drink the blood of the girl (124–126, 391–393, 536–538), and even Hecuba does not call this purpose into question. She objects only that it should be animal and not human blood (260–261). Whether the sacrifice of Polyxena is an appropriate and just way of honoring Achilles is, however, also an ethical and social question, and Euripides allows it to become a focus of the debate between Odysseus and Hecuba (258–331). Such questions as Euripides raises concerning the sacrifice are directed more to moral and ethical issues than to cultic ones.

Achilles has, according to Polydorus' ghost, prevented the Greeks from sailing home (37–39)—an act, like those of most tragic heroes, negatively formulated and, of course, lying beyond the power of the ordinary dead. Neoptolemus' prayer to Achilles, as he makes the drink offering and sheds Polyxena's blood, is that Achilles be kindly (πρευμενής) to the Greeks and allow them all to sail home (538–541), that is, that he stop harming them. This prayer is in fact answered, and in 1289–1290 Agamemnon reports winds favorable for sailing.[101] Achilles has demonstrated his "heroic" power, he has been recognized and worshiped as a hero, and he has heard and answered a prayer.[102]

Of the divinized humans of tragedy considered thus far, each has his own myth and some distinctive features of cult or ritual. A pattern does, however, emerge. There are three general types: (1) deceased kings, worshiped as heroes by their own families; (2) newly made state heroes, who are thought to benefit Athens by bringing harm to former countrymen; (3) those, usually women, who become goddesses as a reward for virtuous and pious action and who confer benefits. All were mortals who were divinized, and the usual division of immortal versus mortal does not serve to distinguish between god and hero here. More important, I have suggested, are the atmosphere surrounding the cult and the function of the individual. Those who are being rewarded for virtuous acts, whose function is conceived of in terms of benefits, and whose rites include feasting and dancing are gods or goddesses. Into this class we may place, as well as the Hyacinthids, also Heracles, Asclepios, and the Dioscuroi. What is most important to their worshipers is their function and cult, not their presumed original status as gods or men. In tragedy the cult of the hero is established not to benefit the hero but to punish his enemies. This, in turn, may and often does bring benefit to the country that received him, but this activity is usually formulated in negative terms, of harming his previous countrymen.[103] The atmosphere surrounding his cult is one of fear, apprehension, and appeasement. One hopes that if the hero can be kept mollified, he will cause no harm.

If we can trust the ancient biographers, Sophocles himself was more than ordinarily interested in hero cult. He himself reputedly was a priest of the hero Halon, helped establish in Athens cults of Asclepios and Heracles, and was himself honored as a hero, Dexion ("The Receiver"), long after his death.[104] His Oedipus of the *Oedipus at Colonus* is in conception very much a hero of cult, and a proper understanding of this may shed some light on lingering problems of interpretation of the play.[105]

Oedipus is a mortal who dies. He is variously imagined or described as "dead" (390, 1509, 1521, 1555, 1691, 1706), "perished" (1580, 1583, 1612–1613), "gone to Hades" (1461, 1551–1552, 1568–1578, 1701, 1706–1707), and a corpse "hidden" in the earth (621–622, 1544–1546, 1775).[106] "Hidden" in the earth recalls the description of Erechtheus but is used equally of ordinary dead.[107] There is no suggestion in the play that Oedipus will have in death a consciousness superior to or different from that of other dead men.[108] His painless death, however, is unique and may be intended by Sophocles as recompense for his life of suffering. He was not struck by a thunderbolt or carried off by a wind at sea (1658–1660). He suffered neither a wound in battle nor death at sea (1678–1682). There were no groans, no pains from disease (1663–1664). He simply vanished. Oedipus had, perhaps, enough sufferings in his life. He is to escape the pains of dying (cf. 1556–1567).

Oedipus will, *post mortem,* help his friends and harm his enemies, a not insignificant ability in the Greek value system of the fifth century. He does this, however, not as a deity by personal involvement but by the power of his tomb and by his curses on his sons. These, once established, bring about their effects automatically. The benefit which he brings to Athens and for which the Athenians receive him is that his tomb will be, like the tomb of Eurystheus, a talisman against the invasion of Attica by his own countrymen. If maintained in accordance with his instructions, it will protect Athens from Theban invaders and make it free from grief.[109] Since Oedipus offers this benefit as a quid pro quo for his own reception, he often describes it in positive terms. But it is, in fact, only a corollary and result of his greater purpose, which is to punish Eteocles, Polyneices, and the Thebans for forcing him into exile.[110] The Athenians, because of their virtue and piety, are to prosper, but only at the expense of Oedipus' sons and countrymen. Oedipus' driving purpose in this play is vengeance on his enemies, and in this he is characteristic of most heroes in tragedy. His curses on his sons, that they perish each at the hand of the other beneath the walls of Thebes, trouble modern critics. The curses seem, in human terms, excessive, and perhaps they are. They are filled with wrath, but wrath, Achilles-type wrath, is a predominant trait in the Oedipus of this play,[111] and it is a wrath common to heroes. Oedipus' wrath at his sons may, on the human level, be disturbing, but Sophocles has chosen in this play to raise Oedipus to the level of hero.

The function of the hero Oedipus is thus largely negative,[112] and the atmosphere surrounding his cult is likewise negative in contrast to that of Olympian gods. Fear pervades: fear of the Eumenides, at whose grove the play is set and where his tomb is to be. Their sanctuary is not to be entered, touched, inhabited, spoken of, or even looked upon (36–45, 125–132, 156–169, 675). Fear hangs over it (39–40, 492). Oedipus' own tomb is to be seen, tended, and known by no one except Theseus. Oedipus himself, alive, is "terrible to look at, terrible to hear" (141). He describes his own nature as "dread" (αἰνά, 212). He is a man of wrath and anger (see above, note 111). He loves his daughters, but he curses Polyneices, Eteocles, Creon, and the Thebans. He is a man who, however involuntarily (266–288, 960–1002), married his mother and killed his father.

The heroization of Oedipus and the power of his tomb received divine validation, like most religious institutions of tragedy, through preordination, through oracles of Delphi.[113] His tomb is a "sacred deposit" (ἱερὰ θήκη, 1763) and is to have a "ground-level hearth" (ἑστία χθόνιος, 1726), an altar of the type usual for heroes. Oedipus is not, however, to receive public worship. Only Theseus and his successors are to know the site of the tomb (1522–1535, 1756–1767),[114] and, in the conventions of Greek religion, without public knowledge public worship is impossible. In this lack of cult activities Oedipus is similar to Euripides' Eurystheus, who expressly forbids any of the usual practices (E. *Heraclid.* 1040–1041). A cult without acts of worship is a self-contradiction in the Greek tradition, and the two poets offer no satisfactory explanation. It is perhaps revealing that no sacrifice to either hero is mentioned in sacrificial calendars or other sources for Athenian religion.[115]

Oedipus was a mortal whom Sophocles heroized, and the *Oedipus at Colonus* gives us a valuable description of the awe, fear, dread, and mystery which enveloped such cults. For interpretation of the play, however, it is most important to remember that heroization benefits not the hero but the society which received him and in which he was heroized. Although our unanswered questions about the *Oedipus Tyrannus* lead us to scrutinize Oedipus' personality in this play, we should be aware that a major, if not the major, concern of the *Oedipus at Colonus* is virtuous and pious versus evil and impious treatment of kin, *xenoi,* and suppliants,[116] and the rewards or punishments arising therefrom. This is, however, a separate issue, one to be discussed later in the context of *xenoi* and asylum.[117]

We may conclude our survey of the cult hero in tragedy with two cases which run counter to the pattern. In a short fragment from Euripides' first (and now lost) *Hippolytus*,[118] someone, presumably the chorus, addresses the now dead Hippolytus:

> O blessed one,
> what honor you, hero Hippolytus,
> received because of your virtuous self-control.
> No other power is greater for mortals
> than that of virtue, because a good return
> from piety comes either beforehand
> or afterwards.[119]
>
> (frag. 446[N])

Μάκαρ ("blessed one"), τιμάς ("honors"), and ἥρως ("hero") indicate that Euripides presents Hippolytus here as a cult hero. This honor he receives because of his virtue and piety; it is a return for them. These lines must be the chorus's response to the institution of a cult of Hippolytus by a *deus ex machina* and served to end the play. Beyond this we can only speculate. This first version of the *Hippolytus* apparently failed in the drama competition, and Euripides rewrote it, correcting what was "unbecoming and deserving censure."[120] The second version, produced in 428, survives but has no similar response to Artemis, the *deus ex machina*. But there we have in full Artemis' prescriptions for the new cult of Hippolytus. She recognizes Hippolytus' "piety and good thoughts" (1419).[121] In return for the evils he has suffered she will give him "very great honors in the city Troezen." Girls before marriage will cut their hair and weep for him, and maidens will always sing about him. The topic of the songs will be Phaedra's love for him (1423–1430). The cultic atmosphere is one of mourning and lamentation, and that agrees with the little we know of Hippolytus' actual cult in Troezen. The hero cult is less explicitly made a reward for virtue here than in the fragment, but a relationship between the two cannot be denied.

The Troezenian cult of Hippolytus, the one at issue in the surviving play and, most likely, in the fragment, had by the first century A.D. acquired some "divine" elements. By then Hippolytus received "honors equal to those of the gods" (ἰσόθεοι τιμαί, Diodorus 4.62.4), and Pausanias, a century later, treats him largely as a god (2.32.1–4).[122] There is, however, no evidence that he was considered a god or godlike in the fifth century, and it is best to leave him as an exceptional case of a mortal who dies and is personally rewarded for his virtue with the honors of a hero cult.

From the *Rhesus,* a play full of peculiarities of language and religion, comes the most bizarre hero/god of Greek tragedy.[123] Late in the Trojan War Rhesus, a famous Thracian king, has come with troops to assist the Trojans. Odysseus and Diomedes stealthily enter the Trojan camp and kill him in his sleep. His divine mother, Musa, the *deus ex machina,* here describes the *post mortem* fate Rhesus is to have:

> He will not go into the black plain of earth.
> I shall ask the netherworld Nymph,
> the daughter of the food-producing goddess Demeter,
> to send up his soul. She is obliged to me
> to show that she honors the relatives of Orpheus.[124]
> Hereafter Rhesus will be to me like one dead
> and not seeing the light, because he will never
> meet nor see me, his mother.
> He will lie, hidden in the caves of the silver-rich land,
> a man/*daimon,*[125] seeing the light,
> a prophet of Bacchus who inhabited the rock of Pangaion,
> a revered god (θεός) to those who know.[126]
>
> (962–973)

Musa's speech here is a muddle of vocabulary, concepts, and categories which are kept distinct in genuine tragedies of the fifth century. It is not even internally consistent. In 962 she says Rhesus will not go to Hades. In 963–964 she promises to ask Persephone to send him "up" (ἀνεῖναι), but from where will Persephone send him "up" if not from Hades? Rhesus will be as a dead man for her, but for others a man/*daimon,* an ἀνθρωποδαίμων. He will be "hidden," as heroes often are, but in caves, not in a tomb. Thus hidden in subterranean caves he will see "the light," that is, daylight, a ludicrous mixture of metaphors and concepts. This poet uses but cannot understand or control the language of fifth-century tragedy.

The divine status of Rhesus, though alien to the religion of tragedy, has some interest in its own right. He is compared, even when alive, to a *daimon* (301), to Zeus (355–359), to a god, to Ares himself (385–387). Such extravagant praise, unparalleled in tragedy,[127] prepares for his future as man/*daimon,* "a god for those who know." The anomaly of Rhesus being dead for his mother but a god for others appears to have been introduced only to allow Musa to be a grieving mother (890–903). How could a Greek mother, divine or other, grieve if her son were to be, for her and for all, a god? The occasional suggestions of mysteries and Orphic elements (943–947, 965–966, 972–973) may be explained without invoking a cult background. Given that Rhesus was Thracian and to be divinized, he was most likely to be drawn into an Orphic context. The Orphic elements are at best superficial: they are not worked into a cultic or conceptual framework for understanding the fate of Rhesus.

Apart from its inconsistency, the religious conception of Rhesus, both alive and dead, seems a product of the late fourth or third century B.C. It was then no longer blasphemous or hybristic to praise kings, emperors, or successful generals in such extravagant language. And, by then, such important public figures were rewarded, *post mortem,* not with hero cults but with divine honors. It is in such a world that Rhesus the ἀνθρωποδαίμων finds his place. But viewed in the context of fifth-century tragedy, Rhesus, like the man/*daimon* he was to become, is a unique creation, and not a very successful one at that.

How do these various tragic heroes relate to those of practised state cult? Deceased kings such as Agamemnon and Darius who were worshiped by their own families obviously had no place in democratic Athens. In addition they are, as I argued, literary fictions, belonging neither to hero cult nor to the cult of the ordinary dead. Most heroes in tragedy are newly made state heroes like Eurystheus and Oedipus, who benefit Athens by bringing harm to their former countrymen. Their function is essentially malignant, though it may have beneficial results for their hosts, and the atmosphere about their cult is one of fear and dread. We have seen some indications that one such view of heroes existed in classical Athens, but contrary to that are the positive views of Theseus, the eponymous heroes, and some local heroes. These heroes of tragedy may be a literary fiction, or, more probably I think, an instance where the tragedians have introduced beliefs and types of divine figures once part of popular religion but in the classical period largely extinct.[128] That is, the Eurystheus and Oedipus type of hero may represent, albeit filtered through the literary tradition, a type of cult fairly common before the Athenians, in the sixth century, gave legendary heroes and their cults new, beneficial roles to play in Athenian democracy and life. The old-style hero, full of wrath and vengeance, a terror to be assuaged, became essentially civilized. The Hippolytus of both *Hippolytus* plays is more the fifth-century, new-style hero, no longer wrathful, no longer a warrior. Rhesus in turn represents the divinized man as he came to be viewed in the Hellenistic period. Given the scanty evidence available, this proposed development of Athenian hero cult is hypothetical, but, correct or not, the state heroes created for the Athenians in fifth-century tragedy appear much more fearful, malignant, and dread-inspiring than those whose cult the Athenians actually practised.

Divine Intervention

Functions and activities of gods, *daimones,* and heroes have been touched upon already. We have examined distinctions between gods and *daimones* and between gods and heroes, but we have also noted the tendency for these distinctions to be broken. The terms "god" and *daimon* are often synonymous, and both can indicate a personalized god or impersonal fortune or "the course of events." Some dead mortals are presented as gods, others as heroes proper. What emerges is a complex structure in which terms such as "god," "the gods," *daimon,* and "hero" move into or apart from one another. Each individual occurrence in tragedy must be judged from the context which the poet has chosen to create. To examine divine intervention, that is, the functions and activities of these divinities, we must draw the lines somewhat differently. The decisive categories, suggested in the preceding pages, are now

1. Individual gods, "the gods" as the Olympian pantheon, *daimones* as equivalent to these gods, and dead mortals considered gods.
2. *Daimon* and "the gods" as equivalent to fortune.
3. Dead mortals as heroes proper.

I have already said much of the activities of the divinities in categories 2 and 3. They are held responsible for much of the unpleasant side of life. Heroes such as Eurystheus and Oedipus bring about evil for their own kin and countrymen. Whatever benefits may accrue for others, the hero's action is derived from hate and hostility. The worshipers' feeling towards them is fear, and, generally speaking, cultic acts are performed to "appease" them and thereby prevent their malicious activity. Misfortune is also the realm of *daimon* as synonym of fortune. Events subjectively considered misfortunes, and chief among these death, are often attributed to this impersonal, cultless *daimon*. In tragedy, more so than in life, such misfortunes may also be assigned to the impersonal collective of "the gods."

Let us now turn to the functions and activities of the first category, primarily individual gods and "the gods" as the collective of Olympian gods. It is this group of whom Pericles said, "We infer their immortality from the honors they have and from the good things they provide us" (Plut. *Per.* 8.6). What follows is a catalogue of their intervention in human life, both as that intervention is described in tragedy and as it is related to beliefs of contemporary popular religion. Certain major areas of divine activity, such as oaths, treatment of *xenoi,* divination, asylum, and justice, will be at most introduced in this catalogue. Each is of major importance and requires full discussion in a more suitable context.

In Euripides' *Suppliants* King Theseus, to prove his claim that good things outnumber the bad in human life, lists the gifts a god gave to mankind:

> Someone said that the worse things are more
> numerous for mortals than the better things.
> I hold the opposite opinion;
> for mortals the good is more abundant than the bad.
> If this were not so, we would not be alive.
> I praise the one of the gods who for us measured out
> a livelihood from the jumbled and bestial world.
> He first put in us intelligence and then gave us
> a tongue as a messenger of words so that
> we can understand the spoken word.
> He gave us the nourishment of food and, from
> the sky, drops of rain for this nourishment,
> so that they may support produce from the earth and wet her womb.
> And in addition he gave us defenses against winter

and the means to ward off the blazing heat of the sun god.
He gave us also journeys over the sea, so that
we might have exchanges with one another for those products our
   land lacks.
By looking into fire and on the folds of entrails [of sacrificed victims]
   and from bird-omens
seers explain things which are
hard to decipher and which we do not clearly understand.
Are we not pretentious when, after
a god has given such equipment for life to us,
these things do not satisfy us?

(196–215)

Theseus speaks of gifts a god gave in the early structuring of the world, at the beginning of human history. Human beings received intelligence, language, food, water, shelter, sea travel, and prophecy. These gifts made human life possible and continued to do so in Theseus' time. The gifts, once made, could presumably continue working, automatically, without additional divine intervention.

Euripides does not identify this divine benefactor.[129] Aeschylus in the *Prometheus* attributes to his title character these gifts and more. His Prometheus claims credit for (1) fire; (2) humans no longer foreknowing the time of their own death—which had been, the chorus says, a "disease"—and living now on "blind hopes"; (3) reason, so that humans could understand what they saw and heard and could build shelters of brick and wood; (4) knowledge of the cyclical movements of the stars, so that they could judge the seasons of the year; (5) numbers and letters; (6) the yoke for plow animals, beasts of burden, and chariots; (7) sailing ships; (8) the arts of prophecy; (9) the techniques of medicine; (10) the mining of bronze, iron, silver, and gold; and, in summary, all the human arts and crafts (πᾶσαι τέχναι, 506).[130] Like those on Theseus' list, once given these gifts could continue on their own without divine supervision.

That Prometheus was chained to a rock for thirteen generations did not reduce or hinder the benefits that humanity continued to garner from his benefactions. They became, as it were, human and not divine responsibility, and that was important for contemporary religion. Even if it were commonly thought that such advances in human civilization had once been caused by

Prometheus or some other god, practised cult was directed primarily to what the gods currently were providing. The Greek religious temper, unlike that of some other peoples, paid remarkably little attention to gratitude for past, particularly distantly past favors. Given the richness of their language, the Greeks of the classical period had relatively few and impoverished ways of expressing gratitude.[131] Greek popular religion was concerned primarily with "now" and "tomorrow." Past favors such as those listed above might indicate the benevolence of some or all gods, but cult was concerned with assuring that benevolence in the present and the future. The past was rather, as it is in the *Prometheus* and *Suppliants,* a matter for literary, mythological, and philosophical speculation.[132]

It is by no means certain that most Athenians shared this view of divine benevolence in man's prehistory. In the famous "Ode to Man" from the *Antigone* (332–375) Sophocles' chorus gives humans sole credit for many of these advances in their culture. They sail the seas, work the land with animals,[133] hunt birds, beasts, and fish, speak, think, build shelters, cure diseases, develop crafts (τέχνη), and live in ordered society. To Sophocles these are human accomplishments, and in none of them does he suggest divine participation. Sophocles' implicit refusal to attribute human progress in such areas to the gods may be a reflection of his own conceptions of man and god, but it was one he shared with several contemporary philosophers.[134] For the common people's view of the debate we have little evidence. Only the cult and festival of Prometheus, as giver of fire,[135] would suggest they inclined towards the Aeschylean view.

In their lists of benefactions neither Euripides nor Aeschylus suggests any divine contribution to early moral or legal life. The gods did not create, either in prehistory or later, the human moral or legal code.[136] There are exceptions to this, and we shall find them important in understanding the gods' relationship to justice as presented by the three tragedians. But by and large, in tragedy and in life moral and judicial standards were created and maintained by humanity, not by the gods.[137]

Some Euripidean characters make strong protests against particular deficiencies, as they see them, in the world order created by the gods.[138] Hippolytus wishes that Zeus had so devised the world that children might be acquired not by sex with women but, like olives, for cash in a market (*Hipp.* 616–624). Medea wishes Zeus had impressed on men a stamp to distinguish good from bad, like the stamp on a gold coin (*Med.* 516–519). The chorus of the *Heracles* want a similar mark of virtue, and they recommend a second lifetime for virtuous men (655–672). Andromache wishes the gods had created a drug to be used against an evil woman just as there are cures against snakebites (*Andr.* 269–272). Each is really an intense wish, not a theological statement, but the last three, and in some ways even Hippolytus' wish in its context, express the longing that the gods had, in the structuring of the world, entered more into the moral realm—a realm which is noticeably missing in tragedy in the more general and programmatic statements of the gods' initial structuring of the world.

As we turn from reported divine intervention in the prehistoric human past to actual, expected, or assumed interventions in the present, we find gods of tragedy providing much of what they did in fifth- and fourth-century popular religion. In *Athenian Popular Religion* I surveyed the areas of divine intervention (18–26), and these included various aspects of war, agriculture, children, safety at sea, and economic prosperity. Each is found in tragedy, some very frequently as the notes below will indicate. I leave aside for later discussion the gods' important concerns with oaths, divination, death, and justice.

The Athenians made prayers, poured libations, and sang paeans before major military undertakings.[139] Just before individual battles they made sacrifices which would indicate to seers or generals whether the omens were favorable. After a successful battle the victors set up a trophy monument and dedicated, either on the site or in a sanctuary at home, some spoils from the battle. This dedication might be either fulfillment of a vow or a "firstfruits" offering. Each of these practices is a regular feature of the religion of tragedy.[140]

Before the battle the prime event is a sacrifice from which omens about the outcome are drawn. "It is man's work," Eteocles says to the female chorus (A. *Th.* 230–232), "to make sacrifices and oracular offerings to the gods" before battle. He bids the chorus to pray that "the gods be 'allies'" (266), and they later pray to the "Zeus-born gods" to "protect the city and the Cadmus-born army" (301–303). Eteocles himself, as a model for an appropriate prayer for such an occasion, prays as follows:

> I say to the city-protecting gods of this land,
> both those dwelling in the plains and those watching over the market,
> and to the streams of Dirce and to the waters of Ismenus,
> if we succeed and if our city is saved,
> we will bloody the altars of the gods with sheep
> and, in the temples, we will set up as trophies
> the spoils taken by spear from the enemy.[141]
>
> (271–278)

If we keep in mind that the site is Thebes, the war defensive, and the text iambic trimeter, we may accept this prayer, *mutatis mutandis,* as a model of a common type of vow.[142]

Where the issue is a single battle, in prospect or retrospect, the attention is more on sacrifices made and examined for what omens they may offer. The taking of omens presumes that the gods had foreknowledge of the outcome of a battle, but from popular sources it is not clear that they were thought to decide this outcome.[143] The presumption in Aeschylus is that they did. His characters give them, explicitly or implicitly, credit for victory and blame for defeat. The gods gave Agamemnon victory over the city of Priam (*Ag.* 524–526, 1335-1336),[144] and in the *Eumenides* Athena promises her Athenians military glory (913–915). The Persians hold gods responsible for their defeat at Salamis (*Pers.* 293–294, 454–455, 513–514, 905–906; cf. 94). To the Persians the defeat was a misfortune, and hence often attributed by them to a *daimon,*[145] but for the Greeks, of course, it was a victory, and Aeschylus presents it, in absolute terms, as good and just.[146] In *Seven against Thebes* too the gods are often assumed to be responsible for military victory or defeat (21–23, 109–180, 265–281, 301–320; cf. 35). There the city is saved and thus prayers on its behalf are answered (301–303). Eteocles himself is killed, but that may be a just punishment for his impieties.[147]

Such explicit references to gods' determining the outcome of wars and battles are not to be found in Sophocles and are scarce in Euripides.[148] In tragedy as in life assignment of divine responsibility for military victory or defeat was rare, and in Aeschylus, where it does occur, it may result largely from his particular concern with demonstrating the justice of the gods. Greeks, even Greek poets, personally fought in many battles and were too experienced in warfare to assume that gods either alone or primarily decided the outcome of military combat.

Individuals in tragedy occasionally express the hope that the gods will be their "allies," their "partners in battle" (σύμμαχοι). As we attempt to understand better how classical Greeks imagined and expressed their relationships to their gods, it becomes important to determine whether a term such as σύμμαχος is employed literally or metaphorically. That σύμμαχος is used when gods are to help in battle or war is understandable, but if it is used of the gods' activities well beyond warfare, it becomes metaphorical and puts the general conception of human relationship to the gods into a certain frame of reference. To put the matter simply, did the Greeks regularly conceive of gods as "allies in battle," or did they do so only in military situations?

Σύμμαχος is used in tragedy almost exclusively in reference to military situations. Eteocles, facing an Argive invasion, urges prayer that the gods be "allies" (A. *Th.* 266). The pro-Athenian chorus in Euripides' *Suppliants,* in the brief interval between Theseus' departure with an army to Thebes and the announcement of his victory, pray to Zeus to be a σύμμαχος to Athens (628–631). In much the same situation the Athenian chorus of the *Heraclidae* claim to be without fear because they have Zeus as their σύμμαχος (766–769). Iolaus expects an Athenian victory because the Athenian divine ally is superior to the Argives':

> We use as allies gods who are no worse than the Argives'
> allies. Hera, Zeus' wife, champions them, but Athena us.[149]
> And I say this contributes to success, to have better gods.
> Pallas will not put up with being defeated.
>
> (347–352)

The claim that our divine ally is superior to theirs seems natural in such situations, but in fact we find it only here.

In Sophocles' *Ajax* Athena, though with heavy irony, speaks of herself as Ajax' ally (συμμάχου, 89–90).[150] With or without irony, σύμμαχος here, however, indicates the quasi-Homeric relationship that Sophocles has established between Athena and the hero. Athena is protectress of the single warrior in Homeric battle (*Aj.* 91–93, 762–769), and in these terms σύμμαχος is appropriate.[151] In his opening prayer to Hermes Chthonios, Orestes asks the god to be his "savior" and "ally" (A. *Ch.* 1–2). In the next prayer he asks that Zeus be his "willing ally" (18–19). In neither is he asking for help in a real military battle, and in each σύμμαχος must be taken metaphorically. The metaphor, however, does not so much define the relationship Orestes has with the god as it reveals his conception of his revenge for his father as a battle to be fought against enemies.[152]

In only two instances does the συμμαχία of the gods appear to be extended beyond the immediate context of war. In Euripides' *Troades* Hecuba understandably laments that the gods have been "bad allies" (469). They did fail the Trojans in war, but Hecuba's cry at this time, given her personal sufferings, seems to go beyond that. So too Dionysus in the *Bacchae* (1341–1343) asserts that the Thebans, if they had been reasonable when they should have been, could have him now as a σύμμαχος. By using that term Dionysus implies that now he is Thebes' "enemy" (πολέμιος), and that is certainly the manner in which he treats the Thebans in the latter half of the play.[153] Here and in the *Troades* Euripides has developed a metaphorical sense of σύμμαχος. Elsewhere in tragedy and popular sources a divine σύμμαχος is, however, simply an ally in battle.[154] One willing to draw negative conclusions *ex silentio* might say that in terms of religious attitude, classical Athenians did not view themselves as personally embattled, as needing divine allies in the everyday battles of life. They fought wars but did not view life itself as a war requiring divine assistance.

The Greeks were not pacifists, and in tragedies war-related prayers concern invasions, defeat, and civil wars, not the avoidance of war in general. The refugee Danaid chorus in Aeschylus' *Suppliants* has been given protection against the pursuing Aegyptiads by the Argives. In gratitude the Danaids make an extensive prayer on behalf of their benefactors, including requests, in rich Aeschylean language, that "wanton Ares" not make the Pelasgian land "slain by fire," that he not "reap mortals in bloody fields" (633–638).[155] They later ask that "strife not bloody this plain of land" with the fallen corpses of its residents, that "the blossom of its youth not be cut down," that "Ares, the man-slaying bed-partner of Aphrodite" not cut down the blossom of the country's young (661–666). Both prayers are directed against a war of invasion by foreigners. The Danaids also pray that the gods grant the Argives "just settlements, without sufferings, with foreigners before the arming of Ares" (701–703). These three prayers, taken together, ask divine help in wars against foreign invaders and in negotiations forestalling war. They go beyond what we usually find in tragedy, and that may be explained, in part, by their integral relationship to the action of this trilogy. Because they took in the Danaids, the Argives face the prospect of an invasion by the forces of Aegyptus,[156] and the Danaids express, though in very general language, the hope that the Argives will not suffer this but will, by a just settlement ("just," to be sure, in the eyes of the Danaids), resolve the issue without war.

The Danaids also pray that "no man-slaying plague attack and rend the city, arming violence among the people and the tear-begetting, danceless, lyreless Ares" (679–682). Here they pray against civil war.[157] The Danaids' presence has brought the threat of civil discord to Argos, and that civil discord may have occurred or been reported in the later, lost plays of the trilogy.[158] In another play Aeschylus' Eumenides make a very similar prayer for the Athenians, their benefactors: may civil war, "insatiable for evils, not roar" in Athens, and may the "dust not drink the dark blood of the citizens" (*Eum.* 976–980).[159] Their wish is that the Athenians may live in political concord, and this prayer may reflect, as does the whole play, Athenian anxieties following the democratic reforms of Ephialtes.[160]

It is noteworthy that prayers to avert war, to settle disputes by negotiation before war, and to escape civil war are to be found exclusively in Aeschylus.[161] His gods, more so than the gods of the other tragedians, involve themselves in affairs of national and international law and justice. This seems to be a particularly Aeschylean conception, one not shared by other tragedians and not attested among the religious practices of his contemporaries. We find no cults devoted to these ends in the fifth century. It is only in the war-weary fourth century, in 374 B.C., that a cult of Eirene (Peace) first appears.[162]

Euripides' Theseus claims that a god gave men "the nourishment of food and, from the sky, drops of rain for this nourishment, so that they may support produce from the earth and wet her womb" (*Suppl.* 205–207). Aeschylus' Prometheus gave men knowledge of the seasons, in all probability for agricultural purposes (*Pr.* 454–458). Sophocles makes the ability to till and farm the soil largely a human accomplishment (*Ant.* 337–352).[163] So much divine intervention the tragic poets variously assigned to prehistorical advancements in agricultural endeavors. In historical times success in all forms of agriculture and animal husbandry was tied to the goodwill of the gods. In prose sources, as usual, the gods' positive contributions are emphasized, with failure attributed to impieties such as perjury or pollution from homicide. Apart from avoiding these, the Athenians attempted to maintain divine favor by proper performance of traditional sacrifices and harvest festivals and, in particular, by first-fruit offerings.[164] In tragedy we often find the negative side, the harm that gods cause or threaten to cause to a country's produce, and it is of interest to discern the reasons given in tragedy for this divine hostility and to see how these reasons accord with conceptions attested for practised religion.

Three factors, apart from human efforts,[165] influence agricultural success in Greece and elsewhere: the fertility of the land itself, sufficient and timely rain, and plant and animal diseases.[166] The gods were involved in each.[167] Zeus was, in tragedy, in life, and everywhere, solely responsible for rain; he is also, of course, the source of thunder, lightning, and, most often, wind.[168] The failure of crops and the death of animals through diseases or similar causes are, in tragedy, linked to the pollution of homicide and to curses. The Erinyes as Aeschylus presents them in the *Eumenides* are the embodiment of both curses and the pollution of homicide,[169] and in anger at the Athenians' failure to convict Orestes they threaten to hurl forth a poison which will blight plant and human life (782–787). Athena knows well that by their curses they can do this (800–803, 829–831). When mollified and transformed by Aeschylus into benevolent spirits, the Erinyes/Eumenides promise the opposite: now they wish for Athens a lasting fertility of crops and animals (904–909, 921–926); now, because of them, no tree and plant diseases are to enter Attica, and Pan is to support the flourishing sheep along with their twofold offspring (938–945). That the Erinyes/Eumenides are made agents of these blessings and harms is uniquely Aeschylus' conception,[170] but similar causes of crop and animal failures are found elsewhere.

The plague upon crops and animals from which Thebes suffers at the opening of Sophocles' *Oedipus Tyrannus* occurs, we learn, because Laius' unpurified killer resides in the city (22–30, 95–107). Upon the same idea is based Oedipus' prayer (269–271) that for those who do not search out the murderer the gods "not send up from the earth any crop." There are indications in the popular sources that such a link between curses, the pollution of homicide, and failure with crops and animals had once existed in practised religion, however attenuated the belief may have been in the classical period. Aeschines reports a sixth-century international agreement, the violators of which (that is, perjurers) are cursed that, among other things, "their land not bear produce" and "their cattle not produce offspring" (3.108–111). We find no such provision in fifth-century treaties.[171] The harm that a polluted murderer could cause his country in its agrarian affairs may also explain, in some small part, his exclusion from religious rituals and, in fact, from the country itself.[172] There is, in any case, no indication from popular sources that Athenians of the classical period continued to attribute crop and animal loss to such causes. We may have here an instance where tragedians hark back to an earlier, once widespread and commonly held belief about the effect of curses and pollution on human efforts to secure food.

With fertility of the land we are in the realm largely of female, maternal deities.[173] Gaia is the "mother of all things," giver and receiver of plant and animal life; she receives the fertilizing rain of Ouranos (or Zeus) and is, of course, the source of agricultural produce.[174] These are facts of nature translated into poetry, but they do have a basis in contemporary cult. A statue of Gaia begging Zeus to rain on her stood on the Acropolis in Pausanias' time (1.24.3), a product, he surmises, of a time of drought. Apparently agricultural cults of Gaia were practised in Attica near the Ilissus, at Phyle, and at Marathon.[175] Gaia seems, however, to represent in literature and cult the earth's fertility only in the most general terms;[176] when specific crops like grain, olives, or wine become the object of concern, Demeter, Athena, and Dionysus come to the fore. In the classical period the Athenians in particular promoted Demeter, whose mysteries they possessed and whose benefits they claimed to have promulgated.[177] Demeter's growth was, we may suspect, at the expense of Gaia, particularly in Attica, where first-fruit offerings of grain were now to be sent to the Eleusinian Demeter. Had the Athenians worked their will, first-fruit offerings from all their subjects would have been sent to their Demeter.[178] In this regard, it is interesting to note, Gaia is addressed only in tragedies which are set in non-Athenian parts of the Greek world. So too she represented "earth" in non-Athenian or international oaths. When Athenians swore oaths among themselves, they usually swore by Demeter.[179]

The myth of Demeter and Kore, some version of it if not the precise one preserved in the Homeric hymn (2), formed the cult myth of the Eleusinian Mysteries, and the mysteries no doubt explicated, among other things, the annual cycle of the birth and death of agricultural crops.[180] Given Demeter's importance in this area, it is surprising how little prominence she and her myth have in tragedy. In the surviving plays she is usually mentioned only in passing, as the mother of Persephone or as a metonym for grain.[181] This may, in fact, result from her close association with the mysteries. Aeschylus himself was accused of impiety for revealing secrets of the mysteries in a play,[182] and he and other tragedians may have taken this experience to heart. The only surviving tragic treatment of the Demeter and Kore myth is in Euripides' *Helen* (1301–1368), and this is an oddly syncretistic, near-eastern account of Magna Mater and Demeter—removed as far as possible, it would seem, from Athens and her mysteries.[183]

In the world of tragedy people do not suffer mundane ailments.[184] Members of the audience might sniffle and cough or nurse a gouty toe, but the most common health concern in the plays is plague or "swarms of diseases" affecting a whole country. The Danaid chorus of Aeschylus' *Suppliants* pray that the Argives escape both.[185] The Erinyes, in Aeschylus' unique conception of them, threaten that they will afflict Athens with plague (*Eum.* 780–787), but elsewhere Apollo is the cause and "stopper" of plague. Aeschylus has the messenger in the *Agamemnon* follow Homer's account (*Il.* 1.43–67) of the plague at Troy, with Apollo hurling his arrows at the army. "Now," the messenger says, "Lord Apollo, be savior and healer" (σωτήρ ... καὶ παιώνιος, 509–513).[186] In Sophocles' *Oedipus Tyrannus* Apollo may not have caused the plague afflicting Thebes,[187] but the Thebans turn to his oracle to find what they might do to end it (40–43, 68–111; cf. 19–21). The plague, much like the famines previously discussed, results from the presence of Laius' unpurified murderer (95–111), and Apollo's oracle reveals this critical piece of information. Apollo's role extends beyond that, however, because at the very end of the prologue the priest prays, in language reminiscent of Aeschylus, "May Apollo who sent these oracles at the same time come as savior and stopper of the disease" (σωτήρ ... νόσου παυστήριος, 149–150). Apollo's association with the plagues of tragedy is fourfold: as Homer's sender of the arrows of plague, as oracular source of necessary information, as the purifying god, and as a healing god.[188] These elements are, of course, interrelated, but the poets generally choose to introduce or emphasize only one or two of them.

Despite his frequent and complex association with plagues in literature, there is little evidence that Apollo played such a role in real life in Athens in the classical period. No historical oracle of Delphi addresses the problem of plague, and in their own plague of 430–426 the Athenians appear to have paid little special attention to Apollo.[189] In fact, as soon as they were able after this plague, they turned their attention to Asclepios of Epidaurus, importing his cult in 420 B.C.

The arrival of Asclepios in Athens at this time must have significantly redirected the Athenians' attention and activity in regard to medicine and religion. His two cult centers, on the south slope of the Acropolis and in the Piraeus, were large, busy, and almost immediately prosperous. But what had the Athenians done before 420? Some, like Aristophanes' Philokleon, may have gone abroad to foreign Asclepieia (*V.* 121–123, produced in 422). Most would have had to be content with various local healing deities and heroes,[190] those whose popularity and activity were probably eclipsed by the late-arriving Asclepios. Despite his role in tragedy, Apollo seems independently to have had little concern with medical healing in Athens either before or after Asclepios.[191] It may be that Asclepios, in addition to drawing to himself various other gods' and heroes' medical activity, also increased for all later Athenians interest in healing through ritual and cult.

The Asclepios of tragedies is not a cult figure. He is the skilled physician of Homer (S. *Ph.* 1437–1438; cf. *Il.* 4.194, 11.518). He is killed by Zeus for returning the dead to life,[192] and there is no mention of his later divine or heroic status. The one possible suggestion of his later role as a healing deity is a tantalizing fragment from Sophocles' lost *Phineus*:

The sight of (the son of Phineus) was restored,
and he was given light in his eyes,
having found Asclepios Paion kindly.[193]

(710[R])

Here it may be appropriate to recall that Sophocles wrote a paean for Asclepios and was instrumental in the introduction of his cult to Attica in 420.[194]

Aeschylus' Prometheus claims he gave humans the medical arts (*Pr.* 478–

483), Sophocles' chorus views them as an entirely human invention (*Ant.* 363–364), and the chorus of Euripides' *Alcestis* treats medicinal drugs as Apollo's gift to the Asclepiadae (969–972).[195] The use of incantations against disease, known from [Hippocrates] *On the Holy Disease* (2.10–15, 4.34), is suggested in Sophocles' *Trachiniae* 1000–1002 and criticized in his *Ajax*: "It is not characteristic of a wise physician to chant incantations when a disease needs surgery" (581–582).[196] Such criticism recalls Pericles' nearly contemporary condemnation of the use of amulets as "silliness" (ἀβελτερίαν), a silliness in which, however, he acquiesced when sick, as no doubt did many others (Plut. *Per.* 38.2).

In Sophocles' *Oedipus Tyrannus* (151–215) we may see the development of the usual associations of god, religion, and plague in a highly original direction.[197] The chorus prays that the plague affecting Thebes end, and their initial appeal to Apollo Paean (154) is understandable because he has provided information on the cause of the plague. Also, the previous speaker, the priest, has invoked him as "savior and stopper of the disease" (149–150). The first part of the ode (151–157), with its references to Apollo's oracle, links the parodos to the action of the prologue. The second part (158–189) begins and ends with an appeal to Athena and also includes addresses to Apollo and the specifically Theban Artemis Eukleia.[198] Athena and Artemis Eukleia are asked for aid, not, I think, because of any specific healing functions they have, but as patronesses of the city Thebes. Athena in particular is, throughout Theban plays, the city's protectress and thus is naturally summoned in times of statewide need, medical or other. Now "the whole people are sick" (169–170), and it is Athena's and Artemis' concern with the whole city that makes them appropriate recipients of this prayer. In its closing stasimon (190–215) the parodos takes a new direction with Sophocles' unique identification of the plague as "Ares, the Raging, who, without bronze of shields, sets me ablaze" (190–192).[199] Having once established this bold metaphor, Sophocles then develops the parodos along lines of Homer's theomachies in *Iliad* 5 and 20–21. From here derive Zeus' antipathy to Ares (5.589–898) and the thought that Zeus might "destroy" this Ares. Also from the theomachies comes the idea that other gods, specifically Apollo, Artemis, and the Theban Dionysus, are to marshal their forces against Ares.

The Deities 59

The desire for children was strong in Greece, so strong that Euripides could term it a "passion" (ἔρως, *Ion* 67, 1227, *Med.* 714–715, and frag. 2[A], 21). One prays for children and successful births to the nymphs, to Artemis, and, once, even to Athena.[200] Infertility, especially among royalty, was a problem worthy of tragedy, and men and women encountering it went to the oracles of Trophonios and Apollo (E. *Med.* 667–681, *Ion*, passim, esp. 64–73, 302–306, 404–409, 534–537) and Zeus of Dodona (E. frag. 2[A], 19–25) to find the cause. Among these causes, in tragedy, are pollution (S. *OT* 172–174) and its like in the curses of Aeschylus' Erinyes (*Eum.* 780–787).[201] Once transformed into the beneficent Eumenides, Aeschylus' goddesses promise "protection of mortal seeds" (909) and will receive, as the primary acts of worship in their cult, first-fruit offerings "before" or "in behalf of" children and the marriage ceremony (834–836).[202] Elsewhere infertility and unsuccessful results of pregnancy fall into that general group of misfortunes caused by "a god" or "the gods" (A. *Ch.* 1005–1006, *Eum.* 660–661; E. frag. 491[N]; cf. E. *Med.* 671).

It seems natural that by and large, women in tragedies appeal to female deities for children and successful births.[203] Women also tend to pray that their children find long and happy lives, men that their children be useful and obedient. As Euripides' Alcestis faces death, she prays to the Hestia of her home that the goddess raise the children, that the boy find a "dear wife" and the girl a "noble husband."[204] She asks that the children not die untimely deaths but rather live "blessed" (εὐδαίμονας), pleasant lives in their fatherland (*Alc.* 162–169). Tecmessa imagines Ajax' mother praying that he come home alive after the Trojan War (S. *Aj.* 507–509). Men, however, are concerned with the benefits their children can offer. Admetus, Alcestis' husband, puts it abruptly: "We have enough children. I pray to the gods that there be benefit (ὄνησιν) from these" (E. *Alc.* 334–335). When Theseus recognizes his son's "good and pious mind," Hippolytus bids him pray that he find "legitimate children of such quality" (E. *Hipp.* 1455). Creon in Sophocles' *Antigone* claims that "men pray to beget and have in their homes obedient children, so that they can repay [their father's] enemy with evils and, equally with their father, honor his friend" (641–644).[205] In *Seven against Thebes* Eteocles says that "Mother Ge, the dearest nurse," raised young men to be "shield-bearers" to defend their country in times of need (16–20). Women too, of course, see the practical benefits of children. The Danaids pray that Argive women may bear "rulers of the land" (A. *Suppl.*

674–675),[206] and the intensely patriotic Praxithea says that women bear children "to protect the altars of the gods and the fatherland" (E. frag. 50[A], 14–15). But in prayers for their own children women of tragedy look to the personal safety and happiness of their offspring, men to the benefits which do or should accrue.

The personages of tragedy are nearly all royal and wealthy. What few religious concerns they express about wealth involve not the acquisition but the preservation of fortunes.[207] The loss of wealth, like other misfortunes, is caused "by a god" (E. frag. 618[N]). In Aeschylean terms great wealth brings the potential for hybris and its punishment (e.g., A. Ag. 946–949, 961–965). Happiness and prosperity (ὄλβος), "dear to all and prayed for," is acquired from "soundness of thoughts" regarding piety and sin (A. Eum. 534–537), and wealth itself is a major component of this prosperity, itself acquired with "a god's help" (A. Pers. 163–164). Apart from this Aeschylean nexus of piety, divine justice, and prosperity, we find in tragedy little divine intervention presumed in man's economic affairs, and this stands in strong contrast to what we know of contemporary religion.

It was contrary to the classical spirit to have, in practised religion, so simplistic and transparent a god as Ploutos (Wealth),[208] and Greeks and especially Athenians turned to established gods to meet their needs in this area. In the fifth century many individual Athenians offered, as dedications, tithes to Athena, sometimes as the fulfillment of a vow, sometimes with the understanding that more success would result in more dedications.[209] Nicias employed the assistance of soothsayers in the chancy and dangerous business of mining (Plut. Nic. 4.2), and others prayed to Zeus Meilichios (Xen. Ana. 7.8.1–6) or, in a family context, to Zeus Ktesios (Isaeus 8.15–16) for personal economic prosperity.[210] Some attempted to ruin their enemies' occupational activities by curse tablets.[211] Similar curses, but statewide, could be added to treaties as punishments for those who violated sworn agreements.[212]

The differences between the tragic and popular religious views of wealth signify little but different areas of interest. Tragic characters, both economically and personally, are above mundane thoughts about earning a living. This no doubt major concern for many members of the audience was simply not a topic for tragedy. The situation is, of course, quite the opposite in Old Comedy and New Comedy, where slaves and low- to middle-class characters and even their gods are often fully engaged in the pursuit of profit.

When Greeks set sail in their small boats on the Aegean and Mediterranean, they exposed themselves and their cargoes to considerable and unpredictable dangers. It is little wonder that then in particular they thought they were entrusting themselves and their fortunes to the hands of the gods.[213] Tragedy, unlike epic, seldom pauses to describe the various prayers, sacrifices, and rituals that preceded, accompanied, and concluded sea voyages.[214] In general terms Poseidon and the Nereids who often accompany him control sea conditions such as waves and currents, whereas the Dioscuroi rescue sailors in distress.[215] Zeus, the producer of all atmospheric phenomena, is usually given responsibility for the winds.[216] In tragedy major exceptions in this regard are to be found in the stories of Iphigeneia and Polyxena as told in the *Agamemnon*, *Iphigeneia at Aulis*, and *Hecuba*. In these stories the Greek fleet is being delayed by a lack of favorable winds, and the Greeks turn to religious means to solve the problem. Iphigeneia and Polyxena are offered as appeasements to the wrath of angry deities. In the mythological tradition Iphigeneia's fate is bound to Artemis and Polyxena's to Achilles, and the deity and hero have, in a sense, displaced Zeus from his usual function.[217] Aeschylus and Sophocles both have Artemis stop the winds, whereas Euripides credits the inability to sail (ἄπλοια) in both stories to Artemis and Achilles but never explicitly says either controlled the winds.[218] Although Artemis and Achilles each had some associations with seafaring,[219] in these plays neither is presented as a sea deity. Each has been offended and must be appeased, but the offenses have nothing to do with seafaring.[220] As a result of the offense each deity would be hostile to whatever undertaking the Greeks might have in mind. The enterprise here is a voyage, but in different circumstances the two deities would equally well have made other ventures impossible until they had been appeased.

It has been claimed that the appeasement of a wrathful god to attain favorable sea conditions was gradually supplanted by simple prayers of request to beneficent gods for those same purposes.[221] If in fact this chronological development did occur,[222] tragedy would reflect the earlier age. Appeasing a wrathful god, by human sacrifice or other means, to obtain favorable sailing would be, like the harmful effects of pollution on crops and animals noted before, an old and by mid-fifth century outmoded idea which tragedians in their archaizing of religious elements chose, in part under the strictures of the mythological tradition, to recreate.[223]

Tragic characters and fifth-century Athenians shared one important belief about seafaring: the gods punish the impious at sea, and thus one should not sail on a ship with a sinner. Andocides (1.137–139) argued in court that his record of safe voyages at sea was proof that he was not an impure and impious man, and Antiphon (5.81–83) claims that the impious man was vulnerable to divine anger at sea and might bring destruction upon his fellow passengers as well as upon himself. Xenophon, in explaining a Persian prince's practice to a Greek audience, also makes the point: "Cyrus considered the piety of his companions also a benefit for himself, reasoning as do those who choose to sail with pious men rather than with those who seem to have committed some impiety" (*Cyr.* 8.1.25). In the popular sources the crime for which the intended victim is punished is always some act of impiety. So too in tragedy.[224] In Euripides' *Electra* the Dioscuroi recommend that no one sail with perjurers (1354–1355),[225] and in Aeschylus' *Seven against Thebes* Eteocles speaks of the death at sea of a man who sails with those who are god-hated (θεοπτύστῳ), hateful to *xenoi,* and unmindful of the gods (602–608).[226]

Sophocles' Oedipus claimed that Athens excelled all other cities in knowing "how to reverence the gods with honors" (*OC* 1006–1007).[227] In Aeschylus' *Eumenides* Athens is the "citadel of the gods, a glory among the Greeks in protecting the altars of the gods."[228] In the same play Athena tells the Erinyes that her city is "most god-loved" (θεοφιλεστάτης, 869). Athenian piety and divine favor are a constant in Athenian tragedy. The tales of great impiety, of *xenos*-killing, of husband- and child-killing, of violation of asylum, oaths, and burial rites, and of blasphemy and murder are all set elsewhere, in Thebes, Argos, Corinth, or in more distant lands. Athens is the scene of pious deeds, the home of pious men and women, and, as in Aeschylus' *Or-*

esteia, Euripides' *Suppliants*, and Sophocles' *Oedipus at Colonus*, the place where impieties committed elsewhere are resolved. We may appropriately conclude and summarize the preceding general catalogue of divine interventions by mentioning the benefits that the tragedians attribute specifically to Athens as a result of the extraordinary piety of the Athenian people.

Athens is Athena's city: she gave her name to it, and the Acropolis is her hill.[229] She is Athens' mother, mistress, and protector.[230] Aeschylus' Zeus is particularly concerned with Athenians because they are under his daughter's "wings" (A. *Eum.* 996–1002 = 1014–1020). Athena gave Athens the olive and watches over the city, but her major role in the Athens of tragedy is military.[231] This is the one function Aeschylus has Athena reserve for herself at the end of the *Eumenides* (913–915). In the same play he also has her found the juridical process for homicide cases (482–484, 570–573, 681–710)[232] and offer Athenians political advice (681–710). This seems an Aeschylean view, a product of his concern for the gods' interest in justice, a topic I reserve for the discussion of Aeschylus himself. Sophocles and Euripides limit her Athenian role to olives and war.[233]

Athens is "holy," "divine," and "well-*daimoned*," a "god-built" city, though in contrast to Thebes and Troy we know of no specific walls or buildings constructed by the gods.[234] Sophocles has a chorus of Athenians credit Poseidon with first teaching them the use of the bit and bridle and of ships (*OC* 707–719).[235] In the battle of Salamis "the gods," a Persian messenger says, protected Athens (A. *Pers.* 347). In what Page (on *Med.* 824ff.) calls a "magnificent hymn to the glory of Athens," the chorus of Corinthian women in Euripides' *Medea*, after calling the Athenians "children of the blessed gods"[236] and praising their wisdom and the city's clear air, says that there the nine Muses begot Harmonia. They also repeat a report that Aphrodite, drawing water from the Cephisus River, gave Athens sweet, gentle breezes (824–845). They wonder how this blessed land will ever receive the unholy Medea, the murderess of her children. Harmonia, Page claims (on 831), is "the *Union* of the nine muses: where these are together, they create a tenth essence, the child of none but of all together." The reference is seemingly to Athens' excellence in all μουσική, with due proportion of each. Here, and only here, is Aphrodite credited with sweet breezes.[237] This ode may be the product only of Euripides' literary imagination, but it may reflect some cult realities. The nexus of Aphrodite, Muses, Cephisus, and flowers is found also in Sophocles' encomium of Athens twenty-nine years later (*OC*

681–693), and Euripides' localization of Aphrodite's benefaction to the banks of the Cephisus is eye-catching. Of the several cults of Aphrodite in Attica,[238] what Euripides describes seems most like that of Aphrodite "In the Gardens," whose cult site has been placed by some near the banks of the Ilissus.[239] We know, unfortunately, little of this cult, or of any association of Aphrodite with the Muses there,[240] or of a like cult beside the Cephisus. In any case this ode from the *Medea* is unique among tragic and prose sources in attributing Athens' literary and artistic accomplishments to the gods and in this regard stands apart from the usual concepts of divine intervention into Athenian life.

This list of divine contributions to Athens is rather meager, and to fill it out we must return to the *Eumenides,* where newly beneficent spirits promise much to just and pious Athenians: that good things will come from the earth, sea, and sky; that the earth, herds, and human beings will be fertile; that the mines will be productive; that neither blight nor plague will afflict the city; that young men will not die untimely deaths; that young women will find husbands; that hated civil war and its bloody battles will never "roar" in the city (903–987).[241] Athena herself guarantees them military success (913–915). Despite the peculiarly Aeschylean assignment of these benefits to the Eumenides,[242] the benefits themselves, as we have seen, are those commonly expected of the gods. They are among the even more extensive benefits the Danaids ask of the gods for the pious Argives (A. *Suppl.* 625–709): that war never burn down the city; that plague never empty the city of men; that civil war not bloody the land; that youth not be killed in war; that the altars be full; that new leaders of the land be born; that Artemis watch over childbirths; that diseases be kept away; that land and herds be fertile; that the poets sing good songs at the altars; that the city reconcile with its enemies before war; and that the citizens honor gods with traditional sacrifices and respect their parents.[243] These two lists of divine benefits promised or prayed for include most of the blessings for which Athenians (and Argives, as an Athenian conceived of them) looked to the gods in literature and life.

In the religion of tragedy the *deus ex machina* plays a famous, not to say notorious role,[244] and nowhere better do we see divergences of religion in tragedy from that of life. Let us begin with the proposition that underlies the *deus ex machina,* namely that gods in bodily form appear to awake mortals and speak to them. Such an occurrence, so common and taken for granted in tragedy, is unattested in all the various sources for popular religion in the classical period.[245] Tragedy represents that mythical time when gods on occasion wined, dined, and conversed with men, when some aristocrats were their children or grandchildren, when gods personally appeared to individuals who were either themselves favored or members of favored families. This conception of divine-human relationships is Homeric and the product of the literary, not religious tradition.

Despite this uniquely literary conception we may still ask how the *dei ex machina* are presented, what they do, and how this is related to the gods of real life. In formal terms the scenes of *dei ex machina* are very similar.[246] Sometimes the chorus or a character recognizes the divine presence before it announces itself, but most often the deity suddenly appears and speaks. He begins with a command, either to hear his words or, more often, to stop some planned or current action. Only then he identifies himself. The content of the speeches varies markedly, of course, according to the circumstances of the play, but most include explanations of the present situation, prophecies about the future, and the establishment of cults. And, finally, the humans immediately and unhesitatingly accept the deity's pronouncements.[247]

The *deus, ex machina,* appears from overhead, and in the four plays where the deity's presence is recognized before he speaks, this aerial path is the only indication of divinity.[248] In each case the chorus and characters cannot identify the deity, and they share the initial reaction and language of the first Taurian cowherd in Euripides' *Iphigeneia among the Taurians*: "There are some *daimones.* . . ."[249] *Daimon* is the *vox propria* for an unidentifiable deity, and it figures in each Euripidean scene, always associated with other similarly indefinite terms ("Who of the gods?" "What divine thing [τίνος θείον] do I perceive?").[250] *Daimon* is lacking only in the *Rhesus* ("What god?" 886), whose author throughout does not follow the tragic or fifth-century conventional uses of the term.[251]

The deity usually begins his speech with a command, more or less peremptorily, depending on whether he is addressing an enemy (as the Dioscuroi to Theoclymenus in E. *Hel.* and Artemis to Thoas in E. *IT*) or a friend (Heracles to Philoctetes in S. *Ph.*). The order may be merely to "listen to my words" or may prohibit an action.[252]

Each *deus ex machina* gives explanations and makes arrangements peculiar to the circumstances of the play, but these explanations and arrangements share some characteristics. In explaining situations which are beyond their control or for which they want higher authority—that is, situations of the type for which men might invoke the gods—these *dei ex machina* usually appeal to Zeus or some form of fate or necessity.[253] Unless some other god has been actively engaged in the plot (as Aphrodite in the *Hippolytus* or Apollo in the *Ion*), the *deus ex machina*, when pressed to provide the ultimate cause, says, "It is fate," "It had to happen that way," "It must be this way," or "Such were the wishes of Zeus."

The *dei ex machina* also prophesy the future. Philoctetes will, according to Sophocles' Heracles, go to Troy, display virtue there, kill Paris with his bow, sack the city, and, after receiving the "best (surviving) player of the war award," bring spoils back to his homeland (*Ph.* 1423–1430). Athena in Euripides' *Ion* gives a detailed account of the future of Ion, Creousa, their descendants, and of the resulting Athenian and Greek tribal structure (1571–1594, 1604–1605).[254] *Dei ex machina* make similar predictions about the future dynasty of the Molossians (E. *Andr.* 1247–1252), about Orestes' wanderings and trial at Athens (E. *Or.* 1650–1652, *El.* 1252–1276, 1290–1292), about the expedition of the Epigonoi (E. *Suppl.* 1213–1226), and about the future of Helen (E. *Hel.* 1662–1675) and Cadmus (E. *Ba.* 1330–1339). The Greeks practised divination, and it might seem only natural to have gods, on stage, giving such information. But in fact the divination which Athenians employed bore little relation to what the *dei ex machina* have to offer. Greeks sought from divination, from oracles as well as from seers and omens, signs of divine approval for planned actions such as war, travel, or marriage. They did not expect from oracles or seers detailed accounts of future events.[255] There was, in the structure of Greek popular religion, nothing remotely similar to the prophecies of the *deus ex machina*.

The *dei ex machina* of Euripides also institute religious cults. The Athena of *Iphigeneia among the Taurians* gives elaborate prescriptions for the site, deities, names, and even ritual of Athenian cults of Artemis at Halae and Brauron (1450–1467). We have already considered (above, pp. 32–34) the provisions that Athena makes in the *Erechtheus* for the Athenian cults of Erechtheus and the Hyacinthids. Similar instructions are given for the sanctuary of the seven heroes who fought at Thebes and for the cults of Hippolytus at Troezen, of Helen as protector of ships, of Dirce, Amphion, and Zethus at Thebes, and of Neoptolemus, Peleus, and Achilles.[256]

The Deities 67

The descriptions Euripidean *dei ex machina* give of non-Athenian cults (for example, of Helen, Dirce, Peleus, and Achilles) are usually general. The individual becomes "a god" and is usually given a function. For Athenian cults (Artemis and Erechtheus), however, the *dei ex machina* give precise locations and details of ritual and priesthood. Their descriptions are also very much in accord with what we know from elsewhere about these cults. It seems that *dei ex machina* describe new cults as they really were to the fifth-century audience, not as the poet personally chose to make them. In the mythical time of tragedy, when gods consort with men, religion is in flux. New cults, new deities, and new forms of old cults appear.[257] The *deus ex machina* often stands at the point of transformation from old to new. The deity sometimes personally causes this change[258] but most often simply reports it. But by describing it the *deus ex machina,* as a divine figure, also reveals the gods' approval of the new deity and new cult. In describing them he ratifies them.[259]

Dei ex machina occasionally make from their elevated position general statements about piety, the gods, and humankind. Although hardly canonical in the manner of the Bible, these and similar statements by seers are as close to the "revealed word of god" as the Greeks come.[260] The poets represent these gods revealing their views and wishes to mankind, and despite the fictitious setting and the literary context it is worth noting what the gods, *ex machina,* have to say on religious matters.

Dei ex machina urge piety. Artemis concludes her speech to Theseus with these words:

Gods do not rejoice when the pious die.
Evil men, however, we destroy together with
their children and houses.

(E. *Hipp.* 1339–1341)

Castor of the sailor-saving Dioscuroi warns against perjury:

Let no one wish to be unjust and
let no one sail with perjurers.
I, a god, speak to mortals.

(E. *El.* 1354–1356)

Perjury is an impiety, perhaps the most common one in real life, and Castor warns that the gods punish the impious at sea.[261] Heracles, in Sophocles' *Philoctetes,* bids Philoctetes and Neoptolemus, as they defeat the Trojans,

> Keep in mind, when you sack the land,
> to be pious in matters concerning the gods,
> since father Zeus considers all other things second to this.
> Piety does not die with mortals,
> it does not perish whether they are living or they die.
>
> (1440–1444)

To reinforce the conventional exhortation to piety, especially in the licentious time of sack and pillage,[262] Heracles adds an inducement, that piety in this life does not die with the body but lives on.[263] These exhortations to piety stand somewhat apart from the immediate circumstances of their plays and for this reason are all the more noteworthy as *ex officio* pronouncements by divinities. The penultimate words of Athena in the *Ion* are much more a direct comment on the action, but they too serve to explain the ways of gods to mortals: "What the gods do may take time, but in the end their acts do not lack force" (1615).

In offering consolation to humans *dei ex machina* also reveal something of their divine world. Castor tells Orestes and Electra, "I and the heavenly gods have pity for much-suffering mortals" (E. *El.* 1329–1330). Artemis tells Theseus, the third victim of Aphrodite's schemes, that "it's only reasonable for mortals to err when gods cause it" ($\theta\epsilon\tilde{\omega}\nu$ $\delta\iota\delta\acute{o}\nu\tau\omega\nu$) (E. *Hipp.* 1433–1434). Thetis bids her husband, Peleus, to stop grieving for the dead, because all mortals are obliged to die; their death "is the decision made by the gods" (E. *Andr.* 1270–1272). And, finally, the Dioscuroi in Euripides' *Helen* may remind us of a point important in understanding the religion in tragedy. Menelaus will not die because, and only because, he is married to Zeus' daughter. "Gods," they say, "do not hate the well-born. Hard labors belong more to those who do not count" (1678–1679). The major characters of tragedy are aristocrats with special family and personal ties to the gods. It is in large part for this reason that they have close and direct relationships and dealings with the gods, and this gives religion in tragedy much of its character. For members of the audience—who would surely be, by the standards of tragedy, among "those who do not count"—religion was a quite different thing.

THREE

Challenges to Popular Religious Beliefs

Characters in tragedy often challenge by word or action beliefs we know to be part of the corpus of Athenian popular religion of the period. Certain beliefs concerning divination, oaths, the rights of *xenoi* and those having asylum, and burial rites are core elements of popular religion and piety,[1] and it is important to see how challenges to them are met. Are, for example, claims of falseness or quackery of prophecy upheld in the denouement of a play? What is the fate of those who violate conventional, religiously sanctioned standards of behavior regarding oaths, *xenoi,* suppliants, and the dead? Are they punished or not? In this chapter I describe the religious beliefs as they appear in tragedy and real life, delineate the nature of the challenge or violation, and, finally, examine the fate of the challenger or violator.

Asylum

Respect for asylum was a lively issue in the fifth century, as we can see from events in just one decade.[2] In 430 in the diplomatic maneuvering preceding the outbreak of the Peloponnesian War, the Spartans demanded that Athens expel those who, like Pericles, were tainted by the pollution of ancestors who two centuries earlier had violated the asylum of the followers of the rebellious Cylon (Thuc. 1.126.1–1.127.3). Cylon's supporters, trapped on the Acropolis and starving, had seated themselves at an altar (presumably of Athena Polias). Their opponents, the nine archons, convinced them to leave the altar with the promise that they would do them no harm. These democrats, however, killed them, some even as they sat "at" or "upon" (ἐπί) altars of the Semnai.³ The perpetrators and their families, labeled "polluted" and "sinners against the goddess," were exiled. Years later, in 508, the Spartan Cleomenes had driven out from Athens those participants in the crime who were still living, and he had cast out from Attica the bones of those who had died. Some exiles later returned, however, and in 430 the Spartans bade the Athenians to banish their polluted descendants, "first of all," according to Thucydides (1.127.1), "helping the gods exact vengeance," but also knowing that Pericles, their archenemy, would be among those "polluted."

The Athenians countered with a demand that the Spartans remove the pollution which they had incurred at Tainaron when they forcibly removed Helot suppliants from the sanctuary of Poseidon and killed them. The Spartans themselves believed that as a result of this impiety they had suffered a major earthquake in the 460s (Thuc. 1.128.1–2). In 430 the Athenians also bade the Spartans to banish the pollution that resulted when, ca. 471, the Spartans had walled up the traitorous general Pausanias, who had taken asylum in a building in the sanctuary of Athena of the Bronze House. Just moments before his death from starvation the Spartans had carried him from the sanctuary (1.128.2–1.135.1).

In 427 Corcyraean oligarchs, defeated in a civil war, took asylum in local sanctuaries (Thuc. 3.70–81). As Athenian generals and soldiers looked on, some of the oligarchs were persuaded to leave the sanctuaries on the guarantee of a trial but then were summarily condemned to death and executed. Some were walled up in a sanctuary of Dionysus and left to die. Most, in desperation, committed suicide in the Heraion. It is the most flagrant and bloody violation of asylum by Greeks of which we have record, and Thucydides uses it to introduce his general account of the horrors and social chaos of civil war (3.82–83).

Several plays center on suppliants lodged in a sanctuary, and here we are able to compare, with more evidence than is usually available, tragic dramatizations to real-life situations. We may begin with two Euripidean plays of the same decade as the events described above. In the *Heraclidae* (ca. 430 B.C.) Heracles' children, mother Alcmene, and friend Iolaus take refuge at the Marathonian sanctuary of Zeus Agoraios in Attica. They are fleeing from Eurystheus, king of Argos, who wishes to complete his persecution of Heracles by killing them.[4] The religious issue in this play is, primarily, the inviolability of asylum itself. Iolaus pleads with the Athenian king Demophon to respect the sanctuary that the Heraclidae have taken (96–97, 220–222). Other countries, bullied by Eurystheus' threats, have driven Iolaus and his refugee band from their sanctuaries (193–196, 954–955). The last hope of the Heraclidae is that Athens, unlike the others, will respect their asylum. Demophon bases his decision to protect the Heraclidae on four factors (236–246): (1) kinship (Pelops was the great-grandfather of both Heracles and Theseus); (2) the obligation to repay the good service which Heracles had rendered to Theseus; (3) the personal and political shame of Athens' yielding to Argive demands for the expulsion of the suppliants; and (4) what Demophon calls the greatest factor (τὸ μέγιστον 238), Zeus, at whose altar the refugees sit. Ethical, political, and religious considerations harmonize and merge to contribute to the just and proper decision. The overriding religious principle, which Demophon himself mentions first, provides the general rule. The moral and political elements put the general rule into a personal and civic context.[5]

The issue in Euripides' *Suppliants,* of the late 420s, is quite different. The chorus of Argive women has taken refuge in a sanctuary of Demeter at Eleusis. They are not themselves in personal danger, and the play turns not on the security of their asylum, but on Theseus' acceptance and fulfillment of their request, proper in religious terms, to obtain the burial which has been denied their sons by the Thebans. The primary question here concerns not asylum but whether Athens as a third party should undertake a crusade to force the performance of traditional religious practices.

In Aeschylus' *Suppliants* the two issues, the personal safety of the suppliants and the granting of their requests, are united. The fifty daughters of Danaus have fled Egypt with their father to escape the unwelcome marriage demands of their cousins, the fifty sons of Aegyptus. The Danaids take asylum in a sanctuary just outside the city Argos. Danaus and his daughters ask king Pelasgus, and through him the Argives, to side with them against the suitors. Their claims to Pelasgus include their kinship with the Argives, the hybris and injustice of the suitors, and the gods' (particularly Zeus') protection of those having asylum. The Danaids threaten, should Pelasgus and the Argives refuse their requests, to commit suicide in the sanctuary rather than submit to the sons of Aegyptus.

In the *Suppliants* elements of asylum and suppliant requests are combined, as they no doubt often were in real life. The person having asylum would almost always have a request to make, and the lines between asylum and suppliant request become blurred. There is, however, a major distinction: one was obliged to respect the asylum and ensure the personal safety of the suppliant, but there is no evidence that one was required—by religious or other constraints—to grant whatever requests a suppliant in a sanctuary might make. Such requests could be, of course, unjust, impracticable, impious, and so forth, and one might easily imagine the social and legal chaos if acceptance of these requests had been automatic.[6] Religious considerations come into play only in maintenance of the rights of asylum and in protecting the personal safety of the suppliant. It is, however, virtually a convention of Greek tragedy (and literature in general) that such supplications by individuals having asylum are just and proper, and also that they are, or should be, granted.[7]

Asylum required physical contact with the altar or at least with the sacred precinct of the deity.[8] Andromache, who in the opening of Euripides' *Andromache* has taken asylum in the sanctuary of Thetis, embraces the cult statue (115; cf. 311) and draws the attention of a potential assailant to the statue's gaze (246). Elsewhere in this play, as more commonly in Greek literature and life, the altar and the sanctuary itself are the guarantors of asylum.[9] Presence *in* the sanctuary was essential, but elements within the sanctuary could be introduced for variety or, as in the *Andromache*, where Thetis is so intimately associated with the action, for special emphasis.

The violation or attempted violation of asylum is an act of violence, violence directed against the gods themselves.[10] It dishonors the gods, is hybristic, and causes pollution.[11] It is unjust, unreasonable, godless, and un-Greek.[12] In the *Heraclidae* Demophon likens it to "robbing" an altar (243–244),[13] which it is in both literal and metaphorical terms, because, as Euripides presents it in the *Ion,* the suppliant becomes the "property" of the protecting deity.[14] There Creousa, in a double-entendre befitting her situation, says, "I give my body as sacred property to the god to have" (1285). In a much misunderstood passage (1287–1289) she labels herself "property" of the god, as Ion had been when he was a temple slave.[15] In simplistic terms, then, to violate asylum was to steal the property of a deity.[16] It was, in life and literature, always condemned.

The ultimate sacrilege was to slay in the sanctuary a suppliant who had gained asylum. It was, of course, "wrong" (οὐ θέμις, *Ion* 1256), and, in addition to the violation of asylum, in tragedy might arouse against the assailant the avenging spirits of the underworld (προστρόπαιον αἷμα, *Ion* 1259–1260). Andromache (E. *Andr.* 260) warns Hermione that Thetis, her guarantor of asylum, will "come after her" if she "bloodies the altar." The bloodied altar was also the focus when the suppliant in desperation committed suicide (Thuc. 3.81) or, as a device to compel attention, threatened suicide in the sanctuary (A. *Suppl.* 457–467; E. *Hel.* 980–987). The pollution would be, as it were, thrice bad: pollution of death, pollution of death in a sanctuary, and pollution of the death of one having asylum in a sanctuary. In tragedy these threats to commit suicide accomplish their purpose. In real life, in Corcyra in 427, the result was quite different.

The rights of asylum were not violated if the refugee left of his own free will, even if blackmail, threats, trickery, or starvation were involved.[17] In Euripides' *Andromache* Menelaus promises that he will spare Andromache's child if she leaves the asylum she has taken (314–315, 380–383). Andromache leaves the sanctuary voluntarily (411–414) and is seized,[18] and Menelaus then refuses to honor his promise (425–432). Euripides has Andromache make no specific protest about the sanctity of asylum, but only a general point: "Do you (Menelaus) think divine things are not divine and do not involve justice?" (439) Had the rights of asylum been violated, Andromache no doubt would have invoked Thetis, from whom she was receiving protection.[19] Once the suppliant voluntarily abandons contact with the sanctuary, the rights of asylum cease to exist, and the individual is no longer protected by religious sanctions. For the guarantor, once he has persuaded the suppliant to leave the sanctuary, to perform what he has promised becomes a matter of justice and personal integrity. Menelaus behaves with "typically Spartan" deceitfulness and is condemned for it. He follows, in fact, one stratagem of the Corcyraean oligarchs of 427. Noble tragic characters like Theseus in Sophocles' *Oedipus at Colonus* and Pelasgus in Aeschylus' *Suppliants* deliver what they promise.

The deity at whose altar the suppliants sit is the primary protector: in the *Heraclidae* Zeus Agoraios of Marathon;[20] in the *Andromache* Thetis; in the *Oedipus at Colonus* the Eumenides for Oedipus and Poseidon for Polyneices;[21] in Euripides' *Suppliants* Demeter of Eleusis; in the *Ion* Apollo of Delphi; in the *Helen* the hero Proteus;[22] in the *Heracles* Zeus Soter and Hestia;[23] for the followers of Cylon, Athena. But in addition to the specific god whose sanctuary is violated, other deities—or, better, "the gods" in general—are concerned. In the *Heraclidae* Zeus Agoraios is primarily responsible, but all the characters as well as the chorus extend concern for asylum beyond this Zeus to all "the gods."[24] This dual involvement is nicely expressed by Iolaus when he speaks of Copreus to the chorus:

(Copreus), dishonoring your gods,[25] drags me by force
from the area in front of the altar of Zeus.

(78–79)

Zeus' sanctuary is being robbed, but all the local gods are being dishonored. Similarly Andromache, whose asylum was under the protection of Thetis, claims (E. *Andr.* 258) that the "gods will know" of Hermione's attempts to burn her out.[26]

It is in this regard that Aeschylus' treatment of asylum in the *Suppliants* is idiosyncratic. In each of the instances described above *one* deity (or *one* corporation, like the Eumenides) possesses the sanctuary and guarantees security. But in the sanctuary where the Danaids stay, the altar belongs to the "assembled gods,"[27] among whom are included Zeus, Apollo, Poseidon, and Hermes (189, 206–223). Each is described individually with his conventional functions. They are presented not as a cult group but as representatives of "all the gods." Their individual identities, as possessors and protectors of the sanctuary, are given no importance. I think Aeschylus does this because he wishes, in this play and perhaps in the trilogy as a whole, to assign to Zeus, without cult restrictions, the protection of asylum and suppliants. What results is Zeus Hikesios ("Of Suppliants"), a deity of function but not, in Athens at least, a deity of cult—a literary creation perhaps of Aeschylus himself, a deity who, universally, watches with a careful eye over mistreatment of suppliants (381–386).[28] This Zeus Hikesios in full justice punishes, sometimes even after death, violators of asylum. His wrath is much

Challenges to Popular Beliefs 75

to be feared.²⁹ Aeschylus did not wish, by making the sanctuary Zeus', to place local and cultic limitations on his universal Zeus. To assign the sanctuary to *one* of the other Olympians would have limited Zeus' role in awkward ways. Better to leave it, as unrealistic as it might be, a sanctuary of "the Olympian gods" in general terms. Then Aeschylus could, as he does so often, appropriate roles and functions (here concerning asylum and suppliants) from local gods and add them to Zeus' portfolio.

The sons of Aegyptus, Egyptians who do not believe in the Greek gods, are understandably ready to drag the Danaids from the Argive sanctuary.³⁰ They, like crows, have no respect for altars (750–752). It is their fate, later in the trilogy, all but one to be murdered on their wedding night by their reluctant brides. In Euripides' *Heracles* Lycus is willing by force to drag Heracles' wife from the altar because he is, he claims, "beyond" or "free from" fears (δειμάτων ἔξωθεν, 723–724). At the play's end his children lie dead, he is blinded, and his existence is one worse than death. Fear of retribution—retribution from the gods in general,³¹ but more specifically from the god of the sanctuary, a fear which Lycus lacked—was no doubt the motivating force behind the maintenance of the rights of asylum. Aeschylus, with his own preoccupations, puts all protection of asylum under Zeus' aegis, and so this fear of reprisal becomes clearly defined and directed: it is "fear of the wrath of Zeus Hikesios." There is no indication, however, that in life or elsewhere in tragedy the matter was so simple.

Ion, in Euripides' play of the same name, mounts a strong challenge against the invariable inviolability of sanctuary (1312–1319).³² This divine law, he argues, is bad and foolish since asylum should be provided only for those who act justly and are treated unjustly. The good and evil should not receive equal treatment. His argument makes some sense, and had these lines survived only as an isolated fragment, they undoubtedly would be paraded as another example of Euripidean criticism of popular religious practices.³³ But in fact we know the context: unbeknownst to Ion, the woman enjoying asylum is his own mother, and had there not been the rule of invariable respect for sanctuary, Ion would have caused his mother's death. Ion and his mother are saved from one of the most awful situations imaginable to a Greek by the very religious law he had criticized. Ion's attack on asylum is answered not by specific words and arguments but by the course of the action of the drama.[34] The principle of asylum and its extension to all people remain unshaken and receive, in Euripides as much as in Sophocles and Aeschylus, strong support. The altar is an "unbreakable shield, stronger than a fortification tower" (A. *Suppl.* 190). The "abode of the gods is a protection common to all men" (E. *Heraclid.* 260).

How, finally, did the gods view their role in matters of asylum? They "help," "protect," and "guard" the suppliant,[35] largely by the expectation that they will punish violators. But how are the gods related to suppliants, and what do they themselves have at stake? Such questions never arise in popular sources, but Euripides and Aeschylus through their characters suggest possible answers. Euripides' Menelaus in the *Helen* (980–987) claims that if he and Helen commit suicide and lie dead in Proteus' sanctuary, it will be a matter of "criticism" (ψόγος) for the hero. In Aeschylus' *Eumenides* (232–234) Apollo claims that if he willingly betrays Orestes, the "wrath" (μῆνις) of the suppliant will be terrible (δεινή) among gods and men. In this situation the god has something to fear. The Danaid chorus of Aeschylus' *Suppliants* in prayer bids Zeus to "respect" (σεβίζου) his suppliants (815–816), and in the *Eumenides* the Erinyes criticize Apollo, who is "respecting" (σέβων) his suppliant Orestes (151). The critical term is σέβω, the *vox propria* for "showing pious respect." In the *Oresteia* σέβω and its cognates are used of personal relationships of a man to a deity, of a mortal to a superior mortal, of a divinity to a superior divinity, and, as here, of a god to a suppliant.[36] When a human being establishes asylum in a god's sanctuary, the god himself is apparently put under an obligation, perhaps even as an inferior in the relationship, and he must, like others, show respect for the suppliant.[37] For him to fail to help is "betrayal" and will bring upon him censure and the wrath of the betrayed suppliant, a wrath which will be, if nothing else, a discomfiture for him among both gods and men.[38]

Whether this conception of a god's relationship to his suppliant can be transferred to popular belief is by no means certain, but it may remind us that worship is a reciprocal relationship. A man may worship a god, but a god must provide a service deserving this worship. In the pragmatic world of popular religion, if a god stopped doing the function expected of him, he would no longer receive worship.[39] For a god to fail to protect his suppliants would blacken his reputation, threaten his credibility, and, in a way, endanger his existence, for in popular religion a god existed primarily to perform his functions.

Xenia

In tragedy a *xenos* may be either a foreign visitor or, in much more specific terms, a citizen of a foreign country with whom one has established a special friendship through exchanges of gifts, mutual hospitality, and a shared dinner table. In the latter case both the guest and the host are termed *xenoi*. The two types of *xenia* must be distinguished, because in the treatment of foreign visitors general social and ethical considerations predominate, whereas for guests and hosts religious sanctions apply.[40]

The Athenians prided themselves on the reception and protection of foreign visitors, particularly when those visitors were victims of injustice in their own countries. This attitude first found expression in tragedy, and the dramatic versions found their way into Athenian prose self-encomia.[41] In the tragedies several foreign visitors take asylum at sanctuaries in Athens (e.g., the family of Heracles in the *Heraclidae* and Oedipus in the *Oedipus at Colonus*), and it is as suppliants, not as *xenoi*, that they have a religious right to protection.[42]

The *xenia* based on the guest/host relationship was, however, a religious matter, and even in the fourth century Demosthenes could be charged with impiety for having tortured and put to death a man with whom he had established this tie (Aeschines 3.223–224). In tragedy the failure to keep a promise to and the deception, robbery, and killing of a *xenos* were all impious deeds which affected one's relationship with the gods. In the *Agamemnon* Aeschylus' Paris, by stealing his *xenos'* wife, set in motion the Trojan War, the punishment of himself and his country, and the events of the *Oresteia*. Aeschylus assigns divine authority in this matter to Zeus Xenios, one facet of his universal Zeus.[43] It was this Zeus who saw to the punishment of Paris and, as accessory after the fact, Troy.[44] He, like Aeschylus' Zeus Hikesios, is primarily a literary deity in conception and presentation.[45] He did not have, so far as we know, a state cult in classical Athens.[46]

The ritual, gods, and appearance of the prophetess Theonoë in Euripides' *Helen* are exotic, but like other such Euripidean characters she is not wholly un-Greek.[47] She scrupulously maintains the ritual of her deities, she is devoted to her dead father, and she urges prayer at the appropriate time (865–872, 998–1001, 1024–1029, 1632). She is particularly Greek in her respect for the obligations of *xenia,* and this is crucial to the action of the play. Proteus, her father, had received Helen from Zeus to shelter and protect. Zeus, Proteus, and Helen were thus *xenoi.*[48] When Proteus dies, his children, Theonoë and Theoclymenus, inherit the obligations of their father's *xenia* with Helen (1028–1029). Theoclymenus intends to violate these obligations by compelling Helen, against her will, to marry him, and by so doing he would be acting impiously.[49] Should Theonoë assist him, she would be betraying her own piety (900–902). She would also be violating her father's wish, but this is a somewhat separate matter, as Helen suggests in 914: "Consider the interests of the god *and* the interests of your father."[50] Also involved are matters of secular justice. These three elements—piety, obedience to paternal wishes, and justice—combine to lead Theonoë to the proper decision to aid in the rescue of Helen and Menelaus.[51] By doing so she rescues Theoclymenus from the impiety he intends (1020–1021) and from the consequences that might have resulted. At the close of the play her own pious and just decisions and actions receive the divine seal of approval from the Dioscuroi appearing as *dei ex machina* (1647–1649).

In Euripides' *Alcestis* Admetus, whose piety lies in exceptionally strong devotion to *xenoi,* is greatly, even miraculously rewarded.[52] In the prologue Apollo says that he saved Admetus from imminent death because of the kind treatment he had received from Admetus when he was forced by Zeus to serve as a common laborer in Pherae. Because Admetus was "holy" (ὅσιος, 10) on that occasion, Apollo has protected him and his house to this day (1–14).[53] The chorus (569–605) implies that Apollo chose Admetus' house for his servitude precisely because it was πολύξενος and ἐλεύθερος, and views the security and fertility which Apollo brought with him (579–587) as leading to the great prosperity which Pherae was presently enjoying (588–596). The chorus approves of Admetus' hospitality towards his current guest, Heracles, and concludes with this general thought: "My soul is confident that a god-respecting man will fare well" (604–605). Admetus is "god-respecting" and "holy" because he respects the obligations of the guest/host relationship. Apollo in the prologue establishes this characteristic of Admetus, and it is stressed throughout the play.[54] As rewards for it Apollo has given Admetus prosperity and even a way to escape an untimely death. These rewards are great, but more are to come.

Challenges to Popular Beliefs 79

Admetus is granted escape from imminent death if he can find one to die in his place. His mother and father refuse, but Alcestis, his wife, accepts. The play is set on the day of her death. Heracles, a *xenos* of Admetus, arrives unaware of the situation. Admetus, in order to fulfill, as he always does, all obligations as a *xenos*, conceals his bereavement from Heracles and entertains him.[55] It is this very act which allows Admetus to recover his beloved and perfect wife. For when Heracles recognizes the true situation, he marvels at Admetus' devotion to his guests (840–860) and determines to return the service by wrestling Alcestis from Death and returning her to Admetus.[56] For his exceptionally pious behavior Admetus receives not only prosperity and release from an untimely death but also the life of his marvelous wife. Nowhere else in Greek drama do we see piety so immediately, graphically, and miraculously rewarded.[57]

The Polymestor of Euripides' *Hecuba*, as the "most unholy *xenos*" (ἀνοσιωτάτου ξένου, 790), is the antithesis to Admetus. He not only deceived and failed to keep a promise to *xenoi*, but he also killed their son, himself a *xenos* under his protection.[58] Polymestor was a Thracian king who had dined with Priam and Hecuba in Troy and was ranked high among their *xenoi* (793–794). Before the capture of Troy Priam had sent to Polymestor his youngest son, Polydorus, and a treasure of gold for safekeeping. When Priam was killed and Troy captured, Polymestor murdered Polydorus and seized the gold. Through Hecuba, the chorus, and Agamemnon, Euripides stresses that by violating the obligations of a *xenos* Polymestor had acted unjustly, shamefully, unholily, and impiously.[59] To Hecuba Polymestor's act revealed that he feared neither those upon the earth nor those below (791–792). She links his action with that of stealing the sacred property of the gods (803–804). To her he is accursed (ὦ κατάρατ' ἀνδρῶν, 716). Her punishment of him is, in part, "for the sake of the gods" (θεῶν ἕνεκα, 852–853).

Euripides has Polymestor the sinner suffer, and suffer badly, in this play. Hecuba avenges his killing of Polydorus by killing his children before his eyes and then blinding him, a fate, he says, worse than his own death (1120–1121). Critics may question whether Hecuba herself was justified in taking this kind of vengeance and in this manner, but Euripides leaves no doubt that Polymestor has committed a sin deserving punishment. As often in Euripides, a sinner is punished, but the motives and ways of the human agent of that punishment are open to question. But the important point in religious terms is that the sinner is punished, and very severely at that.

We thus have in Admetus the man exceptionally pious towards *xenoi* and rewarded for that. Polymestor and the Aeschylean Paris were impious in this same regard, and each was dreadfully punished. Consistently in tragedy φι-λόξενοι are praised or rewarded; ἐχθρόξενοι or ξεινάπαται suffer.

Oaths and Perjury

When an oath has been added, a man is more
careful, for he guards against two things,
the criticism of his friends and committing a transgression
against the gods.

(Sophocles, frag. 472[R])

Oaths were used widely and probably daily by ancient Greeks.[60] They reinforced stipulations of international treaties, they put religious sanctions on magistrates' promises to perform their duties properly and honestly, and they secured major and minor contracts and other financial dealings between individuals. Representatives of each state were chosen to swear the oaths in treaties, and often their names became part of the written record.[61] Athenian young men on assuming citizenship, members of the Boule, generals, jurymen, and probably all in public office swore elaborate oaths concerning their duties. Assertory oaths, guaranteeing that one was telling the truth, were routine. With such oaths witnesses declared the truth of their testimony, fathers and others attested to the qualifications of young men for membership in the deme and phratry (and hence for citizenship), and individuals claimed or disclaimed knowledge of financial transactions, wills, and so on. These oaths were made in the names of numerous gods, almost always those of local cult, who might be related in sundry ways to the action, group, or activity involved. Oaths contained, implicitly or explicitly, a curse on the violator, and perjury was an impiety which brought that curse to fulfillment.[62] For individuals punishment was often the destruction of the perjurer and, perhaps, of his family. I have argued elsewhere that in oath-taking an individual most often faced the choice between pious and impious action, deciding between what was pious and what might bring social or financial gain. For this reason the maintenance of oaths, at the popular level, was often treated as the key element of personal piety.[63]

In tragedy oaths and perjury play a similar but (for reasons to be discussed below) more limited role. International agreements are sealed with an oath, but such agreements in tragedy are unilateral, with one person swearing what he or his people will or will not do. Hence in Aeschylus' *Eumenides* Orestes swears that the Argives will never invade Attica (762–774).[64] Athena, *deus ex machina* in Euripides' *Suppliants,* insists that the same promise, but made by Adrastus to Theseus, be reinforced by an exceptionally formal and ritualistic oath (1183–1209).[65] In the *Eumenides* Aeschylus has Athena herself institute the promissory oath which jurors of the Areopagus court swore (483–484, 679–680, 708–710).

At the end of Sophocles' *Trachiniae* Heracles manipulates his son Hyllus into doing what he most certainly did not want to do, that is, marry his father's concubine Iole. In 1185–1224 (cf. 1239–1240) Heracles assures his son's obedience by appeals to filial devotion, by a handshake, and by a promissory oath with an explicit statement of the attendant curse. The oath is taken on Zeus, commonly invoked in life and tragedy,[66] but doubly appropriate here as Heracles' father. Agamemnon put under oath the suitors of Helen (E. *IA* 57–60, 391–392); Menelaus swore to Agamemnon by their father and grandfather that he would speak his true thoughts (E. *IA* 473–476). The chorus of the *Hippolytus* swear by Artemis that they will not reveal Phaedra's secret (710–714). The daughters of Erechtheus swore that if one were sacrificed all would commit suicide, and for keeping this oath they were honored (E. *Erech.* 65[A], 68–70).[67] In the *Antigone* the guard swears that he did not bury Polyneices nor does he know who did (265–267); Creon reinforces his threat to torture the guard with an oath (304–312) and later asks Ismene to swear that she knew nothing of the burial (535). With an oath Heracles intensified his promise to take vengeance on an enemy (S. *Tr.* 254–257). Neoptolemus twice uses oaths to reassure an understandably suspicious Philoctetes (S. *Ph.* 1288–1289, 1324–1325). The seven heroes against Thebes swore by Ares, Enyo, and Phobos that they would destroy the city or die in the attempt (A. *Th.* 42–48). And with an oath on Dike, Ate, and Erinys Clytemnestra reinforces her claim that "Hope does not walk in the halls of fear" for her.[68]

The most elaborate scene of oath taking is to be found in Euripides' *Iphigeneia among the Taurians* (735–765). Pylades swears he will deliver Iphigeneia's letter to Argos, and Iphigeneia promises him safe passage. They formally dictate to one another the desired oaths. Pylades swears by Zeus,

"Lord of the Sky." Iphigeneia names Artemis, who elsewhere is invoked by women (cf. E. *Hipp.* 713–714) but here is also appropriate as the goddess whom Iphigeneia serves. The curse for both is that they not return home. Pylades adds that if his ship should sink and the letter be lost, the oath should be no longer binding. This proviso leads Iphigeneia to reveal the contents of the letter and thus brings about the mutual recognition of Orestes and Iphigeneia.

In all of the situations described thus far the oath takers eventually fulfill their promises, or, because of other turns in the action (as in *Iphigeneia among the Taurians*), the oath becomes moot. There are, in addition, instances of real or imagined perjury in the plays, and here we can see if the perjurer is, as in life, considered impious and eventually punished for his impiety. Euripides' Eteocles in the *Phoenissae* provides a typical example. He violates his oath to return, after his year's turn at it, the kingship of Thebes to his brother Polyneices. For this, and for this alone, he is described as "impious" and his action as "most unholy."[69] In his false oath injustice and impiety are both involved, but the impiety concerns only the perjury. Eteocles' impiety and injustice are blatant, and he knows exactly what he is doing: "If one must act unjustly, it is best ($\varkappa\acute{\alpha}\lambda\lambda\iota\sigma\tau\sigma\nu$) to do so for the sake of a tyranny. In all other matters one ought to be pious" (524–525). By the end of the play the impious Eteocles lies dead at his brother's hand. This is not to claim that Euripides presents Eteocles' death as punishment for impiety. Other personal defects and errors contributed to Eteocles' death, and these too receive Euripides' attention. But as we see time and again in Euripides, the impious person suffers and dies. The causal connection between the impiety and suffering is seldom made explicit, and many other factors come into play; but almost without exception an individual impious by the standards of contemporary popular religion suffers. As the Dioscuroi, *dei ex machina* in Euripides' *Electra,* proclaim, "Let no one sail with perjurers" (1355).[70]

In the *Medea* Jason and Medea are "living together" in Corinth, a de facto marriage, with children, which is based on an oath Jason had given to Medea. It was at least in part Medea's trust in the Themis (Right) of Jason's oath that led her to leave Colchis with him (205–213). Both view the relationship as a marriage (cf. esp. 1340–1341), but the only religious sanction for it was Jason's oath. To abandon a woman, especially a foreigner, even a woman who had borne one's children, was not a religious offense. In Jason's case, however, it became one because by so doing he violated the promissory oath which he had given. It is the one charge which Medea and the chorus level most frequently and most insistently against him.[71] Many of the charges of injustice made against Jason seem associated with his perjury, and on this basis Medea can invoke the gods as witnesses of the treatment she received from him.[72] Medea also purports to be perplexed at Jason's intentional perjury: "Do you think that the gods (who ruled) then (when you swore the oath)[73] no longer rule? Or do you think that now there are new principles of right and wrong for human beings?" (493–494). The willingness to commit perjury suggests to Medea, as it did to Plato a century later, a fundamental change in religious beliefs and values.[74]

By his perjury Jason endangers, in general terms, the faith people put in oaths taken in the gods' names (410–413, 439–440, 492–495). He himself is "accursed" ($κατάρατον$, 162) and "most hateful to the gods" (467–468).[75] With the loss of his new bride, father-in-law, and especially children he suffers terribly in this play, and we may understand his sufferings at least in part as the "things that happen to impious men" (755).[76] Yet here, as occasionally elsewhere in Euripides, the human agent who effects the punishment[77] of impiety commits a gross impiety in turn. By the murder of her children Medea becomes "impious."[78] Jason also, as a perjurer, loses communication with and support from the gods, as Medea specifically states near the end of the play: "What god or deity listens to you when you are a perjurer and deceive *xenoi*?" (1391–1392). Medea here forewarns the audience of the futility of Jason's final appeals to Zeus (1405–1407) and to the other gods (1410).

Medea's patron and protector is Helios, her grandfather. He was, in the fifth century, not a cult deity in Athens, and Medea's attachment to him is one of several indications of her foreignness to the Greek world. Hecate was worshiped in contemporary Athens, but it is to Hecate's negative, un-Athenian aspects as patroness of sorcery and magic that Medea is devoted.[79] Apart from these deities the decidedly but not completely un-Greek Medea turns to Zeus, Themis, and Ge, all very Greek deities whose involvement can best be explained by their common interest in oaths.[80] Zeus is, of course, the protector or "keeper" of oaths par excellence (169–170),[81] and it is in his role as Zeus Horkios ("Of Oaths") that Euripides presents him throughout the *Medea*. Medea directs numerous appeals to him, and it is only as "keeper" of oaths that he is expected to take an interest in her misfortunes.[82]

By punishing the impious perjurer Zeus is acting with Dike (Justice)[83] and Themis (Right). Themis, who in other plays may have much broader concerns, is defined by Euripides in this play only by her association with Zeus Horkios (160–163, 168–170, 208–212).

Ge appears in the *Medea* in her common role as a nonlocalized guarantor of oaths. An Athenian swearing an oath in his own country to a fellow countryman would normally invoke deities that had local cults, often (for general purposes) Zeus, Apollo, and Demeter.[84] Medea, a foreigner with no city or local cults of her own, and Jason, far from his own country, appeal to more general, less localized deities—Helios and Ge, who, like Zeus and Demeter, represent the sky and land. Helios, elsewhere commonly invoked in oaths, is a particularly appropriate witness of an oath for his granddaughter Medea. Ge replaces Demeter, as she does in other non-Athenian oaths, and Medea has Aegeus, an Athenian traveling abroad, swear by Ge, Helios, and "the whole race of the gods" (735–755).

Jason was a perjurer, Medea an impious murderess of her own children. Helios and Hecate are the objects of Medea's worship. Helios and Ge are made witnesses of the oaths, and Zeus Horkios represents the divine side of the punishment of Jason. Athenian cult did not include these deities in this form, and Euripides, I suspect, avoided involving distinctly Athenian deities in this nasty tale of conflict between two notoriously impious figures.

In two passages, one a fragment and the other problematic, it is claimed that the gods are "understanding" towards false oaths sworn under duress. In Euripides' fragment 645[N] someone is bidden "to think that the gods are understanding when a person, by an oath, wishes to escape death or imprisonment or the violent evils of the enemy."[85] In a much-interpolated section of the *Iphigeneia at Aulis* Agamemnon, hardly a moral authority in this play, tells Menelaus that "the divine" ($τὸ\ θεῖον$) is not unintelligent but is able to understand oaths that have been badly fixed and forced.[86] At best both passages serve to illustrate what we know from elsewhere, that not all characters share the belief in the necessity of unconditionally maintaining oaths. Neither passage is sufficient, however, to throw into question the tragedians' consistent agreement elsewhere with popular beliefs concerning oaths.

The guard in Sophocles' *Antigone* is tragedy's one character who swears a false oath and gets off unscathed. After rough treatment by Creon (304–331), the guard has sworn, surely to himself, that he will not come back to face the king again. Later, despite his oath, he returns bringing the captured Antigone (388–396). The oath is only reported, and no gods or punishment are specified. There is no hint that we are to condemn the guard as impious. The casual taking and breaking of the oath contribute to the *ethopoiia* and make the guard resemble, in this regard, a comic character.[87] A nameless, minor, lowly character can get away with this.[88] Perhaps in this context we should view Orestes' advice, in Sophocles' *Electra,* to the paedagogue to deceive Clytemnestra with an oath. Orestes bids him "add an oath" to his false report of Orestes' death (47–48). The paedagogue, interestingly, does not heed this advice (660–799). It may be, however, what the audience would expect of a lying servant, or Sophocles may be suggesting an ignoble deviousness in Orestes.[89] In any case the false oath is never made, and questions of impiety and punishment become moot.

In Aeschylus' *Eumenides* a god urges perjury. Apollo, as advocate for the accused, argues that the acquittal of Orestes is the will of Zeus which he, Zeus' oracular son, reveals to them. The jurors are to vote in Orestes' favor, for "an oath has no more strength than does Zeus" (621). There underlies this a shocking assumption, that the will of Zeus, the usual protector of oaths, might be at variance with the oath by which Athena, Zeus' own daughter, assured that the jurors would judge justly. Athena herself has previously recognized that simplistic oaths were not sufficient to decide this complex case (429–430), but neither elsewhere in this play nor in all of Athenian forensic oratory is it urged that jurors violate their oaths. The suggestion that the jurors should commit perjury and the rationale behind it, that oaths are inferior to the will of Zeus, are both, I think, intended to be seen as wrong and improper, part and parcel of Apollo's limited, unprincipled, and erroneous view of this moral and legal dilemma.[90] Later Athena again urges the jurors to maintain their oath (708–710),[91] and by doing so they and she reach a settlement of the case in accord with the will of Zeus. Apollo's recommendation of perjury is ignored.

Euripides' Hippolytus delivered antiquity's most famous line on oaths, "My tongue has sworn the oath, my mind has not" (*Hipp.* 612).[92] Thus he angrily responds when he learns that the secret he has pledged to keep was Phaedra's passion for him (601–612). The oath had been sworn, offstage, to Phaedra's nurse, and Hippolytus' words in 612 suggest he no longer feels bound by it. Phaedra assumes Hippolytus will tell the whole story, and this fear contributes to her decision to commit suicide and frame Hippolytus (689–731). Hippolytus, despite this initial reaction, steadfastly adheres to his oath (654–658, 1033, 1062–1063), and for this Artemis herself, *deus ex machina,* labels him "pious" (1308–1309). The maintenance of this oath meant for Hippolytus mental anguish and social and familial upheaval and also eventually contributed to his death. Adherence to it was not easy, and, as 612 reveals, Euripides makes it more than a simple, mechanical reaction. Hippolytus' final decision involves profane as well as religious reasons: "I cannot in any way persuade those whom I need to, and therefore to no purpose I would violate (συγχέαιμι) the oath I swore" (1062–1063). The stakes are high, and here Euripides props up demands of piety with practical reasons. It is, of course, one of the numerous ironies of this play that by piously maintaining his oath to the nurse Hippolytus makes less convincing to his father his very solemn oath of innocence (1025–1033, 1060–1061).[93] "My tongue has sworn the oath, my mind has not" should be viewed as a momentary lapse, an immediate angry outburst by a character who almost immediately (656–658) reassumes and then maintains a proper, even exemplary, attitude towards his oaths. It is ironic and most unfair that this line, spoken by a character proven, in all of tragedy, most loyal to oaths in the most trying and tragic circumstances, should have laid Euripides open to ancient and modern charges of impiety, promoting perjury, and hostility to traditional religion.[94]

In everyday life promissory oaths were employed to involve gods in matters of justice with which they were not inherently concerned. There is no evidence from popular sources that the gods took an interest in human lying, cheating, accepting bribes, giving false testimony, intentionally voting unjustly in a law trial, failing to perform duties as a citizen or government official, or in a host of similar "wrongs." The Athenians brought their gods into these matters by having individuals swear elaborate oaths, with gods as witnesses, not to do such things. If a person then acted wrongly, he became liable not only for legal punishment for the crime but also for punishment from the gods for violating the oath. Divine punishment befell him not because of the illegal act per se but because he violated his oath.[95] In this regard the use of oaths in tragedy is significantly different. In those several plays where the justice of the gods is made an issue, their involvement is direct. They are not motivated or coerced into action by human oaths. They act spontaneously and on their own initiative in ways which are, by human standards, just, unjust, or a problematic combination of the two. The tragedians were concerned, in ways popular religion seems not to have been, with whether the gods are personally and inherently just or unjust.

Aeschylus' *Eumenides* provides a revealing instance of the intersection of the tragic and popular conceptions of divine justice. There we have issues of justice worked out on both divine and human levels. Athena herself, just and wise, attempts to provide a fair trial of Orestes and an equitable mediation of the interests of Orestes, Apollo, and the Erinyes. She becomes involved and operates from her personal concern with justice. When, however, she entrusts the trial of Orestes and subsequent murder trials to human, Athenian judges, she institutes for these jurors and for all such jurors in the future an oath that they will cast their votes "justly."[96] Even in tragedy human, legal justice must be underpinned by an oath, an oath that represents the popular practice of providing religious sanctions for justice in law through promissory oaths. When justice is institutionalized at the human level, it requires such oaths.[97] The gods of tragedy need no such artificial inducements to dispense justice: hence the far more limited role of oaths in the workings of justice in the world of tragedy.

Divination

Oracles and seers are stock in trade of tragedians, and there is scarcely a play in which they or omens, dreams, or other forms of divination are not important determinants of the action. Numerous characters challenge the accuracy of oracles, the ability and veracity of seers, and the significance of portents and dreams. We shall treat these after comparing the divination in tragedy to that practised in everyday life in the fifth and fourth centuries.[98] Separate discussions of oracles, seers, dreams, and omens are required because, although we tend to lump them together under the Latin rubric "divination," they employ different means for often differing purposes and are even, in the plays, occasionally contrasted to one another. This section will conclude with discussions of Euripides' *Suppliants, Iphigeneia among the Taurians,* and Sophocles' *Oedipus Tyrannus,* plays in which several elements of divination are played off against one another and are simultaneously brought into question.

Oracles

The Athenian state turned to the oracles of Zeus at Dodona and of Apollo at Delphi especially on religious questions, for approval of the founding of a new cult, for introducing or changing sacrifices, or for change of status of sacred lands or other sacred property.[99] Oracles were consulted when the Athenians were troubled by a bad portent or religious oversight. The concern, in religious terms, was that planned action be "pious," that it be acceptable to the gods. Of the thirty-four obviously genuine responses from Delphi in the fifth and fourth centuries, twenty-three (68 percent) concerned such religious matters.[100] Nine (26 percent) dealt with war, expeditions, or other matters of foreign policy.[101] For two colonization is the issue, and one is a response to a husband who wants children.[102]

At Zeus' oracle in Dodona inscribed lead tablets preserve more than 150 questions directed to the oracle, and they better than the Delphic evidence suggest the range of private and governmental concerns submitted for oracular consultation. State inquiries, as at Delphi, involved matters of religion and foreign and domestic policy. The citizens of Dodona asked if someone's impurity was causing the bad weather; others asked about moving a temple. States and individuals both inquired to which of the gods they should pray and sacrifice in order "to fare better." People asked about the prospect and paternity of children, about their health, their herds, their commercial ventures, and even about what happened (lost or stolen?) to missing bedding.[103] Inquirers at the oracles sought both answers for troubling questions about present circumstances and indications of success or failure of specific acts which were being planned or undertaken. In the latter the state or individual was simply asking if it "was better and more agreeable" to do or not to do the proposed act.

In the tragedies individuals consult or report oracles on some of these same topics: colonization, plague, infertility of the land, marriage, disease, identity of parents, and childlessness.[104] These matters, often lying beyond the science and control of ancient Greeks, were commonly viewed as areas of divine intervention and thus understandably formed the objects of divination.[105]

One major function of real oracles in the fifth century was the validation and establishment of new or changed cults and sacrifices, a function shared by tragedy but with a noteworthy variation. Tragedy provides divine approval for changes it makes in religious life, but through different means, by preordination through oracles or by immediate validation by *dei ex machina*. The new state hero cults of Oedipus in Sophocles' *Oedipus at Colonus* and of Eurystheus in Euripides' *Heraclidae* receive prior validation. To each man the cult was predicted by Apollo, and each recognizes the fulfillment of the oracle (*OC* passim; *Heraclid.* 1027–1040). Here, as usual, the oracle has validated a new cult, but unlike in life it does so before the event that motivates the establishment of the cult. The *deus ex machina* also provides validation but does so immediately and on the stage. A human being could describe a new cult, but only a god, speaking *ex officio*, could simultaneously describe the cult and represent divine ratification for it.[106] To have the establishment of new gods, heroes, or cults preordained through oracles or immediately ratified by the *deus ex machina* served tragedy's inclination for completeness and economy. A deity or ritual did not become part of official state religion until it had received such validation, and a poet would not want to leave his deity or cult without it. It would, however, be untidy and anticlimactic, at the end of an episode or play, to have to await, for days perhaps, the required stamp of divine approval from Delphi or elsewhere. Thus in tragedy, for reasons of narrative structure and economy, it was a convention that new heroes and other new religious institutions be given prior (through oracles) or immediate (through *dei ex machina*) divine validation.

There are also broader differences between oracles of tragedy and those of real life, in terms both of function and of form. Real oracles treated almost exclusively the present time. They were responses to whether one should *now* make war, make peace, perform sacrifices, build temples and altars, get married, and so forth. A person used oracles and other forms of divination to learn "what he ought, or ought not, to do" (Xen. *Symp.* 4.47–49). A troubling event in the recent past might motivate the inquiry, but the response was directed to present action. The future was never described or predicted. As Dodds puts it, "the primary function of a Greek oracle was to *advise,* not to predict."[107] The inquirer might learn from the oracle that it was "better" to get married, but he did not learn what benefits or results there might be years hence.

A handful, but a famous handful, of oracles in tragedy give explicit descriptions of future events, either of what certainly will happen or what will happen if a condition is fulfilled. The Delphic oracle to Laius, Oedipus' father, is an example of both. Euripides presents it as a conditional prophecy: if Laius begets a son, he will be killed by him (E. *Ph.* 13–23). Sophocles makes it a simple statement of the future: Laius will die at the hands of his child.[108] Aeschylus has Apollo bid or warn Laius "to save his city" by dying without children. His Apollo says nothing of the results to be expected if Laius transgresses this command (*Th.* 742–757). Similarly detailed direct or conditional descriptions of events years in the future are made about Heracles, Oedipus, Eurystheus, and the misfortunes of the Persians.[109] Those about Eurystheus and those in the *Oedipus at Colonus* give prior validation to new cults. Sophocles in particular used oracular statements about the future, as in the *Trachiniae* and *Oedipus Tyrannus,* as a means to develop the irony characteristic of him.

All the demonstrably historical oracles from Delphi and Dodona in the classical period were unambiguous statements about what one should or should not do in a given situation.[110] Aeschylus' Io complains that her father received oracles that were "shifty" ($αἰολοστόμους$) and "difficult to judge" (*Pr.* 661–662),[111] but only four other oracles of tragedy are in fact riddling or otherwise ambiguous. Zeus' oracle told Heracles that he would be killed by one already dead (S. *Tr.* 1159–1163) and would find in time release from his labors (79–81, 821–830, 1164–1173).[112] Apollo told Aegeus that to beget a child he should not loosen the foot of his wine skin until he returned home (E. *Med.* 667–681), and the same god bade Adrastus to wed his two daughters "to a boar and a lion" (E. *Suppl.* 138–146). Heracles understood his oracles only too late, Aegeus needed Medea's help, and Adrastus may have misinterpreted his.[113] Although individuals may challenge the accuracy of oracles and be slow to realize their ultimate truth, the fault usually does not lie with the language of the oracles. Apart from those noted, the oracles of tragedy, like those of life, are straightforward and, with one exception, accurate.

Only one oracle in tragedy is demonstrably false, and Apollo had inten-

Challenges to Popular Beliefs 91

tionally made it so. In the *Ion,* amidst the full ritual of oracular consultation at Delphi, Apollo tells Xuthus that the first person he meets upon leaving the temple will be his own born son. This oracle proves to be false—not obscure, but simply false.[114] Ion, whom Xuthus first meets, was in fact the son of Apollo and Creousa and hence, at most, Xuthus' stepson; but the oracle had explicitly said "born" son (69–71, 534–537), and there was no mistake of interpretation by Xuthus. The chorus, though for the wrong reasons, suspects the oracle (681–685), and Apollo's servant and son, when he discovers the truth, is deeply troubled (1537–1538). Apollo, we are told by a god at the beginning of the play (69–73), will intentionally give this oracle to protect the interests of Ion and Creousa, and, under Athena's orders (1601–1603), the deception of Xuthus will continue beyond the time frame of the play. We may see Euripides' handling of this false oracle as confirming the tragic convention that oracles are true. Euripides thought it necessary to have Hermes advise the audience in the prologue that Apollo would be giving false information through his oracle (69–73). Without this forewarning the audience would have assumed that this oracle, like all other oracles in tragedy, would prove true. Euripides had to prepare his audience for a breach of tragic convention.

Oracles play a significantly different role in the lives of tragic characters than real oracles did for common people. Oracles of tragedy are the product of combining two ideas, one latent in divination and one primarily literary. That an oracle can inform one whether "it is better" to marry or not, or to have a child or not, presumes that the oracular god has detailed knowledge of the future. This logical conclusion was drawn by some[115] but was not acted upon at the popular level, because people did not ask from oracles descriptions of future events. The poets, however, when their purposes required it, gave their oracular gods detailed knowledge of the future.[116] Sophocles' Pythian Apollo can tell Laius his fate years in the future. Poets also have, in differing degrees but apparently far more than average Greeks, what happens happen by the will of the gods. The action of the *Iliad,* viewed from the perspective of the omniscient poet, is the will of Zeus. The future is thus not only known to the gods but determined by their will, and the oracles and oracular gods of literature, unlike those of life, are able to give detailed accounts of these plans and purposes.[117] For these reasons the oracles of literature, unlike those of life, can describe events of the future and, if the poet wishes, explicate the divine purposes behind them.

Seers

Although there is some overlap, practising soothsayers in fifth-century Athens may be divided into seers (*manteis*) and chresmologues. Seers divinized through observation of birds, omens, and signs at sacrifices before military expeditions, battles, and other undertakings. Chresmologues collected oracles attributed to Orpheus, Musaeus, Bacis, and other sundry sources and then provided interpretation of these as a suitable occasion arose.[118] Chresmologues disappear from the Athenian record after the losses in the Sicilian campaign, an expedition for which they and some seers had predicted success.[119] Seers, however, must have weathered the storm of criticism (Thuc. 8.1.1) because we find them still practising in the fourth century. Seers and especially chresmologues are the butt of jokes in Old Comedy, but only seers are portrayed in tragedy. The oracles of tragedy, from the more respectable Apollo Pythios and Zeus Naios, are for the most part unambiguous and are directed to specific situations, not drawn from collections. Hence there was little need in tragedy for chresmologues,[120] and because of their relatively late appearance in the sixth century B.C. and their questionable reputation, they may have been thought unsuited to the heroic age of tragedy.

Although seers like Lampon and Hierocles were prominent citizens in Athens, they had, so far as we know, no official position or appointment, and their activities were usually associated with individual statesmen and generals, not with the government as a whole. Lampon, called both seer and chresmologue, offered his interpretation of a single-horned ram presented to Pericles.[121] He was also, in 443/442 B.C., a leader of the new Athenian colony at Thurii, perhaps in part because of his expertise as a seer.[122] Seers attended some state sacrifices intended to obtain favorable omens, and in 446/445 the seer Hierocles performed, at the state's request, oracle-ordered sacrifices concerning Euboea.[123] Some seers evidently opposed the Sicilian expedition, while those whom Alcibiades "had" (ἔχων) predicted that the Athenians would obtain fame (κλέος) from Sicily.[124] In 394/393 the Athenians gave Sthorys of Thasos citizenship and pay for his help, as a seer, in their victory in the sea battle at Cnidus.[125]

We learn most of the doings of seers from their activities with two Athenian generals, Nicias and Xenophon. Nicias had a seer resident in his home and consulted him both on public affairs and on the silver mines he operated. Seers advised him during the Sicilian campaign, and Plutarch attributes to the momentary lack of an experienced seer Nicias' fatal decision, after an eclipse of the moon, to keep the army in Syracuse for another full lunar cycle.[126]

In the personal account of his adventures with the mercenary force of the Ten Thousand, Xenophon describes how his seers examined signs in sacrifices before various military undertakings. Himself knowledgeable in the mantic arts, Xenophon always followed their advice, sometimes at great inconvenience to himself and his troops.[127] On the one occasion when a general accompanying Xenophon undertook an expedition contrary to their advice, the mission failed and more than five hundred men were lost.[128] At one juncture a seer told Xenophon omens were favorable for his making a speech to the troops and assuming command; another later interpreted for him the omen of a perched eagle screeching on his right.[129] After the campaign, when Xenophon was so impoverished that his resources were scarcely sufficient to get him home, the Phliasian seer Eucleides, after observing a sacrifice made by Xenophon, believed his claims of poverty and told Xenophon that his failure to sacrifice to Zeus Meilichios was its cause. The next day Xenophon sacrificed as advised, and later that very same day men came bringing him pay (*An.* 7.8.1–6).

Some seers were themselves prominent citizens, but others were foreign, freelance consultants to the rich and powerful, especially as they were engaged in military affairs. We know of only one, Sthorys, who was paid by the state, and that was a reward after military success. Little contemporary evidence indicates to what extent such seers were formally or regularly consulted by the state on political or religious affairs.[130] Inscriptions suggest that the state usually turned to oracles on such matters. The seers' primary business was to interpret signs, whether sought or unsought, whether cosmological, animal, or sacrificial, as favorable or unfavorable to an undertaking at hand. Real seers apparently did not predict the future or explain divine purposes. All seers whom the Athenians consulted in classical times were men, and all practised "deductive" divination: that is, they proceeded not by immediate, personal inspiration but by a set of rules, by book-type learning, by the τέχνη μαντική.[131]

This "deductive" mantic craft is among the skills Prometheus claims he gave to men:

> I systematized the many ways of the mantic craft,
> and I first distinguished which dreams ought to come to pass,
> and I made intelligible those hard-to-judge
> chance words and occurrences on the roads.
> I defined exactly the flight of bent-clawed birds,
> telling which ones are, by nature, favorable and unfavorable,
> and what way of life each type of birds has,
> and what hatreds, affections, and gatherings they have with one another.
> And I described the smoothness of vital organs
> and what color the bile should have to be pleasing to the gods,
> and the elaborate conformation of the liver's lobe.
> I, having set afire the limbs wrapped in fat
> and the long loin (of the sacrificial victim),
> led mortals into that hard-to-judge craft,
> and I made clear the fiery signs which were before veiled.
>
> (A. *Pr.* 484–499)

Prometheus claims among his gifts the three most common methods of the mantic art in tragedy and life: ornithoscopy, the observation of the flight of birds; extispicy, the observation of the vital organs, particularly the liver, of sacrificial victims; and empyroscopy, the study of the movements of the flames as they consumed offerings on the altar.[132] The seers' craft is god-given, but practised by mortals. It thus stands between what man accomplishes on his own and what is wholly god-given, such as oracles. Because of this the seers' work can be contrasted to that of the oracle-giving Apollo.[133]

In tragedy Teiresias the Theban, Calchas the seer of the Greek army at Troy, and Helenus, Priam's son and seer of the Trojans, each practise these mantic arts. They interpret dreams and signs from birds and sacrifices. When positively described, they are wise and more than human.[134] They know the truth, the divine, and the "things" of the gods.[135] Seers in tragedies speak "god-spoken words" and give "signs," usually of future success or failure, to those who consult them.[136] Like their counterparts in real life these seers are consulted on matters of war, voyages, health, omens, dreams, and religious needs,[137] but the knowledge they possess and the information they offer are far different. Seldom do they simply report favorable or unfavorable omens from sacrifices.[138] Through their mantic arts and sometimes through their personal wisdom—for Teiresias in particular is a "wise man" figure—they offer detailed descriptions of present situations, of future events, and of the plans and purposes of the gods.[139] In Euripides' *Phoenissae* Teiresias can tell Creon, in the face of the invasion by the Argive army of the Seven, that the cause goes back to Laius and the curses of Oedipus; that if the city is to be saved, no descendant of Oedipus should rule Thebes and Creon's son Menoeceus must die; and that Ares is wrathful because of the killing, long ago, of his "earth-born" snake (867–952). Helenus in Sophocles' *Philoctetes* knows that within the summer Troy will fall when the Greeks obtain the services of Philoctetes and his bow (604–613, 1336–1342). In the *Agamemnon* Aeschylus has Calchas interpret the omen of two eagles, on the right, feeding on a pregnant hare. From this Calchas describes the eventual capture of Troy and sees also the delay at Aulis, the need to sacrifice Iphigeneia to appease the anger of Artemis, and the eventual wrath of Clytemnestra (109–157, 198–204; cf. 249). That seers have this type and range of knowledge is a literary convention, one already established in Homer's Calchas.[140] The knowledge comes primarily from their mantic arts, but (for Teiresias at least) some derives from personal wisdom. Teiresias is "wise," and in Euripides' *Bacchae,* a play very much about differing kinds of wisdom, his words have authority as those of a wise and educated man, not of a seer.[141]

Cassandra, propositioned by Apollo with the gift of inspired prophecy but then doomed by him to have no one believe her, is purely literary, completely outside the framework of practised religion. The Athenians knew and consulted no such prophets in life. For dramaturgical purposes she is a prophet without peer, for she apprises the audience of present circumstances and future events but has little or no effect on the characters, chorus, or course of the action.[142] Analysis of her and of her prophetic skill is purely a literary, not religious topic.[143]

Theonoë, the seeress of Euripides' *Helen,* is, like much else in that play, *sui generis* and forms an integral part of the bizarre religious environment created there. She also serves to introduce our first major criticism of conventional seers. In the prologue Theonoë is described to the audience as daughter of Proteus and sister of Theoclymenus, a woman who knows "divine things, both the things existing and all the things that are going to happen."[144] This knowledge, or capacity for knowledge, she has received from her grandfather Nereus (10–15).[145] The audience, from its familiarity with the conventions of tragedy, would expect Theonoë, who had no prior literary or mythological tradition to identify her, to be either a Calchas/Teiresias figure (a seer who derives prophetic knowledge from the usual skills of bird and sacrifice observation), or, more likely since Theonoë is an unmarried woman, a Cassandra, a woman experiencing personal, ecstatic prophetic inspiration from a god. Initially Euripides allows these expectations to develop. Characters direct to her the kinds of questions about which one usually consults seers. Teucer comes expressly to learn how best to make his way to Cyprus (144–150). Helen and the chorus, offstage, ask her whether Menelaus is still alive (317–320). They learn that he has wandered at sea and is somewhere nearby, shipwrecked (515–539). The audience at this point has neither seen Theonoë nor learned anything of the manner of her prophecy.

One hundred lines before Theonoë's first appearance onstage, Euripides inserts what is perhaps the most direct condemnation of seers and their craft in tragedy. A servant of Menelaus, when he learns that only an image of Helen, not Helen herself, had been the cause of the Trojan War, complains bitterly that neither the Greek nor Trojan seers had ever revealed this to the combatants:

> I saw how worthless and full of lies
> the business of seers is. Unsound are
> the cries of birds and (omens from) the sacrificial flame.
> But indeed it was naive even to think that birds help men.
> Calchas said nothing and gave no indication to the army
> that he was watching his friends dying for a "cloud,"
> nor did Helenus, but the city Troy was destroyed for no purpose.
> You might say, "Because the god did not wish it."
> Why, indeed, do we consult seers? People ought
> to sacrifice to the gods and ask them for good things,
> and dismiss prophecy. That enticement of life
> was wrongly invented, and no lazy man
> ever got rich from (omens in) sacrifices.
> Reason and good planning are the best seer.
>
> (*Hel.* 744–757)[146]

The coryphaeus readily agrees:

> I, an old man, share your opinion about prophecy.
> If someone has the gods friendly, he would have
> the best mantic art for his house.
>
> (758–760)

Menelaus' man considers the seers' failure to provide crucial information proof that their art is worthless and full of lies. He realizes, in retrospect, that it is naive to assume that birds can benefit men in prophecy. He dismisses the one excuse that seers provide, that gods did not want men to know.[147] He proposes rather a religion of sacrifice and prayer without the mantic art and urges "reason and good planning" in prophecy's place.

Most scholars have assumed, rightly I think, that this criticism in a play of 412 B.C. reflects the hostility to seers and chresmologues in the aftermath of the disaster in Sicily.[148] Some seers and chresmologues had provided encouragement to those considering the expedition, and after the defeat the public turned on them (Thuc. 8.1).[149] Chresmologues disappeared from Athenian life, but conventional seers remained, as they do in later plays of Euripides.

The stage is now set for Theonoë's first appearance. One expects she will be either a Calchas or Cassandra. She enters in the face of a strong, perhaps at the time generally welcomed, challenge to the mantic art. Theonoë, it seems, must implicitly or explicitly confirm or refute the validity of the challenge. If she is ineffective and false, she will confirm it. If she proves to be helpful and accurate, she will refute it. The appearance of Theonoë, however, belies expectations. Her entrance onto the stage is unique, befitting neither a Calchas nor a Cassandra. Her attendant carries a torch and sulfur with which to purify, in an odd way, the path before her—an institution, Theonoë says, of "solemn Aether." She has come out of the palace to receive the "pure" or "purifying" breath ($\pi\nu\varepsilon\tilde{\upsilon}\mu\alpha$) of Ouranos, who, like Aether, is not a Greek cultic or mantic figure. This ritual is her $\nu\acute{o}\mu o\varsigma$—and by implication not that of the Greeks (865–872). Euripides has made this prophetess of remote Egypt exotic—in the rituals of her entrance, in the deities she worships, and, no doubt, in her costume. Her method of prophecy, from the little we hear of it, differs from conventional types. She does not employ observation of birds or sacrifices. Unlike Cassandra she does not, despite her close ties to Aether/Ouranos, profess or exhibit direct, ecstatic inspiration from a god. She seems simply to possess knowledge of "divine things, both the things existing and all the things about to happen."[150] And, it turns out, she does know. All that she describes or predicts comes true. But because Theonoë is so exotic, so un-Greek, so different from conventional seers, her knowledge, her accuracy, and even her just and pious character do nothing to meet or ameliorate the earlier challenge against the mantic art in lines 744–760. This attack against an element of popular religion, an element described as it was actually practised in everyday life, remains unanswered.[151]

Euripides needed and wanted a prophetic figure for his plot, and, I suspect, he responded to contemporaries' hostility to conventional seers in 413–412 B.C. by creating, experimentally, a wholly new type of prophet. The remote, Egyptian setting allowed him more than the usual latitude to do this. Whether Egyptian prophets in fact appealed to Aether and Ouranos is of little import. That Theonoë lived in this remote, imperfectly known part of the world allowed Euripides to impart to her whatever exotic rituals, gods, and practices he liked. He experimented with her just as he did with other religious elements in this play.[152]

Theonoë is the focus of what one might call the cult of Aether/Ouranos that is peculiar to the *Helen*.[153] Theonoë calls her entrance ritual a σεμνοῦ θεσμὸν αἰθέρος, and she has left the palace to receive πνεῦμα καθαρὸν οὐρανοῦ (865–867). She knows, of course, the Homeric pantheon (878–891, 1005–1008), and she can recommend prayers to Hera and Aphrodite, with both of whom she has personal concerns (1005–1008, 1024–1027), but it is with the cult of Aether/Ouranos that she is concerned in her own ritual, and it is that which gives her an exotic flavor. In addition, Euripides uses Aether/Ouranos as a thread to bind together disparate events and characters of the *Helen* and to cast over them all an exoticism in keeping with his Egyptian setting. The εἴδωλον of Helen is made of Aether/Ouranos (34, 582–584),[154] and when it has served its purpose, it flies off to its "father" Aether/Ouranos (605–619). The Dioscuroi, we finally learn after initial uncertainties, did not die but became like stars in Ouranos (140, 1495–1500). Not completely dissimilar, the all-knowing Theonoë informs us, is the fate of all mortals, for at death the human νοῦς does not live on, but, rushing into "immortal Aether," has "immortal γνώμη" (1013–1016).

Most of these elements singly can be paralleled in other plays of Euripides,[155] but nowhere except in the *Helen* are they worked so integrally into the fabric of a play. This Ouranic religion does not replace the traditional Olympian religion but is grafted on to it. Hera herself, in an atypical description, is said to dwell among the stars (that is, in Ouranos) (1095–1096), and she achieves her purposes in part through her use of Aether/Ouranos (31–36, 582–586, 605–615). This Aether/Ouranos religion was not part of popular or even literary religion of the time, and Euripides' systematic presentation of it here may be a reflection of his interest in current natural philosophy—especially that of Diogenes of Apollonia.[156] Whatever the source, its presence casts a unifying but exotic aura over the whole play.

The complaint in the *Helen* that Calchas and Helenus did not give pertinent information leads to comments on the illogicality of their methods. Sophocles has Oedipus similarly criticize Teiresias for not helping the Thebans against the Sphinx (*OT* 390–403) or at the time of Laius' death (558–569), but these criticisms arise in an attack on Teiresias' character, not his craft. Oedipus calls him "the evilest of evil men" (334), an accomplice in a plot to kill Laius (346–349), an unscrupulous seeker of wealth and political influence (380–403),[157] an eastern-style priest (μάγος) stitching tricks together, a deceitful wandering priest (387–388), unskilled as a seer (389, 394–396), and a scoundrel (705). It is Jocasta who later turns to more general criticisms of divination, including oracles.[158] Like Oedipus, Creon in the *Antigone* gives Teiresias an honorific reception (991–995) but soon accuses him of venality (1033–1063). He considers Teiresias a "wise seer, but one acting unjustly" (1059).[159] Pentheus in Euripides' *Bacchae* charges Teiresias with profit-seeking and folly (255–257, 345). The Teiresias of Euripides' *Phoenissae* well understands the cause of such criticisms:

> A man who practises the craft of studying omens in sacrifices
> is foolish. If he happens to indicate hateful things,
> he becomes bitter to those for whom he studies the bird omens.
>
> (954–956)

Unlike seers in real life, those of tragedy do, as the chorus of Aeschylus' *Agamemnon* complains, bring forth only "what is fearful to learn" (1130–1135), and they suffer the common fate of messengers bearing ill tidings. Some disbelieve them, some attack their character, and others wish them dead.[160]

Among the numerous and varied criticisms of seers we must note how few concern the principles of the mantic art. Those in the *Helen* are left unanswered; those of the *Oedipus Tyrannus* are refuted by the outcome. Two such criticisms are preserved in fragments:

> The seer who guesses well is best.
>
> (E. frag. 973[N])

> Why, sitting on your mantic thrones,
> do you swear you know clearly the things of the gods?
> Men are not masters of these topics.
> Whoever boasts he knows about the gods
> knows nothing more than how to speak persuasively.
>
> (E. frag. 795[N])

But without having the context we cannot judge whether these attacks are justified or not. Only these four criticisms touch the religious issue; all the others, in various and sundry ways, concern the person of the seer, not his craft.

The seers of tragedy are always right; what they prophesy and what they claim to know always proves true. Criticisms of seers in tragedy have little, I think, to tell us of society's or an individual dramatist's views towards this important part of religious life. They reveal considerably more about how we are to judge the critics than the seers. Those most critical are Oedipus, Creon, and Pentheus. Each will be taken up separately below, but for now we may note that each erroneously faults Teiresias and that the causes, forms, and aspects of these attacks characterize each man quite differently. From each play, however, Teiresias, as a seer, emerges skilled, knowledgeable, and accurate. Whatever Athenians may have thought of seers in real life, the criticisms of them in these plays are unjustified and wrong. We are left with the criticism in *Helen* 744–757, and that, because it attacks the mantic art itself and serves little to characterize a major character and, most importantly, because it is unanswered, remains a strong challenge to an institution of contemporary religion.

Because seers in tragedy are wise about human and divine affairs and because they are always proven to be right, it is worthy noting, as we did for the *dei ex machina*,[161] what they have to say in general terms about religious matters. Only Sophocles' Calchas in the *Ajax* and Teiresias in the *Antigone* offer summary judgments. A messenger reports Calchas' views on Ajax:

The seer said that exceptional (περισσά) and senseless
persons fall into heavy failures from the gods,
a person who, born a human being, does not think as befits a human.

(*Aj.* 758–761)

Teiresias rather affectionately (τέκνον, 1023) warns Creon:

All men err, but when he errs,
that man is no longer without reason and prosperity
who, having fallen into evil, finds a cure and is not unmovable.
Stubbornness incurs the charge of folly and gracelessness
(σκαιότητα).

(*Ant.* 1023–1028)

Both seers speak to faults of the characters,[162] but their comments may be taken more broadly as, perhaps, Sophoclean views of proper religious behavior.

Dreams

Xenophon (*Eq. Mag.* 9.7–9) lists dreams along with sacrifices, omens, and voices as means by which the gods give signs (προσημαίνουσι) to men.[163] Athenians sought out such prophetic dreams at a number of sanctuaries, but they also took unsolicited dreams as prophetic. Those suffering from physical maladies slept in an Asclepieion at Athens or elsewhere and from their dreams apparently received prescriptions for a cure.[164] The sanctuary of Amphiaraus at Oropos provided similar cures by incubation and was probably the site at which the Athenians, in the 330s, bade three men sleep and report their dreams when there arose a troubling question of sacred or profane status of a parcel of land. A dream received there was taken to be "that which the god was commanding," and questions about it would be referred to Delphi (Hyperides, frag. 4.14–18).

The dreams Xenophon reports were unsolicited. When perplexed whether he should assume leadership of the Ten Thousand he dreamed that, amidst thunder, a lightning bolt fell on his ancestral home and set it ablaze.

> He awoke immediately, frightened. In one way he judged the dream good, because when he was in the midst of toils and dangers he seemed to see a great light from Zeus. But because the dream appeared to be

from Zeus Basileus ("The King")[165] and the fire to blaze all around him, he feared that he would not be able to escape the land of the king (of Persia) but would be surrounded by impossible situations. (*An.* 3.1. 11–14)

Xenophon finally took the dream as a favorable sign and assumed command. Later, when he and his troops were hemmed in by a river and hostile troops, he dreamed that he was bound in leg-chains, but the chains, of their own accord, fell off so that he could walk as far as he wished. He naturally took this as a good sign, and omens in subsequent sacrifices also proved favorable. A place for crossing the river was found, and on hearing the news Xenophon poured a libation and bade the men to pray "to the gods who had revealed the dream and ford to bring to pass also the remaining good things." The escape was indeed successful (*An.* 4.3.8–14).

After a workman was seriously injured in the construction of the Propylaea on the Acropolis, a despondent Pericles, as Plutarch reports (*Per.* 13.7–8), received from Athena a dream prescribing treatment. The man was healed, and Pericles erected a bronze statue of Athena Hygieia (Of Health). Smikythe also dedicated a statue to Athena on the Acropolis because of a dream she had had, no doubt from Athena, about her children and herself.[166] Demosthenes evidently claimed that Zeus and Athena sent him a dream announcing, before it was common knowledge, the death of Philip (Aeschines 3.77).

For real-life dreams whose circumstances we know best, the assignment of divine authors is explicable in cultic terms: Amphiaraus, on a question about his property; Asclepios, in his sanctuary, on health matters; Athena Hygieia, whose sanctuary adjoined the Propylaea, on healing an injury.[167] Xenophon credited Zeus Basileus because he thought himself under the special protection of that god during the whole expedition. These were not gods of dreams per se, but gods who, to accomplish their purposes, on occasion employed dreams. The dreams themselves were never thought to be false, but questions did arise about interpretation and the credibility of the recipient.[168] These dreams also all, so far as we know of them, pointed to something good, to something beneficial.

Among the tragedians Aeschylus particularly utilizes dreams. In seven plays he has three characters see visions in sleep: Xerxes' mother, Io, and Clytemnestra.[169] The last serves as the model for the dream Sophocles gives his Clytemnestra.[170] In Euripides only Hecuba and Iphigeneia dream.[171] The world of tragedy has only women dreamers.[172]

The dreams of tragedy are all what we would call nightmares. The Persian queen's surrealistic dream has two beautiful and stately women, Greek and barbarian, yoked like horses to a chariot. The rambunctious Greek breaks up the chariot, throwing to the ground the charioteer Xerxes. Darius stands alongside, pitying his son. A frightened Io is told repeatedly by "visions at night" to surrender her virginity to Zeus, to rendezvous with him in the meadow of Lerna. Aeschylus' Clytemnestra dreamed she bore a snake and wrapped it, like a baby, in swaddling clothes. When she offered it her breast, it sucked out a clot of blood. Sophocles' Clytemnestra saw the dead Agamemnon appear and fix his royal scepter in the ground at the hearth of their home. From it a swelling branch sprouted and cast a shadow over all Mycenae. Hecuba saw a deer dragged from her knees and killed by a wolf.[173] Iphigeneia dreamed that she was back home in Argos sleeping in her bedroom. An earthquake occurred, the palace collapsed, and only a single column, with human hair and voice, remained standing. Iphigeneia then, in her role as priestess, anointed the column as she did victims for the Taurian Artemis.

Because these dreams were unsolicited, the recipients most often do not know their divine source. Sophocles' Electra speculates that her dead father may have sent the vision to Clytemnestra (*El.* 459–460). Hecuba invokes "Lady Chthon (Earth), mother of dark-winged dreams" (*Hec.* 70–71). Euripides elsewhere has the same figure, Gaia, produce dreams (*IT* 1259–1282), and it is quite possible that all tragic dreams described thus far, apart from that of Io, were imagined to have originated in the chthonic world of Gaia and the dead. The nightmares of tragedy come from the underworld, the attested dreams of life from the deities of life, from Zeus, Athena, and the healing gods.[174] The religion of tragedy, like life in tragedy, is much darker than that of the fifth century.

The recipients of dreams in tragedy react, however, much like their real-life counterparts. For interpretation they summon seers.[175] If a question remains, they send to oracles.[176] After the dream they may further test the omens in sacrifice.[177] Because the dreams uniformly portend evil, characters pray and make offerings to avert the evil.[178] Apollo is not the sender of dreams, but he is useful for interpreting them and may receive sacrifices and prayers intended to avert what they portend.[179]

The Clytemnestra of Aeschylus' *Agamemnon* scoffs at the chorus' suggestion that she was announcing the fall of Troy because of a mere dream (274–275), but her heart is ἀνδρόβουλον, "manly in its thinking" (11; cf. 351). The female chorus of Sophocles' *Electra* is prepared to doubt the prophetic power of all dreams and oracles if Clytemnestra's vision is not realized (498–502), but this mild challenge is met when Orestes slays his mother. *Iphigeneia among the Taurians* is unique in that the correct interpretation of a dream is never put forward by a character, and doubt is cast and left pending about the prophetic power of dreams in general.[180]

Omens

Aeschylus' Prometheus claims he taught men to understand dreams, hard-to-judge chance words, occurrences on the roads, and omens from birds and sacrifices (*Pr.* 484–499; see above, p. 47). Several of these we have discussed in the context of the craft of seers, but they and omens from thunder, lightning, and eclipses were also observed and interpreted by laymen.[181] To complete our survey of divination in tragedy we must give a brief account of them.

Seers usually prophesied from "sought" omens (*impetrata omina*), omens which they searched for in sacrifices and in the flight of birds when deliberating a question or proposed action. Tragedy occasionally has an individual act as his own seer in a similar situation, as we know, for instance, that Xenophon did in real life. In Euripides' *Electra* Aegisthus, just moments before he is killed by Orestes, realizes that the signs from the entrails of his sacrificial victim portend "some deceit from abroad" (826–832).[182] In tragedy, however, most omens are "spontaneous" (*oblata omina*), appearing to individuals at critical moments before ventures like journeys, battles, and marriages.[183] Here one had to decide whether or not an event was "ominous."[184] The individual could "make it an omen" or not.[185] In tragedy such ominous events are limited to the flight of birds, chance words, and thunder and lightning, whereas in life they included also rain, earthquakes, eclipses, sneezes, sacrilegious acts, and other such events.[186]

Most omens in tragedy, like oracles, dreams, and seers' predictions, portend trouble. Xerxes' mother, as she sacrificed to avert her dream of the Greek and barbarian chariot-mates, saw an eagle fly to Apollo's altar, where it meekly endured an attack by a hawk (A. *Pers.* 201–210). In the dramatic context of the Greek and Persian battles of 480, neither queen nor audience needed an interpretation. A bird omen warned Heracles that his family was suffering in Tiryns (E. *HF* 596–597); omens in sacrifice told Aegisthus of "deceit from abroad" (E. *El.* 826–832); and ill omens attended Phaedra's departure from Crete and arrival in Attica.[187] Good omens give the observers hope and confidence, bad ones leave them "disspirited."[188] The same sign to opposing forces in the battlefield might indicate opposite fortunes. In Euripides' *Phoenissae* the thunderbolt which struck and killed Capaneus was naturally taken by the Argives as a bad sign. The Thebans interpreted it as a favorable (perhaps literally "on the right") omen from Zeus and attacked (1172–1192). The Thebans then successfully defended their city. A chance word uttered by a servant saved the life of Ion, the young man who became the eponymous founder of the Ionians. As he was about to pour a libation and drink from his poisoned cup, a servant uttered a blasphemous word. Ion, "because he had been raised in a sanctuary and among good seers, made it an omen," broke off the ritual, poured out his cup, and ordered new wine. The plot was discovered, and Ion lived (E. *Ion* 1182–1210). In tragedy these signs are consistently taken seriously and acted upon. The philosophical and rationalistic explanations for such signs and the resulting denigration of them that we find in late accounts of Pericles and Anaxagoras[189] have no place in tragedy. Only Theseus in Euripides' *Hippolytus* (1057–1059) and Oedipus in Sophocles' *Oedipus Tyrannus* (964–967) deny, on principle, the value of such signs, and they do so as they commit other, more grievous errors.

Let us conclude our investigation of divination with a look at three plays—Sophocles' *Oedipus Tyrannus* and Euripides' *Suppliants* and *Iphigeneia among the Taurians*—in which a variety of forms of divination have a role and are subject to extensive criticism by various characters.

In the *Suppliants,* to document his claim that the good things in this world outnumber the bad, Theseus describes to Adrastus the gods' gifts to mortals (195–213). These include the means for sustaining life, intelligence, language, produce from the earth and rain from the sky, shelter, navigation, and, last in the list, the art of seers:

By looking into fire and on the folds of entrails (of sacrificial victims)
  and from bird omens
seers explain things which are
hard to decipher and which we do not clearly understand.

(211–213)

The ranking of the mantic art among other items so essential to human existence reflects the particular prominence which we have seen that divination enjoyed in both the life and tragedy of the times.[190] Several proponents of the modernism of Euripides have, however, claimed that he wrote these lines, and especially those concerning seers, with sarcasm and irony.[191] Whether this is true can be determined only by examining how Euripides treats divination in the rest of the play. If by words and action in the play he debunks seers and their craft, we may look skeptically on Theseus' words. If not, we should turn our gaze to modern critics.

In the *Suppliants* there are two oracles from Apollo of Delphi concerning marriages, one consultation of a seer, and one prophecy from the mouth of Athena. Because Theseus praises only the art of seers, it is appropriate to examine first the one instance of this. Adrastus (155–159), when setting out with the expedition of the Seven against Thebes, failed to consult seers and, even worse (τὸ δὲ πλέον, 158), acted counter to the unsolicited advice of Amphiaraus, the most prominent seer of his time.[192] Adrastus recognizes his folly (156), and Theseus condemns it unequivocally (159, 229–231). In Theseus' view the opposition of the seer indicates that the goodwill of the gods (εὐνοίᾳ θεῶν) is lacking, and, of course, such goodwill is necessary for success.[193] By "dishonoring" the prophecies of the seers Adrastus transgressed the will of the gods (230–231). The manner in which Euripides presents Adrastus ignoring the seers, and the subsequent failure of the expedition, clearly confirm the high value Theseus has placed on this form of divination.

As we extend our discussion to divination in general and consider the oracles of Apollo and the prophecy of Athena in this play, we must remember that Theseus praises only the seers' art and not all divination. Thus even if an oracle should prove false or harmful, it would not necessarily refute Theseus' claims about the mantic art.[194] Two of the three remaining occurrences of divination pose no problems. Athena as *deus ex machina* reveals that the Epigonoi will sack Thebes and avenge their fathers, and this of course comes to pass.¹⁹⁵ And, according to Aethra, her father Pittheus gave her in marriage to Aegeus on the basis of oracles of Apollo Loxias (5–7). To judge by the status and behavior of Aethra and her son in this play, that was a successful marriage, and no criticism can be directed against the oracle.

The case is more difficult for Adrastus, who was bidden by Apollo to give his two daughters "to a boar and a lion" (140). When Tydeus and Polyneices arrived on his doorstep fighting, Adrastus likened their battle to that of two wild beasts and hence gave his daughters to them in marriage. These marriages, of course, proved disastrous for Adrastus and his country,¹⁹⁶ and Theseus points out at length Adrastus' folly in associating his family with these sullied, unjust, and ill-fortuned men (219–225). But what of the oracle? Was it the cause, or did Adrastus make another error like that with the seers? The answer is unclear.¹⁹⁷ The chorus apparently places some of the fault on Apollo (πιϰρὰν δὲ Φοίβου φάτιν, 834). Theseus shows interest in Adrastus' reasoning in interpreting the oracle (139–141) but makes no judgment, favorable or unfavorable, on Adrastus' interpretation or on the oracle itself. Theseus views Adrastus as "yoked by the oracles of Phoebus" (θεσφάτοις Φοίβου ζυγείς, 220) but nonetheless faults Adrastus' good sense in making these marriages.¹⁹⁸ In the text as we have it, Euripides does not make Theseus criticize the oracle itself or claim that Adrastus misinterpreted it.¹⁹⁹ Theseus' attention moves rather to the social and ethical folly of joining a good family to a bad.²⁰⁰ Adrastus clearly did the wrong thing, and the question is, for us, open as to whether this was the fault of the oracle or of Adrastus' judgment in interpreting and acting upon the oracle.²⁰¹ We are left in this play with a confirmation of the value of seers, an accurate prophecy by Athena, a good oracle (on Aethra's marriage), and one problematic for us (on the marriage of Adrastus' daughters). From this play we have thus no reason to question Theseus' (or Euripides') assessment of the value of seers to human life.

In Euripides' *Iphigeneia among the Taurians* two elements of divination, dreams and Delphic oracles, are played off one against the other. In the prologue Iphigeneia recounts a dream: as she slept in her own room back in Argos, an earthquake made her ancestral house collapse; a single column remained standing, and from its capital issued tawny hair and a human voice; and she, performing the ritual she did for human victims in Tauris, sprinkled water on the column (42–55). Iphigeneia takes this dream to mean that Orestes is dead (56–58),[202] and she and the chorus begin funeral offerings and laments for Orestes (61–63, 143–235). But as the audience first learns for sure at line 71, Iphigeneia has misinterpreted the dream. Orestes is still alive. By the end of the play, with the benefit of hindsight, we can see the "proper" interpretation of the dream. Orestes is, in fact, the single column remaining from the collapse (of the male line) of the royal family. He will become enmeshed in the Taurian rituals of human sacrifice performed by Iphigeneia. He will, however, escape death, and in this Iphigeneia misinterprets the dream.

Despite Iphigeneia's claim that her dream was false (569), the course of the action proves it true. Uniquely in this play, however, the accuracy of the prophetic dream is not remarked by any character. Euripides may not have thought it necessary or worthwhile to give the obvious interpretation of the dream or to have pointed to its fulfillment in the usual ways. But the omission may also have resulted from the superiority Euripides has his chorus claim for Delphic Apollo over dreams in this play. In the *Iphigeneia among the Taurians* Orestes' recent life has been orchestrated by the oracles of Delphi. Apollo had ordered him to slay his mother in retribution for her slaying of Agamemnon. Thereupon he bade him to go to Athens to stand trial for the killing. After the trial, when Orestes was still being pursued by some of the Erinyes, Apollo commanded him to go to Tauris, steal the statue of the Tauric Artemis, and deliver it to Athens. Then he would find release from his toils (77–94, 711–715, 937–982, 1012–1015). As in other plays treating Orestes' myth, Orestes and his partisans at particularly dark and desperate moments question Apollo's guidance and oracles. In this play Orestes first expresses uncertainty and bewilderment: "Why, Phoebus, did you lead me again with your oracle into this net?" (77–78). "Persuaded by your words I have come here to an unknown, hostile land" (93–94). Pylades, with his usual calm good sense, advises Orestes, "You must not dishonor the oracle of the god" (105).[203] As Orestes faces imminent death, his questioning becomes sharper: "Even those deities who are called wise are no less deceitful than winged dreams. There is much confusion in divine and human affairs. But one thing alone causes pain, when a man who is not foolish perishes as he does trusting the words of seers" (570–575). Orestes' strongest and most

Challenges to Popular Beliefs 109

direct challenge to the credibility of Apollo comes, as such challenges often do, at a nadir in the fortunes of the protagonists:

> Phoebus, a seer, deceived us.
> By a trick he drove us as far as possible from Greece,
> in shame at his previous oracles.
> I entrusted all my affairs to him and believed his words.
> I killed my mother and now, in turn, I myself am being destroyed.
>
> (711–715)

Pylades offers a bit of encouragement but no real answer to the challenge: "The god's oracle has not *yet* destroyed you, but you do stand near death. But extremely bad fortune is a thing which gives extremely great changes" (719–722). Orestes gives a curt reply, "Keep quiet! Phoebus' words are giving me no help" (723).

In the very next scene (725–899) Orestes and his sister recognize one another, and despair turns to optimism as they make plans for escape and seizure of the statue. The challenge resurfaces only once, in Iphigeneia's prayer to Artemis: "Rescue me and these, or else because of you Loxias' mouth will no longer appear truthful to mortals" (1084–1085). As plans for the escape progress and rescue seems assured, the chorus of Greek women reasserts confidence in Apollo: "Phoebus the prophet . . . will lead you well to the gleaming land of the Athenians" (1128–1131). This is followed (1234–1282) by the longest and most detailed hymn to Delphic Apollo in the Euripidean corpus. The hymn tells a mythical history of the oracle and of Apollo's role there. It describes Zeus' sanction of Apollo's authority and the resulting confidence men can have "in the songs of the oracles at this throne with its crowds of visitors" (1280–1282).

In the end Orestes, Iphigeneia, Pylades, and even the chorus find safe passage back to Greece and, as Apollo had promised, release from their sufferings and labors. All of Apollo's oracles have proved true, and Orestes' doubts and questioning, though understandable, are proved to be mistaken. The full statement of this comes only with Athena's settlement of the issues (1435–1489), but it is hardly in doubt after the magnificent hymn to Pythian Apollo in 1234–1282.

In this same hymn the chorus describes a mythological relationship, unknown from elsewhere, between Apollo's oracles and dreams. When Apollo banished Gaia's daughter from the oracle, Gaia retaliated by sending to mortals dreams that told of "the first things and the things thereafter that were going to be" (1259–1267). Such competition, of course, undercut Apollo's business at Delphi, and he appealed to the ultimate arbiter, Zeus. Zeus decided in his son's favor and took away "truth-in-dreams" (1279).[204] The superiority of Apollo's oracles to dreams is thus established in mythological terms, and we have a precise response to one of Orestes's challenges to Apollo: "Even those deities who are called wise are no less deceitful than winged dreams" (570–571).

Euripides' omission of an acknowledged correct interpretation of Iphigeneia's dream, noted earlier, may result from the superiority to prophetic dreams he gives Apollo in this hymn. The tragic convention that all dreams, properly interpreted, prove true is inconsistent with the denigration of dreams in 1259–1282. Euripides wanted both, a conventional dream and a denigration of dreams. To cover the inconsistency he avoided reference to the dream's fulfillment. Why he chose, somewhat gratuitously,[205] to fault the prophetic power of dreams in 1259–1282 we do not know. It may be significant that *Iphigeneia among the Taurians* is a late play, dated by some to ca. 413, a year or so before the *Helen*, in which there is a similar unmet and gratuitous challenge to the craft of seers.[206]

Three Delphic oracles lie at the heart of Sophocles' *Oedipus Tyrannus*. One told Laius that he was destined to be killed by his own son (711–714), one told Oedipus that he necessarily[207] would kill his father and marry his mother (787–793, 994–996), and the third bade the inquiring Thebans to rid their city of pestilence and plague by eliminating the pollution caused by the presence of the unpunished murderer of Laius (86–136, 241–245, 305–309). These oracles, and the particular ways in which individuals reacted to them, form the core of Sophocles' play. Because Laius feared death at his son's hand, he had him exposed on Mount Cithaeron, and this made it possible for Oedipus later to return unrecognized. Oedipus, to thwart the oracle about himself, fled his presumed home, Corinth, only to arrive in his real home, Thebes. These two oracles are, in form and content, purely literary, unlike any known historical oracle,[208] and, interestingly, it is only against these two oracles that the criticisms described below are directed. The third oracle sets into motion the particular action of the play, Oedipus' discovery of who he is and what he has done. The Thebans are beset by plague and pestilence, and Oedipus, as king, has sent to Delphi to inquire what must be done. Apollo responds that the city should search out the murderer of Laius and, by punishing him, free itself from pollution.[209] In the fifth century some individuals and states did turn to Apollo of Delphi on questions of health, plague, and pollution, and this oracle is modeled from life.[210]

In the *Oedipus Tyrannus* more characters, and for more reasons, criticize oracles and seers than in any other Greek play. This is, I think, not because Sophocles was particularly interested in attacks on or defenses of prophecy, but because, for his plot and to create intricate dramatic irony, he chose to have three oracles at hand and, what is most unusual, *two* characters who question their value. When Teiresias, whom Sophocles makes Apollo's spokesman in this play,[211] is goaded into revealing that Oedipus is Laius' murderer, Oedipus disbelieves, criticizes, and threatens him (297–462).[212] Jocasta bids Oedipus not to trouble himself about a seer's words, because once Laius had received an oracle that he would be killed by his son, and that did not happen (708–725; cf. 852–854). The news that Polybus, whom Oedipus still thinks to be his father, has died in Corinth brings a new round of attacks on the oracle (946–949, 952–953, 964–972). As a result of the questioning of Oedipus and Jocasta, the chorus, which initially had full confidence in Apollo's mantic power (e.g., 406–407), begins to waver. It first questions only Teiresias' knowledge (483–486, 498–501), but later, in reference to Laius' murder, issues a broader challenge:

> Never again will I go in reverence to the untouchable navel
> of the earth nor into (Apollo's) temple at Abae nor to
> Olympia, unless what is happening here shall become an example
>   known to all men.
> Zeus, ruler, if rightly you are called
> "commander of all things," let these things not escape you and your
>   immortal rule.
> For people are now doing away with the old oracles of Laius,
> and Apollo is nowhere illustrious in honor.
> The divine things (τὰ θεῖα) are perishing.
>
> (898–910)

Should the oracle about Laius prove false, and should Oedipus' and Jocasta's criticisms prove true, one can assume that Zeus no longer "commands all things." The practice of worshiping at major sanctuaries and the chorus' whole religious faith are thrown into question.[213] In the end, of course, the oracle about Laius and all else predicted by Apollo and Teiresias come true. Oedipus had killed his father, did marry his mother, and, as Laius' killer, was the cause of Thebes' pollution. The challenge of the chorus is resoundingly met. Zeus in heaven rules, and worshipers will continue to go to the holy "navel." What prevails is the prosaic faith of Creon, who had initially inquired at Delphi (69–111), who was ready to have Delphi substantiate his story (603–604), and who, at the end (1438–1445; cf. 1518–1520), insists that Oedipus' future be decided by Delphi.

The criticisms of prophecy, Apollo, and Teiresias in the *Oedipus Tyrannus* prove wrong, but they are interesting as a review of what one could and did say against the practice in fifth-century literature and life. The criticisms are usually not directed against the god of prophecy himself, though the chorus does complain that if Apollo had wanted them to banish a murderer, it was his task, not theirs, to show who the murderer was (278–279). Oedipus responds, "That is a fair statement, but one man cannot force gods to do what they do not wish to do" (280–281). The chorus makes the point that the gods, here Zeus and Apollo, "know more" than ordinary men, but the same is not necessarily true of seers (498–501). Jocasta, hesitant to fault the god directly, leaves open the possibility that Laius' apparently false oracle came not from Apollo but from his "assistants" (711–712). To Jocasta the case is simple: there is no need to heed the statements of seers because "whatever a god needs he will easily reveal himself" (723–725). When Teiresias refuses to cooperate, Oedipus calls him "a contriving magician, a deceitful beggar-priest who has eyes only for profit and none for his craft" (387–389). He assumes Teiresias is scheming with Creon to gain political power (572–573). He bitingly asks why Teiresias in earlier days had failed to help Thebes against the Sphinx (390–396) and to make the proper investigation of Laius' death (562–569). The only answer given to such questions is the lame but perhaps pious one of Creon, "I do not know, and in matters I do not understand I prefer to keep silent" (569). Two criticisms found in other plays are only alluded to here: that "screeching birds" are hardly fit prophets (964–967), and that a human might, for his own purposes, falsely report an oracle (603–604).

Such are the accusations raised against the god, the seer, and the craft

Challenges to Popular Beliefs 113

and practice of prophecy in the *Oedipus Tyrannus*. Since all prove to be erroneous, the prestige of prophecy is left undiminished or perhaps even enhanced. The source of all the oracles and the patron of prophecy and seers in this play is Apollo Pythios, whose epithet Sophocles nicely links with πυθέσθαι, "to learn by inquiry" (70–71).[214] The question endlessly debated, whether the oracles in some way caused, or merely describe, events in the Oedipus story, is probably insoluble within the framework of the play. Against the occasional suggestions in the text that Apollo somehow "brought these events to pass" stand the apparently voluntary actions of the human beings.[215]

Early in the play Oedipus beseeches Teiresias to (1) "Save yourself and the city," (2) "Save me," and (3) "Ward off all the pollution of the one who has died" (312–313). Unbeknownst to Oedipus, fulfillment of the first and third excludes the possibility of fulfilling the second. Given the circumstances which Sophocles has chosen to construct at the opening of the play, we may imagine roughly the same three requests to Apollo Pythios: "Save the city, save Oedipus, and eliminate the pollution caused by the presence of the murderer of Laius." With the requests put in this form, Apollo Pythios does fulfill the functions historically expected of him: he reveals and thereby eliminates the pollution that is bringing plague and pestilence to the city. The Theban priest at the end of the prologue wishes, or prays indirectly, that Apollo come as "savior" and "stopper of the plague" (149–150).[216] Apollo does that. In a characteristic way Delphic Apollo saves the city, the city whose interests the priest represents. He does not, however, save Oedipus, the subject of our play. Our attention and that of Sophocles is riveted upon Oedipus, but we must not blind ourselves to the larger, familiar religious background in which Oedipus operates as a unique individual.

Amid the manifold uses of the various forms of divination in Greek tragedy we thus have only three unmet attacks on divination as it was practised by fifth-century Athenians: Apollo's intentionally false oracle in the *Ion*; the attack on the craft of seers in the *Helen*; and the denial of truth to dreams at the end of *Iphigeneia among the Taurians*. All three derive from later plays of Euripides, with the *Ion* (ca. 418) being the earliest and the *Helen* (412) the latest. These three, at least six years apart and interspersed among plays where divination is used but not criticized, can hardly be viewed as a sustained attack by Euripides. The great preponderance of evidence from Aeschylus, Sophocles, and even Euripides shows that they had their characters eventually find divination trustworthy, as did most members of the audience.

Death, Burial, and the Afterlife

Death and the afterlife were the areas about which there was the greatest uncertainty in everyday religious life,[217] and that uncertainty is paralleled by the variety of beliefs expressed in tragedy. Let us survey these before taking up the most common challenge to popular religious belief in this area: the denial of burial and burial rites.

Death in tragedy as in life is, as we have seen, often attributed to fortune, fate, daimons, Hades, and Thanatos, all figures without cult and inaccessible to the usual forms of worship. Poets, unlike popular religion, sometimes extended responsibility for it to "the gods" in general and occasionally to individual gods, but even those gods withdraw at death's appearance. The gods of the living have no role or function in death or the world of the dead.[218] The impersonal character and variety of superhuman agents of death reflect that classical Greek religion offered no standard explanation in religious terms for death. There is an occasional strain of fatalism in the tragic view of death,[219] but this fatalism is not founded on religious cult or principle.

The status of the dead is also variously described. Death can be metaphorically and euphemistically described as sleep, the dead as "the sleeping ones."[220] Most dead are, of course, in Hades, but souls are occasionally sent into the *aether*. These alternative destinations are first proposed in tragedy by Sophocles, who has the chorus of the *Ajax* wish that the man who discovered war had, before that invention, "gone into the great *aether*" or Hades (1192–1196).[221] Elsewhere only Euripides speaks of *aether* as the realm of souls, once casually of the ordinary dead (*Or.* 1086–1087) but also of war heroes (*Suppl.* 531–534) and the divinized Hyacinthidae (frag. 65[A], 71–74).[222] Fallen war heroes were even in popular conception a special category, distinct from the common dead and deserving special honor,[223] and it is not surprising to find them sharing a distinction with those rewarded with divinity for their virtue. In the *Helen* Euripides constructs an *aether*-centered religion and has souls of all the dead go to *aether* (1013–1016),[224] as he does also in his quasi-philosophical discussion of Aether and Gaia in a fragment of the *Chrysippus* (839[N]). The thought is that the body returns to earth, the soul to *aether*.[225] The famous epitaph on the fallen Athenian warriors at Potidaea (*IG* I² 945), according to which "*aether* received their souls, Chthon (Earth) their bodies," predates (ca. 432) all the Euripidean treatments of the subject and may well have influenced the dramatist. *Aether* as the abode of the souls may have been a philosophical idea originally, but it was widely familiar in the second half of the fifth century and later and could be played upon by Aristophanes (*Pax* 827–841) and be included in private epitaphs.[226] It was always, however, a minority view.

We may divide conceptions of the life of the dead in Hades roughly into three groups. In all the soul continues to exist, but in the first it lacks consciousness and thought, afterlife is insubstantial, virtually nothing, and for this very reason death is praised or sought as release from earthly sufferings. In the second the souls of the dead mill about, talk among one another, reminisce, and greet their newly arriving relatives. In the third individual souls are rewarded or punished for their actions in life. There is little overlap between these conceptions, and most descriptions of the afterlife in tragedy fall into one group or the other.

Euripides has characters make the stark comment that the dead are "nothing."[227] Aeschylus on occasion denies them thought, joy, and grief.[228] The dead may be denied perception, strength, and the power to affect anything.[229] They are not even "concerned to rise up again" (A. *Ag.* 568–569). This "nothingness" of the dead raises questions why one should make offerings or prayers to them, or even bother to honor or maltreat their corpses.[230] It is, however, characteristic of the uncertain and ambivalent Greek beliefs about the dead that most claims of their "nothingness" come in the plays—Aeschylus' *Choephoroi*, Sophocles' *Electra*, and Euripides' *Troades*—that have the most numerous and most elaborate prayers to a dead person.[231] The nothingness of the life beyond appeals to those beset by miseries in this life. Death is a release from pain, suffering, labor, toil, disease, and evils in general.[232] It is the "greatest bulwark against the many evils" (A. frag. 353[R]). Cadmus in Euripides' *Bacchae* (1338–1339, 1361–1362) even complains that, being sent to "the land of the blessed," he will not "sail the Acheron and be at peace (ἥσυχος)." Macaria, the young heroine to be sacrificed in the *Heraclidae*, wants death to be nothing:

I hope, however, there is nothing. For if we mortals
who are about to die will have worries even there (in Hades),
then I don't know to where someone will turn. For dying
is thought to be the greatest healing drug of evils.

(593–596)

In contrast to this bleak picture of the afterlife stands the world of the cognizant and talkative dead. Clytemnestra bids the dead Agamemnon not to "boast" in the underworld because he has the punishment he deserves for what he did to Iphigeneia (A. *Ag.* 1525–1529). Iolaus, who expects to die, tells Demophon that he will describe to his dead father, Theseus, his good deeds and bring joy to him (E. *Heraclid.* 320–328). As Polyxena goes off to her death, she asks Hecuba what she should report to the dead Hector and Priam (E. *Hec.* 422–423). Cassandra looks forward to her "triumphant" entrance into Hades in the presence of her brothers and father (E. *Tr.* 459–461). Hecuba at one moment expects the dead Hector to tend the dead Astyanax (*Tr.* 1232–1234). Ajax will have something to tell those in Hades (S. *Aj.* 865). Antigone, as several others, plans to rejoin, recognize, and interact with her dead relatives.[233] These souls form, in Hades, a society not unlike that in the upper world, with former kings like Agamemnon (A. *Ch.* 354–362) and Darius (A. *Pers.* 691) retaining their royal status.[234] These dead are pleased or irritated by the praises or criticisms of their fellow spirits and are particularly wrathful at their killers.[235]

These dead are conscious but lack knowledge of current events in the upper world. Darius, whom Aeschylus has conjured up from the dead, needs to be briefed on recent events in Persia (*Pers.* 682–708).[236] Heracles, although a special case as a living person in Hades, knew nothing of the tribulations of his family during his subterranean sojourn (E. *HF* 523–550, 596–597).[237] Unlike the dead who are "nothing," some of this group seem aware of ritual directed to them, whether it be at the funeral or later in drink offerings (χοαί). Teucer does not want Odysseus to attend Ajax' funeral because it would be "vexatious" (δυσχερές) to the deceased (S. *Aj.* 1394–1395). Darius says explicitly that he "received" drink offerings made to him and was persuaded to appear by the ritual laments (A. *Pers.* 685–688, 697).

In Aeschylus' *Choephoroi* the dead Agamemnon is also thought to "have" the drink offerings made at his tomb (164), and Orestes, Electra, and the chorus make elaborate prayers to accompany these offerings. Six times they bid the dead Agamemnon to "hear" them.²³⁸ His "thought" (φρόνημα) survives cremation, and they expect him, like other victims of murder, to be wrathful at his killers (38–41, 400–404).²³⁹ To this end they remind him of the bath and other circumstances of his death (479–495). They invoke him as a partner in obtaining vengeance on Aegisthus and Clytemnestra (142–144, 460, 497–499). Apart from general appeals for pity or help,²⁴⁰ Electra asks him to send Orestes (130–139; cf. 117–121), a prayer which Orestes views as answered by his own arrival (215; cf. 218–219). Electra prays to her father that she be much "more temperate" (σωφρονεστέραν) and "pious" than her mother (140–141). Orestes asks him for control of the ancestral house (480). If Orestes recovers Agamemnon's property, he will establish for his father the traditional banquets of the dead, and Electra will greatly reverence his tomb and bring drink offerings to him at the time of her marriage (480–488). This is, apart from the satisfaction of vengeance, Agamemnon's quid pro quo (cf. 509). If Orestes fails, Agamemnon will be "without honor" (ἄτιμος) amid the dead who receive "good banquets" (483–485). Orestes' final request to the tomb of his father is that Clytemnestra's dream of the snake be brought to pass (540–541), and the dream proves to be as Orestes wished it (928–929).

In cultic terms these are prayers which accompany the pouring of drink offerings at the tomb (*Ch.* 87–99, 129–130, 149).²⁴¹ As Electra ponders what specific requests she should make in this situation, she points to the "custom" (νόμος) of praying that the dead "give back equal things to those sending the offerings" (94–95). The dead should, in usual circumstances, return good for the good offerings loving relatives make.²⁴² Electra varies this formula because the hated Clytemnestra has sent these offerings, but the formula itself may reflect a conventional prayer of popular religion.

Sophocles' Electra in a situation very like that of her Aeschylean counterpart speaks of Agamemnon's "corpse in the tomb" receiving drink offerings (*El.* 440–443; cf. 436), but twenty lines later she has Agamemnon himself in Hades (463). She bids her sister Chrysothemis pray to Agamemnon that he "come as a helper" against their enemies and that Orestes triumph so that hereafter they can give richer offerings (quid pro quo) to Agamemnon. She too credits Clytemnestra's dream to the dead Agamemnon (453–460). Even in this play, however, the chorus and characters express uncertainty whether the dead have consciousness and whether rituals affect them (137–139, 245–246, 1170).

In the *Orestes* Euripides has Orestes, Electra, and Pylades pray to the dead Agamemnon to help and rescue them, particularly in their attempt to kill Helen. They base their claim for assistance on kinship and on the vengeance they took, for Agamemnon's sake, on Clytemnestra. They are eventually rescued, but they do not succeed in killing Helen (796–797, 1225–1242). Because they are not at Agamemnon's tomb, they substitute tears for drink offerings (χοαί) and general laments (οἶκτοι) for ritual ones (γόοι) (1239). Earlier Orestes bade his uncle Menelaus to imagine, as real orators occasionally suggested to their audiences, that the dead man was listening to their words (674–677).[243]

In the *Choephoroi* all that is asked for in prayers to the dead Agamemnon comes to pass, as it does in the similar prayers in Sophocles' *Electra*. But we must remember that Agamemnon and Darius were not common dead. They were former kings, heads of royal dynasties, with special status even in the underworld. They and their cults are more heroic than ordinary, especially to members of their own families.[244] In contrast to the effectiveness of prayers addressed to them stand the appeals to the dead elsewhere in tragedy. Apart from Agamemnon and Darius the dead receive remarkably few addresses and even fewer prayers. Most are to be found in Euripides' *Troades* where Hecuba, Andromache, and the chorus invoke their dead husbands. In 587–594 Andromache bids the dead Hector to come as her defender and take her to Hades.[245] In 673–678 she directly addresses Hector in eulogizing him and their marriage.[246] In 1083–1085 the chorus invoke their "dear husbands" who in death wander without burial, without libations. Andromache (1132–1133), as she leaves Troy, addresses Hector's tomb. In perhaps the most moving scene, at the close of the play (1303–1316), Hecuba falls to her knees, pounds the earth, and invokes her dead children and Priam. The chorus follow her example and call to their dead husbands.

Scholars have commonly, but wrongly, used these scenes from the *Troades* to illustrate that Greeks of the classical period believed the common dead (not only heroes) heard the prayers of the living and might respond to them.[247] In this, insufficient attention has been paid to the context of these scenes and to the same characters' later comments on the nature of death and the status of the dead. In 588–589 Hecuba interrupts Andromache's appeal to Hector with the comment, "Poor woman, you shout for my son who is in Hades," a gentle suggestion, I think, that Hector, because he is in Hades, cannot hear her.[248] Soon thereafter Hecuba concludes this lyric section with the observation, "The dead person forgets his woes" (606–607). Andromache, between her two appeals to Hector, notes that death is better than living in suffering "because the dead person does not perceive or grieve for his misfortunes."[249] She similarly states that Polyxena "has died and knows nothing of her ills" (641–642). Perhaps most telling are her words to her son Astyanax: "Hector will not rise from the earth, snatch up his spear, and come bringing safety to you" (752–753). Andromache may appeal to Hector in moments of high emotional intensity,[250] but in more lucid moments she recognizes the futility of such appeals.

The invocation which Hecuba and the chorus make to the dead in 1303–1316 is most gripping and is accompanied by what would seem to be the appropriate ritual of falling to the ground and beating it with the fists.[251] Hecuba opens the scene with a plea to her dead children to "hear the voice of their mother." The chorus gently suggests the ineffectiveness of this—"You are invoking the dead with your cry"—but then the women are caught up in Hecuba's emotion, fall to the ground, and call upon their "poor husbands down below." In 1312–1316 Hecuba invokes Priam, who is dead, unburied, and without relative or friend, and laments that he "does not perceive" her "destruction." And the chorus knows why: "Because holy black death has covered over his eyes" (1315–1316). What begins as an invocation of the dead ends with observations by all participants on the lack of perception by the deceased.

The invocations of the dead in this play should not be taken as evidence that Athenians in the classical period ordinarily or in fact ever prayed to the common dead and expected to receive something from them. They are natural and intensely human responses to the loss of dear ones, and Euripides has taken pains to suggest gently their futility.[252] These invocations are hardly different from Hecuba's appeals to the city of Troy (601–602, 1277–1279) and even to Hector's shield (1194–1199, 1221–1225). Death is, as Hecuba so succinctly puts it, "nothing" (632–633). Despite the numerous appeals to them, the dead of the *Troades* belong to that group for whom death is "nothingness." Apart from the plays involving Agamemnon and Darius, evidence for prayers to the dead is scanty, and what little there is suggests that such prayers and invocations were ultimately recognized as ineffective.

Our last group of dead, those who are to be rewarded or punished in the afterlife for the deeds of this life, is by far the smallest. Expectations of rewards are rare, tentative, and do not involve the common dead. The chorus hopes that Alcestis, who is imagined as both heroine and god, will receive good things and sit beside Persephone, "if there is (in Hades) anything more for good people" (E. *Alc.* 741–746).[253] Heracles, *deus ex machina* in Sophocles' *Philoctetes*, tells Philoctetes and Neoptolemus that "piety does not die with mortals. Whether they are alive or dead, their piety does not perish" (1443–1444). But here the question, which cannot be answered decisively from the text, is whether Heracles means that piety is rewarded in Hades after death or merely lives on in a dead man's reputation. The latter seems more probable.[254] In tragedy the Land (or Island) of the Blessed, which might seem to be the highest reward, is to be the final abode only of Menelaus (E. *Hel.* 1676–1677) and Cadmus (E. *Ba.* 1338–1339), and they gain admittance solely, it would seem, because they are married to daughters of the gods.[255] Such is the meager evidence for rewards in the afterlife.[256]

There is likewise little evidence for *post mortem* punishments in Sophocles and Euripides. Only Theonoë, the practitioner of an idiosyncratic Aether/Ouranos religion, warns of the punishment of the dead person's Nous (Mind) in the *aether* for crimes like the violation of *xenia* (E. *Hel.* 1013–1016).[257] Aeschylus mentions no rewards after death, but in the *Suppliants* and *Eumenides* he graphically describes judgment and punishment. In those plays the sinner is not "freed" from punishments even by death.[258] Another Zeus (*Suppl.* 230–231), "great" Hades (*Eum.* 273), will judge and punish sinners. Danaus foresees such punishments for violent suitors who take an unwilling bride from an unwilling father (*Suppl.* 227–231), Pelasgus for those who violate asylum (413–416). The Erinyes detail the miseries that await Orestes, the murderer of his mother, after his death.[259] As he suffers in the underworld he will have beside him others who have sinned by treating impiously (ἀσεβῶν) a god, a *xenos*, or "dear parents." Each sinner will have his "deserts of justice" (*Eum.* 269–272).[260] Such *post mortem* punishments for sin are a familiar component of both earlier and later literary and philosophic tradition,[261] but their presence in Aeschylus and lack in Sophocles and Euripides are significant. In Aeschylus we may view them as a product of his concern to demonstrate the justice of the gods—a justice which, if not fulfilled in this life, must be accomplished in the next. In this too he assigns his universal Zeus a role, by identifying him with the "great Hades" whom he has judge the dead.

If we attempt to fit popular conceptions of the dead and the afterlife into the groups of tragic dead we have isolated—the dead who are "nothing," or who are cognizant and conversational, or who are rewarded or punished—we find them belonging almost without exception to the first group. In the *Phaedo* (70A) Plato has Cebes claim that "men" believe that at an individual's death his soul disperses like smoke and ceases to exist. Later (77B) Simmias calls this "the belief of the majority" (τὸ τῶν πολλῶν). Classical epitaphs, funeral vases, and other popular sources offer no description of the lives of the souls of the common dead in Hades or the sky. There is no expectation of meeting dead relatives or of rejoining dead friends. We have no record of any prayer of request to the common dead.[262] The rare expressions of hope that virtue and piety will be rewarded in Hades are riddled with uncertainty.[263] The vast majority of epitaphs simply list the virtues of the deceased, with no mention of future rewards. Although there is little reason for hope in this conception of the afterlife, there is also little to fear, either for the dead or for the living from the dead.[264]

Even if the dead are "nothing," even if they are inaccessible to prayer and ritual and may not even perceive their own funerals, proper and traditional burial rites must be performed. Euripides' *Alcestis* and *Troades,* taken together, provide a reasonably comprehensive picture of the usual and customary funeral rites. Alcestis virtually dies on the stage and parts of her funeral are enacted there. In the *Troades* the characters face the recent, present, or imminent deaths of themselves, of their husbands, sons, and daughters, and of their enemies. Their thoughts, naturally, often turn to rites of burial. The fullest descriptions of such ritual come from tragedy, and these descriptions are generally in accord with the occasional evidence from vase paintings and other fifth- and fourth-century literary and archaeological sources.[265]

The gates of the deceased's house were marked by a vessel of spring water and by a lock of a mourner's hair (*Alc.* 98–103). The corpse would be bandaged if necessary, bathed, garlanded, and dressed in fine garments by a wife or other close relative.[266] The deceased would then lie in state (*prothesis*) for a brief time, probably less than a day, in the courtyard of his house.²⁶⁷ Members of the family and other mourners would visit, wearing black garments and cutting locks of hair.²⁶⁸ This was probably also the scene of formal lamentation, with female mourners tearing their hair, scratching their cheeks and necks, beating their breasts, and singing ritual dirges.²⁶⁹ For obvious reasons pipe and lyre music and the garlands and libations of the symposium were inappropriate to the time of mourning.²⁷⁰

Family members participated in the *ekphora,* the funeral procession from the house to the tomb.²⁷¹ Friends and servants might greet with a gesture and make final parting comments to the dead person as he passed (*Alc.* 609–610, 767–769).²⁷² At the burying, libations (χοαί) of milk, honey, and wine were poured.²⁷³ Honorable burial should be in daylight, not in stealth under the cover of night (*Tr.* 446).²⁷⁴ The tomb should be in the homeland, not abroad.²⁷⁵ The tomb itself was "holy" and under the protection of the gods (*Tr.* 96).

Hippias in Plato's *Hippias Major* (291D) is apparently summarizing popular values when he claims that the "finest thing" (κάλλιστον) for a man is that "being wealthy, healthy, and honored by the Greeks, attaining old age, he give a good burial to his own parents and that, in turn, he be buried well and in a grand manner (καλῶς καὶ μεγαλοπρεπῶς) by his own descendants."²⁷⁶ Hecuba has much the same hopes when she recalls Astyanax' promise to her: "Grandmother, I will cut many a lock of hair for you, and I will bring out bands of friends to your tomb, speaking words of affection there" (E. *Tr.* 1181–1184).²⁷⁷ Admetus, by contrast, in anger threatens his father with the ultimate horror: "You had better hurry and beget other children who will tend you in your old age and who will wrap your corpse in garments and perform your funeral, for I will not bury you with this hand of mine" (E. *Alc.* 662–665).

For mourners there were banquets at the tomb on the third, ninth, and thirtieth days after burial, and later annual presentations of offerings and libations.²⁷⁸ These rituals, like burial, were an important family obligation, and a childless individual might even adopt a son to provide them (Isaeus 2.10). A question in the official examination of archons-elect was whether they "adorned well the tombs of their dead parents."²⁷⁹ The cult that dramatists have their characters pay to the tomb of Agamemnon is modeled on this tomb cult. In Aeschylus' *Choephoroi* Orestes asks his dead father for control over the ancestral home "so that the traditional banquets of men might be established for you. Otherwise you will be without honor among the well-banqueted dead" (483–485).

Common dead had three banquets following their funeral. Those Orestes promises seem annual, more characteristic of hero cults.[280] We have previously noted that the sacrifices and altar at Agamemnon's tomb are features of hero cult.[281] Garlands, hair offerings, and drink offerings are presented at tombs of tragic characters,[282] and they seem no different from those made at the funeral. The drink offerings poured on Darius' tomb are slightly more elaborate, with water and olive oil being added to the usual milk, honey, and wine (A. *Pers.* 609–617). Their purpose, however, is to appease (μει-λικτήρια) and attract Darius' soul from the underworld, and similar purposes of appeasement and help-seeking seem to lie behind the offerings to Agamemnon.[283] There is little evidence that tomb cult for the common dead had such purposes in popular religion, and we should view the tragic treatment of such offerings and appeals to Agamemnon and Darius in the context of hero cult.

What do these funeral and postfuneral rites mean for the dead and for the living? We find in tragedy highly contradictory views. When the dead are imagined as "nothing," one naturally wonders why one should make offerings to them.[284] Then funeral gifts are wasted expense, funeral rites wasted labor.[285] If one thinks the dead have thought and reason much like the living, as Sophocles' Antigone does, the funeral rites take on great significance for the dead themselves.[286] Here the dead are personally aware of the rites they receive and of who performed them.[287]

Two claims about the purpose of funeral rites which have been given great importance in the scholarly literature are each only attested once in tragedy and never in popular sources: that funeral offerings are "appeasements" (θελκτήρια) for ordinary (as opposed to "heroic") dead (E. *IT* 159–166) and that without funeral rites the deceased cannot enter Hades.[288] Neither occurs in the plays most concerned with the denial of such rites.[289] In tragedy funerals are most often described simply as bringing "adornment" or "honor" to the dead.[290] It is in this context that the presentation of precious or treasured clothing, jewels, and other objects is most commonly explained.[291] The honoring of the dead by funeral rites and offerings can obviously benefit the living, socially and psychologically, as well as the dead and does not necessarily presume awareness on the part of the dead.[292] "Honor" or "adornment" is also the purpose of funeral rites given in popular sources.[293]

Another purpose of burial rites was to remove from the world of the living the pollution of death. The clearest evidence of this pollution is the decaying flesh of the visible and tangible body, and burial or cremation eliminated that. One wishes to avoid or remove this ἄγος (S. *Ant.* 255–256), leaving the dead ἁγνός and oneself εὐαγής.[294] Teiresias in the *Antigone* (1015–1022) makes a rationalizing attempt to place the conventional pollution of corpses on a quasi-physical basis when he describes vultures dropping bits of decayed human flesh on the altars of the gods. There is, however, no evidence that popular belief conceived of this pollution so literally or crudely.

For the living the performance of funeral and tomb cult for relatives was, in both tragedy and life, a significant element of personal piety.[295] In court an individual could be labeled "unholy" if he claimed the right to inherit a dead man's property when he had not performed the traditional rites for him ([Dem.] 43.65; Isaeus 4.19). Athenian law freed a son who had been prostituted by his father from all the usual filial obligations, save providing a funeral and the traditional rites when the father was dead (Aeschines 1.13–14). Thucydides (2.47–54) views relatives' failure to provide such rites an indication of moral, social, and religious collapse.

Despite the impiety involved, real-life refusals and failures to perform burial rites did occur in fifth-century Athens. Thucydides describes how the many deaths in the first year of the great plague (430) caused Athenians to forsake their usual practices. "Many turned to the most shameful burials," dumping corpses of their relatives onto others' pyres (2.52.4). I have suggested elsewhere that later revulsion and regret at this led Athenians, as part of a general revival of religious feeling, to reintroduce elaborate, sculptured gravestones in the more prosperous and healthy times ca. 425/424 B.C.[296]

Temple robbers and traitors were by law denied burial in Attica (Xen. *Hell.* 1.7.22). In 462 Themistocles could only secretly be buried in Attica because of the charge of treason outstanding against him.[297] Phrynichus after his death was tried and found guilty of treason, and his bones were exhumed from Attica (Lyc. *Leoc.* 113). Such traitors could, presumably, be buried elsewhere. Plato in his idealized state would refuse, by law, burial to those who voluntarily murdered their fathers, mothers, brothers, or children.[298]

In 430 the Athenians captured six ambassadors from various Peloponnesian states as they were on their way to ask the Persian king to provide money and an alliance against Athens. The ambassadors were brought to Athens, executed without a trial, and "cast into a ravine." The Athenians justified this by the similar treatment Lacedaemonians had given pro-Athenian or politically neutral merchantmen they captured. They too killed their captives as if "enemies of war" (ὡς πολέμιοι) and threw them "into ravines" (Thuc. 2.67). Herodotus reports that the Athenians had similarly treated Darius' heralds who in 490 came demanding Athens' surrender. The issue for Herodotus here is, however, the maltreatment of heralds, not the deprival of burial (7.133). In Athens "casting into the ravine" was, by law, reserved for those who committed capital crimes "against the people" (Xen. *Hell.* 1.7.20; schol. to Ar. *Plut.* 431), and the corpses were left exposed (Pl. *Rep.* 4.439E).

The recovery and burial of one's own and the enemies' dead in warfare posed special problems. Pausanias (1.32.5) reports that the Athenians had buried the Persian dead after the battle of Marathon "because it is in all ways holy (πάντως ὅσιον) to bury in the earth the corpse of a human being." In 425 Nicias, after a victory over the Corinthians, overlooked two of the Athenian dead in the recovery of bodies. After he had left the area he discovered the error and was forced to ask the Corinthians for permission to retrieve them. Since victors usually controlled the battlefield, such a request was a concession of defeat. The pious Nicias chose to renounce his claim to victory rather than leave two Athenian soldiers unburied (Plut. *Nic.* 6.5–6).[299] After their victory over the Spartan navy near the Arginusae islands in 406, the eight Athenian generals were condemned to death and confiscation of property because they had failed, whatever the reason, to recover the corpses of their nearly five thousand dead. Six of the generals were executed, and two never returned to Athens to face trial (Xen. *Hell.* 1.7.4–35; Pl. *Ap.* 32B; Diodorus Siculus 13.100–103).

For the victor to allow the defeated to recover their dead was "the ancestral custom" (τὸ πάτριον), and instances of even temporary refusals or delays are rare. In 424 the Athenians had occupied and fortified the border sanctuary of Apollo at Delion, and after the Boeotians defeated the Athenians in battle there, they refused to allow the Athenians to collect their dead until they evacuated the sanctuary. The Athenians charged that the Boeotians were acting "impiously" and contrary to "traditional practices." The Thebans responded that the Athenians had desecrated the sanctuary. In the midst of this debate the Thebans won a stunning and unqualified military victory, driving the Athenians from the sanctuary. This time the Athenians were allowed to recover their dead, by now numbering nearly a thousand (Thuc. 4.97–100).[300]

After the Thebans defeated the Lacedaemonians at Haliartus in 395, they again refused to allow the defeated a recovery of the corpses, including Lysander, until the enemy withdrew from Boeotian territory. The Spartans in the field agreed to these terms (Xen. *Hell.* 3.5.22–24). Amidst the dozens of battles described by the historians we find only the Thebans, and only in these two instances, bartering for corpses of the war dead. It seems that all, or at least all but the Thebans, thought that in warfare the enemy as well as the other dead were unconditionally deserving of burial and the "customary rites."[301]

Among other accusations of impiety against the Thirty Tyrants—for instance, that they dragged citizens from the sanctuaries—Lysias charged that in 403 they did not allow their victims customary burial. They thought, according to Lysias, that their regime was "more certain and secure" (βεβαιοτέραν) than "vengeance" (τιμωρίας) from the gods (12.96).[302]

Such are the instances of real or threatened denial of burial and burial rites in the classical period. Despite the varying circumstances, all the intentional ones concern dead who might be thought, rightly or wrongly, to have been enemies of the state: traitors, enemies of war (*polemioi*), and opponents in a civil war. As will be seen, it is likewise primarily these groups whose burial rites are brought into question in tragedy, and we may now examine whether the tragedians and their characters uphold the tenet of Athenian popular religious belief that demanded for all except traitors and temple-robbers a funeral and proper burial.

King Creon of Sophocles' *Antigone* orders that Polyneices' body be left unburied, exposed to the ravages of dogs and vultures. In the *Ajax* Menelaus and Agamemnon intend to take vengeance on Ajax by preventing his burial. In Euripides' *Troades* the Greek herald Talthybius blackmails Andromache into silence and acquiescence by threatening to deprive her son Astyanax of burial (735–739). In the *Suppliants* the mothers of the great Argive heroes who had died at Thebes are in Athens to ask Theseus for help in obtaining proper burial for their sons.[303] There is in these plays and throughout tragedy a unanimous and strong condemnation of the violation of burial rites, a condemnation most fully dramatized in the *Antigone* and *Suppliants*. There burial and the attendant rites are viewed not only as the usual practice of all Greeks but as traditions established by the gods.[304] Violation of these rites was characteristic of violent, law-breaking men who failed to "honor" the traditions of the Greeks and their gods.[305] This was a clear-cut act of hybris.[306] Pressing for the observance of the rites in the face of their violation was a matter of justice and of holiness and piety towards the gods.[307] It also brought honor and glory to the individual and state.[308]

In tragedy various arguments are put forth for denying a person burial rites, and each is refuted. It is primarily because Polyneices was a traitor that Creon intends to remove his corpse from Theban territory and deny it burial (E. *Ph.* 1628–1670) or leave it exposed in Thebes (S. *Ant.* 194–206). In both plays Antigone objects that such treatment is "not in accord with traditions" (*Ant.* 449–460; *Ph.* 1651) and makes plans to bury her brother. The *Antigone* dramatizes this decision and the results therefrom, an outcome which Euripides also clearly had in mind when he wrote the *Phoenissae* (e.g., 1744–1746). If Polyneices was in fact a traitor (a point Sophocles does not question) and if Creon's decree legitimately reflects the will of the state (which Sophocles does make an issue; e.g., 683–739), then by Athenian standards Polyneices could be denied burial in Theban territory. In opposition to the "political and legal" position, however, Sophocles puts the views and actions of Antigone. In demanding, performing, and defending the burial of her brother she forcefully expresses her obligations to family and to the "unwritten laws" of the gods. The personalities of Antigone and Creon and broader issues of state versus individual and man versus woman complicate the issue, and, unlike in a legal tract, not all possibilities (such as burial of Polyneices outside of Thebes) are considered. But if we abstract the issue of burial rites from the play, we must conclude that Sophocles in this play opposed exposure and denial of burial even for traitors and enemies of the state.[309]

In Sophocles' *Ajax* Menelaus implies that he can deny Ajax burial on the grounds that Ajax was his enemy in war (*polemios*) (1132).[310] To judge by the respect the Athenians showed the dead of such enemies, the audience would probably not have accepted Menelaus' claim.[311] Menelaus' argument is, however, never directly attacked, because Teucer immediately makes the point that Ajax was never in fact Menelaus' opponent in war, but only a personal enemy.[312] Odysseus then successfully argues that one must not deny burial even to one's most hated personal enemy (1332–1345, 1365).

In Euripides' *Suppliants* a herald from Thebes argues that Capaneus, Amphiaraus, and other heroes had been objects of divine vengeance (494–505). The implication is that some men are so evil or god-hated that they do not deserve burial. The chorus responds briefly that divine vengeance has been sufficient and that the Thebans should not act so hybristically (511–512). At this point Theseus, in the most elaborate defense of burial rites in drama, emphatically restates his claim that it is just and good to bury the dead (526–527). He goes well beyond religious reasons and traditions to demonstrate that it is in accord with current and familiar theory of natural law—"the body should return to the earth, the soul to the *aether*" (531–536)—and is socially advantageous: otherwise those "strong in battle" will become cowardly (540–541).[313] Theseus then debunks with biting sarcasm the notion that the dead, if buried, might harm the Theban land (φόβους πονηρούς καὶ κενούς, 548).

Sophocles also has secular reasons to adduce in defense of burial rites for *all* the dead. Odysseus speaks of basic human feelings, justice, and one's own ultimate fate (*Aj.* 1332–1345, 1365). Teiresias warns of the hatred which can arise within a city when corpses are left unburied (*Ant.* 1080–1083). Euripides, characteristically, has set forth Theseus' arguments formally, logically, and almost clinically. Sophocles offers secular reasons more casually, suggestively, and allusively.

The failure to give burial rites redounded heavily, in tragedy, on the living. The Thebans in the *Suppliants* were defeated in battle by the crusading Athenians. In the *Antigone* Creon lost his son, his wife, and the political authority he held so dear. In the end, in both plays, the dead receive their burial.

Teiresias proffers a systematic account (*Ant.* 1015–1022) of how denial of burial rites affects the relationship of men to their gods. The vultures and dogs, carrying bits of meat from the exposed corpse, literally pollute the altars of the gods. As a result sacrifices will not properly burn on the altars, and, not receiving sacrifices due them, the gods do not heed the citizens' prayers. The city is then "sick." We might like to think that average Athenians had in mind such a pat explanation of the relationship between burial rites, pollution, and the goodwill of the gods. There is, however, only slight evidence elsewhere that such an explanation was widely known or generally accepted.[314] It seems rather to be one of those attempts to rationalize religious practice and myth commonly put in the mouth of Teiresias.[315] No doubt the interrelationship of burial rites, sin, pollution, and the gods of the living and dead was recognized by the average person, but it was hardly understood or articulated in this way. However the various elements are to be explained, in the plays of Sophocles and Euripides the popular tradition of funeral and burial rites for virtually all the dead is strongly defended. And Sophocles in the *Antigone* seemingly removes even one (traitors) of the two exceptions (the other being temple robbers) that the Athenians in real life recognized.[316]

Conclusion

We are now in a position to answer questions posed at the outset of this chapter concerning the presentation in tragedy of some major elements of contemporary popular religion. Are claims of falseness or quackery of prophecy upheld in the denouement of a play? What is the fate of those who violate conventional, religiously sanctioned standards of behavior concerning oaths, *xenoi,* suppliants, and the dead? Are they punished or not?

Prophecies from oracles, seers, dreams, and omens prove true so consistently in Greek tragedy that we can claim their accuracy to be convention. The one false oracle (of Apollo, in Euripides' *Ion*) is, as we have seen, introduced in such a way as to counteract the audience's expectation that it will prove true. Despite the many seers and dreams in tragedy, there are only two unanswered challenges to them (E. *Hel.* 744–757 and *IT* 1259–1282), both from plays produced ca. 412, when other sources reveal a hostility to seers in Athens. Both plays also present counterexamples of successful uses of the same type of prophecy. These two exceptions can carry only slight weight compared to the accuracy ascribed to or assumed for seers and dreams in all the other plays.

Because seers and oracles tell the truth, those who disbelieve them are in the wrong, however persuasive their reasons for disbelief may seem. Oedipus and Jocasta in the *Oedipus Tyrannus,* Creon in the *Antigone,* and Adrastus and Pentheus in Euripides' *Suppliants* and *Bacchae* each disregard or disbelieve seers or oracles, to their loss. Disbelief of an oracle is, by itself, not labeled impious, and the sufferings of disbelievers are not presented as punishments for skepticism. But all the disbelievers are committing an error, the type of error that in the unforgiving world of Greek tragedy contributes to disaster.

It would be going too far, I think, to claim that by having virtually all oracles, seers, and dreams prove accurate the tragedians were consciously supporting a popular religious belief. When tragedians have characters wrongly disbelieve oracles and seers, the purpose seems more to reveal the personality of the character than to demonstrate the validity of the prophecy. But, conversely, we may also say that popular religious belief in the general reliability of oracles, seers, and omens is, with the few exceptions noted, not successfully challenged in Greek tragedy.

Violation of conventional standards of behavior concerning oaths, *xenoi,* suppliants, and burial rites was, however, impious, and in tragedy those impious in these matters are always punished, whether we are reading Aeschylus, or Sophocles, or Euripides. And the punishments, though certainly not always only for the one impiety, are very harsh. By play's end Lycus (asylum, E. *HF*), the Aegyptiads (asylum, A. *Suppl.*), Paris (*xenia,* A. *Ag.*), and Eteocles (oaths, E. *Ph.*) all lie dead. The Thebans (burial rites, E. *Suppl.*) are defeated in battle, and Polymestor (*xenia,* E. *Hec.*), Jason (oaths, E. *Med.*), and Creon (burial rites, S. *Ant.*) suffer, by the standards of tragedy, a fate worse than death. Here, because in distinction from prophecy a socially recognized "sin" is involved and the perpetrators of all such sins are punished, we may claim that the tragedians, purposely or not, lent support to fundamental tenets of popular religious belief. It may be "only" a tragic convention that violators of oaths, *xenia,* suppliants, and burial rites are punished, but it is a convention which coincided with popular beliefs.

Punishment in tragedy is reserved for those who actually commit the sin, not for those who merely think of it, speak of it, or plan it. Menelaus and Agamemnon in Sophocles' *Ajax* wanted to deny Ajax burial but were persuaded otherwise and suffered no punishment. Likewise Admetus threatens in the *Alcestis* not to bury his father, but he does not commit this sin. Hermione in the *Andromache,* Ion in the *Ion,* and Theoclymenus in the *Helen* all threaten and plan violation of asylum but never do it. Hippolytus speaks as though he will violate his oath but never does. Of all these characters only Hippolytus suffers, and then, as will be discussed below, for quite different reasons. In Greek religion what mattered was the action, not the intent and frame of mind. Those who commit impieties are punished; those who merely think or talk of them get off scot free.

On occasion profane as well as religious reasons are introduced in tragedies to defend conventional behavior towards suppliants, oaths, and burial rites. We have seen such factors in the Athenians' deliberations about protecting the suppliant Oedipus in Sophocles' *Oedipus at Colonus* and the family of Heracles in Euripides' *Heraclidae.* The Danaids in Aeschylus' *Suppliants* add secular arguments to their appeal to Pelasgus, and Hippolytus offers practical as well as religious reasons for maintaining his oath in Euripides' *Hippolytus.* In the *Suppliants* Theseus and Aethra have more than religious reasons for securing the burial of the Argive dead. In these instances profane factors are introduced to justify religious practices that presumably could be, and often were, defended by appeals to piety alone. That the tragedians were not always content to justify pious behavior by arguments only from religious concepts will remind us that religion is but one factor among many in the tragedies. Creon did not suffer solely because he violated the burial rites of Polyneices, nor did Eteocles die only because he failed to keep his oath to Polyneices. By pointing to such sins, their basis in popular religion, and the "following" if not "resulting" punishments of the sinners, I make no claim that this complex of ideas is the only or perhaps even the major factor in each situation. Popular beliefs about prophecy, asylum, *xenoi,* suppliants, and the dead, however, recur often and are consistently treated and supported by all three tragedians. As such they form a significant component of the dynamics of Greek tragedy.

FOUR

The Pious and the Impious

I have described numerous popular religious beliefs as they appear in tragedy and, in addition, pious or impious actions and the rewards or punishments resulting from them. Let us now shift the focus to individual characters, examining in particular the reasons, attitudes, and states of mind that tragic poets give to those who behave piously or impiously by contemporary standards. Henceforth we must proceed largely without the control provided by sources for popular religion. Orators, historians, and inscriptions describe some beliefs and label various acts pious or impious, but they scarcely ever tell us anything of an individual's thoughts while performing such actions.[1] The tragedians, however, often have their characters express such thoughts, and they merit study. In default of popular sources we cannot confidently assert that the explanation for impious behavior which a poet has his character give is like or unlike that of the average Athenian, but here the poet's treatment is the best and often the only one we have. At worst we can claim to have isolated tragedians' conceptions of individuals who abided by or violated fifth-century religious beliefs. However, since many tragic characters express widely held religious beliefs about divine intervention, divination, asylum, oaths, and so forth, we might reasonably think that on occasion poets had their characters share with the audience also the reasoning and attitudes associated with these beliefs.

Let us begin with some characters whose religious behavior and attitudes receive only brief but somehow significant mention, and then turn to Creon and Antigone, Hippolytus, Ajax and Odysseus, Pentheus, Teiresias, and Cadmus, and Troy and Athens, each of whose religiosity is central to a play.

The sons of Aegyptus in Aeschylus' *Suppliants* are prepared to violate the asylum that the daughters of Danaus have taken in an Argive sanctuary, and understandably so, because they do not believe in Greek gods. Their herald puts it bluntly, "I don't fear the *daimones* here, for they neither raised me nor brought me to an old age with their sustenance" (893–894).[2] "I revere the *daimones* around the Nile" (922; cf. 923). As a result the Aegyptiads, like crows, have no respect for Greek altars (750–752). They pay no heed to the gods (758–759). In Euripides' *Heracles* Lycus, a Theban king, is willing to drag suppliants from an altar because, he claims, he is "outside" or "beyond fears" (713–716, 723–724).[3] Polymestor in the *Hecuba* has not only violated *xenia* but also denied his victim, Polydorus, burial rites, and to Hecuba this shows that he fears neither "those upon the earth nor those below" (791–792). The common fault for the Aegyptiads, Lycus, and Polymestor, all of whom eventually die or otherwise suffer, is that they lack *fear* of the gods, fear that the gods will punish their sins.

The same Polymestor who violated *xenia* and burial rites has some harsh things to say of the gods:

> There is nothing trustworthy, neither a good reputation
> nor that a person faring well will not (someday) fare badly.
> The gods mix up these things forward and backward,
> imposing confusion so that we may worship ($σέβωμεν$) them in our
>   ignorance.
>
> (E. *Hec.* 956–960)

Some critics have assigned these jaundiced ideas to Euripides' personal philosophy,[4] quite mistakenly, I think. They and other similar views to be examined below are those a dramatist thought appropriate to an impious man, an impious man who in this play is also a lying, murderous Thracian.[5] We have no grounds for attributing these views to Euripides himself.

Eteocles in Euripides' *Phoenissae,* like Polymestor, both commits impiety and reveals other thoughts characteristic of an impious person. He deliberately violated his oath to return the kingship to Polyneices, because, he says, "If one must act unjustly, it is best to do so for the sake of a tyranny. In all other matters one ought to be pious" (524–525). Eteocles consciously chooses impiety for the sake of political gain, and it is not only here that his behavior in religious matters is suspect. He has, he admits, on previous occasions faulted the mantic art and quarreled with Teiresias (768–773, 878–879), whose credibility Euripides takes pains to establish in this play (852–857). Eteocles is also, of Euripides' many characters, the one most inclined to deify abstract concepts.[6] He speaks of Tyranny as the "greatest of the gods" (504–506) and of Caution (Εὐλάβεια) as the "most useful of the gods" (782–783). He even prays to Caution to "save the city" (782–783). This goes well beyond the common tendency to personify abstracts such as Dike (Justice) and put them in the company of the gods.[7] Jocasta, whose speech of rebuttal to Eteocles and Polyneices (528–585) is designed to respond to the predilections of each of her sons, replies in kind to Eteocles' appeal to a deified Tyranny. She questions her son's devotion to Ambition (Φιλοτιμία), "the most evil of the *daimones*," an "unjust goddess" (531–535). She urges him to "honor" Fairness (Ἰσότης), whom she similarly personifies (535–538). We may view Jocasta's deification of Ambition and Fairness as responses to Eteocles' deification of Tyranny. The terms of the argument are set by Eteocles, and Jocasta follows them.

By his perjury and rejection of divination Eteocles shows himself alienated from traditional religion. Cut off from genuine deities, he compensates, it seems, by deifying profane concepts most important to him.[8] Scholars have generally considered such "personification" a sign of deterioration in Greek popular religion,[9] and that Euripides has one of his more despicable characters indulge in the practice may give some indication of his disapproval of this perversion of religion in the 420s.

Medea has much to say of Jason's breaking of his oath to her. She is hardly an impartial judge, but what she says of Jason's perjury is not idiosyncratic. She concludes that he has taken on fundamentally new religious beliefs: "Trust in oaths is gone, and I cannot learn if you think that the gods (who ruled) then (when you swore the oath) no longer rule or if you think that now there are new principles of right and wrong established for human beings" (E. *Med.* 492–494). Nearly a century later Plato too saw perjury largely as the result of changed religious views: "Oaths are no longer appropriate in law suits because now some men do not believe in the gods at all and some think the gods have no concern about us. Others, those who are most numerous and wicked, are of the opinion that if the gods receive flattery and some small sacrifices they help us steal a lot of money and rescue us from great punishments" (*Leg.* 12.948B–D). In Aristophanes' *Clouds* 245–251, 397–402, and 816–830 discussion of oaths similarly raises immediate questions of the nature and power of the conventional gods.

In Medea's view Jason loses communication with and support from the gods by his perjury: "What god or deity listens to you when you are a perjurer and deceive *xenoi*?" (1391–1392). Because Jason sins, the gods do not listen to his prayers, and in fact his appeals to Zeus and the other gods at the end of the play are futile (1405–1414). An Aeschylean chorus gives a chilling account of the gods' unwillingness to hear a hybristic, unjust, and impious man as he flounders at sea:

> Those whom he calls upon hear nothing, and he
> struggles in the midst of the current.
> The god laughs (γελᾷ δὲ δαίμων) over
> the reckless man.
>
> (*Eum.* 558–560)[10]

I have written at length elsewhere of unanswered prayers in tragedy,[11] and point out here only that many such unsuccessful prayers are made by those who, like Jason, have committed an impiety and upset the usual relationship one has with a deity. Polymestor (E. *Hec.* 1066–1068), Eteocles and Polyneices (E. *Ph.* 1359–1376), Aegisthus (E. *El.* 803–810), and Clytemnestra (S. *El.* 634–659) all pray in vain. Their prayers, like Jason's, go unanswered or are answered, to their sorrow, otherwise than they wish. The gods, it seems, do not hear those who act impiously.[12]

Neoptolemus of Euripides' *Andromache* is unique in Greek tragedy in that he sins, recognizes his error, and seeks the god's forgiveness.[13] What then happens is surprising and disturbing but, I think, illustrative of tragic conceptions of punishment for certain types of sin. In the prologue Andromache explains why Neoptolemus is not present to defend her:

> He is in the land of the Delphians where he pays to Apollo
> punishment (δίκην) for the madness with which once,
> having come to Pytho, he demanded from Phoebus
> punishment (δίκην) for Apollo's killing of his
> father (Achilles). He hopes that, if somehow he
> gains Apollo's pardon for his previous errors (σφάλματα),
> he might make the god kindly to him for the future.
>
> (50–55)

Neoptolemus apparently had held Apollo responsible for Paris' arrowshot which killed Achilles (1194–1196) and then had demanded reparation.[14] Peleus also thinks Apollo responsible (1211–1212) but was not so intemperate as to confront him. Andromache and Neoptolemus himself view Neoptolemus' confrontation of the god as an error (50–55, 1106–1108).

A man has sinned; he has recognized his sin and repented of it; and he has come to the god for expiation and forgiveness. In the Christian tradition he would receive forgiveness and be restored to the proper relationship with God.[15] By the Greek standards of human justice, I think, his offer to pay the penalty would be accepted and hostilities would cease. Such, or at least in these terms, is not the result for Neoptolemus. Standing at Apollo's altar he confesses his guilt and announces that he wishes "to pay the penalty for his previous sin" (ἁμαρτίας, 1106–1107). Neoptolemus then enters the temple to consult the oracle, wishing to learn, no doubt, what his penalty is to be. There, as he prays to the god, he is ambushed by the Delphians, and after a furious battle near and even on the altar, he is killed. His body, which lies near the altar, is later dragged by his killers from the temple (1085–1157).

The Delphians, incited by Orestes, commit the murder, but Apollo shares heavily in the responsibility.[16] The murder is committed not only in his sanctuary but at the altar within his temple. All Greeks would assume that, in these circumstances, Apollo would have, if he had so chosen, protected the victim. And, beyond this, it is reasonable to assume that it was Apollo's own voice which rallied the flagging assailants to their final, successful attack against Neoptolemus (1147–1149).

A messenger sympathetic to Neoptolemus concludes his description of these events with a strong protest against Apollo's role in the murder:

> The lord who prophesies to others,
> who for all human beings decides what is just,
> did such things to Achilles' child when the boy was trying to pay due punishment.
> The god, like an evil man, remembered quarrels of long ago.
> How then could he be wise?
>
> (1161–1165)

This strong challenge to Apollo's wisdom and justice is left hanging in the air and is nowhere explicitly answered in the play. There are two likely responses to it and to the fate of Neoptolemus. In other accounts Apollo is angered at the Delphians for the murder of Neoptolemus.[17] He orders special rites for Neoptolemus and grants him the exceptional honor of a tomb and sacred precinct within his own sanctuary. In this account the messenger's challenge could be met by arguing that Neoptolemus suffered but ultimately, because of his suffering, received a fine and timeless reward. This was evidently the version of the myth promulgated at Delphi, and by allusions to details of Neoptolemus' cult myth at Delphi Euripides reveals his familiarity with it.[18] But if Euripides had intended the audience thus to understand the fate of his Neoptolemus, he would, I think, have had Thetis, as *deus ex machina,* point to it in her description of Neoptolemus' future burial at Delphi (1239–1242).

Euripides' Neoptolemus illustrates rather how very wrathful and extreme the vengeance of the gods is once it has been aroused. Neoptolemus acted sinfully and hybristically towards the god; in the tragic convention, by that act his fate is sealed. He has come to Delphi voluntarily to pay the penalty, a penalty which he, judging by human standards, no doubt expects to be moderate and just. The punishment, however, is death. Neoptolemus is virtually sacrificed to Apollo.[19] This exceeds both Neoptolemus' expectations and the witnesses' sense of propriety, but such is the wrath and vengeance of the gods of tragedy. Once a god is angered, as Apollo here, his vengeance may be, by human standards, excessive.[20] The agents of the murder, the Delphians and Orestes, commit impiety by killing Neoptolemus in the temple, but as we have seen elsewhere in Aeschylus and Euripides, a god's vengeance is often accomplished in just this way. A god's wrath is aroused for good reason, but once aroused, in vengeance it exceeds and violates human standards of justice and wisdom. Such is, I think, one reasonable response to the messenger's challenge.

The wrath of the gods, once aroused, results in a vengeance far exceeding that deemed appropriate by humans. We see it here in the fate of Neoptolemus but also, more than thirty years earlier, in that of Aeschylus' Paris, who, because he violated *xenia,* destroyed, in addition to his own life, that of his brothers, father, and city. As tragedy has persons of greater stature and sins of greater magnitude than those found in everyday life, so too it has harsher gods who dispense severer punishments than ordinary people expected of their gods. Harsh gods, more heinous sins, and the lack of a mechanism for repentance, expiation, and forgiveness will make more intelligible the sufferings of Ajax, Hippolytus, and Pentheus as we look at them later.

Creon and Antigone

Even before his first appearance in Sophocles' *Antigone* Creon has made a serious and potentially tragic error. He has denied burial to his nephew Polyneices and intends to leave the body exposed.[21] Creon persists in his error despite warnings and advice from family, friends, and a seer. He suffers terribly in the end, and the life he is to face is, by Sophoclean standards, worse than death.

Creon's error, stubbornness, and punishment have a clarity unlike those of Euripidean sinners such as Hippolytus and Pentheus. The *Antigone* has what the *Hippolytus* and *Bacchae* lack: a strong, clear, single, and dynamic countermodel to the impious man's behavior. Creon has his Antigone.

Creon's error—and this is characteristic of other sinners in Greek tragedy—is one of bad judgment. When he is instructed by Teiresias (988–1090), and when he and the chorus finally comprehend his error (1095–1114, 1261–1353), the talk is exclusively of bad thinking and bad planning leading to error.[22] Creon failed to maintain (σῴζειν) the "established traditions" (1113–1114), in particular the established and unwritten traditions about the burial of the dead. As a result of this he failed to do the proper things, or, more precisely, he prevented the proper and traditional things from being done.

Creon did not intellectually grasp distinctions fundamental to Greek religion, distinctions which emerge with unusual clarity in the antithetical structure and style of this play. There is, of course, the duality of human and divine, a division Creon blurs in his breezy confidence that gods judge the world as he does (e.g., 280–289, 519–522). There are human νόμοι ("laws," "traditions") and divine ones, and they are not necessarily the same. In the *Antigone* Creon's proclamations represent human νόμοι, the product of human (here Creon's) judgment and enforced by human (here Creon's) authority. Opposed, or rather juxtaposed, to them are divine νόμοι, unwritten, the ones at issue in this play governing the proper treatment of the dead (450–460, 1113–1114). These divine νόμοι are based on a divine authority (here Zeus'), are known by tradition, and violations are punished by divine powers (453–457, 1074–1075). Reverence for human authority (Ismene and Creon) dictates respect for human νόμοι; reverence for divine authority (Antigone), respect for the other.[23]

These categories of divine and human are usually in harmony in life and literature. What is good in the one system is judged to be so in the other. They are put into opposition and lines drawn between them only when a person such as Creon throws the system into disarray. The divisions become all the more distinct, of course, when Sophocles, in this play, structures his ideas antithetically.

These human/divine antitheses are familiar to all readers of the *Antigone*. Less well recognized but no less important for the religious thought of contemporary Athens is the play's distinction between "the world of the living" and "the world of the dead" (450–470, 1064–1075). In Greek religion the rules changed abruptly when an individual died, and this was not simply a matter of "not speaking ill of the dead." There was, first of all, a new set of gods. At death the Olympians disappeared, completely and totally. The gods one had worshiped during life were no longer of importance. In their place came, if anything, the hitherto unimportant Hades and his shadowy ilk.[24] One also became subject to a new justice, distinct from the old. In the *Antigone* it is made clear that there is one justice "of the gods above," another of the "gods below": "life above" is ephemeral, "yesterday and today"; "life below" is "always."[25] Creon errs by treating the dead with the justice of the living, and he fails to realize that although in the life above it is proper both to honor war heroes and one's friends and to punish traitors and one's enemies, in death, in the life below, honor (τιμή) must be rendered to all (192–

214, 514–522). Creon has muddled living and dead as well as human and divine[26] and has thereby thrown into disharmony the finely tuned cosmic order.

Creon's confusion of human and divine, life and death, breaks through in one violent, blasphemous, and frightening expression. "You will not," he says to Teiresias, "bury Polyneices in a tomb, not even if Zeus' eagles wish to snatch up his body as food and carry it to the throne of Zeus. Not even so will I, fearing this as a pollution, give him up for burial. For I know well that no man has the ability to pollute the gods" (1039–1044).[27] The thought of eagles carrying bits of decayed human flesh to Zeus himself would have been, to an ancient audience, ghastly. That Creon could imagine allowing such a thing reveals the depths he has reached. Creon's claim that "no man has the ability to pollute the gods" has to it the ring of philosophical and religious theory.[28] It suggests a loftier and purer concept of deity than is generally credited to common folk. This bit of philosophic speculation shows Creon as confident that he understands religious pollution and knows who can pollute what. The business with Polyneices does not, in his judgment, involve pollution. Creon is, of course, tragically mistaken.[29] Teiresias has revealed before this (1016–1022) that although perhaps the gods may not be polluted by men, their altars can be; then sacrifice, prayer, and divination fail. Such is the result of Creon's impious behavior. Creon challenges the religious traditions of his time without understanding them. Even what he thinks he knows he misapplies.

Antigone takes up defense of the divine and the dead, to the detriment, some would say, of the human and living in her life.[30] But for this Creon is in good part responsible, because by his impiety he created a division which need not and should not exist, and he thereby forced Antigone and Ismene to take wholly one side or the other. Ismene chose the human and living; Antigone the divine and the dead. As a result Creon, Antigone, and Ismene all suffer, but Creon suffers most. His life will be more wretched than death. An existence such as his, especially when (as here) it is of his own making, is the ultimate Sophoclean misery.[31]

Creon not only plans an impiety, he commits it *and* perseveres in it. Numerous characters offer him arguments against his plan. Antigone appeals to the unwritten laws of the gods and to basic family feelings and responsibilities. Creon's son, Haemon, puts forth political objections (683–765), and finally Teiresias points out additional religious aspects of the situation

(988–1090). Even the guard and chorus suggest, in cautious terms, their opposition.[32] Despite counterarguments of such variety from relatives, common people, and a seer, Creon persists until the situation has become irremediable. He eventually recognizes his error,[33] but in Greek religious terms that is unimportant. Repentance does not lead to forgiveness, and in quick succession come the deaths of Antigone, Haemon, and Eurydice. The pattern is bad judgment, impious action, persistence in it, and punishment. At some time in this sequence, at a point lying somewhere in or between impious action and persistence in it, the punishment—regardless of the individual's change of heart—becomes inevitable. So Creon and Neoptolemus learn, and so we shall find Hippolytus and Pentheus discovering.

Antigone, of course, views the burial of her brother as pious and in accord with divine laws.[34] In her view the daring burial exhibited her goodness, moral character, and nobility of birth; it would give her "fame" and was a service pleasing to the dead in general and to kin in particular.[35] Antigone recognizes Creon's impiety in "trampling underfoot the honors of the gods" (745; cf. 76–77), but beyond that she little analyzes the religious implications of her behavior or of the burial or lack of it for Polyneices. She simply takes adherence to divine laws requiring burial of the dead as a given (450–460).[36] Here we confront a persistent limitation in our study of the pious and impious in tragedy. Piety and pious acts receive far less attention than their opposites. In literary terms, of course, sin is inherently more interesting than piety. But it must also be noted that in Greek tragedy, literature, and life pious behavior was the usual and ordinary thing. It was expected that one would act piously. What required explanation in the classical period was deviant behavior and the results of it.

We thus learn little detail of religious motives and attitudes of Antigone and other exceptionally pious characters of Greek literature. In conclusion we may stress, however, that Antigone, despite her death, is "rewarded" for her pious action. She attains the Sophoclean ideal of "dying nobly rather than living badly," and she gains for herself the "good fame" ($εὔκλεια$) to which she and so many women of tragedy aspire.[37]

Ajax and Odysseus

In Sophocles' *Ajax*, when the hero thought he had been cheated of the weapons of Achilles, he devised a plan to attack and kill Agamemnon, Menelaus, and other Greek commanders he held responsible.[38] As Ajax set out in the night to accomplish this mission, Athena, in her own words, "stopped him from this delight which would have been incurable and cast upon his eyes hard-to-bear thoughts" (51–52). She drove him mad,[39] and in a deluded state he mistook herd animals and their tenders for his enemies and attacked, captured, tortured, and killed them. Athena's role in this was only to divert Ajax from his attack on the Greek commanders to one on animals and herdsmen. Later, of course, Ajax in shame at the incident commits suicide.

Previously Athena had been an ally and patroness of Ajax (89–90, 116–117), so much in the Homeric model that Ajax could chat with her and even casually refuse her direct request (112–113). Athena turns against him not from any desire to protect the Greek commanders but because of his hybristic behavior towards the gods in general and towards her in particular.[40] In the opening dialogue with Odysseus she makes the delusion of Ajax, usually a very sensible man, an indication of "how great is the strength of the gods" (118–120) and advises Odysseus, as he sees such things, "not himself to say any wrathful word against the gods nor to take on any self-importance" because of wealth or physical strength. In the scales of life "a day lowers or raises up again all human things, and the gods love those who are moderate (τοὺς σώφρονας) and hate the evil (τοὺς κακούς)" (127–133).

Such words from Athena have a general application, and not until lines 756–777 is their relevance to Ajax himself made clear. A messenger here reports the words of the seer Calchas: the wrath of Athena will pursue Ajax for one day, because "exceptional and foolish persons"—individuals "who, born mortal, do not *think* in a way appropriate to a mortal"—fall into weighty failures caused by the gods. Calchas specifies two occasions on which Ajax committed just this error. Once he "boastfully and foolishly" told his father that any "nobody" could have force and victory at Troy with a god's help, but he was confident that he himself would win these even without such help.[41] By this claim he rejected, in the clearest possible terms, the importance and influence of the gods in his life. Another time, when Athena was urging him to battle, Ajax spoke these "terrible and unspeakable" words: "Queen Athena, go and attend other Argives; the enemy will never break through in battle here." "By such words," Calchas sums up, "Ajax acquired the implacable wrath of Athena, because he did not *think* as a man should."[42] Ajax has become god-hated (457–458) because, in the judgment of the seer, he did not "think" properly.

To Ajax may be contrasted Odysseus, who has with Athena a similarly close, Homeric style of relationship. The goddess chats comfortably and familiarly with him and personally and directly protects his interests on and off the battlefield (1–88, 118–133).⁴³ Unlike Ajax, however, Odysseus does not corrupt the relationship by hybris, a hybris that Odysseus' respect for divine authority and power and sense of the limitations of human beings prevent.⁴⁴ In this play Odysseus as a model of proper religious behavior⁴⁵ is also contrasted to the Atreidae, who are eager to take vengeance on Ajax by denying him burial. Odysseus argues effectively and successfully for the burial, that is, for what is just and pious in the situation (1316–1380).⁴⁶

Hippolytus

Euripides' Hippolytus views himself as the model for piety.⁴⁷ The best indication of conventional piety is his adherence, costly in personal and social terms, to the oath he gave to the nurse not to divulge Phaedra's passion for him, and for this Artemis herself, *deus ex machina,* labels him "pious."⁴⁸ Hippolytus' singleminded devotion to Artemis, his maintenance of chastity and purity in the cult of this virgin goddess, and his hymns in her honor suit many modern notions of what religion should be and, as such, have been used as an example of what personal religion must have been to Greeks.⁴⁹ His mystic communion with the goddess, the ascetic life of her devotees, and the beauty of the hymns in her honor are immensely appealing. But to an audience of 428 B.C. such a monotheistic, singleminded dedication must have appeared peculiar,⁵⁰ and we can find no parallels for it in classical literature or life.⁵¹ To Athenians of the classical period any such peculiarity or unconventionality in religion would appear dangerous, but far more dangerous if it also involved rejection of traditional deities and practices. Twenty-eight years after the play was produced, the same two elements, but in reverse order, occurred in the charge of impiety made against Socrates by Athenian prosecutors: "He does not recognize (believe in) (οὐ νομίζει) gods whom the city recognizes (νομίζει), but is introducing other new divine powers."⁵² That Hippolytus is devoted to an odd, uncommon cult is troubling; should it lead him to reject other deities, disaster is imminent. And, of course, Hippolytus does just this. He rejects Aphrodite.

In the prologue Aphrodite gives this rejection by Hippolytus as the single reason she will destroy him: "I honor those who respect my powers, but I overthrow those who are haughty towards me. For there is this characteristic even in the race of gods, they rejoice in being honored by men" (5–8).[53] "Hippolytus, alone of the citizens of this Troezenian land, says that I am the most evil of deities, and he refuses marriage and won't touch a marriage bed" (12–14). Aphrodite claims she does not begrudge Hippolytus the intimacy he has with Artemis (15–20), but "this day I will punish Hippolytus for the sins he has committed against me" (21–22).[54]

Aphrodite sees Hippolytus not only as "neglecting" her and her cult, but as an "enemy" (43, 49) who actively speaks out against her. This situation is not unlike that of Pentheus and Dionysus in the *Bacchae*, with the important exception that Hippolytus, unlike Pentheus, is moral and pious in other aspects of his life. In addition, the action of the two plays begins at different points. In the *Bacchae* most of the acts and words by which Pentheus enters into irremediable hostility with the gods are presented on the stage. In the *Hippolytus* the antagonism has become insoluble before the play begins, and its original causes are only suggested and reflected on the stage.[55]

That the goodwill of the gods—of *all* the gods—must be maintained and that this is accomplished by giving them their due honor, usually in sacrifice, is a fundamental tenet of Greek popular religion.[56] It would neither have surprised nor perhaps have troubled an ancient audience to find a deity punishing an individual who not only neglected but denigrated the honors due her. What Hippolytus initially said or did to "dishonor" Aphrodite occurred before the play's beginning and is not described in detail. What is required, to justify Aphrodite's charge for the audience, are not so much additional blatant and blasphemous words and actions like those of Pentheus, but rather unmistakable indications that Hippolytus holds concerning Aphrodite the views she claims he does.

From his first entry upon the stage Hippolytus gives just such indications. He omits and, when warned by an old servant, refuses even the customary simple greeting to the statue of Aphrodite prominent at the gates of the palace.[57] The old man is worried at this (99–101). "No goddess," Hippolytus replies, "who does her wonders at night pleases me" (106). The old man cautions him, "One ought to give the honors that belong to the deities" (107). Soon thereafter Hippolytus breezily dismisses Aphrodite (113).[58] After Hippolytus departs the old man is quick to pay his own respects to

Aphrodite's statue and hopes to excuse Hippolytus' action as youthful indiscretion (114–120).[59] Hippolytus' behavior in this scene reveals both neglect and more than a hint of distaste and contempt. Aphrodite's charge that he neglects her honors is proved. That he is her enemy is suggested and soon proved, for in 616–624 Hippolytus, reacting to the news of Phaedra's passion for him, imagines a world, ideal to him, in which children would be procured not by sex but, like apples, by money in a supermarket. He is thereby denying Aphrodite her place in the human world and reveals himself as her mortal enemy in the clearest possible terms. And, finally, to Aphrodite's charge that Hippolytus says she is "the most evil of deities" (13) correspond Hippolytus' words to the nurse, "Aphrodite begets wicked behavior in wise women" (642–643). He not only harbors such thoughts, he expresses them publicly. No doubt can remain that Aphrodite has fairly charged Hippolytus with neglect and hostility.

Hippolytus is tragically mistaken—and surely self-deceived—in his claim that he "knows how to reverence the gods" (996). He in fact knows how to revere only one god, and that is why he "labored through the labors of piety in vain" (1367–1369), but he does not realize this fully until the closing scene, where he understands that it is Aphrodite who destroyed him (1401). In his singleminded devotion to Artemis he rejects Aphrodite and persists in that rejection to the end. Such need not happen to normal worshipers of Artemis or Aphrodite. Even the chorus in this play can sing two odes on the powers of Aphrodite (525–564, 1268–1281) and another on the benefits which Artemis brought them (161–169). Artemis the helper in childbirth can hardly be completely disassociated from Aphrodite, the purveyor of the generative instinct.[60]

The disassociation and antagonism of Aphrodisiac and Artemisian elements in the *Hippolytus* result because Euripides made the deities into something which they were not in real religion.[61] He generalized their functions and characters and abstracted them from their usual cultic limitations of appropriate times, occasions, and places in human life.[62] There was a time and place suited to each, and these were observed in cult and practice. In Athens Artemis the virgin was appealed to by young, unmarried women[63] *and* by women in childbirth. Aphrodite represented symbolically and mythically, if not fully in cult,[64] sexual pleasure, and that, for Athenian female citizens, was associated with the marriage bed.[65] The abstraction of Artemis and Aphrodite from their delineated roles in time and place, and the resulting formation of their personae and their antagonism, are literary creations and become part of literary or poetic religion. Whatever criticisms are leveled against them, in this form, have no bearing on the Aphrodite and Artemis of contemporary cult and popular belief. As Barrett puts it in another regard, "This is no denigration of the Olympian religion—such purposes were far from Euripides' mind."[66]

Pentheus, Teiresias, and Cadmus

In the prologue of Euripides' *Bacchae* Dionysus himself tells the audience that he has come to make clear to mortals his status as a god (20–22, 39–42), to win recognition of himself as the son of Zeus, and thereby to defend the good name of his mother, Semele (26–33, 39–42).[67] Semele's sisters have already rejected her claim of Zeus as Dionysus' father, and as a result of this rejection they along with other women of Thebes have been "possessed" or "enmaddened" by Dionysus and are, as maenads ("madwomen"), celebrating Bacchic rites on Mount Cithaeron (26–33).

Pentheus, Agave's son and ruler of Thebes, has, even before his first appearance in the play, established his opposition to Dionysus. By others' reports Pentheus "fights the god" (θεομαχεῖ) and refuses him cult acts of libations and prayers (44–48). He has put under arrest some of the Theban maenads (226–227) and plans to stop the others from their revels (226–232).[68] This sets up, in the clearest possible terms, the confrontation with Dionysus, who has just warned that he will wage war against any who seek by armed force to drive his maenads from their rites (50–52).

In the aged Teiresias and Cadmus the audience are given, still before the first appearance of Pentheus, an extended look at some appropriate ways to acknowledge Dionysus' status as a god.[69] Both Cadmus and Teiresias are respectable and respected men. Cadmus is praised by Dionysus himself for his handling of Semele's cult (10–11), and his noble reputation as founder of Thebes is stressed by Teiresias (170–172). Teiresias himself is conventionally a "wise man" figure, and this wisdom is emphasized (179, 186).[70] They both acknowledge Dionysus to be a new god, son of Semele and Zeus. They are prepared, as best they can, to perform the Bacchic rites and thereby "exalt" and bring honor (τιμή) to him (170–209).[71] They realize that the god wishes such honor from all the citizens (208–209) but are willing, themselves alone, if others refuse, to give him honor in the appropriate way.

Dionysus has, in the prologue, established his demands for recognition as the son of Zeus and Semele, for honor due him as a god, and for freedom for his maenads to practise their rites. Teiresias and Cadmus have revealed how citizens, even those apparently unsuited for the new cult, should recognize the new deity and his rituals. The stage is now set for Pentheus, who in the first thirty lines he speaks (215–247) rejects Dionysus' claim that he is Semele's son by Zeus, contemptuously describes the new arrival as a sleazy, effeminate sorcerer, treats the Bacchic rites as a pretext for drunkenness and illicit sex,[72] and announces his plans to hunt down and arrest more Theban maenads. On each of these points he is committing an error, an error that in a Greek tragedy will be disastrous. The audience already knows he is wrong in rejecting the status and parentage of Dionysus. They also know what Dionysus plans for anyone who opposes his maenads. The audience must, at this point, be uncertain about Pentheus' charges of illicit sex and drunkenness in the rites. They must wait to see how the dramatist chooses to characterize these rites. Euripides eventually portrays the rites of the Theban women as free from the alleged immoralities (677–774, 940) and thereby refutes Pentheus' charges. Pentheus' mistaken notions about the rites take on additional importance later, when his prurient curiosity about them contributes to his decision to spy on the maenads.[73]

In lines 266–810 we find a series of discussions and events that should, if anything could, convince Pentheus of his errors and induce him to acknowledge the new deity and allow his rites. Various attempts are made to persuade him, and each reflects a somewhat different way of looking at religious phenomena. The chorus of Asian maenads, devotees of Dionysus in the broadest sense and therefore not impartial, but not necessarily wrong either, introduce this section of the play with a charge of impiety (τῆς δυσσεβείας) against Pentheus because he does not respect "the gods" or Cadmus (263–265).[74] Teiresias then responds to Pentheus' rejection of Dionysus with a series of sophisticated arguments (266–327).[75] He employs bits of contemporary natural philosophy in his description of Dionysus' functions as a benevolent deity.[76] With some speculative etymology popular in the period he explains the more bizarre elements of Dionysus' birth myth.[77] He stresses Dionysus' future greatness and reminds Pentheus of the limits of human power. He also argues that Dionysus, like Pentheus himself, enjoys being honored. In his own claim, "I will not fight the god" (325), Teiresias recalls Dionysus' description of Pentheus as a "god-fighter" (45).[78]

After the chorus briefly approves Teiresias' speech, Cadmus, Pentheus' grandfather, urges him, even if he does not believe Dionysus is a god, to "lie the lie that brings us credit" and say that he is, because honor will result for Semele and the whole family of Cadmus (333–336).[79] He also reminds Pentheus of his cousin Acteon, who had claimed superiority to a god and was destroyed. He concludes with what becomes a refrain in this play, "Give honor to the god" (328–342). Pentheus responds by intensifying his earlier criticism of Teiresias (255–262) with threats to demolish Teiresias' mantic sanctuary, a clear additional sign of an impious temperament (345–351).[80] After comments on Pentheus' folly and a prayer-like hope that the god will not react against him and the city, Teiresias and Cadmus go off "to the mountain" to celebrate Dionysus' rites (358–369).[81]

The chorus invokes "Lady Holiness" or "Lady Reverence" to witness Pentheus' unholy hybris against Dionysus.[82] They state confidently that the gods, though dwelling far away, observe mortals' activities. Misfortune ($\delta v\sigma$-$\tau v\chi i\alpha$), they say, and divine hostility punish erroneous human thought (370–402, 427–432). A servant arrives leading Dionysus. He describes the miraculous escape of the Theban *bacchae* whom Pentheus had earlier imprisoned, and he expresses his respect and awe for this miracle-worker (434–450). And thus, before the disbeliever Pentheus encounters Dionysus himself, he has heard arguments based on the god's general nature and myth, on his functions, on family ties, and on miracles, from a prophet, his grandfather, and an unbiased servant. One should, perhaps, look not for what is lacking in each argument on Dionysus' behalf,[83] but for what is present. Each is a different, but acceptable facet of Greek (if not Christian) piety, and Euripides has chosen to distribute them among a number of different proponents rather than work them into one harmonious whole. Had Pentheus within him any chord responsive to piety, one of these arguments would have touched him.

In the course of the intricate dialogue with Dionysus, Pentheus not only denies but mocks (467) Dionysus' claim to be Zeus' son. Dionysus implicitly (476), then explicitly (490–502), charges Pentheus with impiety. At the close of this scene Dionysus warns Pentheus that the god is observing (500) and will punish Pentheus for these "hybristic deeds" of denying his existence and treating him unjustly by imprisoning his maenads (516–518). The chorus then restates the birth legend of Dionysus, wonders at Thebes' opposition to him, and prays for Dionysus' help (519–575). The prayer is immediately answered: Dionysus himself appears and announces an earthquake and fire which demolish Pentheus' palace.[84] Dionysus then describes to the chorus Pentheus' deluded and vain attack on the Dionysiac bull, his attempt to put out the fire in the palace, and his assault on the Dionysus-like phantom. Here Pentheus *by action* reveals himself in the most literal terms a "god-fighter": "He, a mortal, dared to enter into battle against a god" (635–636).

Pentheus is unmoved by these miraculous events and by the escape of the Dionysiac stranger from prison. He is deaf even to the god's explanation of them (642–659). He has remained steadfast in his erroneous and impious views despite the words, warnings, and actions of a prophet, a relative, a servant, and a deity. His resolve is untouched by a series of miracles which he personally experienced. He is established, by this point in the play, as incorrigible, deserving whatever punishment the god may have in store. His punishment begins, however, 150 lines later. In the interim a messenger describes more miracles and demands, point blank, that Pentheus "receive this god into the city" for reasons of both the god's greatness and special benefits.[85] This speech is intended not so much to provide additional proof of Pentheus' folly (he has, after all, already experienced miracles and spoken directly with the god) but to prepare for the description of Pentheus' punishment. It reveals the vicious and destructive turn the Bacchic rites may take when violated,[86] and it gives a graphic model of the *sparagmos* that awaits Pentheus.

In the prologue Dionysus was concerned to win recognition and honor as a god and to establish his and his mother's claim that he was the son of Zeus. He there laid down only one specific condition for action, "If the city of Thebes, armed, attempts in anger to drive my *bacchae* from the mountain, I will lead my maenads in battle" (50–52; cf. 790–791). The messenger's speech (728–768) has shown that he could do just that, and it is appropriate that Dionysus' final confrontation with Pentheus focuses on this very issue: Pentheus arranges for his men to make an attack on the *bacchae* (780–786). He will not be dissuaded by Dionysus' warnings, threats, or offers of mediation (787–808). When Pentheus calls for his own weapons so as to join in the attack, he seals his fate—or, better perhaps, he fulfills the specific condition set by Dionysus—and his delusion and punishment begin (809ff).

As Dionysus predicts (857–861), Pentheus dies, slaughtered by his mother as a sacrificial victim to the deity whose existence he denied.[87] Dionysus becomes the victor over the *theomachos*, a fight pitifully easy for the god but agonizing and fatal for the human.[88] The death of Pentheus indicates the power and stature of Dionysus (1030–1031) and affirms the existence of the gods in general (1325–1326).

Pentheus' error throughout the play is misjudgment—his initial misjudgment of Dionysus and his rites, and then his failure to take into account the arguments and evidence which counter his misjudgment. He stubbornly adheres to his initial evaluation despite on- and offstage miracles and despite arguments and warnings from friends, relatives, biased and unbiased observers, and the god himself. Pentheus is clever, quick-witted, quick-tongued, and quick-acting (268–271, 670–671, 780, 820), and all of these contribute to his fatal misjudgments.[89] He has a logical explanation for everything, and he heaps scorn on whatever he judges to be foolish, stupid, and ridiculous (e.g., 248–251, 483). He has a quick mind, but not a good one. In the terminology of the day, he "thinks without thinking well," he is σοφός without having σοφία.[90]

Pentheus' lack of good judgment and wisdom becomes impiety only when, because of it, he misunderstands his relationship to a god. He fails to understand who he is, who the god is, and therefore his proper behavior towards the god.[91] In his error and impiety Pentheus goes far beyond Hippolytus, who rejects *one* deity, Aphrodite, but otherwise exhibits genuine, in fact exceptional piety. Pentheus, who has characteristics of other Greek villains,[92] not only personally rejects Dionysus and his cult but attempts to turn others away from them and heaps mockery and ridicule upon them.[93] Tragedy's most flagrant human mocker of a god becomes, of course, in turn the one most mocked and humiliated (literally and figuratively) by a god.[94]

Pentheus' impiety is presented largely as the result of intellectual error, of rational miscalculation.[95] It is in this light that we can better understand Cadmus' advice to Pentheus: "Even if this god does not exist, as you say, let people say he does in your presence, and lie the profitable lie that he does exist" (333–335). Much the same point is later generalized and expanded by the chorus: "It costs little to think that the divine, whatever it is, has strength" (892–894). To a Christian with faith in one, and only one true

God, such advice would be anathema. To a Greek with a more intellectualized and less emotional belief in a number of quite distinct and various deities, such advice, though not sincere in the Christian tradition nor intellectually rigorous in the ways in which Pentheus takes pride, is, as Cadmus says, prudent, wise, and profitable.[96] It is the "better safe than sorry" wisdom of that common people whose "thought and traditions" (τὸ πλῆθος ὅ τι φαυλότερον ἐνόμισε) the chorus of this play praises in contrast to the cleverness of "exceptional men" such as Pentheus (427–432).[97] Pentheus' wit and hyperrationality prove to be folly, and piety, here towards Dionysus, is made part of true wisdom and morality (1150–1152).[98]

Pentheus, Dionysus tells us, "will come to know (γνώσεται) the son of Zeus, Dionysus, who is, in the end, a god, a god most dreadful (δεινότατος) but also most kind to mortals" (859–861).[99] Pentheus will recognize Dionysus' claims to be the divine son of Zeus and Semele. He will also have understood the two aspects of Dionysus: the force which is benevolent, creative, and life-easing when it is given free rein (ἠπιώτατος)[100] but which, when repressed, becomes violent, destructive, and murderous. In the conventions of tragedy it is sufficient for Dionysus to predict Pentheus' future knowledge. The audience requires no precise indication of it by Pentheus; his recognition that he committed some "errors" is sufficient (1120–1121).[101] For the Greek audience, though not for the Christian, the hero's recognition of his own religious error is not of major importance. For the tragic hero, once he has convicted himself, there is no recantation or repentance leading to forgiveness and salvation, and once dead he breaks all ties with the deities of the living world. What is important is that others, those who will live, learn from his experience. In this play they most surely do.[102]

Troy and Athens

The "goodwill of the gods" was essential to the prosperity of the state. As we have seen, success in warfare and agriculture, and, more generally, good fortune, opportunities for constructive action, and "good hopes" for the future all depended upon it. The goodwill of the gods was the reward for piety, and the Athens described by the three tragedians was exceptional for piety. In Aeschylus' *Oresteia* it is Athena and a jury of Athenian men who resolve the murders, vengeance, and impieties of the house of Atreus. In Euripides'

Heraclidae Athenians protect, against foreign threats, the suppliant family of Heracles; in Sophocles' *Oedipus at Colonus* they harbor the suppliant Oedipus. In Euripides' *Suppliants* they champion and obtain, against Theban opposition, the burial of the Argive warriors. The Athenian kings Theseus (E. *Suppl.*) and Demophon (E. *Heraclid.*) promote the value of seers and prophecy. In the *Medea* the Athenian Aegeus alone keeps his oath and will be rewarded for it. All of these are acts of piety, and for the piety of its citizens Athens enjoyed Athena's gift of the olive and protection in warfare, Poseidon's gift of ships and the bridle, and, from the gods in general, fertility of the earth, herds, and humans, productivity of the mines, husbands for marriageable girls, and freedom from diseases, untimely deaths, invasion, and civil war.[103] All these the Athens of tragedy owed to the "goodwill" of the gods.

Prose sources and tragedies usually describe the benefits which come to a city from the gods. In the *Troades,* however, Euripides looks at the matter in reverse.[104] There he establishes as a major premise that the gods have withdrawn their support from Troy, and he portrays, in the fullest detail found in Greek literature, a city which lacks entirely the goodwill and help of the gods.[105] The results are, to a Greek and to anyone, horrifying.

Troy had, in previous times, enjoyed a good relationship with the gods. In the prologue Poseidon emphasizes that he and Apollo had built Troy's walls and that since that time his own "goodwill" ($εὔνοια$) had never been lacking to the city of "his" Phrygians (4–7).[106] Throughout the play we hear much of the close, we might say intimate, relationships which Cassandra, Ganymede, and Tithonus have had with deities (41–42, 329–454, 820–859). Troy's past associations with the gods had been good, but perhaps not unusually so. Most Greek states, Athens included, prided themselves on roughly similar relationships with specific deities in the mythological past. Troy's ties to the gods in the *Troades* seem very close, mainly because what for most cities was a part of their mythological prehistory is represented dramatically as present and current for Troy in this play. Other states imagined, in their own national mythologies, no less intimate relationships with deities and no less beneficial results in the remote past.

At the end of the play Troy as a city lies virtually destroyed. Its buildings and sanctuaries are leveled and burned. All its men are dead. The male line of the royal house has been exterminated. The surviving women and children have been sent off to various parts of Greece for slavery or worse. Hecuba and the chorus fear that even Troy's glorious name may be lost to the consciousness of mankind (1278, 1319, 1322). For Troy the reversal of fortune is the most extreme that can befall a city.

In the prologue Poseidon reveals, in the clearest possible language, that he has, with reluctance (45–47), abandoned Troy and withdrawn his support (23–27).[107] There is the unmistakable impression that Poseidon's departure means that all pro-Trojan deities have left Troy; as will be seen, this proves to be the case. In the play itself no deity comes to help the city Troy or its few pitiful survivors. Priam's death at the altar of Zeus Herkeios, described early in the prologue (16–17), symbolizes this.[108] Zeus Herkeios is, par excellence, the protector of home and hearth, and that the king of Troy had been killed not only in his own house but at this very altar would indicate to a Greek audience that for the Trojans there was no longer any divine protection.[109]

The departure of the gods from Troy is visibly realized in the destruction and disregard of their sanctuaries and cults. The "(sacred) groves are deserted and the temples of the gods are awash in gore" (15–16). Bloody corpses lie about Athena's sanctuary (599–600). In what may be the most complete catalogue of cult features in Greek tragedy, the chorus lists the losses: "Gone are the sacrifices, the pleasant-sounding noise of dances, the night festivals of the gods, and the golden cult statues" (1071–1074).[110]

In the *Troades* the abandonment of the gods preceded and eventually caused the neglect of cult and sanctuaries. Poseidon stops supporting the Trojans because he is the loser in Olympian power struggles (23–24). The lack of divine support then allows the defeat and devastation of the city. Once desolate, Troy will offer no source of cult for Poseidon, and hence he is leaving (25–27).[111] So too Zeus had abandoned the Trojans. The chorus complains to him, "You betrayed to the Achaeans your temple and fragrant altar in Ilium, the flame arising from cake offerings and the heaven-reaching smoke from myrtle, and the ivy-bearing groves of Ida which are washed by the melting snow, and that glorious, divine place to live, the region first struck by the sun" (1060–1070). The pro-Trojan deities first withdrew their support, and this, in Euripides' version, allowed the stratagem of the Trojan Horse, made by Athena's devices and dedicated to her, to succeed.[112] The resulting devastation included the destruction of sanctuaries and the ruination of cult.[113] There is no hint in this play that the gods withdrew their goodwill because the Trojans neglected cult, the usual concern in popular religion.[114]

We do not learn why Poseidon and the other gods abandoned Troy and allowed the pro-Greek deities to work their will. Poseidon says only that he has been "defeated by the Argive Hera and Athena" (23–24). Euripides' failure to give explicit and understandable reasons for the withdrawal of Troy's divine supporters has led numerous modern critics to complain of the caprice and fickleness of these gods.[115] These critics are, I suggest, mistaken. Euripides does not give reasons because, *in this play*, the problem does not concern him. The pro-Trojan gods had, after all, surrendered Troy well before the dramatic time of the *Troades*.

In the prologue Euripides concentrates attention on a more immediate problem: why has the pro-Greek Athena now decided to destroy the Greeks? To this question he gives an explicit answer completely understandable in religious terms. The Greeks, whom Athena had formerly assisted, had done nothing to punish Ajax who had desecrated *her* temple by dragging Cassandra from there (67–73).[116] Athena thought she had been treated hybristically, and the Greeks had taken no action, had not even said anything, against the impious malefactor. The goddess therefore considered all the Greeks accessories after the fact to the desecration of her temple. Her vengeance would be harsh—the destruction and suffering of all the Greeks— but such is the nature of divine vengeance when it has once been aroused.[117] Athena's stated purpose is that other Greeks learn to be pious concerning her temples and to have proper religious respect for the other gods (85–86). Sin and punishment in these terms were completely in accord with the popular belief that gods personally sought vengeance when their own prerogatives were violated.[118] Euripides in the prologue of the *Troades* centers attention on the religious culpability and divine punishment of the Greeks. He chose not, in this play, to treat the culpability of the Trojans. This does not give us the license to assume a meaningful, pregnant silence and to conclude from that some skepticism concerning the justice and morality of Poseidon and his pro-Trojan colleagues.

From the very beginning of the play the audience knows that, for whatever reason, the gods have abandoned Troy. But the women of Troy do not know this for certain, and this dramatic irony gives heightened pathos to their invocations and prayers. Hecuba, Andromache, and the chorus suspect, at times, that their destruction has come "from the gods" (696, 775–776), that the gods' affection for Troy is gone (858–859). Most interesting in religious terms and most natural in human terms are their reactions. Hecuba ranges from a fatalistic platitude ("I see that the gods sometimes raise up like a tower what was formerly nothing. Other times they destroy what once enjoyed great repute," 612–613)[119] to bitter sarcasm ("The gods were concerned only with causing my sufferings and destroying Troy, the most hated of all cities," 1240–1241).[120] Relatively early in the play she invokes the gods but declares that they have been bad allies. She cannot yet, however, surrender all faith in them: "Despite everything it is proper for any one of us suffering ill fortune to call upon the gods" (469–471).[121] Eight hundred lines later, when she has full awareness of her losses, she abandons even that slender hope. After an anguished appeal to the gods she catches herself: "Why do I call upon the gods? Before they did not listen when they were called upon" (1280–1281). By this time she no longer even maintains the proprieties.

It is in the context of this increasing disappointment with conventional deities that we should view Hecuba's remarkable invocation of Zeus in 884–888. Here she abandons the popular and cultic Zeus who appears elsewhere in the play (1060–1080, 1287–1290) and invokes—to no avail, it should be noted—a Zeus about whose fundamental nature she is now uncertain. He may be Air (γῆς ὄχημα) or the Necessity of Nature (ἀνάγκη φύσεος) or the Reason of Mankind (νοῦς βροτῶν). This Zeus "guides all mortal things according to Justice." This conception of Zeus is drawn from bits and pieces of fifth-century philosophy[122] and is alien to conventional religion, as Menelaus is quick to note ("What strange prayers you make to the gods," 889). Hecuba's invocation is, I suspect, a sign not so much of her enlightened view of religion as of her desperation. It is one of several reactions to the failure of conventional appeals to traditional deities, and it finds no more response than they had.

We should not assume that the inability of the characters in this play to secure and benefit from the gods' help reflects Euripides' view of the human condition in general. He has put these people into a particular and unique situation: life in a city-state which entirely lacks "divine goodwill." The religious issues he raises are (1) why the Greeks lost the goodwill of the gods, and (2) what life for the Trojans was like without this goodwill. These issues are of course related, but they are treated separately. Virtually all Greeks, and particularly the Athenians in the fifth century, thought that *their* states enjoyed the goodwill of the gods, and they made efforts to maintain that happy relationship. They were, thus, unlike the Trojans. But Euripides, writing between the Athenian massacre of the Melians and the launching of

The Pious and the Impious 157

the Athenian expedition to Sicily, provides a cautionary tale.[123] The Athenians, like the Greeks at Troy, could in their success commit gross impieties. The result could well be the godforsaken status of Troy, a city once prosperous like Athens herself.[124] Viewed in this light, the *Troades* would demonstrate not the caprice and uselessness of the gods, but the signal importance to the state and its people of acting piously and maintaining divine favor and goodwill.

Polyphemus

Euripides' *Cyclops* is a satyr play, related to tragedy but burlesque and comic,[125] and discussion of it is not strictly germane to the purposes of this study. But its title character, the Cyclops Polyphemus, is of such interest as a Euripidean description of a totally impious "man" that he requires mention, albeit as an addendum to the treatment of the major sinners of tragedy. In Greek drama Polyphemus is unique in the sheer number of impieties he commits, all in a mere 709 lines. Technically we should not call him an impious "man" because he is, as he claims, "a god born from a god" (231). But in the bizarre world of this tragicomedy Euripides makes little of the Cyclops' divinity and treats him as he would a human character. Twice, in discussions of his impiety, Euripides even calls him a "man" (348, 605). Silenus, the chorus of satyrs, and Odysseus repeatedly label him "impious" and "god-hated."[126] The act by which his impiety is introduced, and the major one throughout, is his maltreatment of *xenoi*. His usual practice is to "feast on" *xenoi* who chance upon his territory. In this play Polyphemus' adversary, Odysseus, is presented as a *xenos* (96, 102) who claims the privileges of *xenia* accorded to shipwrecked men (299–303).[127] To Odysseus' question whether the natives are "*xenos*-loving and holy concerning *xenoi*" (125), the Silenus responds that the Cyclopes slaughter and eat *xenoi* (126–128). Polyphemus not only violates the rights of *xenia*, he also mocks them: once he tells Odysseus that as his gift of *xenia* he will receive the fire and pot in which he will be cooked (342–344); another time his gift is to be the last man eaten (548–551). Most of the references to Polyphemus' impiety are directly linked to this maltreatment of *xenoi*.[128]

But the Cyclops' impiety extends much further. He is, as Odysseus describes him, "a man who has no concern for gods or mortals" (605). He shows no concern for the destruction of religious sanctuaries, even those of his father, Poseidon (288–298, 318–319). Like the impious Eteocles in the *Phoenissae*,[129] in his alienation from the traditional gods he makes other, profane things into "god": wealth (316–317), his own belly ("the greatest of the deities," 334–335), eating and drinking (336–337), and causing himself no grief (338). Polyphemus sacrifices to no god except himself and his own belly (334–335) and has no respect for Zeus or fear of his thunderbolt and rain (320–328). He imitates, à la Salmoneus, Zeus' thunder with his farts (327–328).[130] And, he claims, in terms unthinkable to the average Greek, that "the earth, whether she wishes it or not, *must* fatten my herds by producing grass" (332–333). It is only in a drunken stupor that he can "see the throne of Zeus and all the holy revered group of deities" (578–580). His speech in lines 316–346 offers the single most complete collection of impious attitudes surviving from Greek drama. Odysseus immediately recognizes it as the "thought of an impious man" (348–349) and prays to Athena and Zeus Xenios for assistance (350–355). If Zeus Xenios fails to notice such behavior, then belief in him as a god is vain (354–355).

Like other impious characters in Greek drama Polyphemus, the god-hated beast, is punished: his single eye is bored out by the *xenos* whose rights were being violated. This form of punishment for Polyphemus was, of course, dictated to Euripides by the Homeric tradition. A more human character in a more serious play would have suffered much worse. In any case Odysseus' mild challenge to Zeus Xenios (354–355) has been answered. The violator of a *xenos*' rights has been punished, and Odysseus' warning to the Cyclops (310–312) proves true: "Choose piety instead of impiety because for many people wicked gains bring in turn ($ἠμείψατο$) punishment."

Conclusion

In a survey of the pious and impious characters of Greek tragedy some patterns emerge. We can first distinguish between those who challenge directly, almost face to face, the status, authority, and power of individual Olympian gods from those like Jason, Polymestor, and Creon who commit impieties concerning oaths, *xenia*, burial rites, and such matters. Although, as we shall see in the next chapter, the two groups are not unrelated, the former seem the stuff only of tragedy and literature in the fifth century. The impieties of the latter are like those that average Athenians of the classical period might and occasionally did commit, and to that extent their attitudes and fates may be of more relevance to popular religion.

In their various ways Ajax challenged Athena, Hippolytus Aphrodite, Pentheus Dionysus, and Neoptolemus Apollo. These kings and princes we may class as *theomachoi*, "god-fighters."[131] Euripides evidently coined the verb θεομαχεῖν late in his career specifically to designate such behavior (*Ba.* 45, 325, 1255, *IA* 1408),[132] but the notion of a man fighting a god is as old as Homer. Homeric *theomachoi*, however, have their own divine champions who urge them into physical battle against another deity *and* ultimately protect them. The tragic *theomachoi* act on their own initiative and "fight," alone and in vain, against their divine opponents.[133]

In the encounter with a *theomachos* the deity sees his own honor and status threatened and takes the opportunity to display his power and that of the gods in general. Ajax dismisses the need of Athena's and other gods' help in battle, and for this Athena demonstrates "how great is the strength of the gods" (S. *Aj.* 118). Her punishment of Ajax shows, she says, that man should "not himself say any wrathful word against the gods nor take on any self-importance" because of wealth or physical strength. "The gods love the 'moderate' and hate the evil" (127–133). Aphrodite in the *Hippolytus* honors those who respect her powers but overthrows those haughty towards her. The Dionysus of the *Bacchae* destroys the man who refuses to recognize his divinity and cult. The punishments vary, each suited to the character of the sinner, but the *theomachoi* always lose, and the power of the gods is always reasserted.

In *Seven against Thebes* Aeschylus has a messenger describe individually each of the seven champions of the Argive army.[134] Six of the seven are sinners.[135] The fault of the seventh, the seer Amphiaraus, is that he associates with the impious. Five are described as *theomachoi*, sharing or exceeding the type of hybris that Sophocles' Ajax displayed. Capaneus boasts that he will sack the city whether the "god wishes it or not":[136] not even Zeus, whose thunder and lightning he mocks, will stop him (425–431). To the messenger this boast shows "thought not befitting a human being" (425). Eteocles claims Capaneus is "dishonoring the gods" and foresees disaster for him (440–446). The inscription on Eteoclus' shield says that not even Ares could cast him down from Thebes' towers (468–469). The emblem on Hippomedon's shield is Typhon, Zeus' mortal enemy (491–494). Parthenopaeus swears by his spear, which he reverences (σέβειν) more than a god, that "he will sack the town of the Cadmeians even against Zeus' will" (529–532). Each warrior is overproud of his prowess and goes well beyond Sophocles' Ajax by asserting that he will succeed even against a god's will. Tydeus reveals the same attitude when he continues the expedition despite unfavorable signs from a seer and sacrifices (377–383).[137] Polyneices stands somewhat apart from these *theomachoi*, but he too, by his treason, is thought to be making a direct assault on the gods and their sanctuaries (580–584, [1017–1024]).[138] Each of the *theomachoi*, Polyneices, and even Amphiaraus, guilty only by the company he keeps, dies. The boasts of Capaneus, Eteoclus, and Parthenopaeus are all refuted.

Our second group of sinners, people like Creon, Polymestor, Jason, the Aegyptiads, and the Greeks of the *Troades*, commit impious acts. They too offend the gods, but not so frontally, personally, and dramatically. I reserve discussion of the relationship of impious acts to the dishonoring of the gods for chapter 5 but point out here that although perjury, maltreatment of *xenoi* and suppliants, violation of burial rites, and such acts dishonor the gods in various ways, they differ in both magnitude and quality from the behavior of the *theomachoi*. They are also, to put it simply, more within the range of activity of normal people.

These characters, unlike *theomachoi*, must do, not merely speak of, plan, or threaten the impiety. Capaneus, Eteoclus, Parthenopaeus, and Sophocles' Ajax suffer for their boasts.[139] Creon, Polymestor, Jason, and their like commit impieties and suffer for those; however, as we have seen,[140] characters like Hermione in the *Andromache,* Ion in the *Ion,* Theoclymenus in the *Helen,* and Menelaus and Agamemnon in the *Ajax,* who plan similar impieties but fail or give them up, escape punishment.

The boasts of the Sophoclean and Aeschylean *theomachoi* reveal their frame of mind, and in each instance one has the impression that the boast is not a temporary aberration but an established feature of the character's personality. Ajax, for example, twice, years apart, made much the same hybristic claim. Similarly most of those who in tragedy are punished for impious acts persist in their action and may even commit multiple impieties. Persistence such as we have seen in Creon, Pentheus, Jason, and Hippolytus finds punishment.[141] Polymestor in Euripides' *Hecuba* committed multiple impieties, and the single impieties of Lycus in the *Heracles,* of the Aegyptiads in Aeschylus' *Suppliants,* and of Eteocles in the *Phoenissae* are accompanied by other statements or indications of impious temperament.[142] Seldom and only for insignificant characters such as Lichas in Sophocles' *Trachiniae* is a single impious act sufficient cause for punishment.[143]

When it comes, divine punishment, whether for *theomachoi* or for those otherwise impious, is very severe. It is a vengeance harsh by the standards of human justice in the fifth century B.C., to say nothing of the twentieth century A.D. The lucky sinner loses only his life. Quite often the punishment, in accord with the archaic principle of the solidarity of the family as a single responsible unit, envelops the sinner's family and even, in exceptional cases, his city. To put the issue in Athenian legal terms, the justice of the gods in tragedy is the simple, harsh, unnuanced justice of Dracon, not the mitigated and refined code of the classical period. The characters of tragedy live in the heroic times of the distant past, and into this time are inserted, anachronistically, some ethical values, social and political concerns, and legal concepts of classical Athens. But the system of sin and its punishment as administered by the gods, the gods of Euripides as well of Sophocles and Aeschylus, remains archaic, Draconian.

No less troubling to critics who expect gods to administer a justice enlightened even by twentieth-century standards is that on occasion the gods punish the impious through agents who are themselves impious or otherwise morally culpable. Indisputable cases are Clytemnestra's killing of Agamemnon, Medea's punishment of Jason, Agave's killing of Pentheus, and Neoptolemus' death from Orestes' plots. Others might add, depending on their evaluation of characters, Phaedra's destruction of Hippolytus and Hecuba's of Polymestor.

We have discussed common characteristics of the *theomachoi*, and we may attempt to compose a similar picture of those who are punished for impious acts. They commit the act, not merely think of it or plan it. If they attempt it and fail, they are apparently not punished. They violate unwritten "laws" of the gods or other religious traditions, and they persist in this violation.[144] They do so because they do not "fear" the gods, that is, they do not fear punishment for impieties committed.[145] In this they "think wrongly." In addition to whatever specific punishments they may suffer, they lose the goodwill and support of the gods. Their prayers are not answered or are answered to their disadvantage. They distrust and criticize seers and hence are closed off from this useful religious authority. In their alienation from traditional gods they may adopt abstractions (such as Tyranny or Caution) as gods.

Once persistence in sin has reached a certain point, punishment is inescapable. They may recognize and repent of their error, but this does not remove or mitigate their punishment. The punishment, when it comes, is very harsh, death or a fate worse than death, and may involve as well the destruction of family and homeland.

Opposed to these are the pious who respect the gods, the dead, parents, *xenoi*, suppliants, and oaths. They "think properly," that is, as humans should; they reverence the gods, their laws, and religious traditions. They perform and champion the customary cult acts concerning both gods and the dead. They respect seers and seek and heed their advice. That we learn little of the religious attitudes of such characters suggests that such behavior was the usual, expected, and ordinary thing. Pious behavior was the norm and needed little or no explanation, and this itself suggests the unanimity and strength of popular religious beliefs and conventions for the audience of the fifth century. In tragedy the positive values of piety were virtually unquestioned and hence seldom explicated. When characters challenged or violated them, their actions and attitudes required examination.

We conclude this chapter by introducing for comparison a real-life Athenian who was widely praised by contemporaries and later generations for his piety. Nicias, a prominent statesman in Athens since the 420s and reluctant leader of the ill-fated Sicilian expedition, emerges from both Thucydides' and Plutarch's accounts as exceptionally pious.[146] He performed the choregic duties expected of the wealthy with an expense and beauty previously unknown (Plut. *Nic.* 3.2). In Plutarch's time, five centuries later, two of Nicias' private dedications still were standing, a gilded statue of Athena on the Acropolis and a temple in the sanctuary of Dionysus (3.3). He financed and made lavish arrangements for the chorus which Athenians annually sent to Delos to hymn the god. He dedicated at Delos a bronze palm tree, and he purchased and gave to the god an expensive tract of income-producing land to endow annual sacrifices and feasts. As the Delians performed these sacrifices, they were to ask "many and good things from the gods for Nicias" (3.4–6). As Plutarch notes (4.1), however much these benefactions and dedications were intended to win political favor, they also reflect the piety of the man.

Nicias sacrificed to the gods every day, and he kept a seer in his house to consult on public affairs and his own business operations (4.2). As we noted previously, he once surrendered claim to a military victory rather than leave two Athenian soldiers unburied on the battlefield (6.5–6).[147] In Syracuse he prevented his men from sacking and desecrating a sanctuary of Zeus Olympios. Despite the gold and silver there, he thought no benefit would result and that he would bear the responsibility for the impiety (16.6). Nicias' dependence on omens and seers, termed excessive by ancient and modern political and military historians, led him to delay, because of an eclipse of the moon, the evacuation from Syracuse for twenty-seven days, after which escape became impossible for the Athenians.[148]

In better days Nicias attributed his military successes not to his own "wisdom, power, and virtue," but to fortune and the divine (τὸ θεῖον, Plut. Nic. 6.2). Even Thucydides has him repeatedly express his dependence on the gods in his final speech to his men at Syracuse:

> In my life I have performed what is traditional towards the gods and what is just and without reproach towards men. In return my hopes for the future are still bold. (7.77.2–3)[149]

> Our enemy has enjoyed enough good luck. If we became hated by someone of the gods when we made this campaign, we have now been punished sufficiently. (7.77.3)

> It is reasonable for us now to hope that the "things from the god" will be more gentle, for now we are more deserving of pity than of hate from the gods. (7.77.4)

The parallels of Nicias' piety to that of pious characters in tragedy are too obvious to elaborate, but the soldiers' response to Nicias' tragic death at Syracuse points to an important difference:

> They were disheartened in their expectations from the gods when they reasoned that a man who was god-loved (θεοφιλής) and famous for his many and great services to the gods was suffering a fortune no fairer

than that of the worst and most lowly men in the army. (Plut. *Nic.* 26.6)[150]

These Athenian soldiers on the battlefield suffered a crisis of religious faith in seeing a religious and pious man suffer.[151] Life is not as tidy as literature. In the everyday world pious men like Nicias may suffer.

FIVE

Piety and Honor

Previous chapters have described a number of pious and impious acts and characters in tragedies, especially in the context of challenges to popularly held religious beliefs. Let us now consider piety and impiety more for their own sakes, reviewing briefly what we have seen to be judged one or the other but also adding some new elements. After completing a survey of the pieties and impieties, we must take to heart Socrates' first criticism of Euthyphro: that when asked what was holy or unholy, he gave only particular instances of holy and unholy acts, without investigating the basic nature of the holy and unholy.[1] In this regard we shall take up the relationship of piety and impiety to other Greek virtues and vices and, in particular, their close association to "honoring" the gods and their laws.[2]

My interest here remains what it has been throughout, to learn about popular religion from the evidence of the tragedies. I therefore limit myself to topics in which popular religion and tragedy intersect, that is, to descriptions in tragedy of acts known from popular sources to have been commonly judged pious or impious *and* to more general thoughts about piety and impiety expressed by tragic characters as they reflect upon such acts. Such reflections are rare in contemporary orators, inscriptions, and historians, and we therefore cannot always prove that those in tragedy were or were not shared by average Athenians. But if the three tragedians show agreement on these, as we have seen them do on the designation of pious and impious deeds, we might reasonably expect that the audience shared these views. At worst we shall again have established the consensus of the tragedians. At best we may learn something important of popular religious views of piety and impiety.

Pieties and Impieties

To give structure to the catalogue of pious and impious actions, both those we have already seen and others to be added, I group them according to the social relationship in which they most commonly occur. As major categories I establish pious or impious acts of (1) an individual towards another individual (or group of individuals) unrelated by birth; (2) an individual towards members of his or her own family; (3) an individual towards the city-state; and (4) an individual towards the gods individually or as a group. The gods are affected by all acts of piety and impiety and are thought to reward and punish them; thus the gods' involvement permeates all four categories. But apart from the fourth category, in which an individual directly challenges a god (as, for example, Ajax in Sophocles' *Ajax*), an individual's impious behavior also affects another human being or the country as a whole, and it is in these first three categories that, at the popular level at least, Greek religion and ethics intersect and are mutually supportive. The first three categories, it will be seen, are common to popular religion and tragedy. The fourth category appears primarily, though not exclusively, to be a topic of tragedy and other literary genres.

Individual towards Individual

We have already examined at length the proper and religiously sanctioned behavior towards *xenoi* and those who have taken asylum in a sanctuary.[3] Violation of the rights of either was, in religious terms, impious and godless and could be compared to robbing a sanctuary. In Sophocles' *Oedipus at Colonus* Oedipus expects the Athenians to protect his asylum because they excel in "reverencing the gods with honors" (θεοὺς . . . τιμαῖς σεβίζειν, 1006–1007).[4] To violate asylum "dishonors" the gods and is violence directed against them. The Lycus of Euripides' *Heracles* and the Aegyptiads of Aeschylus' *Suppliants* are willing to drag off a suppliant because they are without fear. The Aegyptiads do not believe in Greek gods and hence have no respect for their altars. They are described by the hostile Danaids as having "impure minds" (δυσάγνοις φρεσίν), as being "excessively haughty" (περίφρονες δ' ἄγαν), and "bold like dogs, paying no heed to the gods" (750–759). In contrast the Argives "respect" (αἰδοῦ and ἄζονται) and "fear" the tokens of supplication, the suppliants themselves, and the wrath of Zeus Hikesios,[5] and they therefore protect the Danaids against the Aegyptiads (345–347, 651–655).

Euripides' Hecuba labels Polymestor the "most unholy *xenos*, a man who feared neither those above the earth nor those below" (*Hec.* 790–792).[6] In the *Agamemnon* Paris "shamed" (ᾔσχυνε) the table of his host Menelaus by stealing Helen, thereby "dishonoring" both the table and Zeus Xenios (401–402, 701–705).[7] The chorus expresses "respect" (αἰδοῦμαι) for Zeus Xenios, who saw to the punishment of Paris (362–366). For Aeschylus impiety thus involves disrespect of the host's table, of the *xenos* himself (*Eum.* 270–271), and of the overseeing deity. Piety is the respect (αἰδώς) of all three.[8] In real life, as in tragedy, violation of *xenia* and asylum was always condemned. But in the world of tragedy, where poets can direct events better than in real life, defenders of *xenoi* and asylum are *always* rewarded and violators are *always* punished.

Oaths, like *xenia* and asylum, were a mechanism for regulating behavior and solving problems between individuals with no close ties of kinship. Oaths could, of course, be sworn by one member of a family to another—for example, by Hyllus to his father Heracles in Sophocles' *Trachiniae* and by Hippolytus to Theseus in Euripides' *Hippolytus*—but that was exceptional.[9] Maintenance of oaths was uniformly termed pious, violation impious. To commit perjury was "to sin against the gods" (S. frag. 472[R]) and might suggest that the perjurer no longer held conventional beliefs about the gods.[10] An oath required "honor" (ἀτιμάσῃς, E. *Hipp.* 611) and "respect" (αἰδεσθείς, S. *OT* 647).[11] By the curse that attended every oath, the perjurer would incur a specified punishment from a designated god. If one held conventional beliefs about the gods, this process was rather mechanical. By violating an oath the perjurer did not "dishonor" a god but simply made the god effect the curse. Theoretically, the god would suffer dishonor only if he himself did not accomplish the punishment specified in the curse. In tragedy that does not happen; as we have seen, the only unpunished perjurer in tragedy is the nameless, menial messenger of Sophocles' *Antigone*.[12]

In popular sources the maintenance of oaths is often treated as the key element of personal piety. As I have suggested elsewhere, that was because it was in this area that the average person most frequently faced temptation to act impiously.[13] But it was also the one area of religious life in which an individual most often, perhaps daily, brought the attention of one god or of a group of gods to his own behavior. By invoking, say, Zeus, Demeter, and Apollo as witnesses to an oath an Athenian invited their scrutiny; a violation of the oath would then bring these potent local deities into action.

In cases of homicide the dominant religious concern in popular religion was pollution. The murderer had committed an impious deed and thus had incurred the pollution of bloodshed.[14] In tragedy most homicides are of closely related family members: Agamemnon, Theseus, and Medea kill their children; Clytemnestra and Deianira their husbands; Oedipus his father and Orestes his mother; and the brothers Eteocles and Polyneices each other. Accounts of these thus reveal little of the religious aspects of homicide per se, because each involves the simultaneous perversion of appropriate, pious behavior towards family members.[15] Nevertheless, in tragedy too the prime religious concern with homicide is the resulting pollution. In Sophocles' *Oedipus Tyrannus* Creon and Oedipus, long before they have any notion of who the murderer of Laius might be, take action as they would against any murderer. He is, they learn from Apollo, a "pollution of the land" (97) and the cause of the plague afflicting Thebes.[16] He is impious and impure (1381–1383). Because this shed blood is "bestorming" the city, the murderer must be banished or killed (100–101).[17] Since the murderer is polluted, Oedipus excludes him from prayers and sacrifices, orders that no one entertain him, and thereby considers himself acting as an ally (σύμμαχος) to the victim, the land, and the god (236–275). At this point both Creon and Oedipus assume that the presence of an unpurified, unpunished murderer is sufficient cause for the plague. Only much later do they learn what Apollo knew from the beginning, that the pollution involved also patricide and incest.

There are numerous other examples. Jason calls Medea's murder of Creon and the princess "unholy" (ἀνόσιον, E. *Med.* 1305). Ajax claims he is going to the seashore to wash off the pollution of killing the herd animals and their tenders (S. *Aj.* 654–656), and Andromache imagines the pollution that would afflict Hermione if she were responsible for her death (E. *Andr.* 334–335).[18] Even after the perfectly justified killing of Lycus, Heracles makes purificatory sacrifices (E. *HF* 922–927; cf. 940). In the *Antigone* Creon takes precautions against pollution when he buries his niece Antigone alive in the tomb (775–776).[19]

In tragedy a fundamental distinction is made between killing *polemioi* (enemies of war) and all others. To kill a *polemios* was neither impious nor pollution-inducing, and it was therefore advantageous in planning or justifying a homicide to define one's personal or political enemy as a *polemios*. The old man and Creousa do precisely that in the *Ion*.[20] In the *Heraclidae* Eurystheus makes the claim that as an acknowledged *polemios* he can be killed without risk of pollution only in the heat of battle, not later as a captive once spared (1009–1011).[21]

In Aeschylus' *Choephoroi* Electra wonders whether it is pious for her to ask the gods that Aegisthus and Clytemnestra be murdered in revenge for Agamemnon. The chorus responds, "How is it not, to repay one's personal enemy (ἐχθρόν) with evils?" (122–123). These lines should not be taken in isolation to mean that it was pious to take retributive vengeance—even to the extent of murder—on one's personal enemies. Electra is bound by another piety, that towards her father, and this has to be balanced against the impiety of homicide and even matricide. Also, in this play Aeschylus presents Orestes' vengeance on his father's killers as a war in which the gods are his allies (see p. 52 above); thus implicitly Agamemnon's murderers become Orestes' and Electra's *polemioi*.[22]

In tragedy as in life the Olympian gods do not intervene to punish murderers. Rather, the presence of a polluted murderer makes prayers and sacrifices ineffectual,[23] with the result that the murderer and all those with whom he associates lose divine support.

One poetic conception of the afterlife, as we have seen, holds that the murdered man remains wrathful at his killers.[24] The chorus of Sophocles' *Electra* express this concisely as they overhear Clytemnestra being killed by Orestes:

Those lying beneath the earth live,
for those who died long ago take the blood of retribution from their killers.

(1417–1421)[25]

There is, however, no evidence that popular religion shared this view either of the afterlife or of punishment of killers.[26] In both life and tragedy the most persistent religious concern was pollution.

Individual towards Family

In tragedy as in life, burial rites and the cult of the tomb were the responsibility of the family, and they devolved upon others only when the family defaulted or, as in war, was not present. Amidst great adversity Antigone secured rites for her brother Polyneices, Teucer for his brother Ajax, Andromache for her son in the *Troades,* and the mothers of the Seven for their sons in Euripides' *Suppliants.* Parents hoped to leave behind children who would provide these rites for them. I have already described in detail the nature of these rites, the obligations of family members, and the uniformly miserable fate of those who violated them.[27] Here let us recall that for the common dead the major purpose of such rites seems to have been not appeasement or admittance to the underworld, but the removal of pollution and the bestowal of honor and adornment.[28] To prevent or omit such rites was impious, unholy, and contrary to "traditional practices" and the unwritten laws.[29] As in matters of homicide, the Olympian gods took virtually no part.

Yet Lycurgus believed that "the concern of the gods watches over all human actions, and especially over those involving parents and the dead" (*Leoc.* 94). Who then are these "gods"? In Euripides they are those of the underworld: Hades, Persephone, and Thanatos (Death) himself.[30] In the *Phoenissae* (1320–1321) to give due honor to the deceased is to show reverence for Hades (χθόνιον θεόν). Sophocles has Teucer wish that Olympian Zeus and Erinys and Dike punish Agamemnon and Menelaus for denying Ajax his rites (*Aj.* 1386–1392). Aeschylus, characteristically, makes these issues a concern of Dike and Nemesis (frag. 266[R]). Of this potpourri of "deities" only Zeus received worship in Athens, and we can only conclude that the oversight of burial rites, like matters of homicide, did not fall into the bailiwick of any specific deity of Athenian cult. Real Athenian deities, as noted before, were far removed from death and its aftermath, and conventional beliefs in these areas appear nondeistic, perhaps predeistic in origin.[31] The tragedians occasionally personalize and enliven them by introducing quasi-divine figures such as Hades, Dike, and Nemesis, but in so doing they reach beyond practised cult.

Religious sanctions also governed relationships between family members, especially those of parents to children, children to parents, brothers and sisters towards brothers, and wives towards husbands. The ultimate perversion of these family bonds was murder, and in tragedy the killing of a parent, child, brother, or husband is always condemned as "unholy" and brings with it pollution.[32] The perpetrator is "impious," even when, as in the case of Orestes and Electra, the murder is done in fulfillment of another obligation of piety.[33] The sin and pollution of kin-killing are so generally accepted and so understandable that we need not dwell upon them. Let us rather direct attention to other aspects of piety and impiety towards family members.

Lycurgus in his prosecution of the traitor Leocrates in 330 B.C. claimed that "it is the greatest impiety not to spend our lives benefiting those from whom we have received the beginning of life and those from whom we have received very many good things" (*Leoc.* 94).[34] He then illustrated his point with the story of a young man who rescued his father, at great personal danger, from the flowing lava of Mount Etna (95–96). In the same vein the Athenians questioned archons-elect whether they treated their parents well ([Arist.] *Ath. Pol.* 55.1–3).[35] An unknown speaker in Euripides' fragment 852[N] summarizes the tragic view:

A man who reverences (σέβει) his parents in life
is, while both alive and dead, dear (φίλος) to the gods.
But may the man who does not wish to honor his parents
not be a fellow sacrificer with me to the gods
nor set sail on the sea on the same boat with me.

The individual who does not honor his parents is an enemy of the gods and therefore corrupts ritual and is subject to punishment from the gods. Honoring (τιμᾶν) one's parents is one of the three major virtues (ἀρεταί), along with honoring the gods and honoring the "common laws of Greece" (E. frag. 853[N]). For the Danaid chorus of Aeschylus' *Suppliants* reverence of parents (τὸ γὰρ τεκόντων σέβας) is the third of the laws of Dike (707–709). In the *Eumenides* the Erinyes stress its importance (545) and claim that those who show irreverence for their parents (ἀσεβῶν . . . τοκέας φίλους) will suffer punishment in the underworld (267–275). Oedipus, of course, committed the two greatest sins against parents, killing his father and having sexual intercourse with his mother, both of which are termed "unholy."[36] In Theseus' view, Hippolytus by forcing himself (as Theseus thought) upon his stepmother acted in an unholy way towards his parents and "dishonored the revered eye of Zeus" (E. *Hipp.* 885–886, 1080–1081). Because they have exiled him and left him an itinerant beggar, Oedipus curses his sons so that they might learn "to reverence" (σέβειν) and "not dishonor" (μὴ ἐξατιμάζητον) their parents (S. *OC* 1375–1379). The chorus of Sophocles' *Electra* sees Electra's attempts to avenge her dead father as an act of piety (461–464), one that shows reverence for the "greatest laws" and for Zeus (1095–1097).[37]

The various obligations of piety have a priority order, and some of life and much of tragedy dealt with the proper ordering of these priorities. Euthyphro, contrary to public opinion and perhaps even that of Socrates, thought that the piety of prosecuting the killer of a hired laborer outweighed the impiety of bringing his own father to trial as the killer (Pl. *Euthphr.* 4D–E). Sophocles' *Trachiniae* provides a similar conflict. When Heracles orders his son, Hyllus, to marry Iole, Heracles' own concubine, Hyllus objects: "Am I to be taught to be impious, father?" Heracles responds as a Greek father: "There is no impiety, if you will delight my heart" (1245–1246; cf. 1247–1251).[38]

Orestes and Electra face a far more grievous conflict: to avenge their father requires killing their mother. The child's obligation towards the father in this situation receives sharpest focus in Sophocles' *Electra*. For Electra a happy life is impossible if her dead father is deprived of the honor of ritual laments (239–243). Electra causes grief for Clytemnestra and Aegisthus so as to give honors (τιμάς) to her dead father, "if there is any gratitude there (in Hades)" (355–356). By killing Aegisthus she foresees winning piety (εὐσέβειαν) from her dead father (968–969). The chorus, in a sense the voice of the community, heartily approves of Electra's devotion:

> By Zeus' lightening bolt and heavenly Themis,
> (those who neglect their parents) are not long
> without suffering.
>
> (1063–1065)

They find her supporting the "greatest laws" (μέγιστα νόμιμα) in piety towards Zeus (τᾷ Ζηνὸς εὐσεβείᾳ) (1093–1097). Sophocles makes little of the religious aspect of the resulting matricide, in contrast to Euripides and Aeschylus, but they too ultimately assert the religious obligation towards the father over that towards the mother in this dilemma.[39]

In popular sources "the gods" in general oversee obligations towards parents. Theseus (E. *Hipp.* 885–886) and the chorus in Sophocles' *Electra* (1063–1065, 1093–1097) see Zeus, father of mortals and immortals, as the protector for fathers. Aeschylus, of course, has his female Erinyes avenge matricide. In this he certainly gives a greater specificity to the divine world than that known to popular religion. Perhaps Sophocles and Euripides do so as well.

The religious obligations towards one's children and brothers are, in tragedy, evident only in violations.[40] The killing of either was unanimously condemned.[41] Apart from this Aeschylus' Electra complains that Clytemnestra possesses an "ungodly" (δύσθεον), in no way "maternal" way of thinking towards her children (*Ch.* 190–191). In Euripides' *Phoenissae* Oedipus' curse on his sons, that they decide ownership of the "house" by the sword, is termed "most unholy" (ἀνοσιωτάτας) by Jocasta (67–68). In *Oedipus at Colonus* Sophocles has Antigone, in her attempts to convince Oedipus to meet with Polyneices, assert a parent's obligation to forgive even the most heinous of his son's violations of filial duties:

> You begot him, and so, father, it is not right (μηδέ . . . θέμις)
> for you to treat him badly in return,
> not even if he does to you the most impious of the most evil deeds.
>
> (1189–1191)

Oedipus accedes to Antigone's plea. Had Theseus in Euripides' *Hippolytus* followed the same principle, he would not have mistakenly caused his son's death. The brothers Polyneices and Eteocles committed impiety when they killed each other, and Iphigeneia would have done so if, however unwittingly, she had caused Orestes' death.[42]

A wife's murder of her husband, unlike the killing of a parent, child, or brother, is not the shedding of kindred blood: that is the reason Aeschylus' Erinyes give for not hounding Clytemnestra (*Eum.* 210–212). But a woman who does this is "godless"; the deed is "impure," "unholy," and "most godless," a "pollution of the land and its gods"; and the husband's death is "impious."[43] Hyllus prays that Dike and Erinys punish Deianira (S. *Tr.* 807–809), and a chorus expects the heavenly gods to send Clytemnestra to her death (E. *El.* 479–484).[44] Even in the underworld Aeschylus' Clytemnestra suffers shame and verbal abuse for her abominable deed (*Eum.* 95–98).

A law credited to Solon excluded adulteresses, like murderers, from the public sanctuaries and allowed summary punishment, except death, for violators of the law. Apparently this law was intended to "keep pollution and impieties out of the sanctuaries," to "motivate temperate behavior, the avoidance of wrongdoing, and a law-abiding desire to stay at home" ([Dem.] 59.85–87).[45] Electra calls Aegisthus' marriage to Clytemnestra "unholy" and Aegisthus "impious" for it (E. *El.* 926–927).[46] Phaedra's adulterous passion for Hippolytus is likewise termed "unholy" (E. *Hipp.* 764–766). The chorus in Euripides' *Ion* complains of poets' songs about women's "unholy marriages of illicit Cypris," when in fact they excel men in piety in this regard (1090–1095). It may well have been because of the impiety of "illicit Cypris" that Aspasia could be indicted for impiety for arranging Pericles' rendezvous with "free women" (Plut. *Per.* 32.1).[47]

Aeschylus' Danaids claim that to take an unwilling bride from an unwilling father is "impious" and "impure," and they foresee punishments for it in the underworld (*Suppl.* 9–10, 227–229; cf. 36–38). Incest, which violates both family and sexual mores, is, of course, unholy and causes pollution (S. *OT* 1011–1013, 1287–1289, *OC* 944–946).

Religious strictures about sex, like the law of Solon, fall more heavily on women. In Sophocles' *Trachiniae* no complaints of impiety arise about Heracles' numerous liaisons, but one can imagine the complaint if Deianira had transgressed but once. Hyllus' fear of impiety in marrying his father's concubine is dismissed by Heracles (S. *Tr.* 1245–1251), and Theseus reacts to Hippolytus' alleged passion for Phaedra as a violation of filial obligations, not as sexual impiety (E. *Hipp.* 885–886). Men like Aegisthus, Oedipus, and the Aegyptiads do not escape criticism in religious terms for sexual misconduct,[48] but these cases have other contributing factors, whereas for women simple premarital sex and adultery bring charges of impiety.

The relations of children to parents, parents to children, wives to husbands, and brothers and sisters to brothers are thus all subject to religious sanctions. One must honor one's dead kin with funeral rites. Children should honor their parents. A wife should reverence her husband, and her adultery is a sin. The male bias is apparent throughout. In the religious domain the father is more important than the mother, the husband than the wife, the brother than the sister. Some extramarital sexual behavior allowed to men is forbidden to women. Violations of these family obligations are unholy and impious and usually cause pollution. Punishments, but of no set type, are expected. Aeschylus, typically, foresees them even in the underworld. But in tragedy no specific gods are regularly involved in these affairs, except Zeus in protecting the rights of fathers.

Individual towards the State

According to Lycurgus (*Leoc.* 129), traitors commit impiety because they "deprive the gods of their ancestral and traditional cults." A traitor betrays "their temples, statues, sacred precincts, their honors established in the laws, and the sacrifices handed down by your ancestors" (1–2). In the classical period young men becoming citizens swore the ephebic oath to maintain or enlarge and better the fatherland, to hold in honor the ancestral sanctuaries, to obey the officials and laws, and not to desert comrades-in-arms on the battlefield.[49] An Athenian citizen who committed treason thus simultaneously committed the impiety of violating his sacred oath.

The heroic age of tragedy does not know such an oath, and the impiety of treason is reduced to its essence: the traitor, if successful, will destroy the sanctuaries, temples, dedications, and laws of his ancestral gods. This is what the Thebans fear from the traitorous Polyneices and the Argive army he leads.[50] In tragedy treason is impious because and only because it results in the "dishonoring" of the ancestral gods and the destruction of their property and cults.[51] As usual in popular religion, the gods of tragedy become involved only when their own interests are threatened.[52] In tragedy, as in life, the gods seem unconcerned with the larger issues of the devotion, respect, and service owed to the fatherland. In tragedy they protect their cults; in life they acted also to punish the perjurer. But in neither do they oversee in broader terms one's relationship to one's country, nor does religion attribute a sanctity to it.

Individual towards God

Thus far we have considered piety as it is manifested in behavior towards other human beings. Here we treat the individual's dealings directly with the gods and their property and cults. As seen just above, treason might well be put into this category, because although it involved fellow citizens and the state, the religious concern was the potential destruction of sanctuaries and cults. The religious aspect of treason is thus essentially only one instance of a larger category of impieties: desecration of sanctuaries, destruction of temples or dedications, and robbing of sacred property. All these are condemned, in tragedy and life, as impiety of the highest order.

When the old servant in Euripides' *Ion* proposes burning Apollo's oracle at Delphi, Creousa refuses: "I am afraid. I now have enough sufferings" (972–975). In the *Bacchae* the impious Pentheus threatens to demolish Teiresias' mantic sanctuary (345–351). Neither plan is carried out. In the *Troades* Athena is angry at Ajax not for what he did to Cassandra but because he did it in her temple and thereby desecrated it. She will punish the Greeks, "so that hereafter they may know to reverence (εὐσεβεῖν) my palace" (69–71, 85–86). Here we may recall that the suppliant in a sanctuary could be viewed as the god's property and thus to violate asylum was tantamount to robbing a sanctuary.[53] Actual temple robbers were, like traitors, denied burial in Attica (Xen. *Hell.* 1.7.22). Heracles, *deus ex machina* in Sophocles' *Philoctetes,* warns that one must reverence even the sanctuaries of the enemy:

> Keep this in mind when you sack the land,
> to reverence things that concern the gods,
> because father Zeus considers all other things secondary.
> For piety does not die with mortals;
> if they live or die, their piety does not perish.
>
> (1440–1444)

Those who violate or destroy sanctuaries, statues, and altars in foreign or hostile lands, such as Xerxes, Agamemnon, and the Aegyptiads, all come to a bad end.[54]

The altars, symbols, and dedications in sanctuaries were part of the "honor" (τιμή) of the gods who possessed them, and to maltreat or destroy them was to "dishonor" the god.[55] In tragedy only Pentheus (towards Teiresias, E. *Ba.* 345–351) and the servant in the *Ion* (towards Apollo, 972–975) intend such a direct affront. For others, insofar as their motives are ascertainable, religious scruples are ignored in their desire for profit (κέρ-δος), usually in the form of booty.[56] In any case all desecrations or destructions of temples, altars, and dedications, at home or abroad, are condemned as impious and are, or are expected to be, punished.

To sacrifice, pray, and sing hymns to the gods was to "reverence" and "honor" them.[57] One "reverenced" and "honored" the holy day, religious song, and sacred implements as one did the gods.[58] A view attested but not common in tragedy and popular sources is that "when one sacrifices to the gods with 'reverence,' even if he sacrifices small things, he finds safety."[59] The infrequency of this view may be because a sacrifice was viewed primarily as a gift to the god;[60] the larger the gift, the greater the honor the god received. In piety as well as impiety, the common view was that the act itself mattered, not the frame of mind behind it.[61] Failure to sacrifice, to make the obligatory offering after a military or other victory, or to celebrate a festival was a likely explanation for an individual's misfortune.[62]

The *theomachoi*, "fighters against the god" such as Ajax, Pentheus, and Capaneus, represent, as we have seen, the most direct challenge to the gods and the greatest perversion of mortals' proper relationship to them. In their various ways they outspokenly and publicly deny "honor" to a god, and instead of being dear (φίλιοι) to the gods become their enemies (ἐχθροί and πολέμιοι). Each and every *theomachos* in tragedy suffers terribly and serves, in the end, to demonstrate the god's power. Fifth-century Athenian history knows of only one man who challenged the gods so frontally. The Melian poet Diagoras scoffed at the Eleusinian Mysteries of Demeter and attempted to turn people away from them, an act directly comparable to that of Pentheus. The Athenians condemned him to death for his impiety, but he fled the city before the sentence could be carried out.⁶³ In tragedy the gods deal directly with such men. In life human justice may have to intervene.

Piety and Justice

The tragedians have characters and choruses, in a wide variety of situations, assert, deny, and doubt that the gods are just.⁶⁴ Some characters claim that the gods help the just and punish or assist in punishing the unjust.⁶⁵ Dike (Justice) herself is represented as a daughter or partner of Zeus.⁶⁶ The father of the gods may be the focus of attention in issues of justice, particularly in Aeschylus, but more often the whole collective of the gods is involved.⁶⁷ Some denials of the gods' justice are made by characters or choruses at momentary lows in their fortunes, only to be proven erroneous later.⁶⁸ Others are never disproven.⁶⁹ Some of the questioning of the gods' justice leads to doubt whether the gods exist or deserve worship.⁷⁰ The justice of the gods is a much-treated topic of literary criticism, both ancient and modern, and that, I think, is its proper arena. As I stated in chapter 1, popular religion seems not to have shared the concern that the gods be just with a justice similar or identical to that expected in human affairs.⁷¹ Justice of the gods is a matter of literary and philosophical speculation, not a major component of everyday religion and cult.

But piety is important to popular religion, and piety (εὐσέβεια) and human justice (δικαιοσύνη) are so intertwined in many poetic texts that some scholars have been misled to think that in fifth-century morality and religion the two are virtually indistinguishable.⁷² They are, however, distinct, and Socrates in Plato's *Euthyphro*, on the one occasion when he himself offers a starting point for the discussion of piety, shows the way. He posits (11D–12D) that piety is a form of justice; therefore everything that is pious must be just, but not everything just need be pious. Likewise everything impious must be unjust, but not everything unjust need be impious. That is exactly the relationship we find in tragedy. Proper worship of the gods is "just."⁷³ Misbehavior involving oaths, *xenoi*, those protected by asylum, parents, and burial rites is often termed "unjust" as well as "impious" and "unholy."⁷⁴ Yet a wide range of unjust behavior, such as lying, stealing, political machinations, and lawbreaking, is never termed impious or unholy. The evidence from tragedy seems to confirm Socrates' proposition, and nothing in the popular sources contradicts it. We may perhaps conclude that in popular religion as well as in literature and philosophy, every impious act was thought also unjust.

Piety, Folly, *Sophrosyne*, and *Hybris*

An impiety was the product of "wrong thinking," as piety was the result of "right" or "safe" thinking. The φρήν (or φρένες), the organ of human rationality,[75] dominates virtually all discussions of piety and impiety. It is the seat, as it were, of religious behavior.

We have already seen that the Creon of Sophocles' *Antigone* committed and persevered in the impiety of denying Polyneices burial because of "bad thinking" and "bad planning."[76] Teiresias tells Creon that Thebes "is sick from his mind" (τῆς σῆς ἐκ φρενὸς νοσεῖ πόλις, 1015) and that he should think (φρόνησον) about these matters (1023).[77] Creon should learn (μανθάνειν) from Teiresias (1031–1032).[78] In their tense dialogue Teiresias promotes the value of good planning (εὐβουλία) and charges Creon with having the sickness of "not thinking" (μὴ φρονεῖν) (1050–1052).[79] As he leaves, Teiresias speaks of Creon's "learning to nourish a mind (νοῦς) better than the mind (τῶν φρενῶν, i.e., thoughts) he bears now" (1089–1090).[80] After the deaths of Haemon and Antigone, Creon laments the "errors of his bad-thinking mind" (φρενῶν δυσφρόνων ἁμαρτήματα), his unprosperous plans (ἄνολβα βουλευμάτων), and his ill-plannings (δυσβουλίαις) (1261–1269).[81] He has come to "learn" (1272) his error and the source of it.

Likewise Pentheus in Euripides' *Bacchae* is led to deny the divinity and honors of Dionysus by bad thinking.[82] Pentheus is more clever than Sophocles' Creon, more quick-witted and quick-tongued, but as we have seen, his cleverness is not wisdom.[83] Unlike the genuinely wise Teiresias (179, 186), he "thinks without thinking well." There are not φρένες in his words, and he does not have νοῦς (269–271). Thinking, he thinks nothing (φρονῶν οὐδὲν φρονεῖς, 332). Pentheus does not think mortal thoughts (τό τε μὴ θνητὰ φρονεῖν) (396) and is mad (μαινομένων) and ill-counseling (κακοβούλων) (399–402).[84] In the god's judgment he is ignorant (ἀμαθεῖ, 480, 490), he does not know what life he is living, what he is doing, or who he is (506).[85] In rejecting Dionysus his φρένες were not healthy (947–948).[86] He is a fool (μῶρος, 369).

Because they are central in these two plays, the follies and the bad-thinking φρένες of Creon and Pentheus are scrutinized by the poets. Other sinners of tragedy, though not described in such detail, have similarly faulty φρένες, whether they think "impurely," "wrongly," "too big," or "in ways not befitting a mortal." The Aegyptiads of Aeschylus' *Suppliants* pay no heed to altars, gods, and asylum; they have "impure" and "haughty" φρένες (750–759).[87] Despite what he later does, Agamemnon recognizes that purple carpets are for gods only and that he should not be honored that way. "To think not badly" (τὸ μὴ κακῶς φρονεῖν), he says, "is the greatest gift of the gods" (A. *Ag.* 921–929). Xerxes, in attempting to yoke the Hellespont, an act treated by Aeschylus as an impiety, was suffering "a disease of the mind" (νόσος φρενῶν, *Pers.* 749–751).[88] The seer Calchas twice accuses Sophocles' Ajax of not thinking in a way appropriate for mortals, and he cites Ajax' two intemperate statements about not needing divine assistance in battle.[89] In the exodos of Sophocles' *Antigone* the chorus concludes:

> To think (τὸ φρονεῖν) is, by far, the first element of happiness.
> One ought to show no disrespect regarding the gods.
> Grandiose words of over-proud men, after paying in return great
>   blows,
> teach one, in old age, to think (τὸ φρονεῖν).
>
> (1347–1353)

In Euripides' *Hippolytus* Aphrodite proclaims that she overthrows those "who think big towards her" (ὅσοι φρονοῦσιν εἰς ἡμᾶς μέγα, 6).[90] Hippolytus' servant thinks he has "planned well" (βουλεύσαντος εὖ) in advising Hippolytus to acknowledge Aphrodite (89). The same servant wishes that Hippolytus had the νοῦς (mind) he ought to have (105). In the *Heraclidae* Iolaus warns about the impious Eurystheus that "Zeus is the punisher of overly high thoughts" (ἀλλά τοι φρονημάτων ὁ Ζεὺς κολαστὴς τῶν ἄγαν ὑπερφρόνων, 387–388).[91] A fool (μῶρος), Poseidon claims, is the man who sacks cities, temples, and tombs and then perishes himself (E. *Tr.* 95–97).[92] The chorus of Euripides' *Bacchae*, a play very much concerned with forms of madness, sees one form in failing "to exalt the things of the gods" (882–887).[93] By contrast, according to a fragment of Euripides (256[N]), "blessed is the man who, having a mind (νοῦς), honors god."

Sophrosyne (σωφροσύνη) is the condition of having safe and sound (σῶος) φρένες.[94] One can, of course, be σώφρων about many matters, but *sophrosyne* about the gods (περὶ τοὺς θεούς) is piety (Xen. *Mem.* 1.1.20).[95] Piety is thus a form of *sophrosyne* as it is of justice. Whether we wish to translate *sophrosyne* as "virtue," "moderation," "self-control," or "temperance,"[96] we should keep firmly in mind its etymology from "safe and sound φρένες." *Sophrosyne* is, as we have seen piety to be, a product of the φρήν, of the mind. Like piety, it is based on rationality, and it may be, as piety is, contrasted to madness (Xen. *Mem.* 1.1.16).[97]

Athena, remarking on Ajax' punishment, warns Odysseus not to "say any wrathful word against the gods."[98] A man should not take pride that he is stronger or wealthier than another, for such human conditions change quickly. "The gods," she concludes, "love the σώφρονας but hate the evil" (S. *Aj.* 127–133).[99]

The messenger in Euripides' *Bacchae*, after seeing and describing the death of the impious Pentheus, concludes with these lines:

To be σώφρων and to reverence (σέβειν) the things of the gods
is best. And I think it is also the wisest possession for mortals who
   use it.

(1150–1152)[100]

Euripides' Hippolytus, who prides himself on his *sophrosyne*, cites as the first proof of it that he "knows how to reverence (σέβειν) the gods" (*Hipp.* 994–996). In a fragment of the lost first *Hippolytus* (446[N]) the chorus claims that Hippolytus receives the honors of a hero because of his *sophrosyne*. "For," it continues, "a good return from piety (εὐσεβείας) comes either before or afterwards."

Of the seven heroes who campaign against Thebes only the seer Amphiaraus is σώφρων (A. *Th.* 568–569).[101] He faults the murderous Tydeus, and he criticizes Polyneices for attempting to sack his fatherland and its native gods. Amphiaraus "harvests the deep furrow in his φρήν" and from there "good plannings sprout forth" (593–594). The messenger concludes his description of Amphiaraus with the pronouncement that "wondrous is he who reverences (σέβει) the gods" (568–596). Eteocles faults Amphiaraus for his associations with impious men, but still, in one line, praises him in terms that we have seen to be closely interwoven: he is "a σώφρων, just, good, and pious man" (σώφρων δίκαιος ἀγαθὸς εὐσεβὴς ἀνήρ, 610).[102]

The prophetic and wise Darius of Aeschylus' *Persae* laments that Xerxes, his son, "being a youth, thinks (φρονεῖ) youthful thoughts" (782).[103] Punishment, he says, for their *hybris* and ungodly thoughts (ἀθέων φρονημάτων) awaits the Persians because when they came to Greece they felt no shame at pillaging the statues of the gods and burning temples. As a result, Greeks altars are destroyed and the sanctuaries[104] of the gods have been uprooted and overturned (807–812). Their punishment, Darius predicts, will show that "a mortal ought not to think (φρονεῖν) excessively high" (ὑπέρφευ, 820). The chorus, he recommends, should use their *sophrosyne* and advise Xerxes "to stop harming the gods with arrogant boldness" (829–830).[105] In the manner characteristic of Greek tragedy Darius associates "thinking" (φρόνημα), "safe thinking" (σωφροσύνη), and piety (εὐσέβεια). Piety is essentially "safe and sound thinking" about the gods. It is a product of reason, not emotion.[106]

In tragedy *hybris* often emerges from discussions of impiety, lack of *sophrosyne,* and injustice.[107] That is not surprising; in the *Phaedrus* Plato treats *hybris* as the opposite of *sophrosyne.* Where thought prevails and leads us, by reason, to what is best, we have *sophrosyne.* When emotion rules and drags us, irrationally, to pleasures, *hybris* is present (237E–238A).[108] Since piety is *sophrosyne* concerning the gods (περὶ τοὺς θεούς), we might expect impiety to be *hybris* περὶ τοὺς θεούς.[109] That proves to be the case, and we see *hybris* often described in ways virtually identical to impiety.

Like impiety, *hybris* περὶ τοὺς θεούς results from faulty φρένες and indicates folly and madness.[110] *Hybris* is unjust and god-hated.[111] It is also often labeled impious or the product of impiety and is associated with disrespect of the gods or with deeds such as violation of burial rites or oaths that are known to be impious.[112] More consistently than the simply impious, hybristic individuals are portrayed as enjoying great success and wealth at the time of their crimes.[113] *Hybris* is often revealed through boasting, not necessarily accompanied by impious action.[114] The hybristic individual is often a *theomachos,* and *hybris,* like impiety, is always punished.[115]

That the sinner exhibits impiety in words and not actions and that the sinner becomes a *theomachos* are, as we have seen, characteristic of religion in tragedy, not in real life. In tragedy wealthy and successful royalty by words challenge the gods directly. In everyday life ordinary people committed ordinary impieties; for them acts mattered, not words. It is not surprising that sources for popular religion show no concern for *hybris* περὶ τοὺς θεούς. Apparently the term *hybris* was not even used in Athenian religion of the fifth and fourth centuries. In court, religious malefactors were charged with impiety, not *hybris*.¹¹⁶ Thus I have treated *hybris* περὶ τοὺς θεούς only summarily here, because, as a topic, it belongs to literary criticism. *Hybris* is a literary, not a popular conception of the relations of god, mortals, and sin.

Piety and Τιμή

Τιμή is both "honor" and the "office" or "function" for which one receives honor. Hence the τιμή of a general may be both his office as general and the honor he receives from fellow citizens for being a general. Τιμή may also be "value" or "an evaluation of worth," and in that aspect is obviously related to "office" and "honor." Τιμή is the last component of piety examined here, and it is, I think, the one that is most complex, most important, and most distinctively Greek. It best defines the status of a god and a Greek's relationship to the gods and to the religious side of life.

Τιμή in its religious context receives an unusually full exposition in Aeschylus' *Eumenides*.¹¹⁷ The Erinyes have a function (τιμή) allotted to them by the Moirae (Fates). In the play this function is demeaned by a god and is virtually eliminated by the course of events. Eventually the Erinyes are persuaded to give up this function and, as Eumenides (Kindly Ones), to take on a new function, one which will be "honored" among men with processions, sacrifices, and other cult acts. In changing from Erinyes to Eumenides they change from hostile and feared spirits with an unenviable function to the more usual form of honored deities benefiting the human race.

Moira spun as the long-term allotment (λάχος) of function for the Erinyes that they pursue until death those who murder blood relatives (*Eum.* 334–340).¹¹⁸ They overthrow families involved in such kin-murders (354–359). Their τιμή is to drive from their homes matricides such as Orestes (208–228).¹¹⁹ But because the Erinyes are daughters of Night and pursue such unsavory business and because, as we have seen, the Olympian gods distance themselves from death and murder,¹²⁰ the Erinyes receive no τιμή from their divine colleagues. They are shunned by them, do not feast with them, and have no share in the "white robes" of Olympian banquets.¹²¹ Mortals feel "awe" (ἅζεται) and "fear" (δέδοικεν) at what they do (389–393). The Erinyes claim that they do not suffer "dishonor" (ἀτιμία), but there is no indication that, as Erinyes, they received cult (393–396).

When Apollo attempts to free Orestes from the religious and legal sanctions for matricide, and when the Athenians and Athena together vote to do this, the Erinyes loudly complain that they are being deprived of their allotted, apportioned function (τιμή). Apollo, they claim, has not been allotted (λαχών) a role in affairs of murder, and by becoming involved he will pollute his true function, the giving of oracles (711–716).[122] He is taking upon himself more power than is just, and he is corrupting the apportionments (μοίρας) of long ago (162–172).[123] Contrary to the law of the gods, he honors a mortal and thereby fails to honor the function of a fellow deity (169–172). Apollo readily admits his disrespect of the Erinyes' function (τιμή, 209).[124] They beg him not to "dock" (ξύντεμνε) their τιμαί, and Apollo replies that he would not, given the chance, accept their τιμαί (227–228). The Erinyes understand why: even without their τιμαί, Apollo is "still called great (μέγας) at Zeus' throne" (229). But for the Erinyes the persecution of kinmurderers is their only τιμή. They must continue to exercise this function (τιμάς) or they perish (747), for as we saw previously, a god without a function ceases to exist.[125] The Erinyes would then suffer laughter (γελῶμαι), the polar opposite of τιμή, and it is in fear of this that they threaten to cast a blight and plague on Attica (778–792).[126] In this way only could they reestablish mortals' "awe" and "fear" for their activities.

It is Athena, a deity wiser than the Apollo of this play, who solves the dilemma. Unlike Apollo she recognizes human society's need for "the fearful good" that watches over human thoughts and constrains individuals to be temperate (σώφρονες), just, and pious, the very benefits the Erinyes claimed their own existence brought (517–543, 690–703). She points out flaws in the Erinyes' simplistic approach to their function (τιμάς) of punishing kin-killers (415–433), but she is keenly aware of and sympathetic to these spirits' concern for their τιμή.[127] The Athenian citizens' vote on Orestes' case did not show, she claims, their ἀτιμία of the Erinyes (794–796).[128] But now that Orestes has been legally acquitted by her vote and the Erinyes have been, de facto, deprived of their function, Athena proposes new τιμαί for the Erinyes both as functions and as honors to be received from these functions.

Henceforth, if the Erinyes agree, their τιμή is to be that "no house will prosper" without them (894–895). They are to provide the many benefits we have described previously: that good things come from the earth, sea, and sky; that the earth, herds, and human beings be fertile; that the mines be productive; that neither blight nor plague afflict the city; that young men

Piety and Honor 185

not die untimely deaths; that young women find husbands; that hated civil war and its bloody battles never "roar" in the city (921–987).[129] They are, in short, to become, as the Eumenides, the cause of countless benefits to Athens. For this function they themselves will be honored.[130] They will have a sanctuary near the Areopagus, "honored (τιμαλφουμένας) by all the citizens" (804–807).[131] They are to dwell with Athena, reverenced in honor (σεμνότιμος, 833), receiving first-fruit sacrifices "before children and marriages" (834–836).[132] Doing good things, experiencing good things, and well-honored (εὖ τιμωμένην), they will share in the god-loved land of Athens (868–869). As property-owning residents of Athens, they can be "honored in every regard" (ἐς τὸ πᾶν τιμωμένη, 890–891). If the Athenians "honor greatly" (μέγα τιμῶντες) the kindly Eumenides and keep their city just, they will be illustrious in all ways (992–995). These honor-loving Eumenides (1033) are led off the stage in an honorific, torch-lit procession, with citizen participants dressed in festival clothes, and amidst promises of sacrifices and τιμαί (1003–1047). Their function (τιμή) is to provide certain benefits to Athens, and as honor (τιμή) for this they will receive worship and a sanctuary, processions, and sacrifices—the full apparatus of the cult they previously lacked. Their new name, Semnai ("Revered Ones"), reflects their new status.

There are elsewhere in tragedy sufficient parallels to demonstrate that this complex of τιμή as function and τιμή as honors expressed primarily in cult is not unique to the *Eumenides* or an idiosyncratically Aeschylean view. It is, I think, a concept central to Greek ideas of the gods and of man's relation to them. As we examine other occurrences of these ideas in tragedy, we may develop a more complete picture of τιμή and its relationship to piety.

A deity's function is his τιμή.[133] The Erinyes consider oracles Apollo's τιμή, and for oracles he is "great" at Zeus' throne.[134] In Euripides' *Iphigeneia among the Taurians* Gaia has once taken away Apollo's oracular τιμή (1267–1269) and Zeus has restored it (1279–1280). In Sophocles' *Oedipus Tyrannus* the chorus worries that if Apollo's oracles prove false, the god himself "nowhere is illustrious in τιμαί," and "the divine things (τὰ θεῖα) perish" (906–910).[135] In each instance τιμή could be rendered simply "honor," but the meaning is deepened and enriched if, as the usage in the *Eumenides* warrants, τιμή is allowed to represent both "honor" and "function." If Apollo loses his function, he also loses his honor. Both are his τιμή, and without that τιμή he is nothing.

Aphrodite has a "royal" τιμή which she alone holds over all creatures (E. *Hipp.* 1280–1281). In poetry, of course, her τιμή involves divine and human sexual activity, and for these "revered deeds" she "is honored" (τίεται, A. *Suppl.* 1034–1037; cf. *Eum.* 213–216). It is for his rejection of these deeds and for refusal of even minimal cult worship of her that Hippolytus is punished.[136] Similarly the Dioscuroi, who rescue men at sea, have "saving τιμαί," surely both as function and as honor (E. *El.* 990–993).[137]

Dei ex machina announce new hero cults in terms of τιμαί. In Euripides' *Hippolytus* Artemis promises to Hippolytus, in return for the evils he suffered, τιμὰς μεγίστας in the city Trozen (1423–1425). By this she means the cult to be rendered to him by unmarried girls (1425–1430).[138] In Euripides' *Antiope* Hermes announces that Amphion and Zethus, the "two white colts of Zeus," will receive honors in Thebes. Zethus probably and Amphion certainly had functions to perform, and both were later worshiped as Theban heroes.[139] For Hippolytus, Amphion, and Zethus τιμαί seem to encompass both function and cultic honors.[140] And, finally, Theseus, though no *deus*, describes Heracles' future cult in Attica in terms of τιμή, sacrifices, and cult buildings (E. *HF* 1331–1333).[141]

The deed for which Prometheus is punished is that he deprived the gods of some τιμή and gave it to men. Fire and the crafts dependent upon it were Hephaistus' τιμή, his "gift of honor" (γέρας), and his "flower," which he had received as his "allotment" from Zeus; Prometheus' "crime" was to steal this τιμή of Hephaistus and give it to humans.[142] Hephaistus is the wronged party, but because fire is a part of the total divine τιμή, a part which Zeus assigned to Hephaistus, the poet makes Prometheus' theft into a violation of the τιμή of all the gods (29–30, 82–83, 945–946). Prometheus also threatens Zeus' personal τιμή, his rule over the gods. Here as elsewhere, Zeus is very much the master of thunder and lightning, but in this play the poet has made him particularly concerned with his rule. That is the γέρας he reserved for himself in the distribution of divine τιμαί (170–171, 228–231). Since Prometheus refuses to reveal the secret that threatens Zeus' rule, he is a vital threat to Zeus' τιμή. Prometheus has damaged the τιμή of Hephaistus and the other gods, and now he threatens the same for Zeus. This crisis must have been resolved in the lost, final play of the trilogy.

For a deity or hero, to have τιμή is to be worshiped in cult. In religious terms, "to honor" is the Greek equivalent of "to worship"; hence a deity's demand for τιμή is, in our terminology, a demand to be worshiped. Hippolytus, Aphrodite says, "honors" Artemis, the sister of Apollo and daughter of Zeus (E. *Hipp.* 15–16). In Sophocles' *Oedipus at Colonus* the chorus of Athenians from Colonus speaks of the Athenian horsemen who "honor" Athena Hippia ("of Horses") and Poseidon (1070–1073). In the *Eumenides* the Pythia describes the adoption of Apollo's cult in Delphi by saying that "the people and Delphos . . . honored (τιμαλφεῖ)" him when he came (15–16).[143] Cadmus bids Pentheus to "honor" Dionysus (E. *Ba.* 342). Hermes orders a servant to "honor" Aphrodite (E. *Alc.* 790–791). And Apollo as *deus ex machina* tells those present at the closure of Euripides' *Orestes* to "honor" Eirene (Peace) (1682–1683). In these and other similar passages, to "honor" the deity is to "worship" the deity.[144] It is the favored way of expressing this concept in Greek.[145] "To worship" in Greek religion is "to render τιμή."

Not surprisingly, gods "rejoice" in being worshiped, that is, in having τιμή, and take a dim view of those who deny it to them. In Euripides' *Hippolytus* Aphrodite gives the most concise, pointed, and famous expression of this point:

I honor (πρεσβεύω) those who respect my powers,
but I overthrow those who are haughty ("think big") towards me.
For there is this characteristic even in the race of gods,
they rejoice in (χαίρουσι) being honored (τιμώμενοι) by men.

(5–8)

She honors those who respect her powers (her functions) and punishes those who "think big," who are too proud of their own powers to respect hers.[146] Like other gods, she rejoices in τιμή. Some modern critics have condemned Aphrodite for these sentiments, thinking that Greek gods should be above concern for mere "honor."[147] If, however, as we have seen, "to be honored" is the Greek equivalent for "to be worshiped," "honor" assumes a far greater significance and Aphrodite's concerns are more understandable. She wants to be worshiped, and few religious faiths have gods so sublime that they do not demand worship and do not reward believers and punish disbelievers. Dionysus too "wishes to have honors (τιμάς) from all people" (E. *Ba.* 208) and, like a human being, "enjoys being honored" (τέρπεται τιμώμενος, 321). In Poseidon's own words it is an indication of Troy's godforsaken status that "the divine things (τὰ θεῖα) are sick and do not wish to be honored (οὐδὲ τιμᾶσθαι θέλει)" (E. *Tr.* 26–27). The abnormal state is for gods not to wish to be honored.

In life and in literature, gods "rejoice" in being worshiped. The *vox propria* is χαίρειν.[148] Aphrodite uses it (E. *Hipp.* 8), and pseudo-Hippocrates (*Aer.* 22.9 [Diller]) says that the gods "rejoice in (χαίρουσι) being honored (τιμώμενοι) and wondered at (θαυμαζόμενοι)."[149] Teiresias advises Pentheus that just as he rejoices (χαίρεις) when many stand on the gates and the city "makes big" (μεγαλύνῃ) the name of Pentheus, so Dionysus enjoys being honored (E. *Ba.* 319–321).[150] Likewise on the few extant actual dedications where a god's reaction to the gift is described, the god is to "rejoice" (χαίροσα) in it (*IG* I² 650, of Athena), or the gift itself is "to cause rejoicing" (χαρίεν, *IG* I² 499).

When gods receive τιμή, they are "magnified," "made greater." Teiresias' remark—see just above—that gods too enjoy it when the city "makes great" (μεγαλύνῃ) their names (E. *Ba.* 319–321) is buttressed by similar expressions elsewhere in the *Bacchae*. Dionysus should "be increased so as to be great" (αὔξεσθαι μέγαν, 183).[151] It is madness not "to magnify the things of the gods" (μὴ τὰ θεῶν αὔξοντας, 886–887).[152] Humans who "think big," that is, who are proud of their own powers, fail to respect the "greatness" and powers of the gods and hence do not render them τιμή. Because they "think big," they scorn—literally "think down on" (καταφρονῶ)—the gods (E. *Ba.* 199). This is, as we have seen impiety to be, an error of the φρήν.[153] The god is then discarded, is "nowhere illustrious in τιμή," and "the divine things perish" (S. *OT* 909–910).[154] To make religious matters ἄτιμα is like "making them as nothing" (A. *Eum.* 213–216). Without τιμή deities cease to exist (cf. S. *OT* 898–910, E. frag. 50[A], 46–49).

Anyone who "dishonors" the gods will suffer punishment. So, as we have seen, Aphrodite warns the audience in Euripides' *Hippolytus* (5–8);[155] so Danaus encourages his daughters (A. *Suppl.* 732–733); so the chorus of *bacchae* advises (E. *Ba.* 884–887).[156] In each of these passages the relationship between ἀτιμία and punishment is explicit, and in the punishment of *theomachoi* we may see at work, with or without specific mention of τιμαί, the same concepts of τιμή as "function" and "honor," of divine existence dependent upon τιμή, and of divine wrath at ἀτιμία. Hippolytus, by his virginal life and in his ideal world, would deny Aphrodite her "function" in human life. He refuses her minimal τιμή in cult acts. Aphrodite faults his τιμή of her and destroys him.[157] Pentheus likewise rejects a god's divine status, the value of his functions, and the cult devoted to him. He not only denies the god his τιμή, he ridicules him and his rites, the very antithesis of τιμή.[158] When Ajax, the proud warrior, denies any need for the help of Athena, the warrior goddess, he is thereby rejecting, for himself, her τιμή both as function and as honor.[159] Capaneus and Parthenopaeus both underestimate the powers of Zeus, as Parthenopaeus does also of Ares. Each, overproud of his own military ability, fails to respect the τιμή of a god powerful in battle (A. *Th.* 422–446, 486–520). By punishing both men, the gods reassert their real τιμή (both as function and honor) to all mortals. Men of "sound φρένες" will henceforth "know themselves"—know their position relative to the gods[160]—and will think and make these gods "great." They will, in short, render τιμή to them.

In tragedy some characters express disrespect for the gods in words, in "proud boasts," but in tragedy as in life gods are "honored" primarily by cult acts. The Eumenides are to receive a sanctuary, sacrifices, hymns, and a procession.[161] In the *Bacchae* Dionysus' devotees "honor" him with his characteristic rituals.[162] Commonly sanctuaries, dedications, hymns, dances, libations, rituals, prayers, festivals, and sacrifices are described as the τιμαί of the gods.[163]

Of these, sacrifice is especially important and has attracted the most attention in ancient and modern scholarship.[164] According to the fourth-century philosopher Theophrastus, "one must sacrifice to the gods for three reasons: either for τιμή or for gratitude (χάρις), or because of the need of good things."[165] Τιμή for the gods was thus only one purpose of sacrifice, but we should be wary of accepting Theophrastus' schematic divisions into *either, or, or.* One sacrifice might serve two or all three of these purposes. Xenophon has Socrates, when asked how to show gratitude to the gods, describe sacrifices both as τιμή for the gods and as a cause of benefits from them (*Mem.* 4.3.15–17).[166] Obviously sacrifices of thanksgiving could also render τιμή to the gods.[167] Characters in tragedy complain that sacrifices, often routine ones made by officials at festivals and intended for the τιμή of the gods, have resulted in no benefits for the givers. They lament, often justifiably, that in these sacrifices the *do ut des* principle had not worked for them.[168] Hence τιμή, gratitude, and future benefits are all recognized purposes of sacrifices (and no doubt of other cult acts), but they are not, as Theophrastus might incline us to think, mutually exclusive.

Sacrifices were widely considered gifts to the gods,[169] and gifts, of course, may serve Theophrastus' same three purposes: to render τιμή, to show gratitude, and to generate a good return. It is to the idea of sacrifice as a gift that Euripides' Medea refers when she says, "The story is that gifts persuade even the gods" (*Med.* 964)—a view which offended Plato years later.[170] The gift of sacrifice, like other cult acts,[171] gave τιμή to the gods, and when Pericles said (ca. 440 B.C.) that "we do not see the gods, but infer their immortality from the τιμαί which they receive and from the benefits they confer upon us" (Plut. *Per.* 8),[172] he surely meant by τιμαί not abstract "honor" but sacrifices, sanctuaries, dedications, hymns, dances, libations, festivals, and the other elements of contemporary cult. In democratic Athens only immortals could be deemed worthy of such τιμαί.

If a person or a city renders τιμή to a god, the god may reciprocate, returning τιμή for τιμή. The Erinyes of the *Eumenides* at last, after being promised τιμαί from the Athenians, accept residency in Athens. They will not, they say, "dishonor" (οὐδ' ἀτιμάσω) the city (916–917).[173] Human τιμή towards the gods is exhibited in cult acts, but the gods show their τιμή by helping mortals. According to the Theban elders, Dionysus "honors" his mother city most highly; therefore they bid him to come and purify it of its "disease" (S. *Ant.* 1137–1145).[174] Euripides' Theseus claims, "When gods honor (τιμῶσι) a man, he has no need of friends. The god helping is enough, when the god wants to help" (*HF* 1338–1339).[175] This help is naturally related to the god's own function (τιμή).[176] In the *Eumenides* Athena will not "put up with not honoring (τὸ μὴ οὐ . . . τιμᾶν) her city for outstanding military contests" (913–915).[177] Oracles are Apollo's τιμή to give, or not to give, as τιμή to mortals (S. *OT* 787–789).

Aeschylus' Agamemnon, as king, is "god-honored" (*Ag.* 1335–1337),[178] and Cassandra claims that neither she, the one time favorite of Apollo, nor Agamemnon will die "dishonored by the gods" (ἄτιμοί γ' ἐκ θεῶν), "for another person, an avenger of us, will come afterwards" (1279–1280). Cassandra and Agamemnon are to receive the τιμή of revenge.[179] In the *Antigone* Sophocles' Creon, although mistakenly transferring principles of the living to the world of the dead,[180] argues that the gods do not "honor" evil men (τοὺς κακούς), those who as traitors attempt to burn their temples and dedications. He presumes that the gods would "honor" their benefactor (εὐεργέτην) (282–289).[181]

The gods' return of τιμή for τιμή completes the cycle.[182] Each god has τιμή as function, and these functions are various and may be different or differently emphasized in different plays. For this τιμή as a function the god is owed and demands τιμή as "honor" and "worship," a τιμή which some characters refuse and demean but most render through sacrifices, dedications, libations, hymns, and other cult acts. In these the god takes pleasure and rejoices. In return for the τιμή received, the god gives τιμή to mortals in the form of help and assistance, usually in the area of his or her own expertise. This whole complex of τιμή led me to state, at the opening of this section, that it, better than any other Greek word, defines the role and status of the gods and the interrelationship of humans and deities.

Τιμή also defines the pious attitude one should exhibit towards parents, *xenoi*, those having asylum, oaths, and the dead. Here we must distinguish carefully to whom or to what the τιμή is owed.

Τιμή is owed to parents both living and dead. One might expect this to be a moral, social obligation, not needing the support of religious sanctions.[183] But in fact most declarations of this obligation include supernatural elements, if not always the gods themselves, and this duty is often listed among other elements of piety overseen by the gods.[184] A fragment of Euripides (853[N]) claims that "there are three virtues (ἀρεταί) you must practice: to honor (τιμᾶν) the gods and the parents who begot you and the common laws of Greece." We shall take up religious aspects of these "common laws" soon,[185] but let us note here that Xenophon (*Mem.* 4.4.20) has Socrates include among the "unwritten laws" the honoring (τιμᾶν) of parents. Aeschylus associates the honoring of the σέβας of parents with respecting *xenoi* and the altar of Dike, for the violation of any of which punishment from the gods will follow (*Eum.* 538–548). Another fragment of Euripides (852[N]) claims that anyone who in life "reverences" (σέβει) his parents is, both alive and dead, "dear to the gods" (θεοῖς φίλος). The speaker hopes that anyone who is unwilling to "honor" (τιμᾶν) his parents will not participate in sacrifices or sail the sea with him. Such, as we have seen, is the common attitude towards perjurers and other sinners.[186] Theseus views Hippolytus' alleged rape of his stepmother as a "dishonoring" of his father but also as an "unholy" act dishonoring the "eye of Zeus." He sees in Hippolytus' death the blow of Dike (E. *Hipp.* 885–886, 1039–1040, 1080–1081, 1171–1172). Oedipus responds to the "dishonor" he received from his sons by cursing them (S. *OC* 1375–1378; E. *Ph.* 872–877), and these curses prove effective. The fulfillment of such curses, though not assigned to the gods, clearly presumes some quasi-supernatural force, the Erinyes or figures akin to them, punishing the dishonoring of parents.[187]

In sum, the pious give τιμή to parents, living or dead, and to refuse it is to run the risk of being cursed or of being punished by the gods for impiety. The τιμή is owed to the parents, however, not to the gods.

By stealing Helen from his host's house Paris shamed (ᾔσχυνε) the table of *xenia*. He and the Trojans were later punished for dishonoring (ἀτίμωσιν) this table and Zeus Xenios (A. *Ag.* 399–402, 699–705).[188] The house of Admetus, the exemplary *xenos*, knew not how to "dishonor" (ἀτιμάζειν) *xenoi* (E. *Alc.* 566–567), and Admetus himself had too much "respect" (αἰδώς) to reject his *xenos* Heracles (823; cf. 857, 1037).[189] Piety towards *xenoi* is "honor" and "respect" towards the *xenoi* themselves. A god's τιμή is not involved unless, as in the *Agamemnon* and occasionally elsewhere in poetry, one specific god is assigned protection of *xenoi*.[190] Gods may punish the "dishonoring" of *xenoi*, but since in cult and most often in tragedy no specific god had the function of protecting them, a god's τιμή was not immediately involved.

In situations of asylum one honors, usually, not the refugee, but the god(s) of the sanctuary.[191] To violate asylum is to "dishonor" the god of the sanctuary and the gods in general, and one who thus dishonors the gods will be punished.[192] If, as we argued above, the refugee is virtually the property of

Piety and Honor 193

the god and one function (τιμή) of a god is to protect refugees in his sanctuary,[193] the ἀτιμία the god suffers in violation of asylum becomes obvious.

In oaths the situation is again different: one honors not the oath-taker or the gods, but the oath itself. Sophocles' Jocasta bids Oedipus to respect (αἰδεσθείς) the oath of Creon (OT 646–648), and the nurse asks Euripides' Hippolytus "not to dishonor" his oath (Hipp. 611).[194]

One purpose of funeral rites and tomb cult was to bring "adornment" and "honor" to the dead. This honoring of the dead, we noted earlier, could benefit the living as well as the dead and did not necessarily presume awareness on the part of the dead.[195] The ultimate perversion of honoring the corpse was to mutilate it. Aegisthus and Clytemnestra reportedly cut off Agamemnon's extremities and tied them around his neck and under his armpits.[196] In Euripides' account Electra claims that Aegisthus further dishonored Agamemnon by drunkenly leaping upon his tomb and pelting it with stones (El. 323–328).

Burial itself is τιμή of the dead.[197] So are the individual acts of the funeral such as bathing, bandaging, dressing, and adorning the corpse with jewelry, the garlands, *ekphora,* drink offerings, and laments: to receive them is τιμή, to be deprived of them is ἀτιμία.[198] Antigone wants the tomb of her brother placed where it is "most honorable" (τιμιώτατον, A. Th. 1002–1003), and the Odysseus of Euripides' *Hecuba* would be content with few earthly goods but wants a tomb "worth seeing," for "that favor (χάρις) lasts long" (317–320).[199] The tomb is, as an epitaph from Sounion puts it, "the gift of honor (γέρας) of the dead" (IG I² 1022). Likewise the elements of the postfuneral tomb cult of Agamemnon—the hair and drink offerings, banquets, and lamentations—are viewed as matters of χάρις and τιμή.[200]

Who is the recipient of this τιμή? In the large majority of cases the dead themselves are honored, but whether they are aware of this honor depends on which conception of the afterlife the poet has chosen to employ for his play.[201] If, as in Sophocles' *Antigone* and Aeschylus' *Oresteia,* the dead are represented as cognizant and talkative in the underworld, then they are "honored" (or "dishonored") among the dead for the rites given (or not) by the living.[202] If the dead are thought "nothing," then the "honor" must be to the deceased's reputation among the living, a reward the living can anticipate but the dead cannot enjoy.[203] Then dishonoring of the corpse means nothing to the dead, and for those in the underworld funeral offerings and rites are wasted effort.[204] Whether the dead are aware of them or not, a proper funeral and tomb would honor the deceased's memory among the living. If, as argued above, popular religion held that life in the underworld was "nothing,"[205] then it, if it followed Euripides' relentless logic, would have shared the view that τιμή was paid to the dead for their reputation among the living, not for their welfare or enjoyment among the dead.

In the burial and the rites of the dead the "nether" gods (A. *Pers.* 621–622), Hades (E. *Ph.* 1320–1321), and Persephone (E. *Or.* 963–964) are occasionally thought to have τιμή at stake, but the more common concern is that by preventing the enemy from recovering his dead or by depriving an individual of burial, one is dishonoring "the things" or "the laws" of the gods, that is, one is dishonoring what the gods hold in honor.[206] By dishonoring these laws one virtually destroys them.[207] It is to these laws that Antigone refers in her famous retort to Creon:

> I did not think that your proclamations had such force
> that you, a mortal, could outstrip the unwritten and unshakable laws
>   (νόμιμα) of the gods,
> for they live not just today or yesterday, but always,
> and no one knows when and from what source they first appeared.
> I was not, fearing any man's idea,
> about to pay among the gods punishment (for the violation of them).
>   (S. *Ant.* 453–460)[208]

These "unwritten laws of the gods" concerning burial are owed τιμή, and Antigone's unwritten laws refer only to treatment of the dead.[209] Thus, in summary, τιμή is owed both to the deceased and to the laws of the gods. A violation of the former is also a violation of the latter.[210]

We need not assign religious sanctions to all "unwritten laws."[211] Those of Pericles in the funeral oration (Thuc. 2.37.3) seem purely secular, although the allusion to them is so brief one cannot be sure. Those which Xenophon has Socrates describe (*Mem.* 4.4.19–25) are, however, in part from popular religion. These are laws shared by all, Greek and barbarian alike, and hence necessarily the creation of the gods and not of humans. They include reverencing (σέβειν) the gods, honoring (τιμᾶν) parents, avoiding incest, and repaying benefactors (that is, *xenoi*). Unlike violators of ordinary human laws, those who offend against these unwritten laws can never escape punishment.[212] Like what Euripides calls "the common laws of Greece" (frag. 853[N]),[213] these laws are associated with "honoring" gods and parents. The virtuous attitude towards these "common laws" was also τιμή.

In tragedy the laws of the gods, whether they are termed νόμιμα or νόμοι, and whether they are described as written or unwritten, concern rites for the dead, τιμή for parents, worship of the gods, respect for asylum, not killing *xenoi,* and not robbing sanctuaries.[214] Although Antigone claims that "no one knows when and from what source they first appeared" (S. *Ant.* 456–457), Aeschylus characteristically has his chorus of Danaids put them among the "institutions of greatly honored Dike" (*Suppl.* 704–709). Sophocles' chorus in the *Oedipus Tyrannus* makes Olympus their father and Aether their mother (863–872).[215] Euripides gives them no author.

These laws are said to be as old as mankind but also ageless, as much in force in the present as in the times of ancestors.[216] They are seen as valid certainly for all Greeks, perhaps for all peoples in the world.[217] If not actually created by the gods, they are of general concern to them. To violate their provisions is to dishonor "the laws of the gods." We can best understand these laws as religious *traditions,* established before the memory of living men—before, as Knox puts it, "the alphabet was invented or the *polis* organized."[218] An Aeschylus or Sophocles might assign them divine creators,[219] but that, I think, is purely literary and philosophical speculation. In popular sources they are referred to simply as τὰ νόμιμα, "the traditions"; the addition of τῶν θεῶν, "of the gods," is poetic.[220]

The most frequently attested provisions of these laws involve the dead, parents, and *xenoi,* precisely the groups, as we have seen, that fall under the protection of no specific god. Here τιμή is to be rendered to humans, not to the gods or a specific god. Because these groups are placed under the umbrella of "the laws of the gods," τιμή owed them becomes a concern of the gods as a group. To dishonor the dead, a parent, or a *xenos* is to dishonor a tradition honored by the gods. Thus individuals recognized as deserving τιμή are brought, though in very general terms, under the protection of the gods.

We have examined the τιμή owed to gods, to parents and *xenoi*, to the dead, and to oaths. The different recipients of τιμή in these different areas can best be understood by reasserting the significance of τιμή as the god's function. In areas where the gods' (or an individual god's) function is clearly demarcated, as in the provision of rain or the protection of refugees in a sanctuary, the gods themselves receive the "honor." Where divine responsibility is diffuse and not assigned to specific deities, as in the protection of parents and *xenoi*, the "honor," which is still important for maintaining proper standards of behavior, adheres to the relevant human (parent or *xenos*). For oaths, where different deities may be invoked and hence the "function" of guaranteeing the oath is split in various ways, the "honor" or "reverence" is accorded to the institution itself, that is, to the oath. And, finally, where there is no divine involvement, as with the dead, the "honor" must be given to the human. In honoring the dead, as in honoring parents and *xenoi*, one does not simultaneously honor specific gods but, in general terms, "the unwritten laws" of the gods, laws over which no one god has jurisdiction. Aeschylus and other poets, both earlier and later, by creating a Zeus Xenios, or Zeus Hikesios, or Zeus Horkios, reshaped the structure and thereby made violations of *xenia*, of asylum, and of oaths direct assaults on the τιμή of Zeus.

I have emphasized τιμή because I find it to be central to fifth-century piety. Τιμή reflects the complex of ideas and attitudes by which Athenians of that time expressed piety. For those who know Greek and are sensitive to etymology, it is no surprise that εὐσέβεια is manifested through τιμή. Σέβας is "reverence," and εὐσέβεια is "good, proper reverence." This "reverence" quite logically is expressed through "honor" (τιμή). When, however, the Greek εὐσέβεια is translated as "piety," or *piété*, or *Pietät*, Roman and Christian ideas of *pietas* and piety inevitably intrude. Faith, devotion, love, humility, and other elements of Christian piety are then, usually unintentionally and often unconsciously, affixed to fifth-century Greek εὐσέβεια.

That done, it seems demeaning to Greek "piety" to limit it to "honor" and "reverence," and scholars comb fringe cults (like Orphism and Pythagorism) and offer psychological interpretations of often poorly known mysteries, initiations, and other rituals to find the deeper emotional feelings they think befit genuine "piety."

Τιμή offers considerably more than a synonym of εὐσέβεια. Because it includes, as well as the "honor" due a god, the god's function and the cult acts rendered to the honoree, it encompasses the whole conceptual framework supporting the simpler term εὐσέβεια. The god has a function (τιμή) for which he is to receive honor (τιμή), and that honor is exhibited in a variety of cult acts (τιμαί). The god then repays the τιμή he receives. The usual Greek relationship between the human individual and a god is not one of devotion and love, as of a child to a father, nor one of fear and servility, as of a slave to a master, but it is like that of a subject to a king. The king has an office and functions (τιμή), and for these he is honored, usually by the freely given gifts of his subjects.[221] In these he delights and takes pleasure, and in return he helps those who honor him.[222] Deprived of the honor due him, the king may become angry, punish his rebellious subjects, and reassert his authority, but that is a perversion of the proper relationship. So too a god has τιμή as function, a τιμή which the god is concerned to maintain. For this the god expects from humans τιμή as honor and worship, and this τιμή is to be rendered in sacrifice and other cult acts. Like a king, a god is justifiably angered when his τιμή as function is not respected, when the τιμή owed him is not given, and he punishes the rebel.

An individual's decision to render τιμή to a god is, as we have seen, a rational decision. It is made by the φρήν, the mind. It is a just and thoughtful recognition of the functions of the gods and therefore of the gods' superiority to mortals. The failure to understand these is folly, *hybris,* and madness. Once the god's function and superiority are recognized, it is only natural to render him τιμή, as both "honor" and "worship," and in Greek religion this worship was given through sacrifices, dedications, hymns, and other cult acts. From these one could with some confidence expect to benefit from the function of the worshiped deity.

In areas where the gods' functions were less clearly apparent, as in the piety owed to parents, *xenoi,* and the dead, the τιμή is directed to humans. But even here, because such groups are of concern to the gods in general, to dishonor them is to dishonor the laws or interests of the gods as a group.

This too was impiety, but not one which affected a specific god. But impiety in these areas, as impiety towards a specific god, was always punished.[223]

The importance of the τιμή complex in the interpersonal relations of the Homeric epics has been recognized and clearly demonstrated.[224] The question arises whether the tragedians, by presenting human relationships to the gods in this context, are utilizing outmoded Homeric concepts to create their heroic world or whether these same concepts of piety and τιμή were still alive in the popular religion of the fifth and fourth centuries. In other words, are there indications in popular sources that the εὐσέβεια/τιμή complex found in tragedy was still the basis of classical religion? If it was, we may with some confidence transfer much of what we have learned of piety in tragedy to popular religion.

Plato's *Euthyphro* offers the best and most complete evidence for the prevalence of this complex at the end of the fifth and the beginning of the fourth centuries. Prosecuting his father for killing a hired laborer, Euthyphro has decided, in real, not merely theoretical terms, that the "holiness" (τὸ ὅσιον) of prosecuting a murderer outweighs the "holiness" of respect due a father. He recognizes that this decision is controversial, and Socrates in effect challenges him to defend it by defining what "holiness" is. Euthyphro is a seer and claims some expertise in religion (3B–D, 13E), but his responses reveal no reliance on esoteric studies or theories.[225] Just as Socrates' opponents in discussions of rhetoric are sophists, so his interlocutor in an examination of piety is a religious expert. Only such a person could, at a moment's notice, articulate and systematize common views of piety, and only from such a person could Socrates expect and demand some rigor of thought about such matters.

Euthyphro's dilemma of which of two pieties to observe is a real one, easily imaginable in everyday life, and he is concerned to make his decision intelligible in terms meaningful to Socrates, family, and peers. His need is not to show that he is acting piously by Homeric standards of Achilles and Hector or by tragic standards of Orestes and Antigone. He is arguing in the here and now of contemporary religious beliefs. The statements about piety and holiness which Euthyphro either makes himself or readily assents to can be summarized as follows. (Socrates, of course, finds flaws in each, but my interest here is not philosophic validity but the value of each statement as a proposition a religious man of the late fifth century might make or accept concerning piety.)

1. Holiness is what I am doing now, to prosecute a person who has acted unjustly concerning murder or thefts of sacred things or committed any other such sin, whether that person be one's father or mother or anyone else. Not to prosecute is unholy (5D–E).
2. What is dear to the gods is holy, and what is not dear to them is unholy (6E–7A). What all the gods love is holy, and what they all hate is unholy (9E).
3. Everything holy must be just, but not everything just need be holy. Holiness is a part of justice (11E–12D).
4. Piety and holiness are that part of justice (τοῦ δικαίου), which concerns service (θεραπείαν) of the gods. This is the kind of service slaves pay their masters (12E–13D).
5. If someone knows how to say and do, in prayer and sacrifice, things pleasing (κεχαρισμένα) to the gods, these things are holy, and such things preserve families and the communal affairs of the cities. The opposites of the pleasing things (τὰ δὲ ἐνάντια τῶν κεχαρισμένων) are impious (ἀσεβῆ), and they overturn and destroy all things (14B).
6. Holiness is a knowledge of sacrificing and praying. Sacrificing is to give gifts to the gods, and praying is to ask them for something. Holiness is a knowledge of making requests and of giving gifts to the gods (14C–D).
7. Holiness is a mercantile craft between gods and men (14E).
8. Our gifts to the gods bring them τιμή, γέρας, and χάρις. Holiness is pleasing (κεχαρισμένον) and dear (φίλον) to the gods (15A–B).

The several points of similarity to the piety of tragedy are obvious: piety includes punishing murderers and those who steal sacred property; the gods love the holy and pious and hate their opposites; holiness is a part of justice; piety is knowledge, that is, it is a product of reason; praying is to ask the gods for something; sacrificing is to give gifts to the gods; proper sacrifice and prayer and holiness in general are pleasing (κεχαρισμένα) to them; the gods give prosperity to persons and cities who please them in worship; the others they destroy. Although Euthyphro demurs at the crudity of the expression (14E), piety is a knowledge of the "business" transactions appropriate between men and gods. He concludes his explication of piety with the statement—for Socrates a frustrating self-contradiction, but a valid expression of the essence of piety in both tragedy and popular religion—that gifts (and here we may perhaps include besides sacrifices other forms of worship) bring to the gods τιμή, γέρας, and χάρις.[226] Τιμή lies at the heart of Euthyphro's final declaration about piety and holiness.

Euthyphro's claim that piety and holiness are justice concerning service (θεραπεία) of the gods, and his comparison of this service to that paid by slaves to masters (12E–13D)[227] conflicts with my earlier statement that εὐσέβεια in tragedy represents a subject's relationship to a king. Θεραπεία and its cognates are used four times in tragedy of service to the gods: once in very general terms (E. El. 743–744); twice in the Ion concerning the Delphians' service to Apollo (94, 187); and once of the rituals performed for Dionysus (E. Ba. 82).[228] Θεράποντες may, of course, be slaves,[229] but not necessarily so. The term designates the "service" the server renders, not, like δοῦλος, the individual's political or social status. Aristophanes (Eq. 58–59, 1261) has citizens giving θεραπεία to the state (Demos).[230] In Homer θεράποντες are freeborn squires to the great heroes, and in other sources θεραπεία is also the service given to one's spouse, parents, children, and xenoi.[231] Θεραπεία thus does not necessarily imply servile status, and hence Euthyphro must define what he means. It is noteworthy that he does not liken it to the θεραπεία a child or adult owes to parents. One does not love or serve a god as one would a parent, nor do gods treat fifth-century humans as their children.[232]

In tragedy there are good kings, like Demophon, Pelasgus, Theseus, and even Oedipus, who earn and deserve the respect and honor of willing subjects. But in democratic Athens the terms "king" and "subject" were abhorred. In the classical period it was unimaginable to Athenians that they would freely render τιμή or θεραπεία to a king. They likewise would loathe being slaves to anyone, but at least for this relationship they had examples in their own society. They knew what θεραπεία a slave owed a master, but they had little or no personal experience of what a subject owed his king. It may be for this reason that Euthyphro chose the model of slave and master, instead of subject and king. Like most similes in Plato it is taken from everyday Athenian life.

We may have here, however, a significant difference between tragic and popular religion. The major characters of tragedy (as of Homer) exercise royal authority. Several interact with gods more personally and directly than did ordinary people. These kings, queens, princes, and princesses see their relationship to the gods as analogous to the relationship of their own immediate inferiors to them, that is, as subjects to royalty. In democratic Athens ordinary people likewise may have viewed their relationship to the gods as they did that of their inferiors to them, but these inferiors were slaves and servants. In any case, we do not find in the *Euthyphro,* or elsewhere, that the human individual's relationship to god, whether it be likened to that of subject to king or of slave to master, was based on fear and humility.[233] It was a matter of τιμή, gifts, worship, and the gods' pleasure in and reward for these.

Apart from the relationship to god as servant to master, Euthyphro's concept of piety—of punishing acts such as murder and theft of sacred property, of the gods loving piety and hating impiety, of piety being a form of justice, of piety being a service to the gods based on reason and on giving sacrifices as τιμή and γέρας, and of the gods' pleasure in these acts of worship—echoes similar thoughts found throughout Greek tragedy. Scattered and fragmentary parallels for Euthyphro's ideas appear in other sources for popular religion, and these are sufficient to demonstrate that his conception of piety was not idiosyncratic.[234] The conclusion seems warranted that most of the fundamental ideas about piety, about the nature of τιμή and its relationship to εὐσέβεια, and about human relationship to the gods that we have found in tragedy may be reasonably accepted as components also of the popular religion of classical Athens. It is here, I think, and not in the highly anthropomorphic gods that we find the religion in tragedy most like, and hence a valuable source for, Athenian popular religion.

In the prologue of Euripides' *Hippolytus* Aphrodite says, "There is this characteristic even in the race of gods: they rejoice in being honored (τιμώμενοι) by human beings" (7–8). In his final statement to Socrates of what the gods receive from men, Euthyphro says it is honor (τιμή), a gift revealing of honor (γέρας), and gratitude (χάρις) (Pl. *Euthphr.* 15A). These two statements, from quite different sources but widely paralleled, express the essence of Greek piety. Had there been a set of commandments for fifth-century Athenian religion, the first would have been "Honor thy gods." Honor, not love, faith, or devotion, was the essential element of Greek piety.[235] Here we may recall Pericles' words: "We do not see the gods themselves, but we infer their immortality from the honors they have and from the good things they provide us" (Plut. *Per.* 8.6).[236]

SIX

The Tragedians and Popular Religion

Previous chapters have frequently noted similarities and differences of religion in tragedy and in fifth-century Athenian life. Here I summarize these similarities and differences, first as they consistently appear in all three tragedians, then turning attention to Aeschylus, Sophocles, and Euripides individually and pointing to ways in which each idiosyncratically presents elements of popular religion. Here we must keep in mind the components of religion in tragedy described in the Preface: (1) the anthropomorphic deities of the Homeric epics; (2) beliefs and deities once part of popular religion but in the classical period virtually extinct; (3) deities, beliefs, practices, and cults of contemporary society; (4) a concern with the morality and justice of the gods; and (5) contemporary or recent philosophical conceptions of deity. The similarities of tragedy and life are obviously to be explained by the third element: that the tragedians employed deities, beliefs, practices, and cults of contemporary society. When the tragedians consistently share a difference from practised religion, we might reasonably speak of a tragic convention. For understanding these tragic conventions and for the differences between the individual dramatists we must look to the other components of the hybrid of religion in Greek tragedy.

Conclusions on the similarities and differences between religion in tragedy and in life and between poets are necessarily general in nature, subject to exceptions. Differences between the poets are largely a matter of frequency and tone, not of single occurrence. Almost any idea expressed about religion or gods in Aeschylus can be paralleled by a line from a play or fragment of

Euripides. The significant differences are those which occur frequently and appear to be emphasized.[1] Against such differences the isolated counterexample cannot be given much weight. Hence in the following pages I stress persistent similarities and differences. The details have been assembled in chapters 2–5. Here I draw from them the general outlines.

The Olympian gods of tragedy are often abstracted from cult limitations of time, place, and function. Whereas Athenians worshiped at different altars, with different rites, on different occasions, and for different purposes Zeus Boulaios ("Of the Boule"), Zeus Phratrios ("Of the Phratries"), Zeus Herkeios ("Of Fences") and Zeus Ktesios ("Of the Stores") in family cult, Zeus Olympios, Zeus Soter ("Savior"), Zeus Horios ("Of Boundaries"), Zeus Teleios ("Of Marriage"), Zeus Naios of Dodona, and so forth, the tragedians, like Homer, tend to represent one generalized Zeus, the Zeus of the epic cycle who is married to Hera, rules on Mount Olympus, and wields the thunderbolt. The worship and the tragic representation of other Olympian deities are analogous to that of Zeus.[2] There are, of course, exceptions, such as the Athena and Apollo of Euripides' *Ion* and the Athena of Aeschylus' *Eumenides,* where the poets have established some ties to Athenian cult.

Once abstracted from cult these same deities may be refashioned. Aeschylus' reshaping of the Homeric Zeus is discussed at some length later in this chapter. Euripides on occasion made Olympian deities into, at least in part, representatives of psychological forces, like the Artemis and Aphrodite of the *Hippolytus* and the Dionysus of the *Bacchae.* In most plays, however, he like Sophocles follows the Homeric model of composite Panhellenic deities living as a family on Olympus and not closely tied to local cults. The Homeric deities and divine machinery are the standard in tragedy, and variations from it reflect personal or dramatic interests of the individual poets.

The tragic poets give to their characters a closer relationship to, more direct contact with, and a better knowledge of their gods than average Athenians enjoyed. Some characters, like Theseus, Heracles, Ion, and Helen, are sons or daughters of gods; others, like Cassandra, Creusa, and Io, are their lovers. In Sophocles' *Ajax* Odysseus and Ajax are intimates with Athena in the Homeric model of the *Iliad* and *Odyssey*.[3] Other tragic figures—men such as Orestes, Hippolytus, and Pentheus—for good or ill, also have close encounters with gods. Numerous other characters and choruses see their gods, usually as *dei ex machina,* and learn directly from them their wishes, plans, and purposes.[4] Real-life Athenians when awake never saw, or even claimed to have seen, Olympian gods.[5] Oracles and seers in tragedy also explain, much more so than their counterparts in real life, the ways and purposes of the gods,[6] so that tragic characters are, by and large, much better informed of what the gods do and why they do it. This degree of intimacy with and knowledge about the gods is thus, compared to popular religion, a tragic convention. It is also a Greek literary convention, found in nearly identical form as early as the *Iliad* and *Odyssey.* Like Homer the tragic poets adopt a pose of omniscience and know which god intervened in each situation and why.[7] Homer, as narrator, may provide this information himself, but tragic poets convey it, if they wish, through seers or the gods themselves. As a result the religion of tragedy has, compared to that of everyday life, far greater specificity. The audience and often the characters know in detail what the gods do and how and why they do it. This is the order that poets, from their superdivine, omniscient posture, can impose on situations which would have been, to ordinary people, often bewildering and inexplicable.

The gods of tragedy provide many of the benefits that their real life counterparts did. Individual gods have special areas of expertise and activity, but, taken together, individual gods and "the gods" as a collective give fertility and health of human beings and their crops and animals. They offer protection against the greatest hazards of Greek life: disease, sea travel, and war. To individuals and states they give economic prosperity. These three major areas of divine intervention—fertility and health, protection, and prosperity—are found throughout Greek tragedy and life. In these matters there are differences between life and tragedy, but they are of detail, not substance.[8]

The gods of tragedy, more than those of life, are blamed for evils.[9] This goes beyond Aphrodite's causing the deaths of Phaedra and Hippolytus or Dionysus' causing that of Pentheus. Throughout tragedy many misfortunes of life, including death, which in popular religion are attributed to fate, fortune, or a *daimon,* are attributed to the collective of the gods. As a result tragic characters—themselves, of course, often in perilous situations—are fearful of what the gods may bring and distrustful of the beneficence of their gods. This fear arises in part because the poets make their characters more aware than ordinary people of the plans and purposes of the gods. But in general terms, the gods of literature are more hostile, less beneficent, and less forgiving than those of popular religion. The sins of tragedy are more heinous than those commonly committed in everyday life, and the gods are more harsh and more feared. In the distilled world of Greek tragedy sins, punishments, and divine emotions are all more potent.

In both life and tragedy the gods were concerned with oaths taken in their name and with the rights of parents, *xenoi,* those having asylum,[10] and the dead. It was the consensus of popular belief that violators in these matters were deserving of punishment. In all the plays of Aeschylus, Sophocles, and Euripides all such violators suffer, and it seems indisputable that the tragedians were thus lending support to these core popular beliefs about piety and impiety.[11] In both tragedy and life those who planned but did not accomplish the violation escaped punishment. What mattered was the action, not the frame of mind.[12]

Tragedy, as distinct from life, frequently presents individuals who directly and frontally assault the τιμή of a god: the *theomachoi.*[13] Although not unknown to epic,[14] the human *theomachos* is particularly a topic of tragedy. Because the *theomachos* overvalues his own prowess, whether of mind or body, he demeans the τιμή (as function, honor, and cult) of the god. Unlike more ordinary sinners in life and tragedy, he may suffer for his boasts alone. His punishment, when it comes, as it always does, is severe. Every *theomachos* dies, and by his defeat and death the τιμή of the god is reasserted.

Because impiety was a form of injustice, the gods who in life and tragedy punish sinners also punish certain forms of injustice. But a wide area of injustice lay outside the realm of impiety, and both tragedy and popular religion, though by different means, attempted to involve their gods in these. Through promissory oaths by new citizens, by jurors, by public officials, by signatories to treaties, and by parties to a contract, and through assertory oaths in legal proceedings, the Athenians attempted to motivate divine interest in and concern for profane matters which otherwise were alien to the gods' functions.[15] The tragedians, as we have seen, rarely use oaths for such purposes and tend rather to make their gods personally interested in justice.[16] That the gods, Zeus in particular, be just is a preoccupation of Aeschylus', but we find also in Sophocles and Euripides characters who assert that the gods are, or should be, just. They invoke the gods to help them in their just causes and often complain bitterly when the gods fail them. In such cases the justice attributed to the gods or demanded of them is identical or similar to that expected in dealings between men.

There is little evidence that the personal justice or morality of the gods was a concern in popular religion. In literature they are first unmistakably an issue in the *Odyssey* and become a focus of attention in Hesiod and Xenophanes.[17] It was from this literary and theological tradition, not from cult, that they found their way into tragedy. After the fifth century they were developed in the philosophical tradition, especially by Plato. Throughout the classical period the justice and morality of the gods remained matters for theological and philosophical speculation, not for cult and worship.

The heroes of tragedy and cult also differ.[18] Some heroes who received cult in real Athenian life, especially Theseus and the eponyms of the ten tribes, were regarded as beneficent, as providing valuable services to their fellow Athenians, and apparently had nothing fearful about their sanctuaries or rituals. But most heroes of tragedy, such as Oedipus and Eurystheus, are hostile, malignant forces who must be appeased and whose cult is pervaded by fear. Their hostility to their own people, left behind in other countries, may benefit the Athenians, but that benefit is primarily a by-product. Here tragedy may reflect the character of older hero cults, whereas the beneficent heroes may be largely the result of politically motivated innovations of the sixth and fifth centuries. In any case the heroes of tragedy are much grimmer and more fearful than those of real life. It is also noteworthy that in tragedy the funeral cults of deceased kings, like Agamemnon and Darius, are presented in the guise of hero cult. As such the dead kings could be invoked and expected to aid the living, beleaguered members of their families.

As their audiences did, tragic characters consult oracles on colonization, plague, infertility of land and humans, marriage, disease, and identity of parents. They question seers about war, voyages, health, omens, dreams, and religious needs. But the conventions of divination in tragedy contribute to a religious atmosphere significantly different from that of practised religion. The responses tragic characters receive, whether they believe them or not, are virtually all accurate and true.[19] This is a convention also found in Homer, a convention of "high" literature but not of comedy.[20] Real oracles were mostly directed to changes in religious cult or to the success of foreign enterprises such as colonization, and real seers tested for their clients the likely success of private and public ventures. Tragic oracles, seers, and *dei ex machina* explain the deeds, plans, and purposes of the gods and offer detailed predictions of the fortunes of individuals and families.[21] Tragic characters are thus better informed of the divine world about them, but as a result characters such as Oedipus and Orestes seem subject, to some degree, to the inevitability of the events predicted about them. Because, unlike in life, the fates predicted by tragic seers and oracles are usually bad, the characters often appear to be functioning in a world of malignant divine forces. The same can obviously be said of Hippolytus, Phaedra, Ajax, and the Trojans, whose misfortunes are all planned and directly predicted by gods themselves, speaking in the prologues.

It is another tragic convention that prophetic dreams prove true and that they are "nightmares" sent from the chthonic world.[22] Athenians of the classical period received their dreams from the Olympian gods, and most of their dreams pointed to good fortune or ways of achieving one's purpose. The oracles, seers, dreams, and predictions of gods in tragedy cast forth a dark cloud under which characters live their lives. Gloom and uncertainty are sometimes increased by riddling or misleading oracles, themselves a literary convention. By contrast, to the ordinary Athenian divination was a positive factor in daily life, a practice that clarified life and was sought out for signs of encouragement in the face of uncertainty. Thus the divination of tragedy, like its conception of the gods and heroes, was more frightening and malevolent than that found in real life.

Both tragedy and popular belief had Olympian gods withdraw at the approach of death, but the tragedians often make individual gods or "the gods"

The Tragedians and Popular Religion 209

as a group responsible for an individual's death. In popular belief death was attributed to fate, fortune, or a *daimon*. In cult, gods were not involved with death and the afterlife. But the tragedians, who introduce such literary figures as Thanatos and Hades, had available, as their dramatic purposes might require, four quite distinct concepts of the afterlife: that the dead were virtually nothing, with no consciousness and no awareness of the doings of the upper world; that the dead in Hades were alert, talkative, and enjoying activities and a society much like that of the upper world; that the ψυχή of the deceased went to the *aether*; and that in Hades sinners were punished for crimes committed while living. The Agamemnon and Darius of tragedy are *sui generis,* both probably of Aeschylus' creation, with a status between that of hero and the cognizant dead. They retain their royal status in Hades but, unlike the other social dead, can be summoned by prayers and offerings to help members of their families in the upper world.

That sinners were punished in Hades for their crimes is a particularly Aeschylean conception, one that he drew from Homer and Pindar. That at death the soul might go to the *aether* is particularly Euripidean, a concept probably taken from contemporary philosophy. The notion that the dead mill about in Hades as if at a remote resort is based, in good part, on the scene of the *Nekyia* in *Odyssey* 11, where Odysseus observes and chats with dead men and women of the past. The first-mentioned conception, that the dead are virtually nothing, at best ψυχαί lacking perception, thought, and strength, is to be found in all three dramatists and is, I have argued above, most like what ordinary Athenians expected the afterlife to be.[23] Death is not thus to be desired, except as an escape from life's miseries, but it is also not to be feared. The many suicides of Greek tragedy lament the loss of the delights of this life; they do not look to pleasures or sufferings expected in the afterlife.[24]

Piety (εὐσέβεια) was a form of justice and a product of "sound thinking." It was a reasoned attitude of "honor" towards the gods, their functions, sanctuaries, cults, and ritual. This honor resulted from a proper understanding of humans' inferiority to and dependence on the gods. Piety also included honor of parents, *xenoi,* those having asylum, oaths, and certain unwritten traditions governing human social, sexual, and religious behavior. To "dishonor" any of these was sin, folly, and injustice, and the malefactor could expect to be punished. Thus far tragedy and popular religion seem to be in agreement. In popular religion one revealed his impiety by action. In tragedy impious and blasphemous words alone are sufficient to bring retribution. In neither case do plans for impious deeds, if not executed, result in punishment.

In tragedy the gods themselves, but often through human agents, punish the impious. For Aeschylus these punishments may take place even in the afterlife. The punishments, when they come, are always severe: death, or suffering worse than death. In real life punishments for impiety were often imposed by human judicial processes, in Athens especially through criminal trials for ἀσέβεια.[25] Even so, in comparison to those for profane crimes, Athenian legal punishments for ἀσέβεια were severe: usually death or exile.

In both popular religion and tragedy the rewards of piety were success in those areas particularly under the gods' control: fertility and health of human beings and their crops and animals, protection in sea travel and war, and prosperity for individuals and states. Hence the consternation and crisis of faith which Athenians experienced when they saw the pious and impious perishing equally in the plague of 430–426 and when the exceptionally pious general Nicias failed, suffered, and died at Syracuse.[26] Life is not as simple as literature. In tragedy the impious eventually suffer, the pious are eventually rewarded. In life the pious occasionally suffered in those areas where they were confident of divine assistance.

Aeschylus

Zeus is the most distinctive feature of religion in Aeschylus' plays. My interest here is not so much Aeschylus' particular conception of Zeus and its literary, particularly Hesiodic antecedents as in how his "Diocentrism" led him to reformulate and distort certain popular beliefs.[27] Fundamental is his assignment to Zeus of functions and responsibilities which, in popular religion, were not his or were not solely his. Simply put, Aeschylus' Zeus grew in stature at the expense of other deities or of different religious concepts. We have seen how, in the *Suppliants,* Aeschylus shifted responsibility for protecting the Danaids to Zeus and from the gods in whose sanctuary they took asylum.[28] For this purpose he employed a Zeus Hikesios—a literary figure, not a deity of Athenian cult—and placed under his protection suppliants throughout the world, regardless of place.[29] Elsewhere in tragedy and in life it was the proprietor (god or hero) of the sanctuary, very much tied to one place, who protected suppliants in that sanctuary and who punished violators.

Xenoi, as guests/hosts, were owed τιμή, and violation of their rights was an impiety. Gods would punish those who dishonored *xenoi*, but in popular religion no particular god's own τιμή was damaged by that impiety. The impiety here was rather a violation of traditional practices.[30] But in the *Agamemnon*, as we have seen, Aeschylus assigns concern for *xenoi* to his Zeus, and this Zeus Xenios, again not a deity of Athenian state cult but of literature, punishes men like Paris who maltreat *xenoi*.[31] Aeschylus has thus gathered two major functions which either were not under another god's authority or were split among various gods and has added them to Zeus' portfolio.[32] In conceptual terms sins against *xenoi* and suppliants are thus much simplified. They become sins against one god, Zeus, and he punishes them. Because he is freed from restrictions of time, place, and circumstances, this Zeus, in these functions, becomes universal.

Aeschylus' Zeus also makes occasional forays into the domain of other deities. In the *Agamemnon* (970–971, 1015–1017) and the *Suppliants* (688–690) his Zeus, beyond simply providing rain and good weather, impinges upon the province of agricultural deities by affecting the produce of the land and "mother earth."[33] For the nether realm Aeschylus proposes an infernal Zeus, identical to Hades, in a specifically Aeschylean role of punishing sinners in the afterlife.[34]

The inspiration for Aeschylus' Zeus came not from cult but from literature. We should not think of Aeschylus as devoted to some exotic, proto-monotheistic cult of Zeus which attributed new functions to the father of the gods. There was, so far as I know, no such cult of Zeus in Athens or elsewhere in the classical period or later. Aeschylus did not, and would not have expected his contemporaries to think that he did, "worship" in ways characteristic of practised Greek religion the Zeus he created in his poetry. Aeschylus was not a prophet of a new Zeus religion. He was not, I think, a religious teacher or reformer.

The genesis of the Aeschylean Zeus is the poet's concern with justice in its many forms, and since in the literary tradition before him, particularly in Hesiod, Zeus had been made *the* protector and dispenser of justice, Aeschylus develops and enriches this association, but he does so for the sake of justice, not for the benefit of Zeus. Under the authority of his Zeus he unites fragmented divine responsibility for suppliants, *xenoi*, oaths, and religious traditions, which, as we have seen, were all matters of justice as well as of piety.[35] He further broadens Zeus' concern by making him the father or throne-mate of Dike, justice personified.[36] He casts the aura of sanctity over his Zeus and Dike with the solemn, sacred, and traditional language of prayer, hymn, and aretology, but both his Zeus and his Dike still remain alien to Greek religious tradition, at home only in the mythological and literary traditions. The audiences of the *Oresteia* and the Danaid trilogy would not have been inspired to found a new cult of Zeus or Dike, but they certainly would have been led to think more deeply and sharply about justice in the human world. This might well have affected their behavior towards one another, but since the Aeschylean Zeus who oversees that process was so remote from cult, the impact on religious belief and practice would have been negligible. The dialogue on the relationship of Zeus and justice was begun in Homer and continuously carried on in literature and philosophy. But to judge from the sources for popular religion, it never penetrated cult and religious practice.

That Aeschylus' Zeus ranges beyond his usual cultic responsibilities, that he oversees all suppliants, all *xenoi,* and all oaths, and that he is the guarantor of justice in general is not a matter of detail, something found, as in Sophocles and Euripides, in only a few lines here and there. Of the six assuredly Aeschylean plays it permeates the *Suppliants, Agamemnon, Choephoroi,* and, in part through Zeus' daughter Athena, the *Eumenides.* In these plays Aeschylus' conception of Zeus forms and shapes the entire religious structure, and it is that which is so distinctive and so alien from popular conceptions of Zeus, deity, and religion.[37]

Aeschylus' concern for justice also led him, again with literary antecedents, to have men punished in the afterlife for the sins and injustices they committed in this life. The Erinyes describe how Orestes, as he suffers in Hades, will see others being punished, those who were impious towards a god, a *xenos,* or their parents (*Eum.* 269–272). In the *Suppliants* those who take unwilling brides and who violate asylum will suffer similar punishments (227–231, 413–416). The judge there will be another Zeus (*Suppl.* 231), great Hades (*Eum.* 273). Like many concerned with justice, both before him and after him, Aeschylus saw that not all impious and wicked people suffer in life. If there was to be unerring justice, punishments must remain for them in the afterlife. In tragedy this a uniquely Aeschylean view, and it was not shared by popular religion.

More consistently and more often than in Sophocles and Euripides Aeschylus' gods determine, or are asked to determine, the outcome of war. This too reflects Aeschylus' particular concern with divine justice. The gods gave victory to Agamemnon at Troy (*Ag.* 1335–1336) and to the Greeks at Salamis (*Pers.* 293–294, 454–455, 513–514, 905–906). Athena promises her Athenians military glory (*Eum.* 913–915), and the Thebans repeatedly pray for military victory (*Th.* passim). All the victories to which the Aeschylean gods contribute are in causes presented by the dramatist as just.[38] The Athenian people, of course, sacrificed, prayed, and took omens before battle and erected dedications after victory, but they do not seem so wholeheartedly to have credited their victories to the gods or to have assumed divine support in war because their cause was just.[39]

In the cause of justice Athena in the *Eumenides* institutes for the Athenians the Areopagus court for the trials of homicide. In doing so she establishes the jurors' oath and rules of procedure.[40] In the same play she also gives the Athenians sage political and moral advice for the welfare of their state (681–710). Elsewhere among the tragedians and in the popular tradition human laws and government are solely a human creation and primarily a human responsibility. Aeschylus' devotion to justice, which led him to adopt a universal, just Zeus, to envision punishment for sin in the afterlife, and to have the gods determine the outcome of wars, here brings a wise and just Athena into the early structuring of Athenian law and government.

Aeschylus, it appears, created the *Mischwesen* of Darius and Agamemnon, neither true heroes with public cult whose tombs and relics are sacred and who must be appeased nor ordinary, powerless dead. Capable of assisting family members who invoke them, they command considerable dramatic attention whether they actually appear (Darius) or not (Agamemnon). If there are antecedents for them in the religious tradition or the cult of the dead, they lie in the Dark or Mycenaean ages and have left no clear trace.

In the literary tradition there are only imperfect models.[41] It is best, I think, to consider them Aeschylus' creation, a new class of "hero" designed to fulfill his dramatic purposes. And apart from the spectacle, which must have been stunning, these purposes included the implementation and explication of justice. In the *Choephoroi* the dead Agamemnon is repeatedly invoked and asked to assist Orestes in his vengeance on Clytemnestra. As late in the trilogy as *Eumenides* 598 Orestes credits his father for his help. Thus Agamemnon is made by Aeschylus, in the *Choephoroi*, into an agent of justice, but his type of intervention is made obsolete, as is that of the Erinyes, by the establishment of the Areopagus court in the *Eumenides*. In the *Persae* Darius, whose ghost appears on the stage, is not an agent but an explainer of justice. He describes with wisdom and authority the injustices and sins of Xerxes and the Persians. We may thus suspect that Aeschylus devised these two unusual "heroes" to serve his cause of promoting justice. His Agamemnon, once established, was imitated, though not always with the same emphasis on justice, by Sophocles and Euripides in their plays on the Orestes theme.

In his vision of the divine world and in his reshaping of religious elements in his poetry, Aeschylus exhibits a boldness which one might compare to Milton's in *Paradise Lost*. His portrayal of the just and universal Zeus is, of course, the prime example of this. Yet even more striking, if the play is his, is the tyrannical Zeus of the *Prometheus,* whose character must have changed substantially in the lost plays of that trilogy if he is to be accommodated to the conception of Zeus we find elsewhere in Aeschylus. Less grand, but no less removed from popular beliefs, are the Erinyes/Semnai Aeschylus created for his *Eumenides*.

From minor cultic deities, the Semnai, Aeschylus created and brought into the theater not only the terrifying, blood-sucking, kin-murder-avenging Erinyes but also the beneficent, much honored, and all-blessing Eumenides.[42] I conclude here with a rather detailed description of them because they illustrate well not only Aeschylus' occasional wide divergences from popular religion in the interest of promoting justice but also some characteristic features of the transformation of popular religion into tragedy.

The Erinyes are variously described from Homer on as the embodiments of curses and of pollution, as avengers of those murdered by kin, and as agents of the justice of Zeus.[43] Although the pre-Aeschylean descriptions of them are not necessarily contradictory, a consistent picture of their functions

The Tragedians and Popular Religion 215

was clearly not established. So far as we can determine, the Erinyes were, to the Athenians, purely literary creatures. In Athens they had no sanctuaries, received no sacrifices, and performed no functions. In short, they were not worshiped by Athenians. For the Semnai we know, by report if not by exact location, three cults, some characteristic "wineless" offerings, cult officials, and the dark, chthonic atmosphere surrounding their worship.[44] But, as so often in Greek religious history, we know least about their function. Their sanctuaries were popular for asylum. The Oedipus of Sophocles' *Oedipus at Colonus* takes refuge at one, as did some real Peloponnesians at the time of King Codrus and as did Cylon's followers in the seventh century B.C.[45] Even Aristophanic characters talk of fleeing to the Semnai.[46]

But providing asylum was a secondary function of a deity. A deity existed to protect the city, provide rain, heal diseases, or make olives grow. That god's *temenos*, once established, might provide asylum.[47] Why some sanctuaries were more popular for this, we do not know. But in any case protection of asylum was a general divine function shared by many gods: it was not their *raison d'être*. The one attested function of the Athenian Semnai of the Areopagus concerned the murder court. Witnesses and principals in murder trials there swore by them, and acquitted defendants sacrificed to them.[48] They were involved, at least to the extent of being witnesses to oaths, with legal proceedings of homicide.

It was from this real but very limited role of the Semnai in the proceedings of the real Areopagus court of his time that Aeschylus created both his Erinyes and his Semnai. He expanded this real role backward to the Erinyes and forward to his new Semnai. The Erinyes derive from his attempts to imagine divine embodiments of the murderous form of "justice by vengeance" represented in the *Agamemnon* and *Choephoroi*. To create them he had available, of course, the varying descriptions in Homer and Hesiod, but he gave them a unified character and function suited to his purposes.[49] He also, with typically grand Aeschylean vision, made them represent not only the old style of justice but the "old" order of the gods against the new order of Apollo and Athena. The transformation of these Erinyes into Semnai, not previously attested and surely Aeschylus' own invention, reflects the changing state of human justice—the change from "justice through private vengeance" to "justice through law"[50]—and, concurrently, the change of vengeful deities of the old order into beneficent deities of the new style. As we have seen, the Erinyes lose their τιμή (both as function and as honor based on that function), but that τιμή is replaced by roles and honors suitable to Aeschylus' new order of things.[51]

Apart from their immediate dramatic purposes, changes in cult and deities in tragedy almost always serve as aetiologies. The cult or deity that results from the change is one held in reverence in Athens or elsewhere in the Greek world. Euripides' *Heracles* ends with the establishment of Heracles' cults in Athens in the places and form known to the audience. This is true also of the Hippolytus cult described at the end of the *Hippolytus* and of the cults of Artemis resulting from the action of *Iphigeneia among the Taurians*. The end point, the status after the change, reflects fifth-century reality.[52] In this regard the Semnai of Aeschylus' *Eumenides* are unique. These Semnai will not serve only as witnesses to oaths in murder trials or even as guarantors of asylum. They become deities who promise to Athens virtually all the benefits the Athenians hoped for from their gods: good things from the earth, sea, and sky; fertility of the earth, the herds, and people; freedom from blight, plague, untimely deaths, and civil war; wealth from mines; and husbands for the young women. They omit only success in battle, and Athena reserves that function for herself. Far from limiting themselves to their historic role, these Semnai have appropriated functions of Zeus, Hera Teleia, Demeter, Poseidon, and of virtually all the gods except Athena. These goddesses, as Athena says, have as their allotment to "manage (διέπειν) all things that concern human beings (πάντα ... τὰ κατ' ἀνθρώπους)" (930–931). Aeschylus has no less boldly created his Semnai than his Erinyes.[53]

Aeschylus' Semnai are an extreme example of what I have termed the economy of Greek tragedy in religious matters.[54] For obvious reasons poets wanted to limit the number of deities they introduced into a single play. One cannot have fifteen or twenty deities crowding the stage. Thus limited, the tragedian may assign, to the deities he does choose, roles and interests well beyond the recognized ones of cult. Here Aeschylus concludes his trilogy with the bestowal of *all* divine blessings on Athens, and as a vehicle for this beatification, however unrealistic it might be, he chose his Semnai. They thus become not merely real witnesses of oaths in the Areopagus court but the bestowers of immeasurably important gifts, all of which were, in real life, credited to a wide variety of other individual and independent gods.

But why were the Semnai chosen for this? It is, I think, because Aeschylus makes them represent the new, enlightened form of justice, the justice to be promulgated by Athena's new Areopagus court. They also reflect in the change of their τιμή (in all its senses) the magnitude of the change from old justice to new justice. The blessings they promise are to come to a *just* Athens. The Athenians will enjoy the blessing of the Semnai only so long as they keep their city "upright in justice" (992–995). There is, throughout, the warning that if the Athenians deviate from the path of justice, they may expect sufferings (927–937). The Semnai, like the Areopagus court (681–706), are to provide to Athens the "mysterious" (τὸ δεινόν) and the "fear" (δέει)[55] that keep human beings on the straight and narrow path of justice (517–525). And thus, although Aeschylus' Erinyes have literary antecedents and his Semnai have a cultic base, what alone explains the remarkable form both have in the *Oresteia* is his interest in the changing forms of justice, not in the reformation of religious beliefs and practices of his fellow citizens.

By concentrating on Aeschylus' differences from popular religion I do not mean to suggest that there is little or nothing of popular religion in his tragedies. In chapters 2–5 we encountered numerous instances of his use of popular religion, many in the form and context found in the popular sources. But unlike Sophocles and Euripides, Aeschylus had a systematic theological scheme in mind throughout, the cornerstone of which is the justice of the gods and of Zeus in particular. When we find Aeschylus remodeling beliefs or deities of practised Athenian religion, the explanation usually lies in this theodicy. Aeschylus' theological system, I have argued, is far removed from popular religion, and the study of it and of the particular character of the "religion" it generates are really subjects of literary criticism and intellectual history, not of *Religionsgeschichte*.

Sophocles

Sophocles is commonly imagined a paragon of "piety," but in his plays he often portrays men and women buffeted by what seem to many to be capricious, amoral, but nevertheless exceptionally powerful gods. The Athena of the *Ajax* and the Zeus of the *Trachiniae* have been particularly faulted for turning on or abandoning their former favorites. For some scholars this creates a paradox: how, if Sophocles was so pious, could he have represented the gods in such an unfavorable light? How could an extraordinarily pious Sophocles let Ajax, Electra, Oedipus of the *Oedipus Tyrannus*, and Heracles and Deianira function in a world in which gods, if they are not actively hostile to the heroes, provide little or no assistance or encouragement in the crises of their lives?[56] The choice has seemed to be either to reject Sophocles' claim to piety or to construct elaborate theories to show that his gods are, despite appearances, just and moral.

Let us first assess what we know of Sophocles' personal piety. His reputation for exceptional piety is a product of modern scholarship: no contemporary source praises him for it.[57] A late and often untrustworthy *Vita* of Sophocles gives some information on his religious activities, and there are anecdotes culled from assorted other sources. After the battle of Salamis in 480, for example, Sophocles, a boy of fifteen or sixteen years, naked and anointed with oil, led the chorus which sang the paean at the victory monument (*Vita* 3). He held the priesthood of Halon, who was apparently a healing hero (*Vita* 11). In the late 420s he was instrumental in the adoption of the Asclepios cult into Athens. He "gave hospitality to Asclepios" (T67[R]) and wrote a paean for him (T73a[R]). For his reception of Asclepios he himself was, perhaps, worshiped as the hero Dexion ("Receiver") (T69[R]).[58] He is also said to have established a cult of Heracles Menytes ("The Informer").[59] Sophocles seems to have been particularly drawn to hero cults, and, if these stories are not all fabrications, they may reflect his literary interest in human "heroes" and in hero cults like that of *Oedipus at Colonus*.[60] If we can trust even some of this biographical data, he was very active in some areas of public cult. We today may consider this a sign of exceptional piety. If the ancients did, they left no record of it. We have no reason to doubt Sophocles' personal piety, but we also do not find it especially commended by his contemporaries or in the ancient biographical tradition—as was, for example, that of Nicias or Xenophon.[61]

Even to expect that personal piety would carry over into a poetic representation of the gods as just, moral, and concerned with human beings is to misunderstand the realities of ancient religion and literature.[62] In popular religion the ancient believer was not, I have argued, concerned that the gods be just or moral in ways identical to those of mortals;[63] hence someone could be pious without claiming that gods were perfectly moral and just. And, secondly, the literary and mythological traditions established in the Homeric epics were so separate from practised religion that poets pious in conventional ways could, remaining within the literary tradition, call into question the behavior, justice, morality, and even the existence of the anthropomorphic gods. Comic poets could even ridicule them without risking the charge of impiety. All this was possible because the anthropomorphic gods of literature were so remote from the core beliefs of practised religion.

Sophocles thus may have been the most pious of the dramatists in his personal life, but we need not expect that either modern or ancient concepts of piety be exhibited in his representations of the mythological world of tragedy. In fact he seems the tragedian least interested, in his plays, in popular religion and the one most willing to distort it for literary purposes. Unlike Aeschylus he refashions it not to promote a consistent theological program but for a variety of literary and dramatic effects. Sophocles' primary interest is the human hero, and he uses both mythological and popular religion, in different ways in different plays, to illuminate facets of human character. Religious obstacles or challenges are only one variety among the many complications that Sophoclean heroes encounter. I find Sophocles' use of religion neither pious nor impious, but essentially opportunistic.

Sophocles' concentration of attention on the human, at the expense of the divine, is suggested by the famous "Ode to Man" in the *Antigone* (332–375). There, as we have seen, he has the chorus of Theban elders attribute to humanity alone the responsibility for many human advances which Euripides and Aeschylus credit to a divine benefactor: people sail the seas, work the land with animals, hunt birds, beasts, and fish, speak, think, build shelters, cure diseases, develop crafts, and live in ordered society.[64] Elsewhere in tragedy and in much of the philosophical tradition most or all of these are boons owed to the gods, but Sophocles makes them human accomplishments, without a word of the participation of the gods. The more Sophocles exalts humanity the less he must credit to the gods.

A number of small but unique features in Sophocles' plays suggest, if taken together, that he was less concerned than his fellow tragedians to maintain verisimilitude to popular religion. The first is a willingness to combine or remodel, in ahistorical fashion, elements of popular practice. Particularly remarkable is his use of the corpse of Ajax (*Aj.* 1168–1184). Ajax' son Eurysakes and his mother arrive to assist in Ajax' funeral, and, as Teucer, Ajax' brother, leaves the stage, he bids the boy to guard Ajax' body. But Eurysakes himself is also guarded by the body, because Teucer, by a curse, makes the corpse into a place of asylum. An asylum was always a sanctuary, a "holy place," to which a corpse, as a "polluted object," was the polar opposite.[65] To make such an unsuitable object into a place of asylum, Teucer must invest it with a supernatural sanction which it does not inherently have. Hence the curse:

> If anyone of the army should drag you (Eurysakes) by force
> from this corpse, then may he, evil as he is, be cast out
> evilly and unburied from this land, and may his whole
> family be cut down root and all, in the same way as I cut this lock of
>   my hair.
>
> (1175–1179)

Such a curse was, of course, unnecessary for protection in a true place of asylum, because the sheltering deity would, without such prompting, punish violators. Teucer's lock of hair does threefold service and may have been the link that suggested to Sophocles this unusual, not to say bizarre, combination of rituals. Hair is first and primarily the appropriate offering of relatives at a funeral,[66] and as such the audience would understand it here in the context of preparations for the funeral. Teucer, however, transforms this funerary hair-offering into a token of supplication (1173–1175), like the boughs or garlands which suppliants usually held as they crouched at an altar or cult statue. Finally, Teucer makes the gesture of the cutting of the lock, the lock which is to be both a funerary gift and a token of supplication, into an act of sympathetic magic, commonly used to reinforce curses: the violator and his family are to be destroyed "in the same way as I cut off this lock of hair" (1179).[67] This threefold use of the lock of hair creates a highly unusual blending of rituals of burial, curse, supplication, and asylum, and by this inventive combination of rites and concepts Sophocles is able to concentrate, dramatically, many of the remaining concerns of the play on one point, the corpse of Ajax.[68]

The puzzling double burial of Polyneices in the *Antigone* (245–258, 278–289, 384–436) may be another example of Sophocles' remodeling of popular ritual for dramatic purposes.[69] Many attempts have been made to understand Antigone's burial and reburial of Polyneices in terms of fifth-century funeral practices, but none has succeeded. Antigone's secret first burial of her brother, the discovery and reaction to it, the second burial, at which she is observed and arrested, and the mysterious, almost supernatural elements attending both burials have a widely recognized dramatic effect and are integral to the structure of the play. But in terms of ritual, questions arise. Was mere covering with dust sufficient to ward off pollution? Did the body need to be ritually reburied, once uncovered? What of the mysterious circumstances—no human traces, no attacks on the corpse by dogs or birds, and the dust storms accompanying the burials? No one of these can be explicated from popular practices or beliefs. The double burial remains unique and mysterious, and I think Sophocles intentionally made it so. To create his dramatic sequence he divided up the usual single ritual of burial, lament, and libations and in the whole went beyond popular practices and even literary conventions.[70] He wanted an intricate, mystery-shrouded structure which would allow him to present the situation and characters from multiple perspectives, and for that he was willing to sacrifice religious verisimilitude.

There are also instances of apparently casual, less purposeful disregard of popular religious beliefs in Sophoclean tragedy. Sophocles offers, in all of tragedy, the one character who violates an oath to no ill effect. He is a minor character, the guard in the *Antigone* (388–396), the oath is only reported, and no gods or curse are introduced.[71] This perjury is unimportant to the action of the play. It may have been introduced to add to the characterization of the guard or to emphasize the great turn of events, but it remains the one exception to an otherwise consistent treatment of oaths in tragedy. In addition Sophocles' Orestes in the *Electra* (47–48) recommends that the paedagogue deceive Clytemnestra with an oath. The recommendation is not followed,[72] but again a Sophoclean character is less concerned about the religious implications of a false oath than were his Euripidean and Aeschylean counterparts.

The contamination of quite distinct rituals in the *Ajax,* the anomalous burials in the *Antigone,* and the disregard of perjury in the *Antigone* and *Electra* may be small points, but their like is not to be found in Aeschylus and Euripides.[73] Together they suggest that Sophocles was less concerned than his fellow dramatists to represent the realities of popular religion. A similar impression, but less subject to proof, arises from the *Trachiniae.*

Sophocles in the *Trachiniae* and Euripides in the *Heracles* both treat the extreme sufferings of Heracles, and in both plays Zeus, as Heracles' father, is prominent. A comparison of their portrayals of Zeus and Heracles[74] offers further indications that Sophocles was less interested in religious verisimilitude and popular religion than, at least, his younger rival. Euripides isolates one cultic aspect of the deity, Zeus Soter ("Savior") and combines that, and that alone, with the epic Olympian Zeus. This Zeus Soter is a deity whose altar (and hence cult) on the stage itself has been established by Heracles

(*HF* 48–50; cf. 54, 521–522). The Athenian audience knew Zeus Soter as the proprietor of the Stoa of Zeus in the Agora, the deity who had "saved" their fathers from slavery in the Persian Wars. By assigning him the epithet Soter, Euripides points explicitly to a cultic function of Zeus and to his moral and, as it were, professional responsibility to "save" his son Heracles and his grandchildren.

Sophocles, rather than developing a single and unified conception of Zeus, introduces a wide range of Zeuses and then binds them together through the paternity of Heracles. We have Zeus Horkios, the Protector of Oaths (1185–1190), Zeus Sender of Lightning (436–437, 1086–1088), Zeus Kenaios, that is, of Cenaeum, a cape on the northwest tip of Euboea (237–241, 287–288, 750–754, 993–1003), and Zeus Giver of Oracles at Dodona (164–172, 1159–1172)—all expressly labeled the "father of Heracles" and thereby linked together and to the epic Zeus of Heracles' myths. Other clearly definable Zeuses in the *Trachiniae* are Zeus Agonios, that is, of the Contest (26), Zeus Oitaios, of Mount Oeta, site of Heracles' funeral pyre (200–201, 436–437, 1191–1216), and Zeus Tropaios, of Victory in Battle (303–306), and they are also surely meant, though nothing is expressly said, to be subsumed under "the father of Heracles." Of all these Zeuses four are defined primarily in terms of their functions (oaths, lightning, contests, victory in battle), two in geographical terms (of Cenaeum and Mount Oeta), and one in both regards (oracles at Dodona). The play also contains numerous references to a Homeric Zeus who lacks cultic restrictions of function and place.[75] The Zeus of Sophocles is a hybrid, an amalgam of various local cultic (Kenaios and Oitaios), functional (oaths, lightning, etc.), and mythological bits which were never found together in such a combination in practised religion. As such he is the type of deity commonly found in epic and lyric poetry, not in life. Euripides' Zeus, however, has his roots more in the cult and religion of the Athenian audience.

The Heracles of Sophocles, like his Zeus, is also primarily a literary, mythological figure. Sophocles' hero will die on the pyre on Mount Oeta in northern Greece; yet there is no clear mention of the cult myth, commonly known at the time, that on this pyre he experienced apotheosis. Sophocles must have intentionally suppressed this familiar element of the Heracles myth. But even if one should grant that some in the audience thought of the Heracles cult on Oeta as they watched the final scene of the play, that was still, to Athenians, a foreign myth, not one of their national history, and a foreign cult, not one in which they participated. In terms of myth and religion, the Heracles of the *Trachiniae,* like its Zeus, is largely Panhellenic and literary. He is, most definitely, not Athenian. Sophocles makes no effort to link Heracles, his adventures, or his cult to Athens.

Euripides, however, plants his Heracles solidly in the soil and national history of Athens. His Heracles had rescued Theseus, king of Athens, from the underworld, and Theseus comes to Thebes expressly to repay to Heracles the favor he received. Heracles becomes, like a host of other figures of tragedy, a beneficiary of Athenian willingness, even eagerness, to give help and sanctuary to people in distress. He is to reside in Athens and receive precincts of land which the Athenians have set aside for Theseus. When Heracles dies these precincts will become centers of his cult. These sanctuaries were those at which the Athenians of the fifth century regularly worshiped and celebrated festivals. The Heracles whom Euripides presents in the *Heracles* becomes their Heracles, a resident of their land. Euripides is dramatizing an aetiology of how Heracles came to be in Athens and why he is worshiped in the places he is. The Heracles of Euripides, like his Zeus, is much closer, both physically and religiously, to the Athenians than is his Sophoclean counterpart.

In contrast to Euripides Sophocles presents his Zeus and Heracles in a mostly mythological, literary, and Panhellenic context. I chose for comparison the *Trachiniae* and the *Heracles* because they involve the same deity, the same hero, and many of the same issues. I recognize that such a comparison cannot constitute "proof" of these differences between Sophocles and Euripides, in part because it would have been exceptionally difficult for Sophocles to construct an Athenian context for this Theban myth of Heracles, but even more because Euripides' side would have looked very different if we had selected some other play of his, such as the *Andromache* or *Hecuba,* for comparison. Nevertheless the comparison still has some value, because it highlights Sophocles' usual way of presenting gods and religion. We find much the same mythological, literary, and Panhellenic—certainly not Athenian and mostly not popular—approach to deities and religion in all his surviving plays, save one. Sophocles was, I think, the least interested of the three dramatists in representing dramatically the religion of his time. Just as he employed the many and heterogeneous Zeuses in the *Trachiniae* as need for them arose, so he introduced, for literary purposes, a heterogeneous mix of mythological, literary, and popular deities, beliefs, and practices into his other plays, with little concern for religious verisimilitude. His dominant concern was the individual human hero, and to that he subordinated everything, including popular religion.

The *Oedipus at Colonus* is the exception, and it shows Sophocles not only capable of but exceptionally skillful at interweaving into the mythological world of tragedy popular, fifth-century deities and cults. This he does not so much for Athens as a whole as for a small district of that country, his own deme Colonus.[76] Written near the end of his long life, set in Colonus, the play recreates, albeit in legendary times, the delights and deities and cults in which Sophocles must have found enduring pleasure and comfort.[77] The demesmen sing of the nightingales, ivy, grapevines, narcissus, crocus, olives, and river of their small district (668–719).[78] In this song and elsewhere are introduced, often with an epithet and description of function, deities who we know were worshiped in Colonus: Poseidon Hippios (of Horses) and Athena Hippia; Demeter Euchloös; Zeus Morios and Athena Moria, protectors of the sacred olives; Prometheus, giver of fire; Aphrodite and the Muses; and Colonus, the hero who gave his name to the deme.[79] Other deities appearing in the ode were certainly worshiped in Athens, some perhaps in Colonus itself: Dionysus, and Demeter and Kore and their Eleusinian Mysteries.[80] Poseidon Hippios as giver of horses and the bit, master of the sea, and patron of the whole district, is given a prominence beyond what his role in the play would require.[81] In this play Sophocles lovingly recreates the landscape and deities and cults of his homeland. No surviving Greek tragedy, not even Aeschylus' *Eumenides,* is more deeply rooted in and more expressive of fifth-century deities and religion.

The Oedipus whose cult is established in this play praises, more than any other character in a surviving tragedy, the piety of Athens.[82] He calls Athens the most pious of all cities, a piety the city demonstrates in protecting his asylum.[83] For this, for their piety, the Athenians are to be rewarded. Oedipus' tomb will protect them against invasion from his Theban kingdom, always a real danger in both legendary and classical times. Like the *Eumenides,* Aeschylus' last surviving play, Sophocles' last play is an encomium and beatification of Athens, and for this Sophocles turned, as Aeschylus had, to practised fifth-century Athenian religion.

The *Oedipus at Colonus* is, however, very much the exception among the surviving plays of Sophocles in its presentation of religion. Elsewhere Sophocles seems, relative to Aeschylus and Euripides, less concerned with and less interested in the religion practised by his fellow citizens. However pious he may have been in his private life, in his tragedies the gods and cults are primarily in the literary, Homeric model. He certainly does not exclude elements of popular religion, as we have seen throughout the previous four chapters, nor is he incapable of developing them, as the *Oedipus at Colonus* magnificently demonstrates. But, relatively, his concentration on the human and heroic usually diminishes the role of the divine and popular.

Euripides

"But Euripidean tragedy is strange water in which to fish for examples of orthodox Greek piety." Such is Bernard Knox's colorful contribution to a distinguished scholarly tradition which sees in Euripides the critic and debunker of what it calls traditional, conventional, popular, or orthodox religion.[84] This view predominated in the nineteenth century and has found its most influential proponents in A. W. Verrall, Wilhelm Nestle, and, more recently, Gunther Zuntz.[85] Euripides' life and Aristophanes' criticisms, as we shall see below, afford this scholarly tradition an ancient springboard, but at its heart lie three elements of Euripidean tragedy itself: (1) occasional representation of Olympian gods as immoral or amoral by human standards; (2) occasional questioning of the veracity of myths; and (3) occasional introduction of recent or contemporary philosophical theory about the gods. To these must be added the modern presumption of "deep irony" pervading the plays of Euripides: the belief that the apparent meaning of words, speeches, scenes, and whole plays is undercut by contrasting imagery and ritual, by inconsistencies of word or action, by allusions to other mythical versions or philosophical theories, and by other such devices.

I have explained in chapter 1 why I reject, for purposes of understanding popular religion, this ironizing approach, which even its proponents recognize would have been intelligible to only a few among the audience.[86] The other three elements are certainly to be found in Euripidean tragedy but have little relevance to the religious beliefs of the audience of the plays. In the first instance, Euripides does present deities—such as Athena and Poseidon in the *Troades,* Aphrodite in the *Hippolytus,* and Dionysus in the *Bacchae*—who are cruel and perhaps unjust or immoral by human standards. But there is no evidence to prove that fifth-century Greeks worshiped such gods as these or expected the gods they did worship to be perfectly moral or just by these standards. The major concerns of practised religion in the most general terms were that the gods existed, that they had some concern for humans, and that some reciprocity existed between humans and gods.[87] The morality and justice of the gods was a concern of literature and philosophy, not of cult. Hence criticisms of the gods in this regard did not affect cult and worship. As for the second element, Euripides does have his characters question the truth of myths such as the judgment of Paris (*Tr.* 971–982), the birth of Helen (*Hel.* 17–21), the feast of Tantalus (*IT* 386–391), and the adulteries of the gods (*HF* 1341–1346). But these are myths which, at least by the fifth century, were literary and divorced from cult. He raises no such questions about aetiological myths for practised Athenian cults. And, third, Euripides does occasionally introduce contemporary philosophical theories, but these need not be viewed as attacks on the cults and religious beliefs and practices of Athenian citizens.[88] Theological speculation, of more interest to some than others, is a regular feature of Greek literature. There is no evidence that such speculation penetrated worship or religious beliefs in classical Athens. To think that poets assumed or hoped that their views would change cult is probably to misunderstand both Greek literature and Greek religion.

The claim that Euripides is a critic of traditional, conventional, popular, or orthodox religion rests on the assumptions that in this "religion" the gods worshiped in life were identical or very similar to the gods portrayed in poetry;[89] that the gods were, as Hesiod, Pindar, and Aeschylus presented them, themselves moral and just by human standards and were, on their own initiative, enforcers of morality and justice in human society; and that the myths of Homer and the epic cycle were taken to be literally true. But the evidence from cult and the prose sources give no indication that any of these propositions is tenable. As we change our conception of what was the traditional, conventional, popular, and orthodox religion in the classical period, we will have to reassess Euripides' relationship to it.

In the preceding four chapters we fished extensively in Euripidean waters and, even without the angler's usual exaggeration, can claim to have caught many examples of orthodox Greek piety. An Athenian's major concerns in popular religion were fertility, of self, of family, and of crops and animals; health and security in times of danger; and prosperity, especially economic, for self and country. In chapter 2 we saw that Euripidean gods, no less than those of Aeschylus and Sophocles, provide these services to humans. When they do not, Euripides offers through his choruses and characters explanations in terms of sin and the resulting punishment. The individual who violates the τιμή of a god (or of the gods) loses divine assistance in just these areas. The punishment for sin may often seem exceptionally severe, but so it was in popular cult. For example, under "old laws" an Athenian could be fined heavily by religious and civil authorities for stealing wood from a sanctuary, whereas a similar crime in a profane setting would be counted only a minor offense.[90]

Piety in popular religion consisted of belief in and reverence for the gods of the city, maintenance of oaths, respect for the rights of asylum and hospitality, observance of tradition and law in cult sacrifices and tendance of the dead, loyalty to country, and proper care of living parents.[91] In Euripides virtually *all* violators in these matters are punished. In chapter 3 we found that all Euripidean characters who commit perjury, who maltreat *xenoi* or those having asylum, who are traitors, or who neglect or violate the rites of the dead eventually suffer. The punishment may arise for other reasons as well, and the human agent of the punishment may be impious too; but in the end *all* violators of conventional, orthodox piety suffer. Conversely those who show exceptional piety in these areas, such as Admetus in the *Alcestis* and Theseus and Demophon in the *Heraclidae* and *Suppliants,* are rewarded. The virtually uniform punishment of sinners and reward of the pious are alone sufficient to belie the notion that Euripides systematically criticizes and debunks the religious beliefs and practices of his audience. They rather point to the conclusion that he is supporting conventional religious beliefs, once these "conventional religious beliefs" are properly understood.

The fundamental error, I have argued, in taking Euripides to be a critic and mocker of traditional religion is mistaking the myths and anthropomorphic gods of literature for the beliefs and deities of practised religion. The view of Euripides as critic of religion is also thought to find support in the testimonia about his life and in the attacks against him by the comic poet Aristophanes, his contemporary. Euripides' biographical tradition, drawing heavily from Old Comedy, is generally unflattering. According to it he had moles, sties in his eyes, and bad breath, was misanthropic and unpleasant to talk to, and hated laughter and women.[92] Given its prejudice, we might expect to find in this tradition some ugly incidents illustrating his alleged impiety. But, to the contrary, we are told that he served as torchbearer in the rites of Apollo on Cape Zoster (*Vita* 17–18) and as winepourer for the dances at rites for Apollo Delios in Athens (Ath. 10.424E–F, citing Theophrastus).

Once, reportedly, Euripides was formally charged with impiety by the demagogue Cleon (Satyrus, frag. 39, col. x = *P.Oxy.* ix, 1176). We know nothing more of this charge and can only speculate on its basis.[93] Aristotle reports a second attack, in his description of methods for countering slander (*Rh.* 1416a28–35). It seems that in a trial involving liturgies and property, a certain Hygiainon accused Euripides of impiety on the basis that he had promoted perjury when, in the *Hippolytus,* he had Hippolytus claim, "My tongue has sworn the oath, my mind has not" (612). I have twice discussed this line, showing both that it is unfairly torn from context for criticism and that Hippolytus eventually exhibits, in the most difficult circumstances, exceptional piety in maintaining just this oath.[94] The court case, moreover, was not expressly for impiety but concerned providing expensive financial services for the state and the value of the principals' property. In this procedure (*antidosis*) the principals exchanged oaths,[95] and it was no doubt in this regard that Hygiainon attacked Euripides. Aristotle presents it as "slander," not as itself a criminal charge. Euripides responded that it was a matter for the theater, not the law court to decide, and we should remember that in the festival at which he produced the *Hippolytus* Euripides won one of the four first prizes he was to receive in his lifetime.[96] The audience must not have found line 612 as offensive in context as Hygiainon found it in isolation. We may surmise that ultimately Cleon's charge was rejected, for there is no evidence that Euripides was punished, and that Hygiainon's accusation probably failed, for Aristotle cites Euripides' response as a model of counterattack against slander.

Hygiainon's recourse to *Hippolytus* 612 serves to introduce Aristophanes' and modern critics' attacks on Euripides' personal piety. The comic poet alludes to *Hippolytus* 612 three times and no doubt gave it the notoriety upon which Hygiainon seized.[97] In one other instance, in Aristophanes' *Thesmophoriazusae* of 411, a widow who has made a "half-bad" living for herself and her five children by weaving garlands used for festivals and sacrifices complains that Euripides has ruined her business:

He, writing his tragedies,
has persuaded men that gods do not exist.

(450–451)

The Athenians, made atheists by Euripides, have no need for the widow's garlands. These two Aristophanic criticisms of religious aspects of Euripides' plays, although the one (on *Hipp.* 612) is unfair and the other isolated, cannot be ignored. The charge of promoting perjury cuts to the heart of popular piety, and the gods mentioned in the *Thesmophoriazusae* are those of cult, not myth. But there is scarcely anything in Euripides' complete plays to justify the widow's charge,[98] and in fact some modern scholars see Euripides as asserting the power and hence existence, if not the morality and justice, of the gods.[99] Without assuming a very deep irony one can hardly think that Euripides meant his audience to imagine that the Athena of the *Troades,* the Aphrodite and Artemis of the *Hippolytus,* and the Dionysus of the *Bacchae* do not, in the tragedies to which they are central, exist. There is likewise no reason to think that he is casting doubt on the Athenian cults of Artemis and Heracles with which he concludes *Iphigeneia among the Taurians* and the *Heracles.*

Support for the widow's claim, like support for modern scholars' attribution of atheism to Euripides, is usually drawn from the fragments.[100] We have seen how misleading this can be in the case of *Hippolytus* 612, and in chapter 1, I pointed out the insurmountable problems in using the fragments of lost tragedies for such purposes. Euripides, somewhat more often than Aeschylus and Sophocles, has characters make blasphemous or impious statements, and from them such fragments have been culled. But in the complete plays, the speakers of such thoughts, when they violate the canons of popular piety, invariably suffer.

The sum of ancient evidence for Euripides' personal impiety comes to little: a charge by Cleon, of which we know nothing; three Aristophanic allusions and one courtroom reference to *Hippolytus* 612; and, last and perhaps alone significant, the widow's complaint in Aristophanes' *Thesmophoriazusae.*[101] Her charge, we must remember, is but a part of a sustained comic assault by women on the "woman-hater" Euripides and, if we are to accept it as historically justifiable, we should do the same for all the attacks on Socrates in Aristophanes' *Clouds.*

Euripides seems, indeed, to have introduced more of the practised religion of his time into his plays than did his fellow tragedians. This includes numerous aetiologies for contemporary cults, maintenance of local particularism of some deities and cults, detailed descriptions of religious rituals, a popular usage of the terms *daimon* and θεός, description of sin and punishment in terms consistent with those of popular religion, and, finally, rewards for conventional piety, especially when Athenians are involved.

Euripidean *dei ex machina* close *Iphigeneia among the Taurians* with a description of the future cults of Artemis at Brauron and Halae in Attica, the *Erechtheus* with the cults of the Erechtheum, the *Hippolytus* with the cult of the hero in nearby Troezen, the *Helen* with Helen's cult as protector of sailors, the *Antiope* with the cults of Dirce, Amphion, and Zethus at Thebes, the *Suppliants* with the cult of heroes who fought and died at Thebes, and the *Andromache* with the cults of Neoptolemus and Achilles.[102] Similarly the future cults of Heracles, those practised by fifth-century Athenians, are explained in the *Heracles,* as is the Corinthian cult of Medea's children in the *Medea*.[103] In a sense the *Bacchae* is aetiological, explaining not only why Dionysus is worshiped in Thebes but also characteristic features of his ritual and myth. Added to these aetiologies which stand out by emphasis or position within a play are numerous lesser ones: the cult of Eurystheus in the *Heraclidae* (1026–1044), the Athenian Arrephoria in the *Ion* (15–26, 267–273), the rituals of the Choes festival in *Iphigeneia among the Taurians* (947–960), and the founding of the Spartan Hyacinthia in the *Helen* (1465–1475).[104]

These aetiologies, especially the major ones assigned to *dei ex machina*, have proved an embarrassment to scholars who see in Euripides a critic of the religion of his time. They wonder that Euripides is "addicted to such accounts of the legendary origins ($αἴτια$) of contemporary things" or consider such aetiologies as "'bonuses' appended more or less gratuitously to the end of the play" or as sops offered to the unsophisticated among the audience.[105] Some draw, somewhat surprisingly, the seemingly more obvious conclusion: "[Euripides'] fondness for tying his story on to a particular cult at the end of the play surely implies that he perceived some value in traditional religion."[106] I would go further. Although such aetiologies are not unknown in Aeschylus and Sophocles (as, for instance, in the *Eumenides* and the *Oedipus at Colonus*), by comparison Euripides shows far more interest than they in the backgrounds and origins of contemporary cults and religious practices.[107] There is also no evidence from the texts that these aetiologies are being introduced to be criticized or ridiculed.

Complementary to Euripides' interest in cult aetiologies is his somewhat more "realistic" depiction of religion. The representation of the gods in Euripides' plays generally is, like that of Aeschylus, Sophocles, and most Greek poets, Homeric,[108] but Euripides characteristically varies it in the direction of practised religion. Cult aetiologies are part of this, but he also occasionally depicts local varieties of cults, gives detailed descriptions of ritual, assigns divine figures the epithets and functions of real cults, and, finally, usually describes sin, punishment, and wrath of the gods in terms familiar to popular religion. Examples of such things can also be found here and there in Aeschylus and Sophocles, but they are not nearly so common or systematic. They each contribute to the greater realism of Euripides' plays, a realism that has been widely recognized from other, nonreligious elements of his tragedy.[109]

The prominence of Apollo in the Delphic *Ion* and of Athena in the *Erechtheus* are only to be expected from any dramatist,[110] but in the *Medea* Euripides gives, beyond what the myth might require, particular attention to Helios and Aphrodite, and it is hardly coincidental that these two deities are central only to the cult of Corinth, the setting of the play. In the *Phoenissae* Eteocles, defending the homeland, appeals to the specifically Theban Athena of the Golden Shield. His brother Polyneices, a Theban too but now living in Argos, turns to Hera, the patroness of the Argolid (*Ph.* 1359–1376).[111] When Euripides set his plays away from the familiar soil of Athens and Greece, he allowed himself greater inventiveness in religious matters. The cult of Artemis in *Iphigeneia among the Taurians,* located at the far shore of the Black Sea, and that of Aether in the Egypt of the *Helen* are described in detail but are very un-Greek in conception. These we shall include among the innovations of Euripides, discussed below.

Earlier in this chapter I described at length how Euripides, in contrast to Sophocles in the *Trachiniae,* created in the *Heracles* a Zeus who had some ties, as Zeus Soter, to Athenian cult. So too the Dionysus of the *Bacchae* is given not only mythological but cultic ties to specifically Theban sacred places and rituals. Such links, established through epithets and references to sacred places and through aetiologies, though not present in all Euripidean plays, are still much more frequent there than in the works of Sophocles and Aeschylus.

Much of what is usually considered the best fifth-century evidence for burial rites, sacrificial ritual, and rites of individual cults is drawn from the plays of Euripides. In chapter 4 we observed how much of the funerary cult is described in the *Alcestis* and *Troades,* whereas such descriptions in Aeschylus seem at variance with fifth-century beliefs.[112] The sacrificial scene in Euripides' *Electra* 781–843 is the fullest fifth-century account we have of this ritual. The *Ion* (passim, esp. 82–237, 414–420) gives us our most vivid fifth-century picture of Apollo's cult at Delphi. And most of what we think we know of the Theban cult of Dionysus comes from the *Bacchae*. These and other brief descriptions of ritual are integral to the plays, not merely tacked on pedantically, and they reveal Euripides' interest in using ritual, ritual often practised by the audience, as a dramatic device.[113] Also more common than in other tragedians are Euripides' references to a god or the collective of the gods as *daimon* or θεός τις, another characteristic of popular religion.[114]

Euripides also, more than his fellow tragedians, describes the complex of sin, wrath of the gods, and punishment in terms common to popular religion. An individual, usually through an act, violates the τιμή (in all its meanings) of a god. Because of this the god becomes angry and punishes the individual. Whether or not one accepts my evaluations of the characters and gods in the *Hippolytus, Bacchae,* and *Troades* (see chapter 4), the pattern of violated τιμή, wrathful god, and punishment of the human is unmistakable. And it was in these terms that popular religion conceived of the nexus of sin and punishment (chapter 5). Euripides often introduces secular motives in addition to religious ones for the punishment of immoral sinners,[115] but that too is realistic and does not undermine these conclusions. The relative emphasis on the religious and secular varies from play to play, but the religious element is always present to some degree. The net effect is that religious thought in Euripidean plays is much closer to popular thought than is, for example, Aeschylus' framework of Ate, Hybris, and Nemesis. Aeschylus' formulation is literary; Euripides', though certainly not completely popular, lies closer in that direction. It may be partially Euripides' proximity to popular belief, not his remoteness from it, that, at least in Aristophanes, generated such a strong reaction.

As a final consideration in stressing Euripides' support of popular religion we may note that in the *Suppliants* and *Heraclidae* piety and its rewards in conventional forms, such as securing burial rites and protecting suppliants, are central. Some scholars see in these "political plays" a temporary lapse in the Euripidean spirit, a failure of nerve.[116] Some admit that Euripides is placing conventional moral law and national traditions into a favorable light but deny religious background to them.[117] Or else the plays are reinterpreted through deep irony.[118] These approaches are, I think, mistaken. In terms of religion two points are salient for these plays: they are set in Athens and they concern acts of piety, not the anthropomorphic gods of mythology. Throughout tragedy Athens is presented as a model of piety.[119] No Athenian commits the horrible impieties of tragedy. Athens is rather where impieties from elsewhere in the world are resolved, whether the perpetrators be Argive, Theban, or barbarian. One could call it a "convention" that Athens was praised for piety in tragedy, but that is probably to misrepresent what a tragic convention is. Rather, neither Aeschylus nor Sophocles, nor Euripides, chose to portray Athens and Athenians as impious. Athenian tragedians, writing plays set in Athens for an Athenian audience, made their homeland and their ancestors pious. It was for Aristophanes and his fellow practitioners of Old Comedy to reveal the follies of the Athenians in their theater.

In these two political plays the Olympian gods have minor roles, and since most of the "religious" criticism that scholars perceive in Euripides is directed against anthropomorphic gods, there is little for them in these plays. In the *Heraclidae* and *Suppliants* Euripides, as he always does, has rewards for characters pious in observing burial rites, maintaining oaths, and protecting asylum. Therefore, with no problematic Homeric gods present but with pious deeds performed and rewarded, these two plays appear "pro-religious." So they are, but they differ little from other Euripidean plays in their respect for the tenets of popular piety.

To stress the support for popular religion in Euripides' plays is not, however, to claim that this aspect alone of "religion" is to be found there. In terms of literary and mythological religion some deities, such as Athena and Poseidon in the *Troades*, are largely Homeric in form, manner, and concerns. The Aphrodite and Artemis of the *Hippolytus* and the Dionysus of the *Bacchae*, while not merely psychological forces, are certainly more developed along these lines than they were in cult or had been in previous Greek literature.

Another characteristic feature of the Euripidean treatment of deity and belief is the occasional introduction of current philosophical theories.[120] Various philosophical ideas appear in individual plays, but unlike the developed theology of Aeschylus they do not permeate the corpus of Euripides' work.[121] Nor are they mere gratuitous digressions; in the play in which each occurs, it has significance for the meaning of the whole. In the *Heracles* Heracles rejects Theseus' somewhat tentative claim ("If the stories of the poets are not false," 1314–1319) that the gods practise adultery, enchain even their fathers to gain tyrannical rule, and, more generally, "sin." Heracles proposes a conception of deity which goes far beyond traditional mythological and popular ideas:

> I do not think the gods enjoy illicit love affairs.
> I have never thought it right nor will I ever believe
> that they tie up one another or that one god is master of another.
> For god, if he properly is a god, lacks nothing.
> These are the miserable tales of poets.
>
> (1341–1346)

The philosophical tradition from which these statements derive had begun nearly a century before Euripides, with Xenophanes of Colophon, who refused to attribute such moral failings to the gods.[122]

In the *Bacchae* Euripides has Teiresias attempt to explain the myth and importance of Dionysus by both scholarly etymology and current philosophical theory. Dionysus was believed to have been born from Zeus' thigh (μηρός) because once Zeus had created a Dionysus image as a hostage (ὅμηρος) to be given to Hera (286–297). Teiresias seems to be borrowing from the philosopher Prodicus in having Demeter represent the "dry" of the world and Dionysus the "wet" wine, and in both being thought gods for their benefactions (274–285).[123] Hence even someone moved only by philosophical theory could find cause to render τιμή to this new god. In the *Troades* much-suffering Hecuba finally invokes a Zeus who may be Air, or the Necessity of Nature, or the Reason of Mankind, a Zeus who "guides all mortal things according to justice" (884–888). The origin of such a Zeus lies in philosophy, and in Hecuba's invocation scholars have detected ideas of Anaximenes, Diogenes of Apollonia, Heraclitus, Anaxagoras,[124] and all those, beginning with Hesiod, who assigned justice to Zeus.[125]

These and similar examples show Euripides' willingness to introduce contemporary philosophical and theological theory into his plays.[126] Such allusions are, however, scattered and determined by the particular needs of the play at hand. They form no systematic whole, and Euripides' apparent interest in philosophy does not grant us license to read philosophical theories into the many plays where the text offers no warrant for it. Euripides' particular innovation in this regard may be his eclectic use of highly specific philosophical theory for dramatic purposes. Aeschylus was no less a philosopher, but he followed one consistent theology well-established in the previous literary tradition.

Euripides' comparatively high respect for the non-Greek, "barbarian" world and for practised religion may also explain another characteristic: his creation, for a particular play, of a realistic but essentially non-Greek religious milieu. For the *Helen,* set in Egypt, he created a religion centered on a divine Aether (see above, chapter 3). Although Aether as a deity is a philosophic conception,[127] Euripides brings the religion alive by giving it its own devotee, rites, and eschatology. He makes this imaginary religion realistic by introducing rituals and terminology which, though not identical to Greek popular religion, were sufficiently similar to allow the audience to recognize it as a religion. Likewise, in *Iphigeneia among the Taurians,* the cult of the Taurian Artemis, at the far edge of the Black Sea and involving human sacrifice, is not Greek but has substance and definition because it is Greek-like. Here we may compare Aeschylus. For the existing cult of the Semnai he imagined the Erinyes as predecessors. But his Erinyes had no cult, no worship, and one can hardly speak of them as religious figures. By contrast Euripides gives to his imaginary predecessor of the Artemis cults in Attica the seemingly real cult of the Taurian Artemis. But it is "seemingly real" only because Euripides was attentive to practised religion and gave necessary elements of that to his imaginary cult.

And, finally, not least among his innovations is Euripides' treatment of myths concerning the gods. Unlike Aeschylus, who refashioned myths to reveal the ultimate justice of the gods and of Zeus in particular, and unlike Sophocles, who employed myths to highlight and challenge human heroes, Euripides seems often to have let the mythological tales run their course in traditional form and then drawn the conclusions about mortals and gods that such tales imply. If one accepts as true the tales of Heracles in the *Heracles,* of Aphrodite and Artemis in the *Hippolytus,* of Dionysus in the *Bacchae,* and of Athena and Poseidon in the *Troades,* one can hardly credit these deities with the same ethics, morality, justice, wisdom, and *sophrosyne* one admires in human beings.[128] Rather than reshape the myths as Hesiod, Aeschylus, and Pindar did, Euripides either let them stand or chose versions which cast these problems into a bright light. As a result, in these plays and others rather harsh criticisms of *mythological* gods are indeed expressed or implied. It is from this approach to myth, if not idiosyncratic at least most developed among the tragedians, that scholars who have equated mythology with real religion find in Euripides a critic of religion. But—to state it a final time—their equation is false. However much Euripides may lay open mythological gods to criticism, he finds no fault with, indeed he supports, the fundamental beliefs and practices of popular religion.

Exodos

I conclude with the lines with which Euripides so often closed his plays:

> Many are the forms of the divinities,
> and the gods bring to pass many things contrary to our expectations.
> That which was expected was not accomplished,
> and a god found a way to bring forth the unexpected.
> So this work turned out.[129]

In the Greek tradition there are many forms of divinities, some mythological, some philosophical, and some popular. They should not be confused. What we had expected to find we did not. Aeschylus, the most theological, is most removed from the practised religion of his time. The "pious" Sophocles shows least interest in popular religion and least attention to its details. Euripides, "the poet of the enlightenment," "the savage critic of conventional religion," "the promoter of impiety," gives to popular religion, properly understood, the strongest and most consistent support. So this work turned out.

Notes

Chapter One

1. The need for material from tragedy to complement the prose sources used in *APR* is noted in reviews by K. J. Dover, *Phoenix* 38 (1984), 197–198, and R. Parker, *CR* 35 (1985), 90–92.
2. The major and highly influential authority here was Wilhelm Nestle, whose *Euripides* and *Vom Mythos zum Logos,* both reprinted (1969 and 1975), have directed much of twentieth-century thought about religion in Euripidean tragedy.
3. See Easterling, "Anachronism in Greek Tragedy"; Bain, *Actors and Audience,* 209–210.
4. On religion versus mythology see Rose, "Theology and Mythology in Aeschylus"; Kitto, *Form and Meaning,* 182–183; Yunis, *A New Creed,* 55 n. 40.
5. On Zeus Ktesios see Nilsson, *GGR,* 1:403–406; Burkert, *GR,* 130.
6. On Athena Polias see Herington, *Athena Polias and Athena Parthenos.*
7. On the Aphrodite and Artemis of the *Hippolytus* and their relation to the deities of cult see Dodds, "Euripides the Irrationalist," 102, and below, pp. 146–147.
8. For an account of myths about the earliest Athenian history and their relation to cults, places, institutions, and national image see Parker, "Myths of Early Athens."
9. See Bruns, "Die griechischen Tragödien als religionsgeschichtliche Quelle"; Gernet and Boulanger, *Le génie grec,* 272–276; Ehnmark, *Anthropomorphism and Miracle,* 68.
10. *APR,* passim, esp. 103. To the beliefs listed should be added, from Yunis's recent study *A New Creed,* that (1) the gods exist, (2) the gods have some thought about men, and (3) there exists some (undefined) reciprocity between gods and men. These fundamental beliefs are, of course, characteristic of virtually all religions and are not distinctively Greek.
11. Nestle, *Euripides,* 51–152. For example, Nestle opens his discussion (52–53) with translations and discussions of six fragments (256[N], 1025[N], 948[N], 800[N], 946[N], 446[N]), in the course of which he merely cites passages from surviving plays.
12. For example, Zuntz (*The Political Plays,* 21) uses fragments (286[N] of the *Bellerophontes* and 795[N] of the *Philoctetes*) to counterbalance the justice of the

gods and the value of divination as portrayed in the complete *Suppliants.* Cf. Zielinski, "L'évolution religieuse d'Euripide"; Nilsson, *GGR,* 1:771–779.

13. Rose, "Theology and Mythology in Aeschylus," 7; Yunis, *A New Creed,* 94. Cf. Kovacs, *The Andromache of Euripides,* 83.

14. *APR,* 98–99.

15. See Ar. *Ran.* 98–102, 1471, *Thesm.* 275–276; Barrett on *Hipp.* 612. Euripides' opponent in a lawsuit quoted the line to show that Euripides was impious, that he urged people to "swear false oaths" (Arist. *Rh.* 1416a28–32). On Aristophanes' and other fifth-century uses of this line against Euripides see Avery, "My Tongue Swore, but My Mind Is Unsworn," 19–24.

16. As noted even by the scholia ad loc.

17. For similar difficulties in interpreting the fragments of new comedy, especially of Menander, see Hunter, *The New Comedy of Greece and Rome,* 139–151.

18. Grube, *The Drama of Euripides,* 43.

19. On historical, literary, and methodological problems with modern attempts to see pervasive irony in the plays of Euripides see Kovacs, *The Heroic Muse,* passim, esp. ix–xi, 1–10, 115–122.

20. See N. Knox, *The Word Irony,* passim, esp. 3–7.

21. Verrall, *Euripides the Rationalist,* 138. Despite the statement of disassociation with Verrall almost obligatory in every modern critical essay, Verrall's fundamental operating principle—that Euripides employed sustained, "deep" irony intelligible to only a few—remains a basis for much of modern criticism.

22. See Nestle, *Euripides,* 71-72, 74: "Der gebildete Athener" and "Der kleinere, tieferblickende Teil der Gebildeten."

23. Zuntz ("Euripides' *Helena,*" 202-204) speaks of the "plain man," a Strepsiades or Euelpides, versus "those able, with cultured sensitivity, to appreciate coherence, necessity and implication where the average spectator was merely delighted or shocked," a Socrates or young Plato; Greenwood (*Aspects of Euripidean Tragedy,* 92–120) of the "intelligentsia" versus the "simple-minded and conventional and orthodox"; Winnington-Ingram (*Euripides and Dionysus,* 6–7), of "an intelligent minority," "an Athenian of intelligence and sensibility, whose social position had allowed him to come into contact with the sophists and to hear Socrates talk." Loraux (*Tragic Ways of Killing a Woman,* viii) gives a full statement of the audience modern criticism implicitly or explicitly assumes: "I would go so far as to say that in the Athenian theater listening was, for the tragic audience, like a sensitive reading, on a par with the 'depth' of the text. In fact, if we follow Jean-Pierre Vernant and think of the member of the ancient audience as a listener with sharp hearing for whom 'the language of the text would be transparent at every level, with all its polyvalence and ambiguities,' we have to credit this all-powerful listener with an attention that, to say the least, could not have been very free-floating; credit him, too, with resources of memory such as we no longer command. He must have had an astonishing ability to compress the long business of unraveling the complexities of the signifier into the short span of a theatrical performance. A fiction, perhaps, but a necessary fiction,

Notes to Pages 8–20   239

which the reader must use when he begins to lose himself in the polysemic depth of the text and the endless quest for resonant echoes." On the pervasiveness of the assumption of such an audience in Euripidean criticism see Michelini, *Euripides and the Tragic Tradition*, 3–51.

24. Burkert, *GR*, 119–120.

25. Discussions of this point are rare, but see Roberts, *Apollo and His Oracle in the Oresteia*, 62–63.

26. For an extensive account of the theory and application of these views see Foley, *Ritual Irony*, esp. chap. 1.

27. See below, pp. 214–217.

28. Guthrie, *The Greeks and Their Gods*, 258.

Chapter Two

1. Or, in more modern terminology, "What Greek religion offered to those brought up within its field of efficacy was both a framework of explanation for human experience and a system of responses to all that is wayward, uncanny and a threat to the perception of order in that experience" (J. Gould, "On Making Sense of Greek Religion," 5).

2. See Willink on *Or.* 1366–1502 and Hall, *Inventing the Barbarian*, 124.

3. On the *magoi* see C. Clemen, "Magoi," *RE* 14 (1928), cols. 509–518 and Hall, *Inventing the Barbarian*, 194 n. 107.

4. Cf. S. *Ant*. 1218.

5. *APR*, 66–68; François, *Le polythéisme*, passim; and W. H. S. Jones, "A Note on the Vague Use of ΘΕΟΣ."

6. *APR*, 58–60.

7. Plutarch claims as his authority for this quotation (*FGrHist* 107 F9) Stesimbrotos of Thasos, a political pamphleteer and scholar of Homer. Although hostile to Pericles, Stesimbrotos is no less reliable than other ancient sources for what Pericles may have said, and in fact may be more trustworthy in that he was his contemporary and "had seen" him (T2 and Jacoby ad loc.).

8. Cf. A. *Th.* 76–77.

9. "How did an ancient Greek *know* that a divine power was at work in the world of his experience? The answer, of course, is that he didn't—outside, say, the fictional worlds of the *Iliad* and *Odyssey*. He had to guess, to wrestle with uncertainty and disagreement, both in discerning the active power of divinity at work in events and, more particularly, in determining what divinity and for what reason." (J. Gould, "On Making Sense of Greek Religion," 9). Cf. Lloyd-Jones, *The Justice of Zeus*, 64; Nilsson, *GGR*, 1:218–219.

10. Viewed in conjunction with ἱλάσκομαι, "to appease," ἵλαος implies a fear that a deity might be angry or offended. Hence the deity is asked to be "kindly" or

"propitious," a euphemistic turn to the idea, "Be appeased if we have offended you." On ἱλάσκομαι see Clay, *The Politics of Olympus*, 242 n. 119.

11. Cf. S. *Ant.* 259–275 (cf. 413–414); E. *Ba.* 714–723.

12. Neither Palaimon nor the Nereids were worshiped in Athens during the classical period. The Dioscuroi, as Anakes, were, but not necessarily as protectors at sea. Note that later in the play, when the Athenian context has been developed and safety at sea becomes a real issue (1414–1419, 1442–1445), Poseidon is the deity involved.

13. For attempts to eliminate the Nereids see Platnauer on *IT* 273.

14. Roughly similar characters in E. *Ba.* 717–723 and *Or.* 903–945 are both in the wrong. See Dodds on *Ba.* 717.

15. E.g., Nestle, *Euripides*, 96; Verrall, *Euripides the Rationalist*, 186.

16. See Powell, "Religion and the Sicilian Expedition."

17. Hdt. 1.60.3–5 and [Arist.] *Ath.Pol.* 14.4, on which see Connor, "Tribes, Festivals, and Processions," 42–47. For other sources see Sandys, *Aristotle's Constitution of Athens*, ad loc. On divine epiphanies, or the lack thereof, in classical Greek religion see Dietrich, *Tradition in Greek Religion*, 94–101. Fox (*Pagans and Christians*, 102–167) can adduce only poetic sources for epiphanies in the classical period, whereas he has abundant epigraphical and other popular sources for epiphanies in the Hellenistic and later periods. For epiphanies of heroes and the god Pan see below, pp. 30–31.

18. See Grube, *The Drama of Euripides*, 55–56.

19. Cf. *Od.* 3.218–222.

20. The guesses of the chorus of Salaminian sailors are wrong but sensible. Artemis Tauropolos was a deity worshiped on the Attic coast, in an area where in historical times Salaminioi dwelled. For Euripides' version of the foundation myth of her cult see *IT* 1446–1469. Artemis is not elsewhere in tragedy or life thought of as causing madness in men, and her link to the action here is not readily apparent. One possible, but partial and not compelling, explanation is that the *Tauro-* of Tauropolos suggested to the Athenians "bulls" and hence Ajax' attack on the cattle (Farnell, *Cults of the Greek States*, 2:449–455; Stanford on *Aj.* 172; cf. Kamerbeek on *Aj.* 172). Her later association with witchcraft (Wilamowitz, *Glaube der Hellenen*, 1:178) is not relevant here. Ajax, both as soldier and as Ajax (cf. 766–775), might well have neglected an obligatory postvictory offering, and Ares and Enyalios, very similar deities but still distinguished in Athenian cult (cf. Oath of Ephebes, Tod, *Greek Historical Inscriptions*, 2:no. 204), could be expected to punish this. Madness too, especially in military situations (A. *Th.* 343–344, 497–498; S. *Tr.* 653–654), is associated with Ares in tragedy.

21. The ἐλαφαβολίαι (178) I take to be an annual festival, but the point is open to dispute. See Stanford ad loc. Cf. *Il.* 9.533–542 for a Homeric rendering of this theme.

22. For a similar analysis of E. *Hipp.* 141–169 see J. Gould, "On Making Sense of Greek Religion," 11. For recognition of the presence of deity in scenes of *deus ex machina* see below, p. 65.

23. For discussions of *daimones* in tragedy and elsewhere see Nilsson, *GGR*, 1:216–222, 739–740; Burkert, *GR*, 179–181; Schlesier, "Daimon und Daimones bei Euripides"; Rivier "L'élément démonique," 78–79; Chapouthier, "Euripide et l'accueil du divin," 209–210; Fraenkel on A. *Ag.* 336, 1341–1342; Barrett on E. *Hipp.* 79–81, 772–775; Broadhead on A. *Pers.* 345–346; Collard on E. *Suppl.* 598b–593.

24. Cf. A. *Pers.* 628–629, *Th.* 174; S. *OC* 864; E. *Andr.* 277, 1226–1230, *IA* 975–976.

25. Fundamental to this development was Plato's designation of Eros as δαίμων μέγας ... καὶ γὰρ πᾶν τὸ δαιμόνιον μεταξύ ἐστι θεοῦ τε καὶ θνητοῦ, *Symp.* 202D–E. Cf. Pl. *Ph.* 107D. See Burkert, *GR*, 331–332.

26. E. *El.* 1233–1235, *Med.* 1391, and *Hec.* 163–164 alone among the hundreds of references to *daimones* in tragedy appear to distinguish between *daimones* and the heavenly gods. Against these cases must be set the many where *daimon* and θεός are used interchangeably, e.g., A. *Suppl.* 893–894, 921–923, *Pers.* 344–347, 513–516, 628–630; S. *El.* 1265–1270, *OT* 885–886, 912, 1378–1379, *Ph.* 446–452, frag. 646[R]; E. *Med.* 966, *Ph.* 1197–1199, *Tr.* 948–949, *Ion* 4, *Or.* 667–668, *Hel.* 1676–1679, *HF* 1242–1243, *IA* 975–976. It may be relevant here that in E. *El.* the deities in question turn out to be the Dioscuroi, mortals made divine and, on their own admission, inferior at least to Apollo (1245). Cf. E. *Hel.* 1660–1661. In any case the Dioscuroi are in succeeding lines, as Denniston notes on E. *El.* 1234, addressed as θεοί (1298, 1328, 1356). Perhaps along similar lines are to be explained the possible "daimonship" of Alcestis (*Alc.* 1000–1005) and Rhesus (*Rh.* 970–971). But these cases remain exceptional, contrary to the usual practice in tragedy, and it is wrong to treat *daimones* as "intermediates between divine and human" in fifth-century contexts as is done, e.g., by M. Robertson ("Greek Art and Religion," 170) and by Denniston on E. *El.* 1234. In view of this E. *Tr.* 56 may well be taken, despite Lee ad loc., as in apposition to 55, not as separate categories.

27. *Daimon* as good fortune: A. *Suppl.* 691–693, *Pers.* 158, 601–602, *Th.* 705–708, *Ag.* 1667; S. *El.* 999, 1305–1306, *OT* 1478–1479, *Ph.* 462–463, 1095–1100; E. *Suppl.* 463–464, 550–555, *Med.* 966, 1228–1230, *Ion* 1269–1270, *Ph.* 1197–1199, *Or.* 667–668; *Rh.* 317, 995–996. Εὐδαίμων and ἀγαθὸς δαίμων represent the positive side of the allotment of *daimones*, for which see Wilamowitz on E. *HF* 440.

Daimon as bad fortune: A. *Pers.* 345–346, 353–354, 472–473, 724–725, 845–846, 909–912, 918–921, 942–943, 1005–1007, *Th.* 705–708, 1001, *Ag.* 1174–1175, 1338–1342, *Ch.* 566; S. *El.* 916–919, 999–1000, 1156–1159, *OT* 828–829, *OC* 76, 1336–1337, 1370–1371, frags. 646[R] and 653[R]; E. *Heraclid.* 934–935, *Med.* 127–130, 671, 1228–1232, 1347–1350, *Ph.* 888, 1265–1266, *Tr.* 98–104, 204, *Hec.* 197–201, *Or.* 341–344, 394, 504, *Alc.* 561, *Hel.* 212–213, 455, 669, *HF* 884–885, 1195, *IT* 203–207, 867, *Hipp.* 241, 771, *IA* 444–445, 1136, *Cycl.* 110, frags. 37[N], 140[N], 273[N]; *Rh.* 56–58, 728, 882–889.

28. E.g., A. *Ch.* 565–566, *Ag.* 1468–1482, 1568–1573; E. *Med.* 127–130, *Ph.* 350–353.

29. *Daimon* viewed as personal: S. *Aj.* 534, *OT* 1193–1196, *Tr.* 909–911, *El.*

1156–1159; E. *Suppl.* 592–593, *Med.* 1347, *Andr.* 98–99, 973–974, *Hec.* 721–722, *Alc.* 499–500, 935–936, *IT* 201–207, *IA* 1136–1137; *Rh.* 995–996.

30. Of cities Troy suffered most. Note that the women of Troy, unlike the poet, assigned such sufferings only to "the gods," not to any specific god (E. *Tr.* 696, 775–777).

31. Euripides stresses Laius' contravention of the oracle by twice, in one line, using σπείρω, the very word Apollo had used to forbid the act (18, 22).

32. On Hades see below, pp. 26–27.

33. In *OT* 35–39 Oedipus is thought to have enjoyed divine support in his encounter with the Sphinx.

34. Teiresias views Oedipus' self-blinding as a "device of the gods" (θεῶν σόφισμα, 870–871) to create an example for the Greek world (if we accept the scholiast's interpretation of this difficult passage).

35. For the Erinyes' role elsewere as effecters of curses see *Il.* 9.454–456, 19.258–260; Hesiod *Op.* 803–804, A. *Th.* 785–791, 885–886, 1054–1056. Cf. E. Wüst, "Erinys," *RE* Suppl. 8 (1956), cols. 101–107; Burkert, *GR*, 197–198.

36. *APR*, 50.

37. A *daimon* pure and simple, as in epitaphs (e.g., *IG* II² 12974, 13087, 13102) and not as a synonym for a "god," is implicated in deaths in A. *Pers.* 918–921, *Th.* 812–813; S. *Aj.* 1214–1215, *Ant.* 832–833; E. *Suppl.* 1006–1008, *Andr.* 1182–1183, *Alc.* 384, *IT* 157–159, *Med.* 1109–1111; *Rh.* 728.

38. Apart from the idea that "it is fate for all mortals to die," fate (μοῖρα, μόρος, πεπρωμένη) is seldom treated as an independent agent of death. The least disputable examples are A. *Pers.* 915–917, *Th.* 975–977 = 986–988, *Ch.* 909–911, frag. 362[R]; S. *Ph.* 331 (but note 334–335), *Ant.* 1328–1332; E. *Hec.* 43–44. Τύχη, not as the event of death (e.g., A. *Eum.* 956–957; S. *Aj.* 1057–1059) but as a cause of death apparently independent of divine control, is to be found only in S. *OT* 263 and frag. 951[R].

39. A. *Ch.* 1006; S. *Ph.* 446–452; E. *Med.* 1207–1210, *Andr.* 1270–1272, *Hec.* 232, frag. 916[N].

40. To a *daimon*: 384, 561, 913–914, 935–936. In 1140 death is termed "Lord of the *daimones.*" To τύχη: 214, 240, 393, 695, 785, 795, 889, 1038. To Μοῖρα: 11–13, 32–34, 523.

41. Cf. 357–362.

42. To Euripides' treatment of Anangke may be compared Aeschylus' description of Thanatos himself, frag. 161[R]:

μόνος θεῶν γὰρ Θάνατος οὐ δώρων ἐρᾶ·
οὐδ' ἄν τι θύων οὐδ' ἐπισπένδων ἄνοις,
οὐδ' ἐστι βωμὸς οὐδὲ παιωνίζεται·

43. On Thanatos, whom Apollo calls "priest of the dead" (25), see Garland, *The Greek Way of Death*, 56–59.

44. A. frag. 255[R]; S. *Aj.* 854–855, *Tr.* 1040–1043, 1085, *Ph.* 797–798, *OC* 1689–1692. Cf. S. *OC* 1556–1578; E. *Hipp.* 1373, 1387–1388.

45. Pausanias (6.25.2) claims that only the people of Elis worship Hades. Garland (*The Greek Way of Death*, 53) notes the taunt in Creon's claim that Antigone (perversely) worships Hades alone of the gods (S. *Ant.* 777).

46. See 112–130, 146–147, 202–203, 357–362, 455–459, 962–990, 1075–1076. This theme, of course, makes Alcestis' eventual rescue all the more miraculous.

47. See discussion of *xenoi*, pp. 77–80 below.

48. Alcestis' return from death is unique even in tragedy, as is Heracles' successful fight against Thanatos which makes it possible. Aristophanes' hypothesis (II) to the play suggests that in fact it is not a tragedy but the fourth play in a tetralogy, the one usually called a "satyr play." But as Seaford notes (*Euripides: Cyclops*, p. 2), "having no chorus of satyrs, it cannot be called a satyr-play, although the theme, and to some extent the mood, is characteristic of the genre." It may be only in the somewhat more fantastic world of such plays that a rescue from death was possible (cf. Seaford, pp. 37–38).

49. Cf. Zeus' powerlessness over death in A. *Eum.* 647–651. In Sophocles' "Ode to Man" (*Ant.* 361–362) only death has been found to be unsolvable and inescapable by man's inventiveness. For popular views see *APR*, 50, 60.

50. See Garland, *The Greek Way of Death*, 148.

51. Cf. Artemis in E. *Hipp.* 1437–1439 and Barrett *ad loc.* Note also A. *Ag.* 1074–1079, *Th.* 857–860; E. *Suppl.* 975–976. See also *APR*, 50; Parker, *Miasma*, 32–73; and Burkert, *GR*, 201–202.

52. Heracles in the *Alcestis* fears he may suffer a similar fate (1135).

53. Lines 132–135 are rejected by Diggle. For the thought compare 146–147. We must remember the exceptional status of Alcestis, described above, when prayers (91–92, 218–225, 251) and sacrifices (132–135) made to rescue her turn out to be effective. Without her husband's close relationships with Apollo and Heracles these prayers and sacrifices would not have sufficed.

54. On *daimones* in Sophocles *OT* see T. Gould, "The Innocence of Oedipus," 378–384, 587–588; Winnington-Ingram, *Sophocles*, 151, 173–178.

55. Taken up, with strong emphasis, by Oedipus at 1311.

56. Previously in the play *daimones* had been used only once as "the gods" (34) and, perhaps not coincidentally, Oedipus had once in passing called Apollo a *daimon* (244–245).

57. Cf. 1478–1479.

58. E.g., A. *Suppl.* 24–26 (see Johansen and Whittle ad loc.), *Ag.* 516–517, and frag. 55[R]. Cf. Thuc. 2.74.2, 4.87.2; Xen. *Cyr.* 2.1.1; Lycurg. *Leoc.* 1; Ar. *Av.* 881. Only once in tragedy is a hero (Colonus) called a θεός (S. *OC* 65). See Nock, "The Cult of Heroes," 141–166 = *Essays*, 575–597; Farnell, *Greek Hero Cults*, passim. Farnell, who divides heroes largely according to their real or presumed origins, has seven categories, each of which has itself considerable variety. In their treatment of heroes and hero cults, Farnell stresses the similarities, Nock the differences. See also Habicht, *Gottmenschentum*, 200–205; B. M. W. Knox, *The Heroic Temper*, 54–59. On hero cults specifically in tragedy see Pfister, *Der Reliquienkult*, 557–572.

59. On the ten tribes and their eponymous heroes see Kron, *Die Zehn attischen Phylenheroen,* passim, esp. 13–31, 242–247; Kearns, "Change and Continuity in Religious Structures after Cleisthenes."

60. For full discussion and bibliography of the reported epiphanies of gods and heroes in historical battles of the classical and Hellenistic periods see Pritchett, *The Greek State at War,* 3:11–46; Speyer, "Die Hilfe und Epiphanie einer Gottheit, eines Heroen und eines Heiligen in der Schlacht."

61. A hero, later identified as Echetlos (or Echetlaios), also appeared to the Athenians at Marathon and later received cult (Paus. 1.15.3, 1.32.5). On his cult see Jameson, "The Hero Echetlaeus."

62. The god Pan had also appeared in the Persian Wars, near Tegea to the Athenian Philippides as he was running to Sparta to request assistance. Pan demanded and eventually received a cult in Athens (Hdt. 6.105–106). There is, however, no evidence that he personally appeared again to an awake Athenian in the classical period. Even in Menander's *Dyskolos* (407–418) Pan reportedly appears to the mother only in a dream.

63. Malkin, *Religion and Colonization,* 17–91, 189–266.

64. Farnell, *Greek Hero Cults,* 361–372.

65. Habicht, *Gottmenschentum,* passim, esp. 195–205; Price, *Rituals and Power,* 23–40, 51–52.

66. Rusten, "ΓΕΙΤΩΝ ΗΡΩΣ: Pindar's Prayer to Heracles (*N.* 7.86–101) and Greek Popular Religion." The numerous apparent heroes and heroines (Alochos, Basile, Epops, Heraclidae, Heroinae, Leucaspis, Menedeios) in the sacred calendar of the Athenian deme Erchia give some indication of how commonly and widely such figures were worshiped (G. Daux, "La grande démarche").

67. On Iatros see Wycherley, *The Stones of Athens,* 181, 193–194. For Sophocles and hero cults see below, p. 218.

68. After his arrival Asclepios may have dominated the healing business in Athens, but he did not monopolize it, as numerous votives to other deities from the fourth century B.C. and later reveal. These have been conveniently collected in van Straten, "Gifts for the Gods," 105–122.

69. Merkelbach, "Die Heroen als Geber des Guten und Bösen."

70. Cf. Austin, *Comicorum Graecorum Fragmenta,* *58; schol. to Ar. *Av.* 1490.

71. Farnell, *Greek Hero Cults,* 365–366.

72. See P. Brown, *The Cult of the Saints,* 5–8.

73. For the sources of the myth see Austin, *Nova Fragmenta Euripidea,* 22–23; Parker, "Myths of Early Athens," 202–204.

74. Mikalson, "Erechtheus and the Panathenaia."

75. On these offerings see Henrichs, "The 'Sobriety' of Oedipus," 98.

76. See below, pp. 114–115.

77. See below, pp. 114–115.

78. On Erechtheus as a god and on his fifth-century cult see Mikalson, "Erechtheus and the Panathenaia." For criticisms see N. Robertson, "The Origin of the

Panatheneia," 233–238. For Erechtheus in Athenian myth, cult, and art see Kron, *Die Zehn attischen Phylenheroen,* 32–83; Parker, "Myths of Early Athens," 193–204.

79. On Heracles, Asclepios, and the Dioscuroi see Burkert, *GR,* 208–215.

80. On the nature of *heortai* see Mikalson, "The *Heorte* of Heortology."

81. Erechtheus was chosen as one of the ten eponymous heroes of the tribes and received cult worship from the members of the Erechtheid tribe. That he could, at the end of the sixth century, be given such a limited role suggests that his importance statewide had waned considerably. See Kron, *Die Zehn attischen Phylenheroen,* 32–55.

82. Mikalson, "Erechtheus and the Panathenaia."

83. On oracles predicting hero cults, and thereby validating them, see below, p. 89.

84. On Athena of the deme Pallene see J. Wiesner, "Pallene," *RE* 18 (1949), col. 247.

85. By descendants of Heracles Eurystheus here means the Dorians, the true Heraclidae.

86. *Eum.* 772–774. These lines may only mean, however, that Orestes will not be hostile to the Argives if they do not attack Athens.

87. Cf. 357–368, 435–444.

88. Orestes' hair offering is surely a delayed funeral gift. Had he been able to attend Agamemnon's funeral, he would have made the offering then. The same may be true of the old man's libation and myrtle garland. Sacrifice on the altar: Denniston on E. *El.* 513 interprets πυρά as βωμός and compares E. *Hec.* 386, *Ion* 1258, *Tr.* 483, and *IT* 26.

89. For numerous parallels see Denniston on *El.* 146–149.

90. Kurtz and Boardman, *Greek Burial Customs,* 215, 237, 301; Garland, *The Greek Way of Death,* 33, 36. The evidence, collected in Garland (110–113), is insufficient to show that animals were sacrificed at tombs of the common dead in the classical period. To support her claim that "it was usual to sacrifice animals" at funerals, Alexiou (*The Ritual Lament,* 8) cites Thuc. 5.11 and Plut. *Sol.* 9, both of which describe hero cults.

91. For Agamemnon as a hero in this play see Langholf, *Die Gebete,* 11.

92. A. *Ch.* 106–121, 130–151, 315–371, 479–509, 540–541; cf. *Eum.* 598; S. *El.* 453–460. For reservations in these plays about the possibility of prayers reaching or affecting Agamemnon see S. *El.* 137–139 and A. *Ch.* 517–518.

93. For Agamemnon as a hero in the *Choephoroi* see Garvie on A. *Ch.* 483–485.

94. Kannicht on *Hel.* 1165–1168 notes the unusual intramural burial but draws no conclusions from it. On intramural burial for heroes see Garland, *The Greek Way of Death,* 88, and Malkin, *Religion and Colonization,* 235.

95. Χαῖρε is the *vox propria*.

96. Note A. *Pers.* 80, 157–158, 634, 642–643, 651, 711, 856. Aeschylus and Isocrates (4.151) presume that the Persians thought their king a god, but there is no

historical evidence that they in fact did. See Price, *Rituals and Power,* 25–26, and Hall, *Inventing the Barbarian,* 90–93.

97. On the fundamentally Greek background of the Darius figure, apart from his status as a god, see Hall, *Inventing the Barbarian,* 89–93.

98. E. Diehl, "Pontarches," *RE* 22 (1953), cols. 1–18; Stengel, *Opferbräuche der Griechen,* 128–129; Hommel, *Der Gott Achilleus,* passim. Achilles may originally have been a "god" in some areas, as Hommel argues, but Euripides presents him as a hero. For criticisms of Hommel's divine Achilles see Hooker, "The Cults of Achilles."

99. Achilles' demand for honor, characteristic of gods and heroes (see below, pp. 186–187), is emphasized throughout: 41, 94–95, 107–115, 304–310. If the πυράν of 386 is an altar (see Denniston on E. *El.* 513), it would be a further indication of Achilles' status as a hero.

100. See below, p. 123.

101. To create a convenient sequence of events Euripides has the favoring winds appear not directly after the sacrifice of Polyxena, as one would expect, but only after Hecuba has taken her vengeance on Polymestor.

102. In E. *Tr.* 622–623 Andromache sees Polyxena's sacrifice as only "a gift to a lifeless corpse" (δῶρον ἀψύχῳ νεκρῷ).

103. On the characteristic "anger" of heroes see B. M. W. Knox, *The Heroic Temper,* 55–57.

104. See below, p. 218.

105. For much that follows I am indebted to Linforth, "Religion and Drama in *Oedipus at Colonus,*" 75–192, esp. 75–129, and Hester, "To Help One's Friends and Harm One's Enemies." The latter also provides extensive bibliography on the relevant topics. For Oedipus' hero cult in Athens see Pfister, *Der Reliquienkult,* 107–114; Henrichs, "The 'Sobriety' of Oedipus"; Edmunds, "The Cults and the Legend of Oedipus." See also Winnington-Ingram, *Sophocles,* 248–279.

106. Cf. 1486–1487.

107. See E. *Erech.* frag. 65[A], 59–60, and above, p. 32. Cf. E. *Ion* 281–282. Of ordinary dead: S. *OT* 967–968, *Ant.* 25, 196, 285, 1039; E. *Hel.* 518–519, *Andr.* 1263–1264, *Hec.* 897; Thuc. 2.34.6; Hansen, nos. 69, 76.

108. The implication of 1486–1487 is that Oedipus, after his heroization, will, like other dead men, lack ψυχή and consciousness.

109. See 72–74, 92–93, 287–290, 455–464, 576–582, 626–628, 644–647, 1489–1490, 1518–1538, 1552–1555, 1764–1765. Oedipus' tomb will protect Athens in much the same manner as the knife, used to perform the oath offerings, protected the city against the Argives in E. *Suppl.* 1205–1209.

110. See 92–93, 399–411, 421–460, 621–622, 646, 784–790, 864–870. On Oedipus' relationships to both his friends and enemies see Blundell, *Helping Friends and Harming Enemies,* 226–259.

111. Note μηνίεις (1274) and μῆνιν βαρεῖαν (1328). Cf. the language of hate in 854–855, 954–955, 1173, 1177, 1197–1199, 1354, 1383–1384. Cf. Rosenmeyer, "The

Wrath of Oedipus"; Winnington-Ingram, "A Religious Function of Greek Tragedy"; North, *Sophrosyne*, 66–68.

112. His function is akin to that of Erinyes (1298–1299; cf. 1432–1434) and avenging spirits (ἀλάστωρ, 787–788) rather than to that of gods.

113. See 84–105, 387–420, 450–454, 621–623, 1331–1332, 1472–1473. On Delphi see below, p. 89.

114. For similar secret rites at the heroine Dirce's grove in Thebes see Plut. *Mor.* 578B and Burkert, *GR,* 212.

115. Pausanias (1.28.7, 1.30.4) mentions a μνῆμα Οἰδιπόδος in the grove of the Semnai and a *heroön* shared with Theseus at Colonus. He was told that the bones of Oedipus had been brought from Thebes to Athens, and this of course contradicts Sophocles' version. See Pfister, *Der Reliquienkult,* 110–112.

116. On *OC* as a suppliant play see Burian, "Suppliant and Saviour."

117. See below, pp. 69–80.

118. On the cult and myth of Hippolytus and on the surviving and lost plays see Barrett, 1–45.

119. ὦ μάκαρ, οἵας ἔλαχες τιμάς,
Ἱππόλυθ' ἥρως, διὰ σωφροσύνην·
οὔποτε θνητοῖς
ἀρετῆς ἄλλη δύναμις μείζων·
ἦλθε γὰρ ἢ πρόσθ' ἢ μετόπισθεν
τῆς εὐσεβίας χάρις ἐσθλή..

120. See Hypothesis II to E. *Hipp.*, τὸ γὰρ ἀπρεπὲς καὶ κατηγορίας ἄξιον ἐν τούτῳ διώρθωται τῷ δράματι.

121. On Hippolytus' piety see below, pp. 144–147.

122. See Pfister, *Der Reliquienkult,* 62–64.

123. Most oddities of the play are discussed in Ritchie, *The Authenticity of the Rhesus,* passim. On the religion see Mikalson, "Unanswered Prayers in Greek Tragedy," 91–92.

124. Rhesus is presented as the cousin of Orpheus (944).

125. Literally ἀνθρωποδαίμων (971), a *hapax* on which see Ritchie, *The Authenticity of the Rhesus,* 159–160.

126. I accept Diggle's ὅς γε in line 972 and his interpretation of the passage; see his "The Prophet of Bacchus."

127. The closest parallel is the Egyptian Danaus' thought to pray, sacrifice, and pour libations to the Argives, the saviors of him and his daughters, as if they were Olympian gods (A. *Suppl.* 980–982).

128. See above, p. ix.

129. Euripides' god may be Prometheus, but not necessarily. Euripides evidently chose not to introduce another specific god—and the ramifications of his myth—into his *Suppliants*.

130. *Pr.* 248–254, 442–506. Cf. Plato *Prt.* 320C–323A; Xen. *Mem.* 1.4.11–18.

131. See Quincey, "Greek Expressions of Thanks"; Versnel, *Faith, Hope, and Worship,* 42–64.

132. On the role of the gods in furthering human civilization, as described in Greek literature and philosophy, see Nestle, *Euripides,* 64–72; Edelstein, *The Idea of Progress in Classical Antiquity,* esp. chap. 2; Dodds, *The Ancient Concept of Progress,* 1–25; Guthrie, *A History of Greek Philosophy,* 2:473–478, 3:60–84. For a comparison of these programmatic statements of man's history by the three tragedians see Havelock, *The Liberal Temper in Greek Politics,* 52–73.

133. In *OC* 707–719 Sophocles' Athenian chorus gives credit for inventing the horse bit and ships to Poseidon Hippios of the deme Colonus.

134. See above, note 132.

135. Deubner, *Attische Feste,* 211–212; Parke, *Festivals of the Athenians,* 171.

136. E. *Ion* 442–443 is an exception, as are "unwritten laws," on which see below, pp. 194–196. Cf. Burkert, *GR,* 248–250.

137. *APR,* 31–38; Guthrie, *A History of Greek Philosophy,* 3:76–79.

138. See Leo, *Plautinische Forschungen,* 113–116.

139. On all Greek religious practices associated with war see Pritchett, *The Greek State at War,* 1:93–100, 105–126, 3:passim.

140. Prayers, vows, libations, and paeans: A. *Th.* 69–77, 87–117, 128–186, 251–255, 266–278, 301–320, 481–485, 626–630; S. *Tr.* 237–241; E. *Suppl.* 628–631, *Ph.* 676–689, 782–783, 1364–1376, *Heraclid.* 770–783, *IA* 1467–1483, 1570–1576. Sacrifices for omens: A. *Th.* 230–232, *Suppl.* 449–451; E. *Heraclid.* 400–409, 488–490, 819–822; *Rh.* 30. Cf. E. *Or.* 1602–1604. Trophies and other dedications: A. *Th.* 271–278, *Ag.* 577–582, *Eum.* 397–402; S. *Aj.* 91–93, 176–178, *Tr.* 182–183, 237–241, 287–288, 750–754, 760–761; *Ant.* 141–143; E. *El.* 6–7, 1000–1001, *Ph.* 1250–1251, 1472–1473, *Tr.* 573–576, *HF* 48–50, *Heraclid.* 695–697, 786–787, 936–937, frag. 369[N], 3–5; *Rh.* 179–180, 469–470.

141. Lines 276–278a are problematical, and I have followed Hutchinson's text.

142. Cf. the scene described by Thucydides (6.32.1) as the Athenians launched their ill-fated expedition to Sicily in 415 B.C.: "When the ships were filled and they had on board all they needed to set sail, the call for silence was made by a trumpet, and they made the prayers customary before setting sail, not individually at each ship but all through the herald. They did this after the soldiers and archons had mixed *kraters* of wine alongside the army and while they were pouring libations from gold and silver cups. The rest of the throng also joined the prayers, the people on land, citizens, and whoever else was well-intentioned towards them. After they had sung the paean and completed the libations, they set sail." Cf. S. *Ph.* 1075–1077, 1469–1471. See Pritchett, *The Greek State at War,* 3:230–237.

143. *APR,* 18–21.

144. In *Ag.* 603 the herald speaks of "a god" saving an individual soldier on expedition.

145. *Pers.* 344–347, 472–473, 515–516, 909–912, 918–921.

146. Cf. *Pers.* 347, "The gods protect the city of the goddess Pallas."

147. See below, pp. 159–160.

148. An exception is E. *Ph.* 1197–1199. Apart from the idiosyncratic *Rhesus* (e.g.,

56–58, 317–320, 728, 882–884, 995–996), Sophocles and Euripides involve gods or *daimones* when (e.g., E. *Andr.* 1182–1183) the emphasis is on death or personal suffering, not on the outcome of the war or battle itself. The god or *daimon* is thus viewed conventionally as an agent of misfortune, not specifically of military victory or defeat. E. *Suppl.* 594–596 is a major exception. Theseus there claims that in his battle against the Thebans he needs just gods to support his just cause. Here, as in Aeschylus, the concern is with the justice of the gods.

149. Cf. *Heraclid.* 770–783, where the chorus, in prayer, justifies its claim to Athena's support.

150. Cf. 116–117.

151. In the same way may be explained *Rh.* 637–638 and 665–667.

152. Cf. *Ch.* 461, 489, 497–499, 584, 729.

153. E. *Ba.* 1341–1343,

εἰ δὲ σωφρονεῖν
ἔγνωθ᾽, ὅτ᾽ οὐκ ἠθέλετε, τὸν Διὸς γόνον
εὐδαιμονεῖτ᾽ ἂν σύμμαχον κεκτημένοι.

We should, perhaps, give εὐδαιμονεῖτε here its etymological meaning, "You would have 'good *daimones*' (or 'a good *daimon*')," not only its metaphorical sense, "You would be 'blessed' (or 'happy')."

154. The "ally" whom Antigone (S. *Ant.* 923) wishes to summon may well be human, not divine, as, e.g., B. M. W. Knox assumes (*The Heroic Temper*, 106).

155. For problems of text and interpretation see Johansen and Whittle ad loc.

156. See Johansen and Whittle on *Suppl.* 934–937.

157. On civil war as the subject of this prayer see Johansen and Whittle on 678–683.

158. The potential for civil discord caused by the Danaids is suggested in 365–369, 397–401, 483–489, and 991–1013; and civil war may have explained, in the lost plays, Pelasgus' disappearance and the Argive failure to continue to protect the Danaids.

159. Cf. *Eum.* 862–865.

160. On political circumstances surrounding the *Eumenides* see Dover, "The Political Aspect of Aeschylus' *Eumenides*"; Macleod, "Politics and the *Oresteia*"; Dodds, *The Ancient Concept of Progress*, 45–63; Podlecki, *The Political Background of Aeschylean Tragedy*, 83–100.

161. This is not to say, of course, that the poets praised war or Ares, its mythological/literary personification. Unless Ares has a cultic or genealogical relation to the action of the play (as in A. *Th.* and *Eum.* and in the *Rhesus*), he is usually described as a force of evil (A. *Ag.* 437–444, 1509–1512, *Eum.* 862–865, frag. 100[R]; S. *Tr.* 653–654, frag. 724[R]).

162. Isoc. 15.109–110. See Deubner, *Attische Feste*, 38; Jacoby, *FGrHist* 3B, suppl. 1:523–526.

163. See above, p. 48.

164. *APR*, 21. Cf. E. *Suppl.* 28–31 and frag. 516[N].

165. Cf. E. *El.* 80–81.

166. On the primitive state of agriculture and its precarious chances for success in the classical period see J. Gould, "On Making Sense of Greek Religion," 6.

167. In E. *Hec.* 592–593 a god can overcome the problem of "bad land."

168. Zeus as cause of rain: A. *Ag.* 1390–1392; S. *OC* 1500–1504, frag. 524[R]; E. *Cycl.* 320–323, *Tr.* 78–79, *El.* 734–736. Cf. Ar. *Ach.* 170–171, *Nu.* 366–368, 1278–1281. For an exhaustive account see Cook, *Zeus,* 3:284–881.

Zeus as source of thunder and lightning: A. *Ag.* 469–470, *Th.* 430–431, 444–446, 512–513, 629–630, *Eum.* 826–828, *Pr.* 358–359, 667–668, 916–923, 992–994, 1016–1018, 1043–1046, 1080–1090; S. *Ph.* 1196–1199, *OT* 200–203, *El.* 823–825, 1063–1065, *Ant.* 128–133, *Tr.* 436–437, 1086–1088, *OC* 95, 1456–1504; E. *Alc.* 3–6, 128–129, *Suppl.* 640, 831, *Hipp.* 683–684, 1201–1202, *HF* 177, *Tr.* 77–81, *Ion* 212–213, *Ph.* 182–183, *Hec.* 474–475, *Cycl.* 320, *Ba.* 90, 596–599, frag. 781[N], 68–69; cf. Ar. *Ach.* 530–531, *Nu.* 366–411, *V.* 323–331. In S. *OT* 469–470 Apollo is armed with his father's lightning bolts and in A. *Eum.* 826–828 they are available to Athena for her use.

Zeus as cause of wind: A. *Pr.* 1043–1046, 1080–1090; E. *IT* 354, *IA* 1323–1324, *Tr.* 78–79.

169. For the Erinyes in this play as curses see *Eum.* 416–417. Cf. note 35 above. On them as agents of pollution see Parker, *Miasma,* 107.

170. See below, pp. 214–217.

171. Nearly identical provisions are part of the curse of the oath which the Greeks purportedly swore before the battle of Plataea in 479, but its authenticity is in doubt (see Tod, *Greek Historical Inscriptions,* 2:no. 204, lines 39–51).

172. On the pollution and exclusion of murderers see Parker, *Miasma,* 104–143; *APR*, 50–52.

173. That Aeschylus occasionally has Zeus, apart from his role as giver of rain, affect the produce of the land and "mother earth" (*Ag.* 970–971, 1015–1017, *Suppl.* 689–690) is characteristic of his Diocentric theology, that is, of his concentration of all divine functions on Zeus. On this see below, pp. 210–213.

174. Gaia as mother: A. *Ch.* 127–128; E. frag. 839[N], 1023[N], on which see Snell in 182A[N]. Plant and animal life: A. *Ch.* 127–128; E. frag. 839[N]. Rain from Ouranos or Zeus: A. frag. 44[R]; E. frag. 839[N]. Cf. E. frag. 1023[N]; Paus. 1.18.7. Agriculture: A. frag. 44[R]; S. *Ant.* 337–341.

175. For evidence of Gaia cults in Athens see Farnell, *Cults of the Greek States,* 3:308–309. Note also *IG* I³ 5, line 3.

176. Apart from fertility of the land Gaia is also associated with oracles: A. *Eum.* 1–4, *Pr.* 209–211, and E. *IT* 1267–1269; with the world of the dead: A. *Pers.* 640–641, *Ch.* 399–489; and with the Asian Magna Mater, A. *Suppl.* 890–892 (on which see Johansen and Whittle), 900–902, and S. *Ph.* 391–402.

177. Mylonas, *Eleusis,* 20–21.

178. *IG* I³ 78. See Burkert, *GR,* 67–68.

179. E.g., Dem. 24.149–151; Aristophanes passim. For Demeter in oaths between Athens and other states see *IG* I³ 14 and 37.

180. See Clinton, "The Author of the *Homeric Hymn to Demeter*"; Richardson, *The Homeric Hymn to Demeter*, 12–30.

181. Mother of Persephone: *Rh.* 963–964. Grain: E. *Ba.* 274–277; A. frags. 44[R], 5 and 300[R], 6–7; E. frag. 892[N], 1–3.

182. For evidence see Radt, T93a–94. For skepticism about this story see Lefkowitz, *The Lives of the Greek Poets*, 68, 172–173.

183. See Kannicht ad loc.

184. On health and Greek religion see Burkert, *GR*, 267–268.

185. *Suppl.* 659–660, 684–687. See Johansen and Whittle on 659–677.

186. On Apollo Paian see Farnell, *Cults of the Greek States*, 4:234–235; Bond on E. *HF* 820.

187. See B. M. W. Knox, *Oedipus at Thebes*, 9–10.

188. Cf. A. *Eum.* 61–63, where, from the Pythia's own mouth, Apollo is ἰατρόμαντις and τοῖσιν ἄλλοις δωμάτων καθάρσιος.

189. The only historical oracle possibly concerning plague is H68 of ca. A.D. 250 (Fontenrose, *Delphic Oracle*). For Apollo's role in the Athenian plague, and for the numerous quasi-historical and literary Delphic oracles on plagues see Mikalson, "Religion and the Plague in Athens, 431–423 B.C.," esp. 218 n. 6.

190. For Pericles' dream, from Athena Hygieia, of a remedy for an injured man see below, p. 102.

191. Apollo as healer, apart from plague: A. *Suppl.* 684–687, *Eum.* 61–63; E. *Alc.* 969–972, *HF* 820–821, on which see Bond ad loc. Outside of drama Apollo as "healer" in Athens appears as a subsidiary member of the healing cults of Asclepios (*IG* II² 47 and 4962A) and Amphiaraus (Paus. 1.34.3). A possible exception in this regard is *IG* I² 310, lines 228–229. See Farnell, *Cults of the Greek States*, 4:233–241.

192. A. *Ag.* 1022–1024; E. *Alc.* 3–4, 121–130. On this myth see Edelstein and Edelstein, *Asclepius*, 2:46–50; Fraenkel on *Ag.* 1022–1024.

193. Παιών and εὐμενής suggest, but do not guarantee, Asclepios' divinity.

194. For evidence see Lefkowitz, *The Lives of the Greek Poets*, 84, and below, p. 218.

195. Euripides' Andromache claims "some god" established cures of snake bites (*Andr.* 269–270).

196. The use of incantations may also be inferred from A. *Ag.* 1019–1021.

197. On this parodos see Ax, "Die Parodos des Oidipus Tyrannos."

198. On Artemis Eukleia see Paus. 9.17.1; Wilamowitz, *Der Glaube der Hellenen*, 1:180–181; Frazer, *Pausanias*, 2:124; Braund, "Artemis Eukleia and Euripides' *Hippolytus*"; Schachter, *Cults of Boeotia*.

199. See Kamerbeek on *OT* 190. In A. *Suppl.* 659–666 and 679–682 Ares is associated with plague but still represents war. See B. M. W. Knox, *Oedipus at Thebes*, 200.

200. For children: cf. E. *IT* 213. To the nymphs: E. *El.* 625–626; on these nymphs see F. G. Ballentine, "Some Phases of the Cult of the Nymphs," 104–105. To Artemis: A. *Suppl.* 674–677; on this Artemis see Johansen and Whittle ad loc. I doubt their contention that Artemis is identified with Hecate here. To Athena: E. *Ph.* 1060–1062. Athena is surprising in this context, but she was the state deity of Thebes, and Euripides here wishes to introduce a particularly Theban myth and theme (1062–1066). Also, Athena's concern for the state as a whole does not exclude concern for an individual's children. Cf. *IG* I² 524.

201. Cf. S. *OT* 269–271.

202. There is no indication that the real Semnai of Athenian cult received any such offerings. The Athenian deity invoked in these areas is Artemis Brauronia, on whom see Cole, "The Social Function of Rituals of Maturation," 238, 243–244.

203. The appeals to Apollo (*Ion*) and Zeus (E. frag. 2[A], 19–25) are to them as oracular gods for information on causes of infertility.

204. On Hestia in tragedy see Bond on *HF* 599. Aeschylus' Eumenides also pray that the "lovely young women" of Athens find husbands (*Eum.* 959–960; cf. 1030–1031).

205. Cf. E. *Med.* 920–921, 930.

206. Reading ἐφόρους with the manuscript in 674, not the φόρους of Page.

207. Cf. S. *El.* 648–649.

208. Cf. E. frag. 153[A]. This Ploutos is, of course, to be distinguished from the Eleusinian Plouton, on whom see Clinton, "The Author of the *Homeric Hymn to Demeter.*" In tragedy Ploutos is imagined as a god only by the mother of the Persian king Xerxes (A. *Pers.* 163–164) and, in a satyr play, by the impious Polyphemus (E. *Cycl.* 316–317). Note also E. frag. 20[N] and *Hel.* 69. Compare Aristophanes, who devotes a whole play to an anthropomorphized Ploutos.

209. Dedications: *IG* I² 408, 411, 415, 485, 499, 585, 615, 623, 625. Cf. *IG* I² 643 and 650. On such dedications throughout Greece see F. T. van Straten, "Gifts for the Gods," 92–96. Vows: *IG* I² 623 and 625. Future dedications: *IG* I² 650, made by a foreigner.

210. In A. *Suppl.* 443–445 Zeus Ktesios is intimately associated with domestic wealth.

211. Wünsch, *Defixionum Tabellae,* nos. 87, 95; Peek, *Kerameikos,* 3:no. 9.

212. Aeschines 3.108–111. Cf. Dem. 54.40–41.

213. See Wachsmuth, Πόμπιμος ὁ Δαίμων, 50, 203, 424, 433; Burkert, *GR,* 266–267.

214. For an exhaustive description of such prayers, rituals, and sacrifices in the Greek and Roman world see Wachsmuth, Πόμπιμος ὁ Δαίμων, passim.

215. Poseidon and Nereids: E. *Tr.* 82–84, 88–91, *IT* 1414–1418, 1442–1445. Cf. A. *Suppl.* 218–219. Dioscuroi: E. *El.* 990–993, 1347–1356, *Or.* 1636–1637. In E. *Hel.* 1495–1505 the Dioscuroi are to "send" the favoring winds from Zeus. Cf. E. *Hel.* 1663–1665. See Kannicht on *Hel.* 1495–1511. In E. *El.* 1241–1242 the Dioscuroi stop the "terrible tossing of the sea." In A. *Ag.* 661–663 the herald attributes the

rescue of Agamemnon's ships from the engulfing storm to "some god" (θεός τις). Agamemnon holds the gods of his homeland responsible for his successful return (810–812, 852–853).

216. A. *Pr.* 1045–1046, 1084–1087, *Suppl.* 33–36; E. *IT* 354, *IA* 1323–1329, *Tr.* 78–79. In E. *IT* 1487–1489 Athena, *deus ex machina,* orders winds to send Orestes to Athens.

217. The indications of Achilles' hero status in the *Hecuba* are his ability to cause ἄπλοια, his demand for a sacrificial victim, and his answering of a prayer. See above, pp. 37–38.

218. A. *Ag.* 146–150, 192–204; S. *El.* 563–572. In E. *Hec.* and *IA* Achilles and Artemis are responsible for the Greeks' ἄπλοια (*Hec.* 37–39, 109–112, 538–541, *IA* 87–92, 358–359, 1491–1497; cf. *IA* [1521–1527] and [1570–1576]), and that ἄπλοια is caused by the lack of favorable winds (*Hec.* 900, 1289–1290, *IA* 10–11, 351–352). Nowhere in Euripides, however, is it said explicitly that Achilles or Artemis caused the unfavorable winds, nor are they asked to send favorable ones. In the only direct comments on the subject in these plays, Agamemnon claims that "a god" is not sending favorable winds (*Hec.* 900), and the chorus, in a problematic passage, wishes Zeus were not sending unfavorable ones (*IA* 1323–1329). Kovacs (*The Heroic Muse,* 105, 140 n. 22, 145 n. 58) would have the gods, not Achilles, cause the windlessness of the *Hecuba.* For him Achilles simply stops, by a display of his displeasure, the Greeks from sailing.

219. In the Black Sea, on Leuke, and in the region of Olbia, Achilles had, in the Roman period, a major cult as Pontarches ("Ruler of the Sea"). There are slight indications that his role as protector of sailors in the Black Sea (though not the epithet Pontarches) may have existed as early as the fifth or fourth century. Euripides was familiar with the cult of Achilles on Leuke, whatever form it had in the fifth century (*Andr.* 1259–1262, *IT* 434–438). Achilles was worshiped in this area as a god and not, as in the plays, as a hero. On cults of Achilles see above, note 98.

There are scattered references to an Artemis Limenitis ("Of the Harbor") and Neosoös ("Ship-Saver"), but they date only from the Hellenistic period (Ap. Rhod. 1.569–572, *Anth. Pal.* 6.105). See also Farnell, *Cults of the Greek States,* 1:430–431. For Artemis "Of the Lagoon" in E. *Hipp.* 145–150 and 228–231 see Barrett ad loc.

220. The causes for Artemis' wrath, when given, are all associated with her usual functions *on land* as protectress of animals (A. *Ag.* 134–159, on which see Fraenkel on 158; S. *El.* 563–572). See Farnell, *Cults of the Greek States,* 1:430–431. The offense to Achilles, his companions' failure to accord him due honor (*Hec.* 40–43, 113–115, 303–320), similarly is unrelated to seafaring. On further possibilities for the concerns of Aeschylus' Artemis see Lloyd-Jones, "Artemis and Iphigeneia"; Clinton, "Artemis and the Sacrifice of Iphigeneia in Aeschylus' *Agamemnon.*"

221. Wachsmuth, Πόμπιμος ὁ Δαίμων, 127–131. For such "request" prayers in tragedy see A. *Suppl.* 130–132; S. *Ph.* 528–529, 1075–1077, 1469–1471. For a sacrifice see E. *Hel.* 1581–1588. For a storm destroying and endangering a fleet and caused by the wrath of the gods see A. *Ag.* 634–635, 649.

222. The evidence from the archaic and classical periods, collected in Wachsmuth, is too scanty and heterogeneous to demonstrate this development convincingly.

223. The offerings before the sailing of the Sicilian expedition give no indication of wrathful deities (Thuc. 6.32.1–2). Henrichs ("Human Sacrifice in Greek Religion," 208–224) has shown as fictitious the human sacrifices reportedly (Plut. *Them.* 13.2–3, *Arist.* 9.2, *Pelop.* 21.3) made before the naval battle at Salamis. On the harmful effects of pollution on crops and animals see above, pp. 54–55.

224. E. frag. 852[N], where the impiety is failure to honor a parent.

225. In 1347–1353 the Dioscuroi claim they will rescue at sea only those to whom "holiness and justice" (ὅσιον καὶ τὸ δίκαιον) are dear, not those who are "loathsome and polluted" (μυσαροῖς).

226. In the biographical tradition it is claimed that Protagoras, Diagoras the Melian, and Diogenes the Cynic, each allegedly impious, perished at sea. See Lefkowitz, "Was Euripides an Atheist?" 162.

227. Cf. *OC* 260–261, 1125–1126.

228. A rough translation, one of several possible, of the bold and dense Greek of *Eum.* 917–920:

οὐδ᾽ ἀτιμάσω πόλιν,
τὰν καὶ Ζεὺς ὁ παγκρατὴς Ἄρης τε
φρούριον θεῶν νέμει,
ῥυσίβωμον Ἑλλά-
νων ἄγαλμα δαιμόνων·

Cf. the translation by Lloyd-Jones (*The Eumenides*, 67): "An outpost of the gods, / guardian of the altars of the Greeks / and the delight of the immortals."

229. Athena's city: A. *Pers.* 347, *Eum.* 79, 667–668, 707–708, 772, 858–862, 1017–1018; S. *OC* 107–108; E. *Suppl.* 377, *Heraclid.* 770–773, 922–923, 933–934, *Med.* 771, *Hec.* 466, *HF* 1323, *Ion* 8–9, 30, 211, 453–454, 871, 1297, 1574, 1578, 1584, *IT* 960, 1014, 1441, 1452, 1480–1481, *El.* 1319–1320, frag. 65[A], 57 and 77; *Rh.* 941. Eponymous: E. *Ion* 8–9, 1555. Acropolis: E. *Ion* 12.

230. E. *Heraclid.* 770–772:

ἀλλ᾽, ὦ πότνια, σὸν γὰρ οὖ-
δας [γᾶς], σὸν καὶ πόλις, ἇς σὺ μά-
τηρ δέσποινά τε καὶ φύλαξ

"Mother" is a bold epithet for this motherless, husbandless, virgin, and childless goddess, and it is not attested elsewhere. It appears here, perhaps, from the maternal concerns of the chorus, and does not reflect the usual relationship of Athena to her people. See Zuntz, *The Political Plays of Euripides,* 121–122.

231. S. *OC* 694–706; E. *Tr.* 801–803 and frag. 50[A], 46–49. On the olive as a part of Athena's cult see Burkert, *GR,* 141. Military role: A. *Eum.* 913–915; E. *Heraclid.* 770–783 and frag. 41[A]. Cf. E. *Suppl.* 1230–1231.

232. Euripides twice describes Orestes' trial before the Areopagus. In *El.* 1258–

1269 he follows the more usual tradition that the first trial there was of Halirrothios, a trial in which Athena played no role. In *IT* 1469–1472 he seems to credit Athena with establishing the precedent that equal votes mean acquittal for the defendant.

233. These functions correlate with the two aspects of Athena Polias which Herington (*Athena Parthenos and Athena Polias*, 44–47) isolates: the fertility goddess of the Erechtheum with her olive-wood cult statue and the armed, warrior goddess of the Parthenon.

234. Holy: S. *Aj.* 1221–1222; E. *Tr.* 218–219, *Med.* 824–826, *El.* 1319–1320. Divine: E. *Tr.* 218–219. Well-*daimoned*: E. *Tr.* 207–208. God-built: S. *El.* 707; E. *Hipp.* 974, *IT* 1449.

235. On cult of Poseidon Hippios in Athens see below, p. 303 n. 79.

236. Cf. Isoc. 5.124–126.

237. In A. *Eum.* 905–906 Athena asks these for Athens.

238. See Farnell, *Cults of the Greek States*, 2:732–733.

239. Paus. 1.19.2. More recent scholarly opinion (e.g., Burkert, *Homo Necans*, 150–154; Parke, *Festivals of the Athenians*, 141–143) has followed Broneer (*Hesp.* 1 [1932], 52) in placing the cult on the north slope of the Acropolis.

240. On altars of the Muses near the Ilissus River and in the Academy see Paus. 1.19.5, 1.30.2. Cults of the Muses were established in Athens at least by the fifth century (*IG* I² 324, lines 62 and 91; cf. Aeschines 1.10). Cf. *Rh.* 941–942.

241. On the benefits the Semnai give to Athens see Macleod, "Politics and the *Oresteia*," 136–138. Cf. also the drinking song which, addressed to Athena, asks that the city and its citizens be free from "griefs, civil wars, and untimely deaths" (Page, *Poetae Melici Graeci*, no. 884).

242. See below, pp. 214–217.

243. On this ode see Johansen and Whittle on A. *Suppl.* 630–709. The Eumenides' list culminates with the avoidance of civil war, and this may reflect political anxieties of 458 B.C. (see above, p. 53). The Danaids' prayer ends with requests for piety among the citizens, surely because the Danaids' present and future safety depends so heavily on the Argives' pious respect for asylum and suppliants. Of the Eumenides' promises the Danaids omit only two, success of the mines and that girls find husbands. The first reflects the importance to Athens of the silver mines at Laurion; the second, perhaps, the Danaids' own avoidance of marriage.

244. On religious aspects of *deus ex machina* see Collard, *Euripides: Supplices*, 407–408; Langholf, *Die Gebete*, 123–127; Barrett on *Hipp.* 1283; Schmid and Staehlin, *Geschichte der griechische Literatur*, 1.3:705. For general studies see Spira, *Untersuchungen zum Deus ex Machina bei Sophokles und Euripides*; B. M. W. Knox, "The 'Medea' of Euripides," 206–211 = *Word and Action*, 303–306; Grube, *The Drama of Euripides*, 73–79, 395–396. On the use, or rather nonuse, of the *machina* by Euripides' *dei ex machina* see Taplin, *The Stagecraft of Aeschylus*, 443–447.

245. See above, p. 21.

246. The *deus ex machina* occurs in S. *Ph.* 1409–1451; E. *Suppl.* 1183–1226, *Hel.* 1642–1679, *Hipp.* 1283–1439, *IT* 1435–1489, *Or.* 1625–1690, *Ba.* 1330–1378, *Andr.*

1231–1272, *El.* 1238–1356, *Ion* 1553–1618, *Erech.* frag. 65[A], 55–117, *Antiope* frag. 48 [Kambitsis], 67–103; *Rh.* 890–982.

247. Cf. E. *IT* 1475–1476. The one exception is the Orestes of the *Orestes,* who expresses momentary concern that the voice he hears is not Apollo's, but τινὸς . . . ἀλαστόρων. Given his previous fits of delirium (215–238, 255–279), his fear is understandable. In the end, however, he obeys (1666–1670).

248. E. *Andr.* 1226–1230, *El.* 1233–1237, *Ion* 1549–1552; *Rh.* 886–889. See esp. E. *El.* 1235–1236.

249. See above, pp. 19–20.

250. *Andr.* 1227–1230, *El.* 1233–1235 (on which see note 26 above), *Ion* 1549–1552.

251. See above, pp. 43–44. Other unusual features of Musa's scene as *deus ex machina* include the lyric laments (895–903, 906–914) and Hector's failure even to acknowledge the presence of the deity (952–961, 986–992). For a defense of the scene as Euripidean see Ritchie, *The Authenticity of the Rhesus,* 132–135, 339–340.

252. To listen: E. *Suppl.* 1183, *IT* 1436, *El.* 1238, *Hipp.* 1283–1284. Prohibition: S. *Ph.* 1409–1410; E. *Hel.* 1642–1643, *IT* 1435, *Or.* 1625, *Erech.* frag. 65[A], 55–57, *Antiope* frag. 48 [Kambitsis], 67–68.

253. Zeus: S. *Ph.* 1415, 1440–1444; E. *Andr.* 1269, *Or.* 1633–1634, *El.* 1247–1248, 1282–1283, *Hipp.* 1331–1334, *Hel.* 1669, *Ba.* 1333, 1340–1341, 1349, *Erech.* frag. 65[A], 99–100, *Antiope* frag. 48 [Kambitsis], 70 and 96 (cf. 104–106). Fate, necessity, and related expressions: S. *Ph.* 1439–1440; E. *Andr.* 1268–1269, *Or.* 1652–1656, *El.* 1247–1248, 1264, 1290, 1301, *Hel.* 1646, 1652–1655, 1660, 1676–1677.

254. For the variants and details of which see Parker, "Myths of Early Athens," 205–207.

255. See below, pp. 88–93.

256. The seven at Thebes: E. *Suppl.* 1211–1212, on which see Collard. Hippolytus: E. *Hipp.* 1423–1430. Helen: *Or.* 1635–1637, 1683–1690, *Hel.* 1666–1669 (on which see Kannicht ad loc.). Dirce, Amphion, Zethus: E. *Antiope* frag. 48 [Kambitsis], 80–85, 98–99, 112–115. Neoptolemus, Peleus, Achilles: E. *Andr.* 1239–1242, 1253–1258, 1260–1262.

257. See above, pp. 13–14.

258. Thetis will make (ποιήσω) her husband Peleus a god (*Andr.* 1253–1256). Artemis "will give" (δώσω) Hippolytus "very great honors" in Troezen (*Hipp.* 1423–1425), and Athena has "made reside" (κατῴκισα) the souls of the Hyacinthids in the sky (*Erech.* frag. 65[A], 72).

259. On this see below, p. 89.

260. On statements by seers see below, pp. 100–101.

261. Perjury: see below, pp. 80–87. Punishment at sea: see above, p. 62.

262. Cf. A. *Th.* 343–344, *Ag.* 338–347, 524–528.

263. For the interpretation of line 1444 see below, p. 120.

Notes to Pages 69–72   257

Chapter Three

1. *APR*, passim.

2. On asylum see Stengel, "Asylon," *RE* 2 (1896), cols. 1881–1886; Strohm, *Euripides*, 17–32; J. Gould, "Hiketeia"; Burnett, *Catastrophe Survived*, 159–166; Parker, *Miasma*, 181–186. I treat here only suppliants in a sanctuary. In tragedy there are numerous examples of ritual supplication of one individual by another, outside a sanctuary (e.g., S. *Ph.* 484–485; E. *Hec.* 145, 239–246, 273–278, 342–345, 737–753, *Or.* 382–384, *IA* 900–901, 911, *Med.* 709–715), but this practice is scarcely attested for the classical period. For the ritual and the few classical examples see J. Gould, "Hiketeia." In using this type of supplication the tragedians are either reviving an archaic practice or are simply following Homer, who makes wide use of the ritual.

For the dates and other sources of the following episodes, all drawn from Thucydides, see Gomme, Andrewes, and Dover, *A Historical Commentary on Thucydides,* ad loc. For other fifth-century episodes involving asylum for the Athenians see Hdt. 6.108 (Plataeans at Athenian altars); Xen. *Hell.* 2.3.52–56 (Theramenes at altar in Bouleuterion); Lys. 13.24 (Agoratus and others at altar in Mounychia); Andoc. 1.44 (Mantitheos and Apsephion at altar in Bouleuterion); Andoc. 2.15 (Andocides at altar in Bouleuterion); Plut. *Per.* 31.2 (Menon, in Agora).

3. For how the Cylonians got from the Acropolis to the sanctuary of the Semnai near the Areopagus see Plut. *Sol.* 12.1.

4. On the *Heraclidae* see Fitton, "The *Suppliant Women* and the *Herakleidai*."

5. A comparable mixture of motives led the Athenians to respect Oedipus as a suppliant in Sophocles' *Oedipus at Colonus*. Oedipus himself emphasizes the significance of piety towards the gods (258–285, 1003–1013; cf. 919–923, 1179–1180), but Theseus and the Athenians are particularly influenced by the affront to Athens' sovereignty, by the rewards Oedipus promises, and by Oedipus' own pitiable condition (107–110, 282–288, 455–463, 631–637, 902–928, 1012–1013). On this blend of political and religious motives see J. Gould, "Hiketeia," 90.

6. Cf. *Heraclid.* 259. Cf. also the situation that Tiberius faced, centuries later, of uncontrolled use of asylum in Greek cities (Tac. *Ann.* 3.60).

7. Cf. S. *OC* 1179–1180. This is not true of supplications formally and even ritualistically made to one individual by another, without the element of asylum. For numerous examples of refusal of this kind of suppliant request, especially in Homer, see Gould, "Hiketeia," 78–82.

8. Helen, for example, must desperately scurry back to the *temenos* of Proteus to reestablish her asylum (E. *Hel.* 541–547).

9. Altar: E. *Andr.* 161–162, 260, 357–358, 411, 427, 565–567. Cf. *Ph.* 274–275, *Hel.* 800, *HF* 48, 974, *IA* 911, *Suppl.* 267–268, *Heraclid.* 61, 121–124, 196, 238–239, 243–244, 249, etc., frag. 1049[N]; S. *OC* 1158; A. *Suppl.* 83–85, 190, 482, 751–752; Lys. 12.98. In the context of asylum the altar was, in Aeschylean language, δαιμόνων σέβας (*Suppl.* 85), a pregnant phrase, a literal meaning of which is "an object the

gods revere." See Johansen and Whittle ad loc. Sanctuary: E. *Andr.* 42–44, 117–140, 161–162, 253, 262–263, 380, *Suppl.* 721–723. Cf. Lys. 12.98.

10. Violence: E. *Heraclid.* 71, 79, 102, 243, 249, 254, 286, etc.; S. *OC* 922. Against the gods: E. *Heraclid.* 97, 112–113, 221–222; A. *Suppl.* 812.

11. Dishonors gods: E. *Heraclid.* 72, 78; S. *OC* 277–278; A. *Suppl.* 732–733. Hybristic: E. *Heraclid.* 924–925, *HF* 260–262; A. *Suppl.* 426, 817–821, 880–881. Pollution: A. *Suppl.* 366–367, 375, and E. *Heraclid.* 71, 264, all refer to pollution resulting from the simple violation of asylum. Other references to pollution in this context probably include the death of the suppliant (A. *Suppl.* 472–473, 618–620, 654–655; Thuc. 1.126–128, 1.134). See Parker, *Miasma*, 146, 183–185.

12. Unjust: E. *Heraclid.* 104, 254; cf. A. *Suppl.* 381–386, 395–396, 402–406, 429–430, 437; S. *OC* 920–923. Unreasonable: E. *Heraclid.* 101, 369–370. Godless: E. *Heraclid.* 107, *HF* 255; A. *Suppl.* 762; S. *OC* 275–283. Un-Greek: E. *Heraclid.* 130–131. Cf. A. *Suppl.* 893–894.

13. Cf. A. *Suppl.* 927.

14. Property of a god: S. *OC* 921–923; A. *Suppl.* 423–424.

15. *(Κρ.) ἀλλ' οὐκέτ' ἦσθα Λοξίου, πατρὸς δὲ σοῦ.*
    (Ιω.) ἀλλ' ἐγενόμεσθα πατρός· οὐσίαν λέγω.
    (Κρ.) οὐκοῦν τότ' ἦσθα· νῦν δ' ἐγώ, σὺ δ' οὐκέτι.

These lines are, I think, to be understood as follows:

Creousa: "No longer were you Apollo's, but your father's."
Ion: "I was born from my father. I'm speaking of 'property.'"
Creousa: "You were Apollo's property at that time. I am that now, but you no longer are."

Cf. Grube, *The Drama of Euripides*, 274.

16. Συλᾶσθαι is the *vox propria*. Etymologically it is the direct opposite of ἀσυλία, the status enjoyed by the sanctuary and its occupants. See, e.g., E. *Heraclid.* 243–244, *Hel.* 61, *Med.* 728; A. *Suppl.* 610, 927; S. *OC* 919–923. Cf. A. *Prom.* 761.

17. To set a fire and burn the suppliants out, as Lycus intended to do to Heracles' father, mother, and children, was impious and hybristic (*HF* 242–246, 255, 261, 284–285). Hermione in the *Andromache* threatens to "burn out" Andromache (253–260), an act reflecting her general disrespect for the rights of asylum (161–167, 246–263). She later finds herself in need of asylum (859), and her blasphemous predictions (161–167) about the goddess Thetis all prove false (1243–1245).

18. Her later claim that she was "dragged" from the altar (565–567) is either incorrect or high metaphorical.

19. Had Euripides wished to continue divine protection for Andromache here, he would have had her require Menelaus to swear an oath to fulfill his promise. Euripides, however, portrays Menelaus as deceitful, not impious.

20. Euripides may have chosen Zeus Agoraios, "Zeus of the Marketplace," to anchor the play in local Athenian cult and also to emphasize the political and social

factors which elsewhere in the play are prominent in the decision to protect the suppliants. For the cult of this Zeus in Athens see Wycherley, *The Athenian Agora*, 3:122–124.

21. Poseidon is chosen for convenience and economy. To have Theseus nearby and demonstrate his piety, Euripides has him sacrificing, naturally enough, to his father, Poseidon. The setting, once established, is then convenient for the discovery of the suppliant Polyneices. Poseidon has no intrinsic relation to Polyneices or his supplication.

22. On Proteus as a hero see above, p. 36. A *heroön* was exceptional as a place of asylum, as both Menelaus (*Hel.* 800) and Kannicht (ad loc.) note. In A. *Ch.* 336–337 Electra's description of Agamemnon's tomb as a place of asylum appears metaphorical. For Theseus' sanctuary as a place of asylum in Athens see Christensen, "The Theseion."

23. On Zeus Soter in this play see Mikalson, "Zeus the Father and Heracles the Son in Tragedy"; and below, pp. 221–222.

24. E. *Heraclid.* 33, 72, 78, 97–98, 101, 113, 260, 264, 903.

25. Cf. 221–222.

26. Cf. A. *Eum.* 232–234, E. frag. 1049[N].

27. I.e., ἀγώνιοι θεοί, A. *Suppl.* 188–189, 242, 333, 355. See Fraenkel on A. *Ag.* 513.

28. In Homer Zeus Hikesios is the protector of the suppliant who appeals, not in the context of asylum, to another person, as he is also in Sophocles and Euripides: *Od.* 9.267–271, 13.213–214, 14.386–389, 16.421–423; S. *Ph.* 484–485; E. *Hec.* 342–345, frag. 16[P], line 15. Zeus Hikesios as protector of asylum may well be Aeschylus' creation.

29. A. *Suppl.* 192, 347, 359–360, 381–386, 413–416, 426–427, 478–479, 615–620, 641, 811–816. See Johansen and Whittle on *Supp.* 381–386.

30. A. *Suppl.* 751, 755–759, 893–894, 921–923. When the Greek Danaids attempt to convince Pelasgus, a Greek, to respect their asylum and supplication, they invoke a specific Greek god, Zeus Hikesios. But when the chorus, Pelasgus, and other Greeks attempt to argue many of the same points with Egyptians, they naturally speak only of the gods in general (750ff.). Cf. the association of asylum and belief in the existence of the gods humorously exploited in Ar. *Eq.* 30–34.

31. Cf. E. frag. 1049[N].

32. Cf. *Ion* 1253–1255, 1275, 1279–1281, 1309.

33. Similar criticisms of asylum arise in frag. 1049[N] from Euripides' *Oedipus* (see Snell, 554a[N]): "When a man who is unjust sits at an altar, I would bid the tradition (νόμον) farewell and, not fearing the gods, would take him off to court. A bad man ought always to suffer badly." Someone probably said this of Oedipus, but since we know nothing of the speaker or the context, we cannot take this as Euripidean criticism of popular religion. It may well, as in the *Ion,* turn out to be exactly the opposite.

34. Cf. Burnett, "Human Resistance and Divine Persuasion in Euripides' *Ion,*" 103 n. 36.

35. A. *Suppl.* 381–386, *Eum.* 232–234; S. *OC* 1285–1286; E. *Hel.* 801, 1086.

36. Human to deity: e.g., *Ag.* 338–339, 515, 925, *Ch.* 644–645 (cf. 55–57), *Eum.* 12–13, 22, 270–271, 725–726, 897, 910 (cf. 1018–1020). Mortal to superior mortal: e.g., *Ag.* 258, 785, 925 (Cf. 833), *Eum.* 270–271, 545–548. Divinity to superior divinity: A. *Eum.* 435. I owe these observations to Sean Mulholland. On τιμή owed to *xenoi* see below, p. 192.

37. Cf. A. *Suppl.* 83–85, on which see Johansen and Whittle. On a similar concept, as expressed through the term αἰδώς as well as σέβας see J. Gould, "Hiketeia," 86–90.

38. Cf. 232–234. "Betrayal" is commonly felt when gods do not assist mortals as they were expected to: A. *Th.* 104, 169, 251; E. *HF* 342–343, *Tr.* 1060–1070, *Ion* 438. See Yunis, *A New Creed,* 83, 131.

39. To Robert Garland I owe the example of the heroes Aeacidae. After the Aeginetans had sent the heroes to help the Thebans in battle and the Thebans were once again defeated by the Athenians, the Thebans sent the Aeacidae back to Aegina and asked for men (Hdt. 5.80–81).

40. Plato seems not to observe this distinction and has foreigners in general protected by Zeus Xenios, even in commercial transactions, largely because they are helpless and "more pitiable" (*Leg.* 5.729D–730A; cf. 12.953E). On social, political, and religious elements of *xenia* see Herman, *Ritualized Friendship,* esp. 124–125; J. Gould, "Hiketeia," 90–94.

41. In tragedy: A. *Eum.* passim; S. *OC* 261–262; E. *Heraclid.* 329–330. In prose: e.g., Lys. 2.11–16; Hdt. 9.27; Dem. 60.8; Isoc. 4.52, 10.31, 12.168–171.

42. The foreign visitors who appeal to the gods or to piety have in each instance taken asylum (A. *Suppl.* passim; S. *OC* 258–265; E. *Heraclid.* 93–94, 107–108, 112–113, 416–418). In S. *OC* 632–633 Theseus claims he has a military-based *xenia* (δορύξενος κοινὴ ... ἑστία) with Oedipus, but Oedipus makes no reference to this *xenia*. Shipwrecked sailors were a special case: in Euripidean drama at least they were *xenoi* with a form of asylum protected by the gods (*Hel.* 449; cf. *Cycl.* 299–303).

43. Zeus Xenios: *Ag.* 60–71, 355–402, 534–537, 699–716. Cf. *Suppl.* 627–629, 670–673. Euripides has "the gods" assist Menelaus in punishing Paris (*Tr.* 867–868). For the Homeric version of this see *Il.* 3.351–354.

44. *Ag.* 60–71, 355–384, 699–705 (on which see Fraenkel ad loc.), 744–749. Throughout tragedy Zeus Xenios seems to oversee only the guest/host *xenia*. A. *Suppl.* 627–629 and 670–673 may be an exception, but the situation there is complicated because the Danaids are *xenoi* who have asylum *and* claim ties of kinship. On Zeus Xenios see Farnell, *Cults of the Greek States,* 1:73–74; Herman, *Ritualized Friendship,* 125.

45. On Zeus Hikesios see above, pp. 74–75.

46. The phratry Thymaitis had a sanctuary of Zeus Xenios, probably in the fifth century (*IG* I² 886). There is also attested a late (112/111 B.C.), private cult of him, probably in the Piraeus (*IG* II² 1012). On both see Wycherley, "The Olympieion at Athens," 178.

47. On Theonoë see below, pp. 95–98.

48. Comparable is the relationship of Priam, Polymestor, and Polydorus in Euripides' *Hecuba*.

49. Cf. 1638.

50. Cf. 1647–1649.

51. Menelaus too claims the rights of a *xenos* as the victim of a shipwreck (449, 479–480) and casually reminds Theonoë of this status in his arguments to her (954).

52. On Admetus' devotion to *xenia* see D. M. Jones, "Euripides' *Alcestis*"; Burnett, "The Virtues of Admetus." For φιλοξενία as a virtue in Athens see *IG* I² 530, line 3; Hansen, no. 67.

53. Cf. 23, 41–42. Cf. also A. *Eum.* 723–726.

54. Cf. 8, 476, 537–605, 747–772, 809, 822–823, 830, 854–860, 1012–1018, 1037–1040, 1151.

55. The servant who questions Admetus' reception of Heracles in these circumstances (747–772) could not be expected to appreciate the obligations by which a royal, aristocratic, and "respectful" master feels himself bound. Cf. 600–601, 859–860. On *xenia* as primarily an aristocratic institution see Herman, *Ritualized Friendship*, 162–165. Throughout (cf. 551–552, 809, 822, 1012–1018, 1037–1040) we are made to think that Admetus goes well beyond the ordinary in fulfilling his duties as a *xenos*.

56. Had Admetus refused Heracles hospitality because of his own sorrow and grieving, Alcestis most surely would not have been saved. Cf. 68–69, 1119–1120, 1128, 1147–1148.

57. Cf. 604–605, 1147–1148.

58. Failed promise: cf. A. *Ch.* 704–706; E. *Med.* 1391–1392 and frag. 667[N]. Killing of son: in Sophocles' *Trachiniae* (260–283) Heracles killed, by deceit, the son of a *xenos* who had given him a poor, hybristic reception. Sophocles has Olympian Zeus angry only at Heracles' deceitful tactics. Otherwise the son deserved to die because of his father's treatment of Heracles. Isocrates (12.121–122) associated the murder of a *xenos* with crimes like incest and the murder of a brother, father, or mother. Cf. Hes. *Op.* 327–334.

59. Polymestor, speaking in his own defense (1132–1182), avoids calling either himself or Priam or Polydorus a *xenos* and thereby never responds to the real charge, namely that he violated the obligations of *xenia*. Agamemnon, who makes the final judgment in the case, is not misled (1240–1251). On Polymestor's injustice, impiety, etc., see 714–716, 788–794, 803–805, 852–853, 1004 (sarcastic, of course), 1023–1034, 1086, 1233–1235, 1247–1248. Polymestor's actions and words reveal other faults as well: he has denied Polydorus burial (47–52, 781–782, 796–797); he lies, though not under oath, to Hecuba about Polydorus' fate (989–993); he desires to take vengeance on the Trojan women by eating their bodies (1071–1074, 1125–1126), a thought which Agamemnon terms "barbaric" (1129). On Polymestor's crimes see Meridor, "The Function of Polymestor's Crime"; Hall, *Inventing the Barbarian*, 107–110.

60. See Plescia, *The Oath and Perjury*; *APR*, 31–38, 98–99.

61. For fifth-century examples see Thuc. 5.18.9–19.2, 23.1–24.1, 38.1–3, 42.1, 47.1–12; *IG* I³ 37, 39, 40, 53, 62, 75, and 76.

62. According to Thucydides the Spartans, in retrospect, thought they had suffered the loss at Pylos in 425 and other misfortunes of the Archidamian War because they had violated their oath-bound treaty with the Plataeans in 429 (7.18.2; cf. 2.71.2–3, 2.74.2).

63. *APR*, 31–38, 98–99.

64. This oath is unique in that Orestes promises that he himself, as a dead hero, will punish violators. He thus makes the oath and simultaneously becomes its superhuman guarantor.

65. On which see Jeffery, "The *Battle of Oinoe* in the Stoa Poikile," 55. For fifth- and fourth-century examples of the weakness of international agreements not secured by oaths see Plescia, *The Oath and Perjury,* 59.

66. See p. 263 n. 81.

67. See above, pp. 32–34.

68. A. *Ag.* 1431–1434, on which see Fraenkel ad loc. Unlike his fellow tragedians, Aeschylus on occasion has characters swear by triads of deities (here Dike, Ate, and Erinys; in *Th.* 42–48 Ares, Enyo, and Phobos), as was common in formal state oaths. See Usener, "Dreiheit"; Dover on Ar. *Nub.* 1234. The use of abstractions as witnesses (Dike, Ate, and Phobos) is peculiar to Aeschylus. That Parthenopaeus in *Th.* 529–532 swears by his spear rather than by a god is probably an indication of his hybris. See below, pp. 159–160.

69. Cf. 481–483, 491–493, 609–610.

70. See above, p. 62. Similarly Lichas in Sophocles' *Trachiniae* violates his oath on Zeus to tell Deianira the truth, and though no explicit connection is made, he dies at Heracles' hands (378, 398–399, 427–428, 436–437, 772–784; cf. 427–428).

71. Cf. 20–23, 160–163, 168–170, 410–414, 439–440, 492–498, 510–511, 1391–1392.

72. Injustice associated with perjury: 165, 208, 577–578, 692, 767, 802. Gods invoked as witnesses: 20–23, 160–163, 168–170, 208–212, 332, 1351–1353.

73. So the force of the τότ' in 493.

74. See Pl. *Leg.* 12.948B–D. Cf. *Rep.* 2.364B–365A, *Leg.* 10.885B, 905D–907B. Similarly in Aristophanes' *Clouds* 245–251 a discussion of oaths leads quickly to questions of the nature of the gods.

75. On 467–468 see Page ad loc.

76. In strong contrast to Jason stands the Athenian Aegeus. He too swears an oath to Medea, but he will keep it and as a result will acquire the offspring he has long desired. Once again an Athenian serves as the exemplar of what is decent and pious (709–758).

77. Cf. 1013–1014.

78. Cf. 796, 1268–1270, 1282–1289, 1327–1328, 1371–1373, 1383.

79. On Helios and Hecate in Athens and in this play see Mikalson, "Unanswered Prayers," 84–86, 97–98.

80. On Medea's "Greekness" see Mikalson, "Unanswered Prayers," 84–86, 97–98; B. M. W. Knox, "The *Medea* of Euripides," 211–218 (= *Word and Action*, 306–311).

81. E.g., S. *Ant.* 184, 304–314, *Tr.* 1185–1190, *Ph.* 1289, 1324, *OC* 1767; E. *Hipp.* 1025–1031, *IT* 749; *Rh.* 816–819.

82. If we accept as genuine the closing lines of the exodos (1415–1419), Zeus' importance to this play is emphasized, because only here among the five versions of these lines (*Alc.* 1159–1163, *Andr.* 1284–1288, *Hel.* 1688–1692, *Ba.* 1388–1392) is Zeus specifically named. See Kovacs, "Treading the Circle Warily," 268–269.

83. Cf. 157, 208–209, 764–767, 802.

84. Plescia, *The Oath and Perjury*, 6; Usener, "Dreiheit," 19.

85. Cf. Sophocles frag. 932[R], where there is no mention of divine punishment for false oaths made by a woman in labor.

86. *IA* 394a–395:

οὐ γὰρ ἀσύνετον τὸ θεῖον, ἀλλ᾽ ἔχει συνιέναι
τοὺς κακῶς παγέντας ὅρκους καὶ κατηναγκασμένους.

394a is lacking in the best manuscripts.

87. Cf. 264–267. By contrast Oedipus in *OC* 650 thinks requiring an oath of Theseus would be treating him as though he were κακός. But later he apparently exacted an oath from Theseus (1636–1637, 1767).

88. Cf. the elaborate and delightful false oath of Silenus in E. *Cycl.* 262–269, the curse of which calls for the destruction, not of himself, but of his "children," the satyrs. The satyrs then reply in kind (271–272).

89. Lying servant: cf. S. frag. 933[R]. On the possibility of Orestes' deviousness see Schein, "Electra, A Sophoclean Problem Play," 72–73.

90. On Apollo's arguments as advocate see Roberts, *Apollo and His Oracle in the Oresteia*, 60–72; Winnington-Ingram, "The Role of Apollo in the *Oresteia*."

91. Cf. *Eum.* 679–680, the same advice but from the chorus.

92. See above, p. 7, and below, p. 228.

93. On Hippolytus' piety concerning oaths see B. M. W. Knox, *Word and Action*, 220–221.

94. See above, p. 7, and below, p. 228.

95. *APR*, 31–38. On gods, justice, morality, and oaths see also Burkert, *GR*, 246–254.

96. *Eum.* 482–486, 708–710. For the jurors' oath in Athens see *APR*, 31–32.

97. Cf. S. *Ant.* 368–369, θεῶν τ᾽ ἔνορκον δίκαν.

98. On divination, in life and literature, see Nilsson, *Geschichte der griechischen Religion*, 1:164–174; Nock, "Religious Attitudes of the Ancient Greeks"; Parke, *The Oracles of Zeus*; Pritchett, *The Greek State at War*, 3:47–153, 296–321; Fontenrose, *The Delphic Oracle*; Burkert, *GR*, 109–118; Bächli, *Die künstlerische Funktion von Orakelsprüchen, Weissagen, Träumen*; Parker, "Greek States and Greek Oracles"; Smith, "Diviners and Divination in Aristophanic Comedy"; Mikalson, *APR*, 39–49.

99. For specific examples see Yunis, *A New Creed,* 44 n. 14.

100. Fontenrose, *Delphic Oracle,* divides the responses of Delphi into historical (H), quasi-historical (Q), legendary (L), and fictional (F) and provides a catalogue of each group (244–416). H2, 7, 9–13, 15–17, and 21–33 all concern *res divinae* at least in part.

101. Fontenrose, H4, 5, 8, 11, 13, 15, 19, 20, 22. For a more inclusive treatment of such oracles see Pritchett, *The Greek State at War,* 3:296–321.

102. Colonization: Fontenrose, H6, 14. For a full account of Delphi's role in colonization see Malkin, *Religion and Colonization,* 17–91. Desire for children: Fontenrose, H34.

103. On these tablets see Parke, *The Oracles of Zeus,* 100–114. The largest collection is in Carapanos, *Dodone et ses ruines,* 68–83. Cf. Plut. *Mor.* 3.386C, 3.408C.

104. Colonization: E. *Ph.* 638–648, *Hel.* 144–150. Plague: S. *OT* passim. Infertility of land: S. *OT* passim; E. *Ion* 303. Marriage: A. *Pr.* 829–835; E. *Suppl.* 5–7, 138–146, 219–221, 832–833. Disease: A. *Eum.* 60–63. Identity of parents: S. *OT* 774–793; E. *Ph.* 33–37. Childlessness: E. *Med.* 667–681, *Ion* passim, esp. 303, 404–409, *Ph.* 13–23, frag. 2[A], 19–25.

105. On divine intervention see above, pp. 45–64.

106. For examples of these foundations see above, pp. 32–33, 41–44, 65–67. The cult of Oedipus also receives immediate validation through the mysterious god's voice, which has the function if not the form of a *deus ex machina* (*OC* 1623–1628).

107. Dodds, *The Ancient Concept of Progress,* 177 n. 3. Cf. Gernet and Boulanger, *Le génie grec dans la religion,* 286.

108. S. *OT* 711–714, 787–793, 852–854, 994–996. See Dodds, "On Misunderstanding the *Oedipus Rex,*" 41 (= *The Ancient Concept of Progress,* 69).

109. Heracles: S. *Tr.* 76–81, 164–172, 821–827, 1159–1174. Oedipus: S. *OT* 787–793, 994–996, *OC* 621–628, 969–973; E. *Ph.* 1703–1707. Eurystheus: E. *Heraclid.* 1026–1044. Persians: A. *Pers.* 739–741. Cf. E. *Cycl.* 696–700.

110. Fontenrose, *The Delphic Oracle,* 20.

111. Cf. S. frag. 771[R]; for problems of interpretation see Pearson on S. frag. 771.

112. On these oracles see Bowra, *Sophoclean Tragedy,* 150–154; Kirkwood, *A Study of Sophoclean Drama,* 78–79.

113. See below, pp. 105–107.

114. Owen (*Euripides: Ion,* xx) and B. Gauger (*Gott und Mensch im Ion,* 79–89) argue, unsuccessfully I think, that the oracle should be viewed as ambiguous, not false. See Yunis, *A New Creed,* 135 n. 64.

115. Xen. *Ap.* 13, *Symp.* 4.47–49, *Eq. Mag.* 9.9.

116. Cf. E. *Ion* 5–7.

117. E.g., A. *Eum.* 19, 614–618; E. frag. 13 [P], 8–13.

118. On seers and chresmologues see Fontenrose, *The Delphic Oracle,* 152–165; J. Oliver, *The Athenian Expounders of the Sacred and Ancestral Law,* 1–17; Jacoby,

FGrHist, on 328 T2; Th. Hopfner, "Mantike," *RE* 14 (1928), cols. 1258–1288; Burkert, *GR*, 111–114; Roth, "Teiresias as *Mantis* and Intellectual in Euripides' *Bacchae*"; Smith, "Diviners and Divination in Aristophanic Comedy." On the role of seers in military affairs see Pritchett, *The Greek State at War*, 3:47–153.

119. On the role of seer in the Peloponnesian War and Sicilian expedition see Radermacher, "Euripides und die Mantik," 504–510. In the late fifth century Lampon and perhaps other seers were also ridiculed for their role in the (ultimately) unsuccessful colony Thurii, which the Athenians founded in 443/442 B.C. See Malkin, *Religion and Colonization*, 98–101.

120. For apparent chresmologues, in an Athenian context, see E. *Heraclid.* 403–405, 488–490.

121. Plut. *Per.* 6.2–3. On Lampon's religious and political activity see Yunis, *A New Creed*, 69–70. On Philochorus see Jacoby, *FGrHist* 328 F67.

122. Fontenrose, *The Delphic Oracle*, 156; Jacoby, *FGrHist*, on 328 T2; Malkin, *Religion and Colonization*, 97–101. On seers' role in colonization in general see Malkin, 92–113.

123. At state sacrifices: [Arist.] *Ath. Pol.* 54.6. Hierocles and Euboea: *IG* I² 39; Jacoby, *FGrHist*, on 328 T2.

124. Plut. *Nic.* 13.1–4.

125. Osborne, "Honours for Sthorys (*IG* II² 17)." On the activities of the Athenian seer/chresmologue/politician Diopeithes see Connor, "Two Notes on Diopeithes."

126. Plut. *Nic.* 4.2, 14.6, 23.1–24.1. Cf. Thuc. 7.50, where the delay is recommended by seers.

127. E.g., *An.* 5.2.9, 6.4.12–22, 6.5.2, 6.5.8, 7.8.10, 7.8.22.

128. *An.* 6.4.23–26. Cf. *Hell.* 4.8.36–39.

129. *An.* 5.6.28–29, 6.1.22–24.

130. But cf. *IG* I² 39 described above, p. 92. Jacoby, *FGrHist* on 328 T2, following Cicero *De Div.* 1.43.95, attributes to seers a major role in Athenian deliberations on religious matters and on foreign and domestic affairs.

131. Cf. Isoc. 19.5–7. On deductive versus inductive prophecy see Th. Hopfner, "Mantike," *RE* 14 (1928), cols. 1258–1288.

132. These same three methods are credited by Theseus in E. *Suppl.* 211–213 to his divine benefactor. See S. *Ant.* 998–1022 and E. *El.* 826–833 (where Aegisthus acts as his own seer) for the fullest descriptions of these procedures in tragedy. For details on extispicy see Pritchett, *The Greek State at War*, 3:73–78.

133. E.g., E. *El.* 399–400, *Ph.* 954–959.

134. Wise: S. *OT* 484; E. *IT* 662, *Ba.* 179, 186; *Rh.* 65–66. Cf. S. *Aj.* 783. More than human: S. *OT* 297–299; E. *Hec.* 87.

135. S. *OT* 297–299, *Ant.* 1091–1094; E. frag. 795[N]; *Rh.* 65–66.

136. God-spoken words: θέσφατον, E. *Ph.* 766–768, *Suppl.* 230; θεσπίζω and cognates, S. *Ant.* 1054, 1091, *Ph.* 610; E. *Ph.* 903, 907, 911, 971. The same words are used of Apollo's oracles: e.g., S. *OC* 388, 969–970, 1472; E. *IT* 120–121, 937,

1013–1014, 1255, 1438, *Andr.* 296, 1161, *Hel.* 148–150, *Ion* 685, 729, 755, 779. Cf. S. *OC* 1427–1428, 1516–1517. Signs: E. *Suppl.* 211–213, *Ph.* 955, *Hel.* 749.

137. War: A. *Th.* 24–29, 377–383, *Ag.* 109–157; S. *Ph.* 604–613, 1336–1342; E. *Ph.* 766–773, 834–959, 1255–1258, *Suppl.* 155–161, 229–231, *Heraclid.* 340, 400–409, 488–490, 819–822, *IA* 88–92; *Rh.* 63–69. Voyages: A. *Ag.* 109–157; E. *IT* 15–24, *IA* 88–92. Health: S. *OT* 284–462; E. *Hipp.* 236–238. Omens: A. *Ag.* 109–157. Dreams: A. *Ch.* 32–41, 551; E. *Hec.* 87–89. Religious needs: concerning sacrifice of Iphigeneia, A. *Ag.* 109–157, E. *IT* 15–24, *IA* 88–92; of Menoeceus, E. *Ph.* 931–941. Concerning pollution of murder, S. *OT* 284–462; of unburied dead, S. *Ant.* 998–1032. In neither life nor literature do seers institute new cults or festivals.

138. E.g., A. *Th.* 24–29, 377–383; E. *Ph.* 1255–1258, *Suppl.* 155–161, 229–231.

139. Present circumstances: S. *OT* 284–462, *OC* 1298–1300; E. *IT* 15–24. Cf. E. *Hec.* 743–744, *Hipp.* 1055–1059, 1320–1322, *Hel.* 749–751. Future events: A. *Th.* 617–618, *Ag.* 109–157; S. *Ph.* 604–613, 1336–1342; E. *Ph.* 867–952, *IA* 88–92. Plans and purposes of the gods: A. *Ag.* 109–157; S. *Aj.* 756–779; E. *Ph.* 931–941, *IT* 15–24, *Hipp.* 236–238, frag. 795[N].

140. *Il.* 1.68–113, 2.322–330.

141. S. *Ant.* 1059, *OT* 484; E. *Ba.* 170–369, esp. 179, 186, 368–369. On Teiresias in the *Bacchae* see below, pp. 147–151.

142. A. *Ag.* 1072–1330; E. *Tr.* 352–461, *Andr.* 293–300, frag. 42b[N].

143. On Cassandra in Greek tragedy see Mason, "Kassandra."

144. On which see Kannicht on *Hel.* 13–15.

145. In the mythological tradition Nereus is renowned primarily for justice and honesty, not for prophecy (Hes. *Th.* 233–236; cf. *Hel.* 922–923, 1002–1004). For possible associations of Nereus with prophecy see Detienne, *Les maîtres de vérité*, 29–50.

146. On possible interpolations here see Burnett, *Catastrophe Survived*, 86–87; Kannicht ad loc.

147. Cf. E. *Ion* 374–377; Ar. *Av.* 963–965.

148. Kannicht on *Hel.* 744–760; Radermacher, "Euripides und die Mantik."

149. See above, p. 92. In 414 there was also some hostility towards the seers from the problems at Thurii. See above, note 119.

150. On the form of Theonoë's mantic knowledge and on other unusual features about her see Zuntz, "Euripides' *Helena*"; Kannicht, *Euripides: Helena*, 1:71–77; Conacher, *Euripidean Drama*, 294–297; Parker, *Miasma*, 93–94; Matthiessen, "Zur Theonoeszene."

151. See comments in this regard in *Euripide*, 238, and Matthiessen, "Zur Theonoeszene," 696.

152. See, e.g., the unusual syncretism of 1301–1368, the unique Aether/Ouranos religion described below, and the use of a hero shrine for asylum (797–801, on which see above, p. 36). See also Hall, *Inventing the Barbarian*, 150–151.

153. See Matthiessen, "Zur Theonoeszene," 699–704.

154. Cf. E. *Ba.* 292–293.

155. On this see Kannicht on 1013–1016.
156. See Kannicht's extensive commentary on passages cited.
157. Cf. E. *IA* 520.
158. See below, pp. 110–113.
159. Cf. E. *Hel.* 919–923.
160. Cf. E. *IT* 531–533.
161. See above, pp. 67–68.
162. On Creon and Ajax see below, pp. 139–144.
163. On dreams see Dodds, *The Ancient Concept of Progress,* 176–185, and *Greeks and the Irrational,* 102–134; H. Kenner, "Oneiros," *RE* 18 (1959), cols. 448–459; Th. Hopfner, "Traumdeutung," *RE,* ser. 2, 6 (1937), cols. 2233–2245; Messer, *The Dream in Homer and Greek Tragedy*; Kessels, *Studies on the Dream.*
164. *IG* IV² 121, 33–41. See Edelstein and Edelstein, *Asclepius,* 2:139–158.
165. Cf. *An.* 6.1.20–24.
166. *IG* I² 524, the crucial part of the text of which, however, is restored.
167. Asclepios had not yet arrived in Athens, and Pericles could not entrust his workman to him.
168. *APR,* 40.
169. A. *Pers.* 176–230, 517–526, *Pr.* 640–672, *Ch.* 32–41, 523–531, 928–929. I leave aside A. *Eum.* 94–139, where the dead Clytemnestra appears onstage as a dream image to the sleeping Erinyes. This is like other dreams in that the recipients are female and the dream emanates from the underworld.
170. S. *El.* 410–427, 459–460, 498–502, 644–647.
171. E. *Hec.* 68–97, 702–707, *IT* 42–62, 148–156, 348–350, 569–571.
172. Noted by Messer, *The Dream in Homer and Tragedy,* 51, 84, 93, 98. The single exception, as so often, is in the *Rhesus* (780–788), where Rhesus' charioteer dreams that wolves are attacking his master's horses. Aeschylus' Eteocles (*Th.* 710–711) briefly reports "true sights of sleep apparitions," but of these we learn nothing more. On this passage and for reservations about the convention that only women dream in tragedy see Kessels, *Studies on the Dream,* 163–165.
173. Diggle, following Wilamowitz, rejects these lines (90–91). If we accept all his deletions (73–76, 90–97), we learn nothing of the content of Hecuba's dream except that it portends evil.
174. Cf. Messer, *The Dream in Homer and Tragedy,* 57–58: "The immediate source of dream in tragedy is to be found *not in religion and cult,* but in the *literature,* that is, the source of the dream in tragedy is a bookish, artistic source."
175. A. *Pr.* 484–486, *Ch.* 32–41 (on which see Garvie ad loc.), 551; E. *Hec.* 87–89. Cf. A. *Pers.* 224–227.
176. A. *Pr.* 658–672.
177. A. *Pers.* 201–211.
178. A. *Pers.* 201–230, 517–526, *Ch.* 44–46, 523–550; S. *El.* 406–410, 426–427, 630–659; E. *Hec.* 79–82, 96–97 (on which see Diggle ad loc.). Cf. Xen. *Symp.* 4.33.
179. A. *Pers.* 205–206; S. *El.* 630–659.

180. For discussion of this dream see below, pp. 107–110.

181. That Prometheus omits meteorological omens from his otherwise rather complete list may not be accidental. Such signs were credited to Zeus, if to anyone, and for Prometheus to assist men in understanding signs sent from Zeus may have seemed incongruous with the Zeus/Prometheus antipathy at the core of the play.

182. One would expect to have a seer attending a ruler at a sacrifice, but by eliminating him Euripides has simplified the scene, accelerated the action, and removed a potential (and "holy") defender of Aegisthus.

183. Journeys: A. *Ag.* 109–159, *Eum.* 770, frag. 95[R]; E. *Hipp.* 757–762. Cf. Thuc. 6.27.3, 7.79.3; Plut. *Per.* 35.1–2, *Nic.* 23. Battle and war: A. *Ag.* 109–159; E. *Ph.* 1187–1192. Marriage: E. *IA* 607–610, 987–989.

184. E. *IA* 988–989. Cf. Thuc. 6.27.3, 7.79.3; Plut. *Per.* 6.1–3, 35.1–2, *Nic.* 23.

185. A. frag. 95[R]; E. *Ion* 1187–1193, *IA* 607–610.

186. In tragedy: Birds: A. *Pers.* 205–211, *Ag.* 109–159; S. *OT* 964–967; E. *Hipp.* 1058–1059, *HF* 596–597. Chance words: E. *IA* 607–610, *Ion* 1187–1193. Thunder and lightning: E. *Ph.* 1187–1192. Cf. Xen. *Ap.* 12. In life: Rain: Thuc. 7.79.3. Earthquake: Thuc. 8.6.5, Plut. *Nic.* 10.6. Eclipse: Plut. *Per.* 35.1–2, *Nic.* 23. Sneeze: Xen. *An.* 3.2.9. Sacrilegious act: Thuc. 6.27.1–3. Plutarch reflects the interests of his own age when he lists the following four signs the Athenians reputedly disregarded when they decided on the Sicilian expedition (*Nic.* 13.1–4): the mutilation of the herms; a man's self-mutilation at the altar of the twelve gods; ravens in Delphi attacking an Athenian dedication; Athenians fetching on an oracle's command the priestess of Athena from Clazomenae and finding her name to be Hesychia (Peace).

187. E. *Hipp.* 757–762, on which see Barrett ad loc.

188. Good omens: E. *IA* 607–610. Bad omens: ἀθυμέω and its cognates are the *voces propriae*: A. *Eum.* 770; E. *El.* 831. Cf. S. *OT* 747; Thuc. 7.79.3.

189. E.g., Plut. *Per.* 6.1–3, 35.1–2, *Nic.* 23.

190. Cf. Nilsson, *Greek Popular Religion,* 123–139. For relevance of divination to the *Suppliants* see Collard, p. 166.

191. Nestle, *Euripides,* 71. Norwood (*Essays on Euripidean Drama,* 154) rejects these lines as un-Euripidean *because* of their praise of divination.

192. In the *Heraclidae,* also a play of the 420s, Demophon, king of Athens, in similar circumstances is meticulous in seeing that the seers and oracles are consulted and in studying and comparing their responses (399–409, 673, 819–822). Compare Aeschines' allegation that Demosthenes sent out Athenian troops to Chaeronia in 338 despite unfavorable omens (Aeschines 3.131).

193. Cf. *Suppl.* 211–213, 229–231, 496–505, 594–597, 608–616, frag. 352[N].

194. Nestle (*Euripides,* 71) and Zuntz (*The Political Plays,* 7) fail to observe this distinction.

195. Athena's revelation of the future is accurate, clearly the prime requisite of divination, whether or not it shows the gods to be just, fair, or kindly. On the latter see Conacher, "Religion and Ethical Attitudes in Euripides' *Suppliants,*" 26.

196. But not until the defeat of the Argives by the Thebans. In Euripides' other

account of this oracle (*Ph.* 408–425) Polyneices, before his death and the failure of the expedition, seems reasonably content with the marriage (424–425), but the potential for disaster was evident (580–582). In the *Phoenissae* characters make no judgment on Apollo or Adrastus concerning this oracle.

197. See the discussions of Conacher, "Religion and Ethical Attitudes in Euripides' *Suppliants*," 17–18; Gamble, "Euripides' *Suppliant Women*: Decision and Ambivalence," 398–399. Zuntz (*The Political Plays*, 7) oversimplifies the situation and, apparently, lays all the blame on Adrastus.

198. Before an Athenian court of law no consideration of "compulsion" by oracles would have arisen (*APR*, 48). Theseus' concentration on social, moral, and ethical issues (219–225), viewed in this regard, is quite realistic.

199. Adrastus acknowledges the difficulty of interpreting the oracle: Φοίβου μ' ὑπῆλθε δυστόπαστ' αἰνίγματα, 138.

200. Euripides likewise has Theseus move from primarily religious considerations to profane ones in his criticisms of Adrastus for ignoring the seer's warning before the expedition (155–161).

201. The answer, I suspect, lies in ὡς ζώντων θεῶν (221) or what originally stood in their place. Of attempts to make sense of this unparalleled phrase, even the best (Conacher, "Religion and Ethical Attitudes in Euripides' *Suppliants*," 18: "As if the gods were like human beings, directly interfering in political affairs") must read far too much into ζώντων and are unconvincing. I follow Collard (on *Suppl.* 220–221) in rejecting the possibility of ζώντων. It is clearly in this half line that Theseus rendered his judgment on the oracle or on Adrastus' use of it. But that is now lost. For our purposes it is best not to recommend an emendation such as Scaliger's δόντων for ζώντων (accepted by Diggle), which necessarily turns the balance one way or the other.

202. Cf. 348–349.

203. Accepting, with Diggle, ἀτιστέον for the manuscript's κακιστέον. The text of Orestes' response to Pylades (120–121) is also problematic.

204. On ἀλαθοσύναν of 1279 see Platnauer ad loc.

205. Grube (*The Drama of Euripides*, 118–119) thinks this hymn has "little dramatic relevance."

206. For the date see Platnauer, p. xvi. On the challenge to seers in the *Helen* see above, pp. 95–100.

207. Dodds ("On Misunderstanding the *Oedipus Rex*, 41 = *The Ancient Concept of Progress*, 69) stresses that the oracle did not involve a condition ("If you . . . , then . . ."). It was, as Sophocles presents it, a simple statement of what was to happen.

208. See above, pp. 88–90.

209. Cf. 69–72, 95–107, 132–136, 149–150, 241–245, 305–309.

210. On Apollo and the Athenian plague of 430–426 B.C. see Mikalson, "Religion and the Plague in Athens, 431–423 B.C.," 217–225. Pausanias reports (10.11.5) that the residents of Cleonae, suffering from the same plague, were told by Delphi to

sacrifice to the rising sun. They did so, found relief, and dedicated a bronze goat to Apollo at Delphi.

211. Cf. 284–286, 376–377, 410. Sophocles creates or, better, emphasizes a special closeness of Teiresias to Apollo in the *Oedipus Tyrannus,* thereby interlocking Apollo's oracles and Teiresias' pronouncements. Elsewhere too seers are occasionally linked to Apollo (S. *Ph.* 841–843; E. *Ba.* 328, *Hyps.* frags. 22 and 60 [Bond], 25–26; cf. *Il.* 1.72, *Od.* 15. 244–245) and Apollo is sometimes even called a seer ($\mu\acute{\alpha}\nu\tau\iota\varsigma$, A. *Ag.* 1202, 1275, *Ch.* 559, *Eum.* 18, 169, 595, 615; E. *IT* 711, 1128, *Ion* 387, 682; cf. S. *OT* 965; A. *Eum.* 61–63, 715–716, frag. 350[R]). Often, however, Teiresias and the other seers appear independent of Apollo and do not, when challenged, invoke his authority: e.g., Teiresias in S. *Ant.* and E. *Ph.* (note lines 954–959), Calchas in A. *Ag.*; S. *Aj.*; E. *IT, Hel.*, and *IA.* It should also be recalled that in tragedy Prometheus, or Theseus' divine benefactor, not Apollo, taught men the mantic arts (above, pp. 46–47). We thus should recognize the special purpose in Sophocles' close association of Apollo and Teiresias in the *Oedipus Tyrannus.*

212. See above, p. 99.

213. On the relationship of Jocasta's and Oedipus' criticisms of oracles to this ode see Winnington-Ingram, *Sophocles,* 179–200.

214. The same Delphic god is called Phoebus (71, 96, 133, 149, 163, 279, 285, 712, 788, 1011), an epithet explained explicitly in A. *Eum.* 7–8 and allusively in E. *IT* 1252–1269.

215. Apollo responsible for events: 376–377, 720–722, 1329–1330. Cf. 738, the "plan" of Zeus. Voluntary actions: in 1329–1330 and 1349–1355, e.g., are contrasted, as strophe and antistrophe, Apollo's involvement and the free choice of individuals.

216. On Jocasta's prayer to Apollo Lykeios (not Pythios) in 911–921 see Mikalson, "Unanswered Prayers," 87.

217. *APR,* 74–82. For general studies of Greek concepts and practices concerning death, funerals, and the afterlife see Garland, *The Greek Way of Death*; Kurtz and Boardman, *Greek Burial Customs*; Burkert, *GR,* 190–199; Parker, *Miasma,* 32–73; Alexiou, *The Ritual Lament,* 4–23, 102–103, 131–205; Humphreys, "Family Tombs and Tomb Cult in Athens."

218. See above, pp. 25–28.

219. A. frag. 362[R]; S. *Ant.* 1328–1332, frag. 951[R]; E. *Hec.* 43–44, frag. 916[N].

220. A. *Ag.* 1451, *Eum.* 704–706 (on which see Dodds, *The Ancient Concept of Progress,* 49); S. *OC* 621. Cf. A. *Ch.* 318, 495; S. *Tr.* 1040–1042, *El.* 436, *Ph.* 856–861, *OC* 1578, 1706.

221. Cf. Stanford on *Aj.* 1192–1194. For other possible meanings of these lines, especially in reference to *aether,* see Jebb on 1192 and Kamerbeek on 1193.

222. On the Hyacinthidae see above, pp. 32–34. Cf. E. frag. 971[N].

223. Plut. *Per.* 8.6, *Arist.* 21; Thuc. 3.58.4; *APR,* 78–79; Garland, *The Greek Way of Death,* 89–93.

224. See above, p. 98. On 1013–1016 see Kannicht ad loc.

225. *Aether* and Hades are, quite obviously, mutually exclusive abodes for the same souls. If we follow Denniston's interpretation (ad loc.) of E. *El.* 59, γόους τ' ἀφίημ' αἰθέρ' ἐς μέγαν πατρί, Electra imagines her father's soul in the *aether*, but sixty-three lines later (122–123; cf. 144) in Hades. Inconsistency of beliefs about the afterlife is common but need not be assumed here. Electra's point in this soliloquy is only, I think, that she is speaking her laments openly, but to no living audience. E. *Suppl.* 1139–1141,

αἰθὴρ ἔχει νιν ἤδη,
πυρὸς τετακότας σποδῷ·
ποτανοὶ δ' ἤνυσαν τὸν Ἀιδαν.

offers a curious muddle (noted by Denniston on E. *El.* 59) of these ideas. The *aether* "holds" those who have melted away in the ash of the fire, but the dead, winged, make their way to Hades. Apparently here cremation releases the souls into the *aether*, only for them to fly away to Hades.

226. *Aether* as philosophical idea: see Wilamowitz, *Der Glaube der Hellenen*, 1.368; Guthrie, *The Greeks and Their Gods*, 262–264; Kannicht on E. *Hel.* 1013–1016; Collard on E. *Suppl.* 531–536; Nestle, *Euripides*, 160–163. In epitaphs: *IG* II² 11466 and 13104–5.

227. E. *Tr.* 632–638, *IA* 1250–1252, frag. 532[N]. Cf. E. *Alc.* 381.

228. *Ch.* 517–518 (for the problems of which see Garvie ad loc.), frag. 266[R]. Cf. E. *Or.* 1084.

229. Perception denied: E. *Alc.* 404, 726, frag. 176[N]. Powerlessness: E. frags. 450[N], 532[N].

230. A. *Ch.* 517–518, frag. 266[R]; S. *El.* 137–139; E. *Hel.* 1421, frags. 176[N], 640[N].

231. Such discrepancies incline some to emend the texts. See, e.g., Garvie on A. *Ch.* 517–518. Garvie (p. xxxiii) finds a literary purpose in some such discrepancies in the *Choephoroi*.

232. A. *Ag.* 567–569, *Suppl.* 802–803, *Pr.* 747–754, frag. 255[R]; S. *El.* 1170, *Tr.* 1173, *OC* 954–955, frag. 698[R]; E. *Suppl.* 86, 1000–1005, *Tr.* 271, 606–607, 641–642, *Heraclid.* 591–596, *Alc.* 937–938, *Hipp.* 1370–1373, *Or.* 1522, frags. 449[N], 833[N]. See Johansen and Whittle on A. *Suppl.* 802–803.

233. S. *Ant.* 73–77, 867–868, 891–903. Cf. A. *Ag.* 1555–1559; S. *Ph.* 1208–1212, *OT* 1371–1373; E. *Hec.* 422–423, *El.* 1143–1145, *Tr.* 459–461, 1234, *Alc.* 363–364.

234. On A. *Ch.* 354–362 see Garvie ad loc. So too the chorus in S. *El.* 837–841 imagines the dead hero Amphiaraus still "ruling" under the earth.

235. Pleased/displeased: A. *Eum.* 94–99; E. *Hec.* 551–552. Cf. A. *Ch.* 483–485, *Ag.* 1526–1529; E. *Hec.* 136–140. Wrath at killers: A. *Ch.* 40–41, 324–327; S. *El.* 1417–1421.

236. Cf. S. *El.* 1066–1069; *Od.* 11.487–540. See Garland, *The Greek Way of Death*, 2.

237. Heracles certainly has not heard Megara's invocation of him and descriptions of her plight, an invocation she prefaces with "If any voice of (living) men is heard in Hades" (490–496).

238. *Ch.* 4–5, 139, 157, 332, 459, 508. Cf. 315–318. The frequent repetition of this request "to hear," a request usually made at most once in prayers to Olympian gods, may reflect the uncertainty whether the dead do really hear prayers. Cf. A. *Pers.* 634–640; E. *Or.* 1231–1234, 1241–1242.

239. Cf. 143–144 and 324–331.

240. Cf. 130, 147–148, 332–333, 502. As late in the action as *Eum.* 598 Orestes claims his father is sending him help from the tomb.

241. On which see below, pp. 122–123.

242. Cf. 147–148, *Pers.* 220–222; E. *Alc.* 1004–1005.

243. Lys. 12.99–100; Dem. 19.66, 20.87; Isoc. 9.2, 19.42; Lycurg. *Leoc.* 136. In the *Orestes* Clytemnestra's tomb cult is also prominent. Helen, who spends her time weaving "gifts" for her dead sister (1431–1436), has Hermione deliver hair- and drink-offerings and pray to her to have an "appeased" (πρευμενῆ) way of thinking towards Helen, Hermione, Menelaus, and even Orestes and Electra (112–123). When Hermione returns, she claims she has received from Clytemnestra just this πρευμένειαν (1323).

244. See above, pp. 35–37.

245. I follow Diggle on the assignment of speakers in 587–594. For the problems involved see Lee ad loc.

246. See Schadewaldt, *Monolog und Selbstgespräch*, 178–181, 252–254.

247. E.g., Langholf, *Die Gebete*, 11.

248. Cf. E. *Alc.* 404.

249. Cf. 636–638. The text of 638 is problematical, but the sense is clear.

250. Cf. E. *Andr.* 523–525.

251. Cf. *Il.* 9.568–569; E. *El.* 678.

252. Cf. Dover (*Lysias and the Corpus Lysiacum*, 178), who writes, in another context, "People who believe that they can find in Homer, Aischylos, and Sophokles pervasive religious and philosophical doctrines often arrive at findings which are vulnerable simply because they have not made enough allowance for accurate portrayal of the subtlety and irrationality of human beings as they really are." Cf. Grube, *The Drama of Euripides*, 52: "And a dramatist who made his characters behave and speak with perfect logic in matters of religion would be a poor dramatist indeed."

253. Cf. E. *Heraclid.* 591–593. On Alcestis as both heroine and god see above, p. 35.

254. Cf. E. *Andr.* 775–776. See Linforth, "Philoctetes, The Play and the Man," 149–150; Kamerbeek on S. *Ph.* 1440–1444.

255. Cf. *Od.* 4.563–569. See Dodds on *Ba.* 1330–1339; Kannicht on *Hel.* 1676–1679; Hommel, *Der Gott Achilleus*, 18–20.

256. Frag. 837[R] of Sophocles is famous for its apparent reference to the Eleusinian mysteries:

Thrice-blessed are those who go to Hades after seeing
these rites. For them alone it is possible
to live there, but the others have all evils.

See Richardson, *The Homeric Hymn to Demeter,* 311–312.

257. See above, p. 98. Dale, on *Hel.* 1013, describes these lines as "a piece of high-toned but vague mysticism appropriate to Theonoë."

258. Ἐλεύθερος and cognates are Aeschylus' preferred expression: *Suppl.* 416, *Eum.* 175, 340.

259. *Eum.* 175–177, 267–275, 334–340, 387–388.

260. A. *Th.* [1017–1019], an interpolated passage, claims that even when dead a traitor who has dishonored his ancestral gods will acquire their ἄγος.

261. See Dover, *Greek Popular Morality,* 261–268; Adkins, *Merit and Responsibility,* 140–148.

262. "To sing laments at a tomb" became a proverbial expression for "wasting one's time in appeals." See Garvie on A. *Ch.* 926.

263. *APR,* 79–82.

264. Garland, *The Greek Way of Death,* 17–18, 48, 66, 122 and "Γέρας Θανόντων: An Investigation into the Claims of the Homeric Dead."

265. On which see Garland, *The Greek Way of Death*; Kurtz and Boardman, *Greek Burial Customs*; Alexiou, *The Ritual Lament,* 4–23.

266. Bandaged: E. *Tr.* 1232–1233, *Ph.* 1669. Bathed: E. *Tr.* 1152, *Alc.* 159–160, *Hec.* 609–613, 780, *Ph.* 1667; S. *Aj.* 1404–1406, *Ant.* 900–901, 1201, *El.* 1139–1140. Garlanded: E. *Tr.* 1143–1144, 1247, *HF* 525–526, 562. Dressed: E. *Tr.* 377–378, 1143–1144, *Alc.* 662–664, *Med.* 1034, *HF* 329, 702–703, 1360, *IT* 627, *Hec.* 578, *Or.* 1066. By a close relative: E. *Tr.* 377–378, 390, 1143, *Alc.* 662–665, *Hel.* 1275, *IT* 627; S. *El.* 1138–1142. Alcestis, who foresees her own imminent death, like Socrates in the *Phaedo* and Oedipus in S. *OC* (esp. 1597–1603), does some of these acts for herself (*Alc.* 158–161). See Garland, *The Greek Way of Death,* 14, 24. For tragic characters who sing their own funeral dirges see Alexiou, *The Ritual Lament,* 112–113.

267. On *prothesis* see Garland, *The Greek Way of Death,* 23–31.

268. Black garments: E. *Alc.* 427, *Hel.* 1088, 1186–1187, *IA* 1438, 1448. Cf. Plut. *Per.* 38.4. Hence Death is called "black-robed" (*Alc.* 843–844). Locks of hair: E. *Alc.* 426–427 (in 428–429 Admetus orders that even the horses' hair be shorn), *Tr.* 480, *El.* 91, *Ph.* 1524–1525, *IT* 172–173, 703, *Suppl.* 973–974, *Hel.* 367–368, 1187–1188, 1224, *HF* 1390, *IA* 1437; S. *Aj.* 1173–1179 (on which see below, pp. 219–220). Antigone (E. *Ph.* 1524–1525) calls hair offerings the "first fruits" of grief and mourning.

269. E. *Tr.* 480–482, 793–794, 1235–1236, *Alc.* 103–104, *HF* 1025–1027, 1389–1390, *Suppl.* 71–86, *El.* 144–150, *Andr.* 1197–1198, 1209–1212, *Hec.* 650–656, *Hel.* 164–178, 370–374 (Greece herself mourns), 1087–1089, *Or.* 960–964; A. *Th.* 852–860, *Ch.* 429–433; S. *El.* 870. On such laments see Alexiou, *The Ritual Lament,* 11–14, 102–103, 131–205.

270. E. *Alc.* 430–431, 1015–1016. The "god below" was ἀσπόνδῳ (424, but note Diggle's text). Cf. S. *OC* 1220–1223.

271. On *ekphora* see Garland, *The Greek Way of Death*, 31–34.

272. Cf. A. *Ch.* 9; E. *Suppl.* 772–775, 802–804.

273. E. *IT* 159–166 (the fullest description of these libations), 634–635; S. *Ant.* 430–431, 901–902. On such offerings see F. Graf, "Milch, Honig, und Wein"; Stengel, *Opferbräuche der Griechen*, 126–145, 178–190.

274. Cf. A. *Ch.* 429–436.

275. *Tr.* 378–379, 389; S. *El.* 759–760; A. *Ag.* 506–507. Cf. Fraenkel on *Ag.* 435: "In the later fifth century the bodies of Athenians who fell in battles abroad were as far as possible cremated on the battlefield . . . ; the ashes were afterwards collected and, again so far as was practicable, sent back home." In having ashes returned to the homeland (as in A. *Ag.* 434–436) the tragedians follow fifth-century, not Homeric practices. Cf. Garland, "Γέρας Θανόντων: An Investigation into the Claims of the Homeric Dead," 16.

276. Garland, *The Greek Way of Death*, 22.

277. Cf. E. *Tr.* 381–382, *Med.* 1032–1036, *Hec.* 430; S. *OC* 1704–1708.

278. *APR*, 97; Garland, *The Greek Way of Death*, 104–120; Alexiou, *The Ritual Lament*, 7, 31–32; Rohde, *Psyche*, 116–174.

279. Cf. Xen. *Mem.* 2.2.13; [Arist.] *Ath.Pol.* 55.3.

280. See Farnell, *Greek Hero Cults*, 352–355; Nock, "The Cult of Heroes."

281. As in E. *El.* 91–92, 513–515. See pp. 35–36 above.

282. Garlands: S. *El.* 457–458, 894–896; E. *El.* 323–325, 512, *Or.* 1321–1322. Hair: A. *Ch.* 7, 168–180, 197–200, 226; S. *El.* 51–53, 448–451, 900–901; E. *El.* 91, 515, *Or.* 96, 113, 128, *IT* 172–173, 703. Drink offerings: A. *Ch.* and *Pers.* passim; S. *El.* 51–53, 406, 439–446, 893–895; E. *El.* 323–325, 511–515, *Or.* 96, 113, 1321–1322.

283. See above, pp. 35–37. In Sophocles' *Electra* Clytemnestra sends offerings to Agamemnon's tomb to ward off her bad dream (on which see above, pp. 102–104) and as expiation for the murder (406–448). The drink offerings to the hero Achilles (above, pp. 37–38) are also to be κηλητηρίους (E. *Hec.* 535).

284. See above, pp. 115–116.

285. E. *Hel.* 1421, frag. 640[N]. Cf. E. *Tr.* 1248–1250.

286. See above, pp. 116–119.

287. Creon (S. *Ant.* 196–197) speaks even of the rites "going down" to the corpses.

288. Offerings as appeasements: in A. *Ch.* 14–15 Orestes thinks the drink offerings may be μειλίγματα for Agamemnon. Rites ensure entry to Hades: E. *Tr.* 1081–1085. Murray's (and Diggle's) text of E. *Suppl.* 62 would introduce the same concept there, but the text is highly uncertain. The ghost of Polydorus (E. *Hec.* 1–58) has *left* Hades to obtain proper burial of his corpse. Contrast Homer's ghost of Patroclus (*Il.* 23.71–76), who needs burial to enter Hades. On the latter see Garland, "Γέρας Θανόντων: An Investigation into the Claims of the Homeric Dead," 8–14.

289. As stressed, for the *Antigone* and *Ajax*, by Kitto, *Form and Meaning in Drama*, 147–148, 181–182.

290. Hence the prominence of κόσμος and its cognates in the context of funerals and tomb cult: S. *Ant.* 395–396, 901, *El.* 1139, 1401; E. *Alc.* 149, 161, 613, 618, 631, *Andr.* 1160, *Hec.* 578, 615, *Suppl.* 78, *HF* 329–334, 548, 703, *Tr.* 1147, 1200, 1208, *IT* 632, *Hel.* 1062, 1068, 1279, 1414, *Or.* 611; Thuc. 2.46.1; Xen. *Mem.* 2.2.13, *Hell.* 6.1.6, 6.4.7; Isaeus 8.22, Dem. 18.287, 20.141, 60. 13. Cf. E. *Ba.* 857–859.

291. A. *Th.* 1002–1003, [1017–1025], [1046]; S. *Ant.* 21–25, 207–210, 284–285, 395–396, 900–904, *El.* 1139, *Aj.* 1386–1392, frag. 4[P], 20–23; E. *Alc.* 160–161, 612–613, 618–619, *Tr.* 1200, 1208, *HF* 329–335, 548, 702–703, *Med.* 1035, *Hec.* 578, 609–618, *IT* 632, *El.* 323–325, *Ph.* 1319–1321, *Hel.* 1279. Cf. S. *El.* 1139.

292. Rites as honoring the dead: S. *Ant.* 284–285. Dead may be unaware: E. *Tr.* 1248–1250. Cf. E. *Suppl.* 78.

293. Thuc. 2.35.1 and *IG* I² 1022, to which compare E. *Heraclid.* 597–599.

294. This is most fully expressed by verbs in the *Antigone*: ἀφαγιστεύειν (247), καθαγνίζειν (1081), ἁγνίζω (545), ἐφαγνίζω (196). Cf. E. *Alc.* 1143–1146 (where the process must be reversed for the recovered Alcestis), *Suppl.* 1211, *Or.* 39–40 and schol. ad loc. See Kurtz and Boardman, *Greek Burial Customs*, 149–150; Pearson on S. frag. 116; Parker, *Miasma*, 32–73.

295. E. *Hel.* 1277; S. *El.* 237–243; *APR*, 97.

296. Mikalson, "Religion and the Plague in Athens, 431–423 B.C.," 223–224.

297. Thuc. 1.138; Plut. *Them.* 23, 32. Themistocles' burial in Attica may not have been made until the fourth century. See Gomme, Andrewes, and Dover, *A Historical Commentary on Thucydides*, at 1.138.6; Malkin, *Religion and Colonization*, 224.

298. Pl. *Leg.* 9.872A–873B. Cf. 9.874B.

299. In the oath the Greeks purportedly took in 479 before the battle of Plataea, they swore to bury the allied dead and to leave no one unburied (Tod, *Greek Historical Inscriptions*, 2: no. 204, lines 30–32).

300. It should be noted that the Boeotians won this great victory at a time when, according to the Athenians, they were acting impiously. In such regards life is not as tidy as literature.

301. For a contrary (unsupported) view see Connor, *The New Politicians*, 51. Cf. O. Taplin, *CR* 26 (1976), 119.

302. The Thirty allowed to Lysias' brother Polemarchus a humble, dishonorable burial, clearly one not appropriate to his wealth and station (Lys. 12.18). Elsewhere in this speech Lysias claims members of the Thirty did or would violate oaths and asylum (12.9–10, 96–98).

303. The *Suppliants* is usually dated 424–420 B.C., and many see in it a direct response to the Theban refusal to return the Athenian dead after the first battle of Delion in 424. See Collard on E. *Suppl.*, pp. 8–14. It seems a particularly Theban trait, in literature as well as in life, to disrespect the burial rites of their enemies.

304. Usual practice: S. *Ant.* 1113–1114; E. *Suppl.* 311, 526, 537–541, 671–672. Ordained by the gods: S. *Ant.* 76–77, 449–460, 519–521, 921–928, 1070–1075; E. *Suppl.* 19, 563. Cf. S. *Aj.* 1130–1131, 1342–1345.

305. Violent: S. *Ant.* 65–67, 1073; E. *Suppl.* 308. Cf. S. *Aj.* 1334–1335. For βίαιον similarly contrasted to εὐσεβές see E. *Hyps.* frag. 60.40 [Bond]. Traditions not honored: S. *Ant.* 76–77; E. *Suppl.* 19, 301–302. Cf. S. *Aj.* 1129, 1343–1344.

306. E. *Suppl.* 512, 575, 630–633, 728–730, 743–744. Cf. E. *Ph.* 1663; S. *Aj.* 1091–1092, 1151, 1384–1385. Electra (E. *El.* 894–904) responds to Orestes' suggestion that they expose Aegisthus' corpse as prey for the beasts and birds with a sense of shame at maltreating corpses (νεκροὺς ὑβρίζειν) and with fear of the ill will it would arouse among her fellow citizens. She specifies no divine sanctions. The Dioscuroi (1276–1277) eventually make provision for the burial of Aegisthus. Cf. S. *El.* 1487–1490.

307. Justice: S. *Ant.* 449–460, 921–928; E. *Suppl.* 65, 328, 526, 564. Cf. S. *Aj.* 1108–1110, 1334–1335. Piety: S. *Ant.* 74, 921–928; E. *Suppl.* 39–40, 123, 367, 373, 559.

308. S. *Ant.* 71–72, 502–504, 511, 693–695, 699; E. *Suppl.* 78, 306, 315, 367–368, 373–374.

309. Teiresias' argument (*Ant.* 1015–1022) from the pollution of altars by bits of flesh from corpses would require the burial of all men no matter what crimes they had committed. See above, p. 124.

310. Cf. *Aj.* 1062–1068, 1089–1092, 1108–1110, 1128–1132, 1150–1155, 1332–1335, 1343–1345, 1348–1349, 1383–1395.

311. See above, pp. 125–126.

312. *Aj.* 1133. In the *Antigone* the thought of Creon similarly moves from punishing Polyneices the traitor (194–206) to Polyneices the personal enemy (519–522). The reasons for the transition may be seen in 182–190.

313. Cf. E. *Hec.* 328–331; Lys. 2.7–10. Aethra, in discussing the same topic, similarly moves from specifically religious considerations to a broader political and social context (297–331). The salient point is not that Theseus fails to emphasize religious considerations in his decision to secure the burial of the Argive dead (Conacher, "Religion and Ethical Attitudes in Euripides' *Suppliants*," 20) but that he adduces additional ethical, social, and even natural-law arguments in support of the religious convention. At the end of his argument he returns to the fundamental point: it is a νόμος παλαιὸς δαιμόνων (563).

314. Lys. 2.7, an account based on tragedy. See Parker, *Miasma*, 44.

315. Cf. his explanations of the powers and birth myth of Dionysus in E. *Ba.* 272–327.

316. See above, pp. 124–126.

Chapter Four

1. See above, pp. 14–15.
2. On this use of *daimon* see above, pp. 22–29.
3. See above, p. 75.

4. Nestle, *Euripides*, 43, 234.

5. On the Thracian character of Polymestor see Hall, *Inventing the Barbarian*, 107–110, 126, 137–138.

6. Cf. Rawson, "Family and Fatherland in Euripides' *Phoenissae*," 124.

7. The following abstracts are called θεοί, are the recipients of prayers of petition (not merely invocations), or are otherwise clearly presented as gods. Aidos (Respect): E. *HF* 556–557, *Ion* 337. Anangke (Necessity): E. *Alc.* 962–983 (see above, pp. 26–27). Chronos (Time): S. *El.* 179. Dike (Justice): A. *Ag.* 381–384, *Ch.* 244–245; S. *Aj.* 1389–1391, *OT* 274–275, *Ant.* 451–452; E. *Med.* 1389–1390, *Or.* 1242–1243, *Ba.* 991–996 = 1011–1016. Dokein (Appearance): E. *Or.* 782. Eirene (Peace): E. *Or.* 1682–1683, *Ba.* 419–420, frag. 453[N]. Elpis (Hope): E. *IA* 392. Eris (Strife): E. *Ph.* 798–800. Eutychein (Success): A. *Ch.* 59–60. Good Thinking (ἡ φρόνησις ἀγαθή): S. frag. 922[R]. Hosia (Holiness): E. *Ba.* 370–378. Kratos (Force): A. *Ch.* 244–245. Lethe of Evils (Forgetting): E. *Or.* 213–214. Lype (Pain): E. *Or.* 398–399. Nemesis: E. *Ph.* 182–184. Nike (Victory): E. *IT* 1497–1499, *Ph.* 1764–1766, *Or.* 1691–1693. Nous (Reason): E. frag. 1018. Penia (Poverty): E. frag. 248[N]. Ploutos (Wealth): E. frags. 20[N], 153[A]. Pronoia (Foresight): E. *IA* 864. Knowing One's Friends (τὸ γιγνώσκειν φίλους): E. *Hel.* 560. On such abstractions as gods see Langholf, *Die Gebete*, 49–50, 138–141; Nilsson, "Kultische Personifikationen"; Bond on E. *HF* 556; Wilamowitz on E. *HF* 557; Dodds on E. *Ba.* 370–372; Burkert, *GR*, 184–186; Grube, *The Drama of Euripides*, 41–42.

8. Cf. A. *Ch.* 55–60 and the discussion of Polyphemus in E. *Cycl.*, below, pp. 157–158. The impious Eteocles is, not surprisingly, most ready to question on religious terms the propriety of Polyneices' invocation of the deities of Thebes (604–608). It is also inconsistent, but human, that before the life-and-death struggle with his brother, Eteocles prays to a "real" god, the Theban Athena (1372–1376).

9. *APR*, 111.

10. Cf. A. *Ag.* 396–402.

11. See Mikalson, "Unanswered Prayers."

12. Cf. E. *Ph.* 605.

13. On Neoptolemus see Burnett, *Catastrophe Survived*, 151–156.

14. On his first trip to Delphi Neoptolemus may have intended to sack Apollo's temple, a dramatic act of impiety (1092–1095).

15. On this see Kovacs, *The Andromache*, 72, 79, 103 n. 40, and *The Heroic Muse*, 19–20.

16. Cf. 900, 1002–1006, 1202.

17. For the myth and its sources see Fontenrose, *Python*, 397–401, 418–426. On Pindaric treatments of Neoptolemus see Most, *The Measures of Praise*, 157–182; Lloyd-Jones, "Modern Interpretation of Pindar," 131–137.

18. Neoptolemus' alleged intent to sack the temple (1095), the fight at and on the altar (1123–1138), Neoptolemus' "pyrrhic" dance (1135), and the corpse lying near the altar (1156) each allude to a feature of the Delphic myth of Neoptolemus/Pyrrhus, for which see Fontenrose, *Python*, 397–401, 418–426.

19. Euripides even places Neoptolemus on the altar of Apollo (1123).

20. News of Apollo's possible future involvement in the killing of Neoptolemus immediately brings to the chorus' mind remembrances of Apollo's punishments of Clytemnestra and Troy, neither of which they can fully comprehend (1010–1036). These lyrics prepare the way for the messenger's protest in 1161–1165.

21. On religious aspects of the *Antigone* see B. M. W. Knox, *The Heroic Temper*, 91–116; Winnington-Ingram, *Sophocles*, 117–149, esp. 147–149. On the impiety of denying burial rites see above, pp. 124–128.

22. Bad thinking: φρήν and its cognates, 726–727, 755, 1015, 1023, 1051, 1090, 1104, 1261. On the importance of this concept throughout the play see Knapp, "A Point in the Interpretation of the *Antigone*." Bad planning: βουλεύω and its cognates, 1026, 1050, 1098, 1242, 1265, 1269. Error: ἁμαρτάνω and its cognates, 1023–1027, 1260–1262. Cf. 710–727, 753–755.

23. Cf. 58–99, 449 ff, 744–745, 872–874.

24. See above, pp. 25–28.

25. Cf. 280–289, 441–460, 514–523, 921, 1064–1075. Ephemeral versus eternal: 456–457. Cf. 74–77.

26. Most clearly exemplified, of course, in keeping the dead Polyneices above ground, in the world of the living, while at the same time burying the living Antigone (1068–1075).

27. Sophocles has prepared for this horrific statement of Creon's by emphasizing much more than is usually done in tragedy that the alternative to proper burial is attacks by carrion (29–30, 205–206, 257–258, 696–698, 1015–1022; cf. 1080–1083). It is noteworthy that Creon regularly has Zeus on his lips. The first two mentions are innocuous: he makes him a witness of his proper civic behavior (184), and he swears by him that he will punish the guards if they do not catch the person giving Polyneices burial rites (304–305). Thereafter, however, the tone becomes ominous. In 486–489 he uses the name of Zeus Herkeios, protector of the family unit, to emphasize that he will not shelter even a family member from the punishment he proposes. In 658–659, while disallowing all considerations of family, he likewise perversely refers to Zeus as protector of the family ("Let Antigone sing her hymns to Zeus Synaimos"). The epithet Synaimos, apart from the play on Haemon's name, stresses the Zeus who protects blood kin. These two uses of Zeus' name suggest disrespect and flippancy towards the deity. They prepare the way for the clear blasphemy of 1039–1044.

28. Cf. E. *HF* 1232.

29. Parker (*Miasma*, 33; cf. 145) considers "this rejection of plain fact as lunatic defiance."

30. B. M. W. Knox (*The Heroic Temper*, 91) speaks of her "obsessive concern for the dead." Cf. Winnington-Ingram, *Sophocles*, 134.

31. Cf. 1165–1171, 1306–1311, 1324–1332.

32. Cf. 278–279, 724–725, 802–805, 1100–1101. Cf. also 504–509, 692–700, 733.

33. Cf. 1105–1114, 1261–1276, 1317–1325.

34. Pious, however sarcastically she expresses herself: ὅσια πανουργήσασ᾽, , 74; ἐπεί γε δὴ τὴν δυσσέβειαν εὐσεβοῦσ᾽ ἐκτησάμην,, 923–924; τὴν εὐσεβίαν σεβίσασα, 943. In accord with divine laws: 76–77, 449–460.

35. Virtue and nobility: 37–38, 72. Fame: 502–504. Pleasing to dead: 74–77, 89, 559–560; to dead kin, 897–904.

36. Antigone does show particular concern for Polyneices qua brother (45–46, 80–81, 466–468, 502–504, 511–517, 899), and in this vein Sophocles or someone else chose to introduce the remarkable argument that she would go to such extraordinary lengths to bury a brother but not a husband or children (905–920). A significant objection to these lines is that the argument runs counter to all descriptions of the obligations of burial in literary and popular sources from Athens and elsewhere. A woman was obliged to see to the burial of her husband and children. I leave it to others to decide whether this and other objections to 905–920 are sufficient to deny them to Sophocles. For a defense of these lines see B. M. W. Knox, *The Heroic Temper*, 103–107.

37. Noble death: 96–97, 461–470; cf. 72. Good fame: 502–504, 511, 692–695, 699, 817–822, 925–928. It is in her victory and fame that Antigone's momentary doubts, expressed in 921–928, find their response. Her enemy is mistaken and suffers. Antigone dies, but her fight is won; her brother is buried, her εὔκλεια is assured, and she "died well."

38. On relevant issues see Winnington-Ingram, *Sophocles*, 11–72; Kitto, *Form and Meaning in Drama*, 179–198.

39. See above, pp. 21–22, on who did and who did not recognize Athena as the agent of this.

40. From all that has preceded, especially 756–777, the audience recognizes that Tecmessa mistakenly thinks Athena acted solely or primarily for Odysseus' sake (952–953).

41. Ajax' folly is stressed by repeated references (758, 763, 766). According to Sophocles' Electra (*El.* 563–576), by a similar kind of boasting Agamemnon brought upon himself the wrath of Artemis.

42. The impiety of the hero is not central in this play but is necessary to motivate Athena's hostility to him. The "impious" side of Ajax' character is not developed, though that tendency does occasionally come to the surface, as when he says to Tecmessa, "Don't you realize that I am no longer obliged to please the gods?" (589–590), a statement which shocks her religious sensibilities (591). Ajax' wrath at the gods is also troubling, and the chorus momentarily rejoice when they think he has given it up (743–744).

43. Athena is his φύλαξ (36), the *vox propria* for this type of Homeric relationship.

44. Respect for the divine: e.g., 86, 1332–1335, 1343–1345. Human limitations: 86, 121–126, 1365.

45. The initial presentation of Odysseus (1–126) and his later defense of the burial rites for Ajax belie the chorus' and Tecmessa's hostile judgment of him (e.g., 955–960, 971). Cf. 1374–1375, 1381–1388, 1398–1399.

46. See above, pp. 121–128.

47. *Hipp.* 82–83, 656, 993–996, 1060–1061, 1364–1369. On religious aspects of the *Hippolytus* see B. M. W. Knox, *Word and Action,* 220–227; Grube, *The Drama of Euripides,* 177–197; Conacher, *Euripidean Drama,* 28–53; Dodds, "Euripides the Irrationalist," 102; North, *Sophrosyne,* 79–81; Barrett on E. *Hipp.* 79–81; Köhnken, "Götterrahmen und menschliches Handeln in Euripides' *Hippolytus*"; Schlesier, "Der Stachel der Götter"; Yunis, *A New Creed,* 111–121.

48. Cf. 611–612, 656–658, 1033, 1062–1064, 1307–1309. On the oath see also above, pp. 85–86.

49. E.g., Festugière, *Personal Religion,* 10–18.

50. This is suggested by Theseus in the troubled lines 952–954.

51. As Barrett notes (on 79–81), individual elements of Hippolytus' worship and attitudes can be paralleled, but not their combination in any form like this. On Hippolytus' *not* being an Orphic see Lucas, "Hippolytus."

52. Pl. *Ap.* 24B–C, 31C–D, *Euthphr.* 3B; Xen. *Mem.* 1.1.2–3, *Ap.* 24; *APR,* 92–93, 96–97. On the substance of the charge against Socrates see Yunis, *A New Creed,* 62–66.

53. Cf. 1402.

54. Cf. 48–50.

55. On the different starting points of the *Bacchae* and *Hippolytus* see Conacher, *Euripidean Drama,* 59; Grube, *The Drama of Euripides,* 401; Burnett, "Pentheus and Dionysus," 18–24.

56. See below, pp. 176–191.

57. On the nature of such greetings see Burkert, *GR,* 75.

58. Compare the language of 113 and 1058–1059.

59. The danger into which Hippolytus has placed himself is obvious also from the nurse's words to Phaedra: "The Cyprian goddess is unendurable if she flows over one in abundance. She gently goes after the one who yields. But when she catches one who views himself exceptional and too good for her, she treats him violently" (443–446).

60. See Burkert, *GR,* 150–151.

61. Cf. 359–361.

62. The usual means by which Greek poets refashioned the popular religion to create the artifice it became in poetic literature.

63. In E. *IA* the sacrifices made to Artemis at the beginning of the marriage ceremony (718, 1110–1114) may also be viewed as rites to symbolize the conclusion of maidenhood in preparation for a new stage of life. On hair offerings of maidens in the Artemis cult see Barrett, *Euripides: Hippolytos,* p. 4.

64. As suggested in 537–540.

65. For Aphrodite's association with connubial sex see the marriage song in E. *Phaethon* 227–244 (Diggle).

66. Barrett, *Euripides: Hippolytos,* p. 155.

67. Dionysus' demand to be recognized as a "god born from a god, the son of

Zeus" encompasses the individual claims and is central from beginning to end: 1 (ἥκω Διὸς παῖς), 26–33, 39–42, 47–48, 466–468, 581, 603, 859–861, 1340–1343, 1349. On the *Bacchae* see Grube, "Dionysus in the *Bacchae*"; Deichgräber, "Die Kadmos-Teiresiasszene"; Dodds, *Euripides: Bacchae*, xi–l; Diller, "Euripides' Final Phase"; Burnett, "Pentheus and Dionysus"; Winnington-Ingram, *Euripides and Dionysus*; Schlesier, "Der Stachel der Götter"; Roth, "Teiresias as *Mantis* and Intellectual in Euripides' *Bacchae*"; Yunis, *A New Creed*, 77–81.

68. In this Pentheus is comparable to Lycurgus, who attempted, among other things, to stop Dionysus' maenads and suffered for it (S. *Ant.* 955–965; *Il.* 6.130–141).

69. For summaries of the differing interpretations of this controversial scene see Dodds, *Euripides: Bacchae*, pp. 90–91; Conacher, *Euripidean Drama*, 62–63; Musurillo, "Euripides and Dionysiac Piety."

70. Some modern critics discredit Teiresias, ipso facto, because he is a seer. That is mistaken on two counts. In the *Bacchae* Teiresias is not speaking as a seer (368–369) but as a wise man (σοφός), whose personal wisdom is stressed in this play (179, 186). Even Winnington-Ingram (*Euripides and Dionysus*, 57) must concede that in this play "the 'wisdom' of Teiresias has the verdict of history." Secondly, as we have seen (above, pp. 92–101), in the conventions of Greek tragedy seers are not conniving, meretricious, profit-obsessed charlatans. It is only wrongheaded characters who judge them to be such. On Teiresias see Dodds, *Euripides: Bacchae*, pp. 91, 93.

71. The aged Teiresias and Cadmus may look ridiculous attempting in their Bacchic garb the Bacchic dances and gestures. They recognize that (204–205), and Pentheus seizes upon it (248–254). What is and is not ridiculous, however, like the question of who is and who is not mad, becomes a motif of the play, and eventually the audience will realize that Pentheus is not the best judge of this. "Exalt": αὔξεσθαι as what a god gets from dances and rites (183, 209). See Skutsch and Rose, "*Mactare—Macula?*" 223; Dodds on *Ba.* 183; and below, p. 188.

72. Cf. 453–459.

73. Cf. 471–476, 485–488, 811–816, 829, 912–916, 1061–1062.

74. Impiety: if δυσσεβείας is the correct reading (see Dodds on *Ba.* 263). On respect for parents as piety see below, pp. 170–173, 191–192.

75. Webster (*The Tragedies of Euripides*, 271) nicely terms Teiresias the "modernist churchman" here. Cf. Lefkowitz, "Impiety and Atheism in Euripides' Dramas," 74–75.

76. The association of wet and dry elements with Dionysus and Demeter and their role as benefactors suggest Prodicus' influence. See below, p. 234.

77. See Dodds on *Ba.* 286–297, and Roth, "Teiresias as *Mantis* and Intellectual in Euripides' *Bacchae*," 62.

78. Apart from E. *IA* 1408, where Achilles praises Iphigeneia for giving up her resistance to being sacrificed, θεομαχεῖν occurs only in this play and is used only in relation to Pentheus (45, 325, 1255; cf. 794–795). The idea of "man fighting god" is

familiar from earlier literature and drama (see Kamerbeek, "On the Conception of ΘΕΟΜΑΧΟΣ"), but Euripides may have coined the verb itself to suggest the exceptionally impious and heinous actions of Pentheus.

79. See Dodds on *Ba.* 334.

80. Teiresias' sanctuary really existed (Paus. 9.16.1), and a pious man does not make threats to destroy sacred property. Compare the recommendation of the misguided and impious old man in Euripides' *Ion* who recommends burning down Apollo's oracle (972–975; cf. 1045–1047).

81. Cf. the unsuccessful prayer to Aphrodite by the old servant on Hippolytus' behalf in E. *Hipp.* 114–120. See Dodds on *Ba.* 360–363 and his p. 238. To Pentheus' attempts to turn Teiresias and Cadmus from the rites of Dionysus might be compared the attempts of the notoriously impious Diagoras of Melos to turn celebrants away from the Eleusinian Mysteries. On Diagoras, who was criminally charged with impiety, see *APR,* 136 n. 6; Woodbury, "The Date and Atheism of Diagoras"; Winiarczyk, *Diagorae Melii et Theodori Cyrenaei Reliquiae* and "Wer Galt im Altertum als Atheist?" 164–166.

82. Cf. Dodds on *Ba.* 370–372, Ὁσία πότνα θεῶν: "Ὁσία or ὁσιότης may be defined as the quality of scrupulousness, especially in religious matters, which makes a man keep within the limits of what is permitted (ὅσιον)."

83. Most critics look at the limitations or failings of each view. See, e.g., Winnington-Ingram, *Euripides and Dionysus,* passim, esp. 40–58, 116–167; Roth, "Teiresias as *Mantis* and Intellectual in Euripides' *Bacchae,*" 59–63.

84. On different views of the reality of the earthquake and fire see Dodds, *Euripides: Bacchae,* pp. 147–150; Winnington-Ingram, *Euripides and Dionysus,* 182–185.

85. Miracles: 666–667, 704–713, 716, 726–727, 755–758, 760–764. Demand: 769–774. On the messenger's speech see Winnington-Ingram, *Euripides and Dionysus,* 88–99.

86. Later made explicit by Dionysus, 859–861.

87. Characteristically Euripides is willing to use one impiety to punish another. Agave's killing of her son Pentheus was "unintentional," but, like Heracles' killing of his children in E. *HF,* was nonetheless impious. See below, p. 173. When Dionysus had urged Pentheus "to sacrifice" to the new deity, Pentheus grossly perverted sacred language to suggest his sacrificial victim would be the maenads on Mount Cithaeron (794–797). He had it nearly right.

88. Cf. 439, 621–622, 636–637, 640. See Grube, "Dionysus in the *Bacchae,*" 46. On the victorious Dionysus in this play see also Winnington-Ingram, *Euripides and Dionysus,* 24–30.

89. Cf. E. frag. 1032[N].

90. Cf. 268–271, 332, 387–397, 480–506, 655–656, 947–948, 1150–1152.

91. Cf. 506 and Dodds ad loc.

92. To the faults listed by Dodds (pp. xliii, 97, 100), add a quick temper (670–671) and certain types of prejudice against seers (255–260, 345–351), foreigners

(483), and women (passim, esp. 785–786). For Pentheus' repressed Dionysiac traits see Winnington-Ingram, *Euripides and Dionysus,* passim, esp. 159–161. One also has the impression that Pentheus' objectionable manner did not crop up overnight (358–359, 670–671, 1255–1257). The best that can be said of him is that usually "he was fond of his old grandfather" (Dodds on *Ba.* 1302–1329).

93. Cf. 250, 272, 286, 322, 467, 1080–1081, 1293.

94. Cf. 810–861, 912–970, 1024–1152.

95. Largely, but not solely. His general temperament, in addition to his haste to judge, speak, and act, is occasionally criticized (670–671, 991–1001).

96. Cf. E. frag. 256[N]. This lack of "faith" or "genuine piety" has troubled some critics about Cadmus. See, e.g., Winnington-Ingram, *Euripides and Dionysus,* 54.

97. See Dodds ad loc.

98. Cf. 200–203, 387–402, 483–484, 489–490, 655–656, 882–896, 1008–1010, 1301–1304.

99. "In the end" (ἐν τέλει) is problematical. See Dodds on *Ba.* 859–861. On δεινός see Jebb on S. *Tr.* 476 (appendix).

100. Cf. 1341–1343.

101. Cf. Dodds on *Ba.* 1117–1121.

102. Agave and Cadmus: 1249–1250, 1303–1305, 1325–1326, 1340–1349, 1374–1378.

103. On Athens, her piety, and support received from the gods see above, pp. 40, 62–64.

104. On religious aspects of the *Troades* see Scodel, *The Trojan Trilogy of Euripides,* esp. 130–137; Kovacs, "Euripides, *Troades* 95–7: Is Sacking Cities Really Foolish?"; Lefkowitz, "Impiety and Atheism in Euripides' Dramas"; Yunis, *A New Creed,* 81–87.

105. Here are realized the fears expressed by the chorus in A. *Th.* 219–222.

106. Euripides here ignores the Homeric version, in which Poseidon is a bitter enemy of Troy (*Il.* 14.357–378, 21.435–460). For a possible reason see Lee on *Tr.* 7. I disagree with Fontenrose's interpretation of τῶν ἐμῶν Φρυγῶν as well as with his distinction between the city of the Trojans and the Trojans themselves. See Fontenrose, "Poseidon in the *Troades*"; Wilson, "Poseidon in the *Troades*: A Reply"; Fontenrose, "A Response to Wilson's Reply."

107. On this prologue see O'Neill, "The Prologue of the *Troades.*"

108. Cf. 483.

109. Zeus' lack of concern for Troy is stressed elsewhere in the play (1060–1080, 1287–1292).

110. Cf. 148–152. The reference of 1075–1076 remains to be ascertained. See Yunis, *A New Creed,* 83 n. 12.

111. Cf. Yunis, *A New Creed,* 82–83.

112. Athena's involvement with the Trojan Horse is also significant. She contributed to its construction (9–12, 561), and it was a dedication to her, placed in her

sanctuary on the Acropolis in a festival atmosphere (525–526, 532–536, 539–541). Destruction emanating from the sanctuary of the Acropolis deity, like Priam's death at the altar of Zeus Herkeios, reflects the totally godforsaken status of the Trojans. Cf. 46–47, 72.

113. Cf. 26–27 and E. *Andr.* 1025–1027.

114. The chorus in E. *Andr.* 1009–1027 describes much the same situation. Apollo and Poseidon, for an unknown reason, withdrew their support from Troy, and, as a result, "no longer has the altar fire with its fragrant smoke gleamed for the gods" (1025–1027).

115. E.g., Conacher, *Euripidean Drama*, 134–137; Scodel, *The Trojan Trilogy of Euripides*, 132–135; Sartre, "Why the *Trojan Women*?"

116. Ajax' impiety is that he violated Cassandra's asylum in Athena's temple, not that he raped her there. See Scodel, *The Trojan Trilogy of Euripides*, 67; Lee on E. *Tr.* 453; Mason, "Kassandra," 82, 89.

117. In Poseidon's own words, Athena's love *and* hate are excessive (68).

118. *APR*, 27–30, 103–104.

119. Cf. 101–104.

120. The text of these lines is, however, problematical. Cf. 1242–1245.

121. Cf. E. *Ion* 1619–1620.

122. See, e.g., Lee on *Tr.* 884–888; Norwood, *Essays on Euripidean Drama*, 15; Zuntz's comments in *Euripide*, 158; Conacher, *Euripidean Drama*, 142; Scodel, *The Trojan Trilogy of Euripides*, 93–95, 100, 135; Guthrie, *A History of Greek Philosophy*, 2:323–324; Lefkowitz, "Impiety and Atheism in Euripides' Dramas," 72–74; Yunis, *A New Creed*, 85 n. 16.

123. For bibliography on the relationship of the Melian massacre and this play see Conacher, *Euripidean Drama*, 136. For chronological problems in associating the two see Kip, "Euripides and Melos."

124. Poseidon warns in the prologue, "A fool is the man who sacks cities and after causing the abandonment of temples and tombs, the sacred places of the dead, himself perishes" (95–97). This is usually taken to suggest that such a person perishes because of the impiety of causing desolation of temples and tombs. However, in a full analysis of the text and context of the passage ("Euripides, *Troades* 95–7: Is Sacking Cities Really Foolish?") Kovacs has demonstrated that impiety consists only in desecrating temples and tombs, not in causing their abandonment by razing cities. According to Kovacs, Poseidon speaks here not of the impious man but of one who perishes, by his own folly, after great success as a sacker of cities.

125. See Seaford, *Euripides: Cyclops*, pp. 1–48.

126. Impious: 26, 30–31, 310–311, 348, 378, 438. God-hated: 396–397, 602.

127. Cf. E. *Hel.* 449 and p. 261 n. 51 below.

128. Cf. 30–31, 288–289, 310–311, 334–349, 377–378, 396–397, 693.

129. See above, pp. 134–135.

130. For a different interpretation of this passage see Seaford ad loc.

131. Women of tragedy either decline (Deianira in S. *Tr.* 491–492) or are praised

for declining (Iphigeneia in E. *IA* 1408) to be god-fighters. Aeschylus' Orestes, like these women, chooses not to make the gods his ἐχθροί (*Ch.* 900–903).

We should not depreciate the strong term *theomachos* by applying it to those "unworthy" of it. Burnett (*Catastrophe Survived*, 122) labels the Creousa of E. *Ion* a *theomachos*, but Creousa lacks, among other things, the persistence of true *theomachoi*. Likewise we should not, with Winnington-Ingram (*Sophocles*, 147), call the Creon of S. *Ant.* a *theomachos*. He opposes the unwritten laws but had no intention to confront the gods directly. On the relationship of these unwritten laws to the gods see below, pp. 194–195.

132. On θεομαχεῖν and related expressions see Nestle, *Euripides*, 428 n. 73; Kamerbeek, "On the Conception of ΘΕΟΜΑΧΟΣ"; Diller, "Euripides' Final Phase"; Dodds on E. *Ba.* 45.

133. Hippolytus' devotion to Artemis contributes to his antipathy to Aphrodite, but Artemis herself neither incites nor protects Hippolytus in his encounter with Aphrodite.

134. Cf. 375–396, 422–436, 457–471, 486–500, 526–549.

135. On the impiety of these and on Amphiaraus see Podlecki, *The Political Background of Aeschylean Tragedy*, 35–40.

136. Cf. E. *Suppl.* 498–499.

137. See above, pp. 92–100, 106.

138. Cf. S. *Ant.* 198–201, 282–289. See below, p. 175.

139. Cf. A. *Th.* 438–443, 550–551, 563–567, 794, frag. 1[P], 15–18; S. *Ant.* 128–133, 960–963, 1348–1353, *El.* 563–573, *Tr.* 280–283. Cf. also E. *Or.* 4–10 (of Tantalus) and *Ba.* 337–340 (of Actaeon) and 386–388.

140. See above, p. 130.

141. Cf. Teiresias' advice to Creon, S. *Ant.* 1023–1028, and above, p. 101.

142. See above, pp. 74–75, 79–80, 130, 134.

143. See above, p. 262 n. 70.

144. Xenophon's Socrates (*Mem.* 4.4.19–22) makes it a distinctive feature of the gods' νόμοι ἄγραφοι that, unlike human laws, men cannot escape punishment for violation of them. On νόμοι ἄγραφοι see below, pp. 194–195.

145. Cf. Lys. 6.19.

146. Nilsson, *Geschichte der griechischen Religion*, 1:784–785.

147. See above, p. 125.

148. Thuc. 7.50.4; Plut. *Nic.* 23.1–6. On Nicias' religious attitudes and their importance to the Sicilian expedition see Powell, "Religion and the Sicilian Expedition."

149. Cf. Isoc. 15.281–282.

150. Cf. Thuc. 7.86.5 and adespota, frag. 1b[K].

151. A similar crisis of faith arose for some of the same reasons among the whole of the Athenian populace during the years of the plague (431–426). See Mikalson, "Religion and the Plague."

Chapter Five

1. Pl. *Euthphr.* 6D.
2. On piety in general see Gernet and Boulanger, *Le génie grecque dans la religion*, 354–370; F. Pfister, "Kultus," *RE* 11 (1922), cols. 2120–2122; Dirlmeier, "ΘΕΟΦΙΛΙΑ–ΦΙΛΟΘΕΙΑ"; Kroll, *Theognis-Interpetationen*, 214–217; Kaufmann-Bühler, "Eusebeia"; Dörrie, "Überlegungen zum Wesen antiker Frömmigkeit"; Burkert, *GR*, 272–275.
3. See above, pp. 70–80.
4. Cf. 275–278.
5. On Zeus Hikesios see above, pp. 74–75.
6. On Polymestor see above, pp. 79–80.
7. On Paris and Zeus Xenios see above, p. 77.
8. Cf. A. *Eum.* 546–548. As Barrett (on E. *Hipp.* 1258–1259) puts it succinctly, "when one feels αἰδώς towards a suppliant or ξένος, one αἰδεῖται the gods who protect him."
9. See above, pp. 80–87. When Menelaus swears an oath to his brother Agamemnon (E. *IA* 473–476), he invokes as witnesses not the gods but their grandfather Pelops and father Atreus.
10. See above, pp. 83, 135–136.
11. Cf. S. *OT* 653; A. *Eum.* 483–484 (the text of which is problematical), 679–680.
12. See above, p. 85.
13. See above, p. 80.
14. *APR*, 50–52. On pollution of homicide see Parker, *Miasma*, 104–143.
15. On which see below, p. 171.
16. Cf. 236–243, 313.
17. Cf. E. *Or.* 481, 500–502, 900.
18. Cf. *Andr.* 491, *IT* 381–383.
19. Cf. 889 and A. *Suppl.* 262–266.
20. E. *Ion* 1045–1047, 1290–1295, 1334. Cf. A. *Th.* 679–682; Thuc. 3.56.2. See Parker, *Miasma*, 112–113. In Sophocles' *Ajax* Menelaus, in wishing to deny Ajax burial rites, attempts (wrongly) to label him a *polemios*. See above, p. 127.
21. Cf. 961–966 and Thuc. 3.58.3. To the hyperbole of Peleus' speech to Menelaus in E. *Andr.* belongs the claim (614–615) that Menelaus killed Achilles and was a polluted man for it. See Stevens ad loc.
22. As Parker notes (*Miasma*, 112), Plato in the *Laws* has a far more comprehensive list of homicidal acts he would free from pollution: "killing of a night thief, or of a footpad in self-defence; killing of a person sexually violating a relative of the killer; killing in defence of a relation"; or killing in self-defense during a civil war (Pl. *Leg.* 9.869C–D, 874B–C). None of these acts occurs in tragedy, and we therefore cannot judge the tragedians' treatment of them.
23. Cf. E. *Or.* 1602–1604, *HF* 1281–1284.

24. See above, p. 116.
25. Cf. 482–487.
26. *APR*, 50–52.
27. See above, pp. 121–128.
28. See above, pp. 123–124.
29. See above, pp. 139–142.
30. Hades: E. *IT* 167–168. Persephone: E. *Or.* 960–964. Thanatos: in E. *Alc* 843–851 Heracles imagines Thanatos himself partaking of the blood sacrifices at the tomb.
31. See above, pp. 25–28.
32. Murder of a parent: A. *Ch.* 1016–1017, *Eum.* 40, 151–154, 210, 230–275, 280–283, 653–656; S. *OT* 1011–1013, 1440–1441, 1519, *OC* 944–945; E. *Or.* 374, 481, 546, 562–563, 827–828, 1624, *IT* 934–957, 1168–1178, 1200, 1209–1229. Of a child: A. *Ag.* 206–211, 219–220, 1417–1420; E. *Med.* 796, 846–850, 1268–1270, 1284–1289, 1323–1328, 1346, 1371, 1383, 1406–1407, *Hipp.* 1286–1287, 1447–1453, *IA* 1104–1105, 1185–1190, 1317–1318, *HF* 1155–1156, 1161–1162, 1219, 1232–1233, 1302, 1324–1325. Of a brother: A. *Th.* 679–682, 734–738, 829–831; S. *Ant.* 172; E. *IT* 870–872. Of a husband: A. *Ag.* 1493, 1517, 1643–1646, *Ch.* 46, 525, 966–967, 986, 1027–1028, *Eum.* 600–602; S. *El.* 124–126, 245–250, 1380–1383, *Tr.* 1037; E. *El.* 479–484, 1170–1171, *Or.* 24–26, 500–503, 515, 518–519, 925, 935–937.
33. This dilemma is concisely expressed in E. *Or.* 546–547 and 562–563.
34. Cf. S. *El.* 1058–1062.
35. *APR*, 99–100.
36. S. *OT* 1287–1289, *OC* 944–946; and see note 32 above.
37. Cf. 967–969.
38. The impiety for Hyllus would lie in his living with the woman who, though indirectly, caused his mother's death. See 1233–1237.
39. Religious aspect of matricide: E. *IT* 934–957, 1168–1178, 1200, *Or.* 374, 481, 546–547, 563, 827–830, 1624; A. *Ch.* 1016–1017, *Eum.* 40, 151–154, 210, 230–275, 280–283, 653–656. Preference accorded to father: E. *El.* 973–977, *Or.* 546–547, 562–563; A. *Eum.* passim.
40. Electra, however, thinks that vengeance on Aegisthus and Clytemnestra would win a reputation for piety from (the presumed dead) Orestes as well as from Agamemnon (S. *El.* 967–969).
41. See above, note 32.
42. Polyneices and Eteocles: A. *Th.* 679–682, 734–738, 829–831; S. *Ant.* 172. Iphigeneia: E. *IT* 870–872.
43. The woman is godless: A. *Ch.* 46; S. *Tr.* 1037. Cf. E. *El.* 645, 683. The deed is impure, etc.: A. *Ch.* 986; S. *El.* 124; E. *El.* 1170–1171; pollution, A. *Ag.* 1643–1646. Husband's death is impious: A. *Ag.* 1493; E. *El.* 677.
44. Cf. S. *El.* 1380–1383.
45. *APR*, 87–88, 99.
46. Cf. 600.
47. Dover ("The Freedom of the Intellectual," 28) casts doubt on the historicity of this charge of impiety against Aspasia.

48. Cf. E. *El.* 1260–1262. In E. *Tr.* 41–44, 249–255, Agamemnon's impiety is not that he "wedded" Cassandra but that is so doing he acted counter to Apollo's wish that she remain a virgin.

49. Tod, *Greek Historical Inscriptions,* 2: no. 204. See *APR,* 33–34; and Siewert, "The Ephebic Oath."

50. A. *Th.* 580–583, [1017–1024]; S. *Ant.* 198–201, 282–289; E. *Ph.* 604–606.

51. A. *Th.* 14–16, [1017–1019].

52. Cf. Burkert, *GR,* 248.

53. See above, pp. 72–73.

54. Xerxes: A. *Pers.* 807–814. Agamemnon: A. *Ag.* 338–347, 524–528 (if, against Fraenkel, we accept 527; see Fraenkel and Page and Denniston ad loc.). Aegyptiads: A. *Suppl.* 750–759. On E. *Tr.* 95–97, often cited in this regard, see above, p. 284 n. 124.

55. A. *Th.* 14–16, *Ag.* 577–582; E. frag. 50[A], 46–49. Cf. A. *Eum.* 538–542.

56. A. *Ag.* 338–347; S. *OT* 883–896. Cf. A. *Eum.* 538–542.

57. A. *Suppl.* 1024–1025, *Th.* 236; S. *Aj.* 710–713; E. *IA* 673–676.

58. A. *Ag.* 245–247; E. *IT* 958–960, *Hel.* 1473–1475 (on which see Kannicht ad loc.).

59. E. frag. 946[N]; Porph. *Abst.* 2.16; Isoc. 7.29–30. See *APR,* 101–102.

60. See below, pp. 189–190.

61. The philosophers, and especially Plato, did not share this "common view." See Meijer, "Philosophers, Intellectuals and Religion," 245–259.

62. S. *Aj.* 172–181; Xen. *An.* 7.8.1–6. See above, p. 21.

63. See above, p. 282 n. 81.

64. On the justice of the gods of cult see Nilsson, "Die Griechengötter und die Gerechtigkeit"; Yunis, *A New Creed,* 45–50.

65. Gods helping the just: A. *Suppl.* 77, 402–404, *Ag.* 810–828, 912–913, *Eum.* 911–912; E. *Suppl.* 594–597, 1145, *Ph.* 154–155, 256–260, *El.* 1350–1356, *IA* 1034–1035, *Or.* 1650–1652, frag. 584[N]. Gods punishing the unjust: A. *Suppl.* 402–404, *Ag.* 362–402, 810–829, 1577–1582, *Eum.* 267–275, 538–565, *Th.* 597–614; S. *Ph.* 1035–1042, frag. 4[P], line 11; E. *Hipp.* 675–677, *El.* 483–484, 1168–1171, *HF* 772–773, *Heraclid.* 901–908, *Tr.* 867–868, *Med.* 802, *Or.* 1361–1365.

66. A. *Th.* 662–663, *Ch.* 948–952; S. *OC* 1381–1382; E. *Med.* 764, frag. 151[N].

67. Zeus: A. *Suppl.* passim, *Th.* 597–614, 626–630, *Ag.* 355–402, 1563–1564, *Ch.* 244–245, 306–314, 382–409, 641–645, 788–789, *Pr.* passim; S. *Aj.* 1389–1391, *El.* 209–210, *OC* 1381–1382, *Ant.* 449–455; E. *HF* 209–212, *Tr.* 884–888, frags. 506[N], 832[N]. The collective of the gods: A. *Suppl.* 78, *Th.* 602–608, 626–630, *Ag.* 396–402, 810–829, 912–913, 1577–1582, *Ch.* 462, *Eum.* 558–565, frag. 301[R]; S. *Ant.* 368–369, 921–928, *OT* 883–896, *Ph.* 1035–1042, frag. 4[P], line 11; E. *Suppl.* 594–597, 608–616, 1145–1146, *Heraclid.* 906–908, *Ion* 1619–1622, *El.* 479–484, 583–584, 1168–1171, *Ph.* 154–155, 256–260, 467–468, *Hipp.* 675–677, *IA* 1034–1035, *HF* 772–773, 813–814, *Tr.* 867–868, *Med.* 802, *Or.* 1361–1362, 1650–1652, *Hel.* 900–904, 914–916, frags. 584[N], 585[N], 606[N], 835[N].

68. S. *El.* 245–250, *Ant.* 921–928, *OT* 883–896; E. *El* 583–584, *HF* 209–212, *IT* 560, *Suppl.* 608–616. The many claims of injustice against Apollo in the *Ion* seem, at least to Creousa and the chorus, refuted by the outcome of the play (1609–1622).

69. E. *IA* 1034–1035. On the unresolved charges against Zeus in S. *Tr.* and E. *HF* see Mikalson, "Zeus the Father and Heracles the Son in Tragedy."

70. S. *OT* 883–896; E. *El.* 583–584, *IA* 1034–1035, frag. 577[N].

71. For the involvement of gods in many matters of justice through oaths see above, pp. 86–87.

72. As in, e.g., A. *Suppl.* 395–396, 404, *Th.* 597–598; S. *Ph.* 79–85, 1049–1051, *OC* 823–825; E. *Alc.* 1147–1148, *Ph.* 524–525, *Hipp.* 1080–1081, *Heraclid.* 901–908, *Ba.* 991–996 = 1011–1016. Among modern scholars see, e.g., Versényi, *Holiness and Justice*, passim, esp. 1–9.

73. E. *Heraclid.* 901–903, *Ba.* 991–996 = 1011–1016, 997–1000.

74. Oaths: E. *Ph.* 491–493, *El.* 1349–1356, *Med.* 802, frag. 645[N]. *Xenoi*: A. *Th.* 597–614, *Ag.* 362–402, 758–781, 810–829, *Eum.* 267–275, 538–548. Cf. E. *Alc.* 1147–1148. Asylum: E. *Heraclid.* 101–104. Parents: A. *Suppl.* 707–709, *Eum.* 267–275, 511–548; E. *Hipp.* 1080–1081. Burial rites: S. *Aj.* 1389–1391, *Ant.* 921–928.

75. The φρήν, the diaphram or lungs, had been, since Homer's day, viewed as an organ of thought, as what we would call the mind. The plural, φρένες, may be the mind itself or thoughts emanating from it; φρονεῖν is "to use the φρήν." On the φρένες see Ireland and Steel, "Φρένες as an Anatomical Organ in the Works of Homer." In this section my translations are even more literal than usual, to maintain the pervasive presence of φρήν.

76. See above, pp. 139–142. On the importance of φρόνημα and ἀφροσύνη throughout the *Antigone* see Knapp, "A Point in the Interpretation of the *Antigone*"; Kirkwood, *A Study of Sophoclean Drama*, 233–239.

77. Cf. 996.

78. Cf. 992.

79. Cf. 1103–1104.

80. Cf. E. frag. 256[N].

81. Cf. 904, 1098, 1240–1243.

82. Cf. Yunis, *A New Creed*, 79.

83. See above, pp. 147–152.

84. See Dodds on *Ba.* 395. Cf. 326, 358–359, 884–887.

85. Cf. 358.

86. Cf. 311–312, 1301–1302.

87. Cf. 104–110. Contrast Pelasgus' deliberations and the Danaids' reaction (407–419, 640–642), where the need of φροντίδος σωτηρίου is stressed.

88. Cf. 782, 808, 820.

89. Cf. μὴ κατ' ἄνθρωπον φρονῇ, 761; οὐ κατ' ἄνθρωπον φρονῶν, 777. Cf. 758, 763, 766. See above, pp. 142–144. Cf. A. *Th.* 425, 438–439, *Pers.* 820.

90. Cf. 114–115, 118–120, 445–446.

91. Cf. A. *Pers.* 827–828.

92. For the interpretation of these lines see above, p. 284 n. 124.

93. Cf. S. *OC* 1536–1537; A. *Suppl.* 104–110; Xen. *Mem.* 1.1.14.

94. Chantraine, *Dictionnaire étymologigue de la langue grecque*, s.v. σῶς; North, *Sophrosyne*, esp. 1–84; Witte, *Die Wissenschaft vom Guten und Bösen*, 10–24; Lloyd-Jones, "Ehre und Schande in der griechischen Kultur."

95. Cf. Xen. *Mem.* 4.3.2–18.

96. Barrett on *Hipp.* 79–81. No single English word adequately translates *sophrosyne*. To avoid repeated laborious periphrases I transliterate the term.

97. On madness as an antithesis of piety see A. *Suppl.* 104–110; S. *OC* 1536–1537; E. *Ba.* 882–887.

98. On Ajax, his φρένες, and his impiety see Winnington-Ingram, *Sophocles*, 11–56; North, *Sophrosyne*, 58–61; and above, pp. 142–144.

99. Cf. A. *Pers.* 772. See also Headlam on A. *Eum.* 520 (quoted with approval by Dodds, *The Ancient Concept of Progress*, 59 n. 3): "σωφρονεῖν is synonymous with γνῶναι σεαυτόν, *to know your place* in relation to the gods and to your fellowmen." Cf. North, *Sophrosyne*, 4–6, 35.

100. Cf. E. *Ba.* 329, 504, 1341–1343.

101. The φρένες of each of the other heroes are criticized by the messenger, Eteocles, or the chorus: Tydeus, 387 (cf. 410); Capaneus, 425, 438–439; Eteoclus, 483–484; Hippomedon, 497–498; Parthenopaeus, 536–537, 550–551; Polyneices, 661, 671. On their lack of *sophrosyne* see North, *Sophrosyne*, 39–43.

102. Cf. S. *El.* 307–309, 464–465; E. frag. 388[N]. In *Suppl.* 925–927 Euripides' Theseus sees Amphiaraus praised by the gods by being snatched up alive and buried, together with his chariot. He clearly has in mind Amphiaraus' oracular cult at Oropos.

103. On Darius see above, pp. 35–37. On *sophrosyne* in the *Persae* see North, *Sophrosyne*, 35.

104. Or "statues" (ἱδρύματα, 811). See Broadhead ad loc.

105. On problems of interpretation with these lines see Broadhead ad loc. Cf. E. *Tr.* 85–86.

106. Cf. E. frag. 256[N]; Xen. *Mem.* 4.6.2–4.

107. On *hybris* in fifth-century life see MacDowell, "*Hybris* in Athens"; Ober, *Mass and Elite*, 208–214.

108. Cf. Pl. *Symp.* 196C.

109. Cf. Pl. *Leg.* 10.884–885B.

110. In this and the notes immediately following I distinguish between passages where *hybris* is certainly the topic of discussion ("explicit") and those where it appears to be ("probable"). *Hybris* resulting from faulty φρένες: (explicit) A. *Suppl.* 104–110, *Pers.* 807–808, 820–831, *Eum.* 532–537; E. *Hipp.* 473–475, *Ph.* 1111–1112; (probable) A. *Th.* 422–426, *Pers.* 745–772; S. *Aj.* 127–133. From folly: (explicit) S. *Aj.* 1150–1154. From madness: (explicit) A. *Suppl.* 104–110; S. *OC* 1534–1538; (probable) S. *Ant.* 128–137, 960–965.

111. Unjust: (explicit) A. *Ag.* 758–781, *Eum.* 517–565; E. *Ba.* 516–518. Godhated: (explicit) A. *Th.* 501–503, *Suppl.* 81; S. *Tr.* 280; (probable) S. *El.* 563–573.

112. Impious: (explicit) A. *Pers.* 807–831, *Ag.* 758–771, *Eum.* 532–548, *Pr.* 82–83; S. *Aj.* 1150–1154, *OC* 1534–1538; E. *Tr.* 69–71, 85–86, *Ba.* 374–375, 516–518 (cf. 553–555), 1296–1297, 1347, *Ph.* 1663; (probable) A. *Th.* 563–567; S. *Ant.* 960–965, 1348–1353.

113. Prosperity: (explicit) A. *Ag.* 758–781, *Eum.* 558–565; S. *OT* 873–879, *El.* 792–794; (probable) A. *Ag.* 377–378, frag. 154a[R], 15–19; S. *Aj.* 127–133.

114. Boasting: (explicit) S. *Tr.* 280–283; (probable) A. *Th.* 422–446, 465–469, 563–567, frag. 154a[R], 15–18; S. *Aj.* 127–133, *Ant.* 128–137, 960–965, 1348–1353, *El.* 563–573.

115. *Theomachos*: (explicit) Aegyptiads, A. *Suppl.* passim; Hippomedon, A. *Th.* 501–503; Paris, A. *Ag.* 758–781; Pentheus, E. *Ba.* 516–518, 1296–1297; Xerxes and Persians, A. *Pers.* 745–751, 807–831. Cf. E. *Hipp.* 473–476; (probable) Agamemnon, S. *El.* 563–573; Ajax, S. *Aj.* 127–133; Capaneus, A. *Th.* 423–446; S. *Ant.* 128–137; Creon, S. *Ant.* 1348–1353; Eteoclus, A. *Th.* 465–469; Lycurgus, S. *Ant.* 960–965; Parthenopaeus, A. *Th.* 563–567. Punishment: (explicit) A. *Pers.* 807–831, *Suppl.* 104–110, *Ag.* 758–781; S. *OC* 1534–1538, *Tr.* 280–283. E. *Tr.* 69–73, 85–86, *Ba.* 516–518, 1296–1297; (probable) A. *Th.* 438–446, 563–567, *Eum.* 552–565, frag. 154a[R], 15–18; S. *Ant.* 128–137, 960–965, 1348–1353, *El.* 563–573.

116. On such trials for impiety see Derenne, *Les procès d'impiété*; Rudhardt, "La définition du délit d'impiété d'après la législation attique"; Dover, "Freedom of the Intellectual"; MacDowell, *The Law in Classical Athens*, 200–202; Yunis, *A New Creed*, 59–72; Winiarczyk, "Wer Galt im Altertum als Atheist?"

117. For the τιμή of the Erinyes and in the *Oresteia* in general see Macleod, "Politics and the *Oresteia*," 138–144; Podlecki, *The Political Background of Aeschylean Tragedy*, 78–80. On τιμή and γέρας in Homer see Benveniste, *Le vocabulaire des institutions indo-européennes*, 2:43–55; Clay, *The Politics of Olympus*, passim.

118. Cf. 415–421, 845–846. An individual's *moira* is literally his "portion," often, as here, personified. Cf. *Eum.* 172, 476.

119. Cf. 415–421.

120. See above, pp. 25–28, 169. Cf. *Eum.* 471–472.

121. Cf. 349–352 (for a different interpretation of these lines see Lloyd-Jones, *The Eumenides*, 33), 385–388, 394–396, 417, 721–722, 791–792.

122. Cf. 208, 323–327.

123. As the Erinyes claim he did in the house of Pheres for Admetus (723–728). In Euripides' *Alcestis* Thanatos complains that by saving Admetus, Apollo is unjustly "delimiting and ending" the τιμάς of the nether gods (29–31).

124. Cf. 179–197, 721–722.

125. See above, pp. 76–77.

126. Cf. 837–846 = 870–880.

127. Cf. 794–807, 824, 833, 848.

128. The Athenians may actually have voted, by a margin of one, against Orestes. Athena voted for acquittal, making a tie and thereby granting acquittal. See Wilamowitz, *Aischylos Interpretationen*, 183–185; Podlecki, *Aeschylus: Eumenides*, 211–213.

129. See above, p. 64.

130. The Erinyes/Eumenides thus change from one to the other of the two classes of gods described by Isocrates (5.117): from gods overseeing "misfortunes and vengeance" and *not* "honored" (οὔτε ... τιμωμένους) with prayers or sacrifices, to gods who give "good things" and receive, in turn, temples and altars.

131. Cf. 854–855, τιμίαν ἕδραν. On religious connotations of τιμαλφεῖν see Fraenkel on *Ag.* 922.

132. Cf. 856–857.

133. Herodotus (2.53.2) claims Hesiod and Homer "made" the theogony for the Greeks, gave the gods their epithets, distributed their τιμάς and τέχνας, and revealed their outward forms (εἴδεα). So long as we limit ourselves to poetic conceptions and remember that Hesiod and Homer are representatives of a tradition, Herodotus' statement appears accurate. "Honors" and "crafts" are closely linked by Herodotus (τιμάς τε καὶ τέχνας), and the historian seems to be unpacking the complex of ideas (as both "honor" and "function") inherent in τιμή. Cf. Pl. *Phlb.* 61B–C.

134. If with Diggle we accept Valckenaur's οὐκ ἀτιστέον in E. *IT* 105, Pylades warns Orestes not to "dishonor" Apollo's oracle.

135. For the whole passage see above, p. 111.

136. See above, pp. 144–147. Cf. A. *Eum.* 215–216.

137. On function here see Denniston on E. *El.* 993.

138. In the first, lost *Hippolytus* the hero also receives τιμή, but its nature is not revealed in the surviving fragment (446[N]). It is possible that a description of cult honors, like those in the preserved *Hippolytus*, may have preceded these lines.

139. E. *Antiope* frag. 48 [Kambitsis], 86–103, on which see Kambitsis ad loc.; *Suppl.* 662–663.

140. On Achilles' demand for and receipt of τιμή in E. *Hec.* see above, pp. 37–38. A living person's religious duties could also be termed τιμαί: e.g., Iphigeneia's priesthood of Artemis (E. *IT* 748, 774–776) and Theonoë's prophetic ability (E. *Hel.* 13–15).

141. For the τιμαί of new cult heroes in the classical period see Thuc. 5.11 (Brasidas); Xen. *Hell.* 7.3.12 (Euphron); Paus. 1.32.5 (Echetlaios). Cf. Plut. *Thes.* 33, 35. For the practice of designating the worship and cult of heroes as τιμαί see Malkin, *Religion and Colonization*, 189–240.

142. A. *Pr.* 7–8, 29–30, 38, 48, 82–83, 107–108, 542–543, 945–946.

143. On τιμαλφεῖν see note 131 above.

144. Cf. A. *Th.* 77, 236, *Ch.* 255; E. *Heraclid.* 901–903, *Hipp.* 107, *Ba.* 1007–1010, frags. 50[A], 46–49, 256[N], 286[N] line 10.

145. Cf. Burkert, *GR*, 271: "In Greek virtually the only expression for the concept of religion is honours of the gods, *theon timai*."

146. On "thinking big" see above, p. 180.

147. E.g., B. M. W. Knox, *The Heroic Temper*, 6: "Hippolytus and Phaedra, Heracles, Pentheus, and many another are victims of gods whose power is exercised, as

they expressly tell us, for no other purpose than their own aggrandizement or the vindication in the sufferings of humanity of their own wounded self-esteem."

148. Cf. Lys. 6.33; Xen. *Mem.* 4.3.16; Pl. *Phdr.* 273E, *Criti.* 119D, *Leg.* 6.759B. On the concept of χάρις in religion and reciprocity between men and gods in this regard see Yunis, *A New Creed,* 101–107. On the "rejoicing" element of χαίρω, χάρις, and their cognates see Versnel, "Religious Mentality in Ancient Prayer," 47–49.

149. Cf. E. *Hipp.* 106, *Andr.* 566, *IT* 35–36, 384, frag. 794[N].

150. Cf. E. *Alc.* 53, where Thanatos "enjoys" (τέρπεται) his τιμαῖς. Cf. also 55.

151. Cf. 209, 273–274, 309, 329, 770, 1031. The same language appropriate to deity is used of Mount Cithaeron in S. *OT* 1086–1095.

152. Cf. E. *HF* 840–842.

153. See above, pp. 179–183.

154. In S. *OC* 277–278 may be expressed an antithesis between "honoring the gods" and "considering them 'fools,'" but the critical word, †μοίραις† or μώρους (278), is uncertain. Cf. E. *HF* 840–842.

155. Cf. 1402. See above, pp. 144–145.

156. In A. *Eum.* 538–565 Dike (Justice) is presented as a god, and the suffering of one who "dishonors" her and her altar is graphically described.

157. See above, pp. 144–147.

158. See above, p. 283 n. 93.

159. See above, pp. 142–144.

160. See above, note 99.

161. A. *Eum.* 833–836, 854–857, 1003–1038.

162. E. *Ba.* 191–192, 206–209.

163. Sanctuaries: E. *HF* 1331–1333. Cf. *Ion* 130; Xen. *Mem.* 1.1.14. Dedications: A. *Ag.* 577–582 (cf. 922); cf. E. *HF* 375–379, frag. 50[A], 46–49. Hymns: E. *Heraclid.* 777–783, *Hipp.* 55–56. Dances: E. *Heraclid.* 777–783, *Ba.* 206–209, 220, frag. 65[A], 77–80. Cf. S. *OT* 1086–1095. Libations: E. *Or.* 1686–1688. Rituals: E. *Heraclid.* 777–783, *IT* 959–960, 1458–1461. Prayers: A. *Suppl.* 627–628, *Th.* 230–236; E. *El.* 192–197, *HF* 607–609. Festivals: E. *Heraclid.* 777–783, *IT* 959–960, 1458–1461. Sacrifices: A. *Suppl.* 704–706, *Ch.* 255–257; E. *HF* 1331–1333, *Heraclid.* 777–783, frag. 65[A], 77–80. Theseus speaks sarcastically of Hippolytus' "honoring" the smoke of the writings of Orpheus (E. *Hipp.* 953–954).

164. Rudhardt, *Notions fondamentales,* 289–290; *Le sacrifice dans l'antiquité.*

165. Περὶ Εὐσεβείας, frag. 12 [Pötscher, 42–44] = Porph. *Abst.* 2.20. On the philosophers' views of sacrifice as τιμή and piety see Meijer, "Philosophers, Intellectuals and Religion," 245–259.

166. Cf. A. *Eum.* 1028–1031; E. *Ba.* 284–285. Cf. E. *Hel.* 753–754.

167. A. *Ag.* 86–91, 261–263; E. *Alc.* 1154–1158, *Or.* 1137–1139. Sophocles' Clytemnestra (*El.* 278–281) has made into a monthly festival, replete with choruses and sacrifices, the day on which she killed Agamemnon. The honorees are "the saving deities." For prayers of thanksgiving see E. *El.* 415–416, 761–764. Cf. S. *Ant.* 330–331.

168. On unprofitable sacrifices to Olympians see A. *Ag.* 1167–1171; S. *Tr.* 993–995; E. *Tr.* 1240–1242. Cf. A. *Th.* 174–180, *Eum.* 106–110.

169. Nock, "The Cult of Heroes," 149 (= *Essays*, 582–583). Cf. Burkert, *GR*, 35, 46, 66, 93. Aeschylus' Thanatos "does not passionately desire gifts, and therefore you might accomplish nothing by sacrificing or pouring libations" (frag. 161[R], 1–2). Cf. A. *Ag.* 88–91. On sacrifices as "gifts" and for salutary warnings on interpreting the meaning of sacrifices see Kirk, "Some Methodological Pitfalls." On gifts and the wide range and significance of gift-giving by men to men and to gods in Homer see Finley, *The World of Odysseus*, 61–65, 100–103, 132–133, 148.

170. See Pl. *Rep.* 3.364B–365A, 390E, *Alc.* 2.149E, *Leg.* 10.885B, 905B–907B.

171. On votive offerings as "gifts" to the gods see Yunis, *A New Creed*, 103–106.

172. Note plural τιμαί. On the benefits see above, pp. 18–19.

173. Contrast Troy in E. *Andr.* 1014–1018.

174. Cf. *Hymn. Hom. Ap.* 88; Bacchyl. 9.98, 10.12.

175. Diggle (ad loc.), following Nauck, deletes these lines. The same thought, though not in the context of τιμή, occurs in E. *Or.* 667–668. For the chorus of the *Bacchae* it is a γέρας from the gods to be victorious over one's enemies (877–880 = 897–900).

176. Cf. Xen. *Cyn.* 1.1–2.

177. According to Herodotus (1.60.5), the heralds who preceded Pisistratus and his fake Athena into Athens announced to the citizens, "Receive with good will Pisistratus, whom Athena herself has honored (τιμήσασα) most of all men and whom she brings back to her Acropolis."

178. Cf. *Ag.* 42–44, *Pers.* 762–764; Xen. *Hier.* 8.5. Cf. *Il.* 1.174–175, 277–279, 11.45–46 (on which see E. Benveniste, *Le vocabulaire des institutions indo-européennes*, 2:49–55).

179. Ἄτιμοι here, as Fraenkel on *Ag.* 1279 notes, clearly alludes to "unavenged" but is not simply equivalent to ἀτιμώρητοι. Ἄτιμοι is a pregnant word, suggesting both the vengeance and the "honor" which Cassandra and Agamemnon are to receive from that vengeance. Cf. Garvie on A. *Ch.* 142–143.

180. See above, pp. 140–141.

181. If the text of Sophocles frag. 247[R] is correct, "wisdom" may be a product of the τιμή a god returns to man. For the expected "Alone is wise the man who honors god" the fragment offers "Alone is wise the man whom a god honors." On text see Radt ad loc.

182. A god may also have χάρις towards a man: E. *Heraclid.* 767–768. Dedications may be one form of showing τιμή for such χάρις (A. *Ag.* 581–582). On this see Yunis, *A New Creed*, 101–107.

183. Cf. E. *Alc.* 658–660; S. *Aj.* 506–507; Pl. *Leg.* 10.886C; Isoc. 1.16.

184. Cf. Pl. *Leg.* 10.931A–E. On piety owed parents see above, pp. 170–173.

185. See below, pp. 194–195.

186. See above, p. 62.

187. There are also indications that parents should "honor" their children: The-

seus, "respecting" (αἰδούμενος) the gods and his son, "because he is from me," claims not to take pleasure in Hippolytus' sufferings (E. Hipp. 1257-1260). Clytemnestra claims that in sacrificing his daughter Agamemnon did not honor (οὐ προτιμῶν) her (A. Ag. 1415-1418). Cf. S. El. 1426-1427, OC 1273-1274; E. Ion 615.

188. For Zeus Synestios (704) as Zeus Xenios see Fraenkel on Ag. 704.

189. Αἰδώς and its cognates are commonly used also in these contexts. On Admetus as exemplary xenos see above, pp. 78-80.

190. On Zeus Xenios see above, p. 77.

191. For refugees who do receive τιμή see S. OC 1273, 1278 (where the refugee is also Oedipus' son); E. Heraclid. 101. In OC 285-288 Oedipus demands τιμή not as a person having asylum but as a "holy" (ἱερός), "pious" (εὐσεβής) man bringing benefits to Athenian citizens.

192. Dishonor to god or gods: A. Suppl. 732-733; E. Heraclid. 69-72, 78-79. Cf. S. OC 275-281, 1006-1013; E. Hel. 980-987. See above, pp. 72-75. Punishment: A. Suppl. 732-733. Cf. S. OC 275-281.

193. See above, pp. 72-73.

194. Cf. A. Eum. 213-214. In OT 653 "respect" is owed to Creon, now "great" in his oath. In the context of oaths αἰδέομαι and its cognates are more common than τιμή and related forms. Cf. A. Eum. 483-484, 679-680, 710.

195. See above, p. 123.

196. A. Ch. 434-443 (on which see Garvie on Ch. 439); S. El. 444-445. Cf. E. frag. 176[N].

197. Burial and the funeral: A. Th. [1017-1025, 1046]; S. Aj. 1332-1342, 1356, Ant. 21-25, 207-210, 284-285, 514-516, 913-915, OC 1409-1410. Cf. Thuc. 2.35.1, 2.36.1; Pl. Leg. 1.632C. In Homer burial and funeral rites are γέρας θανόντων (on which see Garland, "Γέρας Θανόντων: An Investigation into the Claims of the Homeric Dead").

198. Elements of the funeral: A. Suppl. 116, Ch. 429-443, Th. [1022-1024]; S. Ant. 900-904 (cf. 430-431), El. 1212-1214 (if Electra refers to lamentations due as τιμή at funerals); E. HF 1360-1361, Alc. 618-619, Ph. 1318-1321, 1664-1670, El. 323-325, Suppl. 78. Euripides' Medea (Med. 1032-1036) expresses her previous "sweet thought" that, duly buried by her children, she would be the object of envy (ζηλωτόν) to men.

199. Cf. S. Aj. 1164-1167.

200. Elements of tomb cult: A. Ch. 96-99, 193, 200, 320-322, 483-485, 510-511 (on which see Garvie ad loc.); S. El. 239-243, 443-445, 908. These need not, however, be considered representative of the ordinary dead; as we have seen above (pp. 35-37), the dead Agamemnon was presented as a type of hero. Cf. Thuc. 3.58.4.

201. Dead person honored: A. Suppl. 116, Ch. 200, 434-443, 483-485; Th. [1046]; S. Aj. 1342, Ant. 21-25, 207-210, 514-516, 900-904, El. 443-445, OC 1409-1410; E. HF 1360-1361, Alc. 618-619, Ph. 1320-1321, 1670, Hec. 317-320, Heraclid. 597-599, frag. 176[N]. Cf. E. Med. 1032-1036; Thuc. 2.36.1, 3.58.4; Pl. Leg. 1.632C, 11.927B; IG I² 1022. Deceased's awareness of honor: cf. Pl. Leg. 11.927B. On the various conceptions of the afterlife see above, pp. 114-121.

202. S. *Ant.* 21–25 (on which see B. M. W. Knox, *The Heroic Temper,* 91–92); A. *Ch.* 483–485 (on which see Garvie ad loc.). Cf. A. *Eum.* 95–96.
203. Dead honored only by reputation among the living: E. *Suppl.* 78. Such a view is implied by the emphasis on the τιμή of a tomb prominent to men: A. *Th.* 1002–1003; E. *Hec.* 317–320; *IG* I² 1022. Cf. E. *Med.* 1032–1036.
204. Dishonor to corpse irrelevant to the dead: E. frag. 176[N]. See above, p. 115.
205. See above, p. 121.
206. S. *Ant.* 76–77:

σοὶ δ' εἰ δοκεῖ,
τὰ τῶν θεῶν ἔντιμ' ἀτιμάσασ' ἔχε.

Cf. S. *Aj.* 1129–1131; E. *Suppl.* 16–19, 301–302. On prevention of burial see above, pp. 121–128.
207. S. *Aj.* 1343–1344; E. *Suppl.* 311, 561–563.
208. "Laws" may be too strong for νόμιμα (especially in contrast to νόμους of 452), but "customs," "ways," and other simple translations are too weak. Νόμιμα θεῶν are here "proper and sanctioned modes of behavior established by the gods *or* of concern to them." On νόμιμα and this passage see B. M. W. Knox, *The Heroic Temper,* 94–98.
209. B. M. W. Knox, *The Heroic Temper,* 94–98.
210. Cf. S. *Ant.* 745.
211. On the unwritten laws see Ehrenberg, *Sophocles and Pericles,* 22–50, 167–172; Guthrie, *A History of Greek Philosophy,* 3:76–79, 117–131; Hall, *Inventing the Barbarian,* 184–190.
212. The "natural" ways in which incest and violations of *xenia* are punished are unfamiliar to Socrates' interlocutor and appear the product of philosophic speculation, not popular religion. But there too no specific god is involved.
213. If, as Stobaeus claims (3.1.80), these lines come from Euripides' *Heraclidae,* the "common laws" may refer more specifically to asylum. But the lines are not to be found in our manuscripts of the *Heraclidae.*
214. Rites for the dead: S. *Aj.* 1129–1131, 1343–1344, *Ant.* 449–460, 1113–1114. Parents: A. *Suppl.* 701–709 (in these lines piety towards *xenoi* and gods may also be "institutions" of Dike; see Johansen and Whittle ad loc.); S. *El.* 1095–1097; E. frag. 853[N]. Cf. Xen. *Mem.* 4.4.19–25. Worship: S. *El.* 1095–1097; E. *Ba.* 201–203, 890–896 (on both of which see Dodds ad loc.). Cf. Xen. *Mem.* 4.4.19–25. Since men believe in the gods by νόμος ("tradition"), Euripides' Hecuba can claim that νόμος rules the gods, that the gods are inferior to νόμος (*Hec.* 798–800). Cf. Xen. *Mem.* 4.6.2–4. Respect for asylum: E. frag. 1049[N] (if, in fact, the νόμος here is a νόμος τῶν θεῶν). Safety of *xenoi*: E. *Hec.* 798–805. Cf. Xen. *Mem.* 4.4.19–25. Not robbing sanctuaries: E. *Hec.* 798–805.
215. In S. *Ant.* 450–455 Antigone may be implying that the νόμιμα concerning the dead are Zeus' and Dike's creation. Cf. S. *El.* 1095–1097.

216. S. *OT* 870–872, *Ant.* 456–457; E. *Ba.* 201–203. Cf. *Ba.* 895–896.
217. E. *Suppl.* 311, 526–527, 538, 671–672, frag. 853[N]; Xen. *Mem.* 4.4.19–25. Cf. S. *OT* 865–870.
218. *The Heroic Temper,* 97.
219. The creators they propose—Dike and Olympus—are not deities of cult.
220. Cf. Lys. 6.10 for divine concern for ἄγραφοι νόμοι of the Eumolpidae. In a summary of Euripides' *Heraclidae* Isocrates (12.169) speaks of the πάτριος νόμος concerning burial as "assigned by a divine power" (ὡς ὑπὸ δαιμονίας προστεταγμένῳ δυνάμεως). In popular religion the emphasis is on the ancestral tradition of the νόμιμα, that is, τὰ πάτρια νόμιμα, not on their divine origin.
221. On the variety and nature of "gifts" Homeric man gave his king see Finley, *The World of Odysseus,* 61–65, 100–104, 132–133.
222. The similar attitude one should have towards kings (or military commanders) and gods is particularly clear in S. *Aj.* 666–677. Cf. Dover, *Aristophanic Comedy,* 32: "The Greek's relation with one of his gods was essentially the relation between subject and ruler. A ruler is a person whose actions and decisions cannot always be predicted or explained by his subjects; he can be placated, in normal times by normal tribute; he makes rules—which he himself does not necessarily obey—and punishes subjects who break the rules; but he does not concern himself with what lies outside the province of his rules, and a prudent subject will pay his tribute, obey the rules, and keep out of the ruler's way."
223. Cf. Lys. 6.10.
224. Adkins, *Merit and Responsibility,* 62–64; Jaeger, *Paideia,* 1:8–12. For a survey of the importance of τιμή in Greek culture see Lloyd-Jones, "Ehre und Schande." For the division, on the mythic level, of the τιμαί of the Olympian gods see Clay, *The Politics of Olympus.*
225. For attempts to find theological and philosophical expertise in Euthyphro see Roth, "Teiresias as *Mantis* and Intellectual in Euripides' *Bacchae,*" 63–65; Hoerber, "Plato's *Euthyphro,*" 95–98.
226. On χάρις and the reciprocity concerning it between humans and gods see Yunis, *A New Creed,* 101–107.
227. Cf. Pl. *Phd.* 62C–E.
228. Θεραπεύω and its cognates are widely used of service to the gods outside of tragedy: e.g., Pind. *Ol.* 3.16, *Pyth.* 3.109; Hdt. 2.37.2; Lys. 6.51, Xen. *Mem.* 1.2.64, 1.4.10–13, 18, 2.1.28, *Oec.* 5.12, 5.20, 11.8, *Symp.* 4.49, *Eq. Mag.* 7.1, 9.9, *Cyr.* 7.2.15, 8.1.24; Isoc. 3.20, 7.29, 10.56, 11.24, 15.281–282; Pl. *Rep.* 2.362C, 4.427B, 4.443A, *Phdr.* 252C, 255A, *Leg.* 4.716D, 5.740C, 9.878A, 11.930E, *Epin.* 988A, [*Def.*] 412D–413A, 415A; Theopompus *FGrHist* 115 F344. One may likewise "serve" a holy day (Hdt. 3.79), sanctuaries (Thuc. 4.98), and the ancestral traditions of funerals (Lys. 2.81). Hesiod (*Op.* 135–139) provides an early and concise statement of the nexus of θεραπεία, sacrifice, and honor: those who were unwilling to serve (θεραπεύειν) the gods and to sacrifice were buried in the earth by Zeus because they were not giving τιμάς to the Olympian gods. On the concept of θεραπεία θεῶν see Burkert, *GR,* 273.

229. E.g., E. *Suppl.* 762–763. Cf. *Or.* 221–222.

230. In the *Knights,* however, Demos is represented as a δεσπότης (58). Cf. Isoc. 15.70.

231. Squires in Homer: e.g., *Il.* 1.321, 5.580, 8.119, *Od.* 4.23. Service to spouse: E. *Ph.* 1548–1549. To parents: Pl. *Rep.* 4.425B, 5.467A, *Men.* 91A, *Leg.* 10.886C; Lys. 19.37, 24.6; Xen. *Mem.* 2.2.13; Isaeus 2.18, 2.25, 2.36, 2.45. Cf. E. *Ion* 109–111, 181–183, *Ph.* 1686. To children: E. *HF* 632–633. To *xenoi*: Pl. *Leg.* 4.718A; Pind. *Ol.* 13.3.

232. Lloyd-Jones, *The Justice of Zeus,* 3, 33. Euripides' *Ion* is a special case. As a foundling raised in the sanctuary Ion is virtually, and views himself as, a temple slave (131–132, 182, 309, 327). He serves (θεραπεύω) those that feed him and the temple that raised him as others would serve their parents (109–111, 181–183; cf. 129–130, 151–152). On Ion's status in this regard see Yunis, *A New Creed,* 122–125.

233. Cf. Burkert, *GR,* 189, 273. The Dionysus cult described in Euripides' *Bacchae* is exceptional in what it expects of devotees and in its Eastern character; there the Asian *bacchae* call Dionysus "master" (δέσποτα, 582), and even Teiresias says that "one must be a slave" (δουλευτέον, 366) to the gods. Cf. E. *Cycl.* 709. E. *Or.* 418 is to be explained by Orestes' (unusual) dependence on the orders of Apollo at this time of his life.

234. These topics rarely arise in forensic and deliberative orations but are to be found mostly in philosophical or protreptic discussions of piety. Hence most of the references below come from philosophers or others musing about the nature of piety. For a very similar nexus of piety, τιμὴ τῶν θεῶν, and knowledge see Xen. *Mem.* 4.6.2–4. Cf. E. frag. 256[N]. On the τιμαί of gods and heroes, especially as exhibited in festivals, sacrifices, prayers, and dedications: Porph. *Abst.* 4.22 (on Draco's law); Lys. 2.80; Lyc. *Leoc.* 1, 26, 88, 97, frag. in *FGrHist* 392 F2; Hyperides 6.43; Thuc. 5.11; Xen. *Mem.* 1.1.14, 1.3.3, 1.4.10, 4.3.13–17, 4.6.2–4, *Oec.* 11.9, *Ages.* 1.34, *Eq. Mag.* 3.2; Isoc. 1.13, 5.32, 5.117, 14.60; Dem. 19.86, 257, 280; Theopompus, *FGrHist* 115 F344; Pl. *Symp* 190C, *Alc.* 2.148E–149A, *Rep.* 3.386A, *Leg.* 4.717A, 4.723E, 7.809D, 7.815D, 8.828D, 10.899D, 11.931A, *Epin.* 977A, 980A–B, 985D, *Ep.* 357C, [*Def.*] 414A–B; Arist. *Eth. Nic.* 8.1160a; *IG* II² 5501. Cf. Pl. *Symp.* 188C, *Leg.* 5.726A–728C; Dinarchus 1.94; Apollod. 3.14.1; *IG* II² 4334, 5501. In the ephebic oath (Tod, *Greek Historical Inscriptions,* 2: no. 204) Athenian youth swore they would honor (τιμήσω) the "ancestral sanctuaries" (line 16). On sacrifices and dedications as "gifts" to the deity: Hdt. 1.87.1; Xen. *Mem.* 1.3.3; Pl. *Alc.* 2.149E, *Leg.* 4.716D–717B, 10.905D; *IG* II² 4373, 4548, 4596, 4602, 4888. For more dedications see Yunis, *A New Creed,* 104 n. 6. On gods' "taking pleasure" (χαίρω and cognates) in sacrifices, dedications, and other forms of worship: Hdt. 1.87.1; Polyxenus, frag. 1 [Müller]; Xen. *Mem.* 1.3.3, 4.3.16, *Eq. Mag.* 3.2, *Cyn.* 13.16–17; Lys. 6.33. Cf. *IG* I² 650, II² 4319; Ar. *Pax* 385–389; Pl. *Symp.* 188C, *Leg.* 11.931A. On τιμαί of the dead among the living, or, though always expressed with uncertainty, among the dead and nether gods: Lys. 2.80; Dem. 60.34; Aeschines 1.14; Thuc. 3.58; Hdt. 1.30.5; Pl. *Hipp. Mai.* 291D–E; Isoc. 9.1–2; *IG* II² 7863, 7873. Cf. Isaeus 2.36.

235. Compare the four definitions of piety collected in [Pl.] *Def.* 412D–413A: piety is (1) justice concerning the gods, (2) a voluntary ability to serve the gods (δύναμις θεραπευτικὴ θεῶν ἑκούσιος), (3) a correct understanding concerning the honor (τιμή) of the gods, and (4) a knowledge of the honor (τιμή) concerning the gods. Cf. Burkert, *GR,* 271: "In Greek virtually the only expression for the concept of religion is honours of the gods, *theon timiai.*"

236. Cf. Arist. *Eth. Nic.* 1102a3–4.

Chapter Six

1. Nilsson, *Geschichte der griechischen Religion,* 1:772.
2. For Artemis and Aphrodite in E. *Hipp.* see above, pp. 146–147.
3. See above, pp. 21–22, 143.
4. See above, pp. 64–68.
5. See above, p. 65.
6. See above, pp. 87–101.
7. See above, p. 26.
8. E.g., in Athens, at least after 420, Asclepios had the healing functions usually given to Apollo in tragedy. Similarly in classical Greece success in seafaring was sought by sacrifices to beneficent deities, especially Poseidon. In tragedy problems with seafaring are usually overcome by appeasing an angry deity.
9. See above, pp. 17–29, 138–139.
10. It seems a convention of tragedy, in fact of all Greek literature, that requests by individuals having asylum are just and are, or should be, granted. See above, pp. 71–72.
11. See above, pp. 129–131.
12. See above, pp. 160–161.
13. See above, pp. 147–151, 158–162.
14. See above, p. 159.
15. See above, pp. 86–87.
16. See above, pp. 86–87, 178–179.
17. See above, pp. 86–87. For arguments that Zeus dispenses justice in the *Iliad* see Lloyd-Jones, *The Justice of Zeus,* 1–27.
18. See above, pp. 29–45.
19. On Apollo's false oracle in the *Ion* see above, pp. 90–91.
20. Cf. Parker, *Miasma,* 15: "while in high literature the seer is always right, in comedy he is always wrong."
21. It is a tragic convention that oracles and *dei ex machina* give prior or immediate validation to new cults. In life such validation was usually sought from Delphi *post factum.* See above, p. 89.
22. It also seems to be a tragic convention that only women have prophetic dreams. See above, pp. 102–103.

23. See above, p. 121.
24. On Antigone in Sophocles' *Antigone* as an exception to this see above, p. 123.
25. See above, p. 291 n. 116.
26. Mikalson, "Religion and the Plague in Athens, 431–423 B.C." On Nicias see above, pp. 162–164.
27. On Zeus, religion, and justice in Aeschylus see Rose, "Theology and Mythology in Aeschylus"; Solmsen, "Strata of Greek Religion in Aeschylus" and *Hesiod and Aeschylus*; Lloyd-Jones, "Zeus in Aeschylus" and *The Justice of Zeus*, 84–103; Winnington-Ingram, "A Religious Function of Greek Tragedy"; Kiefner, *Der religiöse Allbegriff des Aischylos*.
28. See above, pp. 74–75.
29. On Zeus Hikesios see above, pp. 74–75.
30. See above, p. 192.
31. On Zeus Xenios as a literary deity see above, p. 77. Cf. A. *Suppl.* 627–629.
32. See above, pp. 192–193, 194–196.
33. Cf. A. *Suppl.* 583–585.
34. A. *Suppl.* 156–160, 230–231, *Ag.* 1385–1387, *Ch.* 382–385, *Eum.* 273–275, frag. 273a[R]. Cf. S. *OC* 1606; E. frag. 912[N].
35. Among the tragedians Aeschylus alone makes Zeus and Dike authors of τὰ νόμιμα. See above, pp. 194–195. On Zeus Hikesios and Xenios in Homer see Lloyd-Jones, *The Justice of Zeus*, 5. On justice and piety see above, pp. 178–179.
36. See above, p. 178.
37. Cf. A. frag. 70[R]. The justice of Zeus may well have been a central issue also in the lost plays of the Promethean trilogy.
38. See above, pp. 50–51.
39. See above, pp. 49–53. For the one instance in Euripides where the Athenians expect divine support because their campaign is just see E. *Suppl.* 594–596 and p. 249 n. 148 above.
40. Euripides in *IT* 1469–1472 follows Aeschylus' version of the founding of the Areopagus but does not make it into an exemplum of the justice of the gods. He seems merely to be following Aeschylus' account of the fate of Orestes. See above, p. 254 n. 232.
41. See above, pp. 35–37.
42. According to the *Vita* (9) of Aeschylus, the appearance of the chorus of Erinyes so terrified the audience that children fainted and women miscarried. On the story see Taplin, *The Stagecraft of Aeschylus*, 372, 438 n. 2; Calder, "*Vita Aeschyli* 9."
43. On the Erinyes and Semnai in Aeschylus, literature, myth, and cult see Rose, "Theology and Mythology in Aeschylus"; Solmsen, *Hesiod and Aeschylus*, 178–224; E. Wüst, "Erinyes," *RE* suppl. 8 (1956), cols. 82–166; Winnington-Ingram, "A Religious Function of Greek Tragedy" and *Sophocles*, 205–216; Dietrich, *Death, Fate,*

and the Gods, 91–156; Henrichs, "The Eumenides and Wineless Libations" and "The 'Sobriety' of Oedipus"; A. L. Brown, "The Erinyes in the *Oresteia*"; Lloyd-Jones, "Les Erinyes."

44. See Paus. 1.28.6–7, 1.30.4, 1.31.4; and above, note 43.
45. Paus. 7.25.2–3; Thuc. 1.126.11; Plut. *Sol.* 12.1; and above, pp. 69–70.
46. Ar. *Eq.* 1311–1312, *Thesm.* 224.
47. See above, pp. 69–77.
48. Paus. 1.28.6; Dinarchus 1.47; schol. to Aeschines 1.188.
49. Solmsen, *Hesiod and Aeschylus,* 178–224; Winnington-Ingram, "A Religious Function of Greek Tragedy," 21; Parker, *Miasma,* 125.
50. For criticisms of this traditional view see Lloyd-Jones, *The Justice of Zeus,* 90–95.
51. See above, pp. 183–185.
52. See above, pp. 13–14.
53. If we accept the contention of, e.g., Dietrich and Lloyd-Jones (above, note 43) that the Erinyes were deities worshiped in archaic Athens, then the Erinyes of the *Eumenides* would not be so much Aeschylus' personal creation as his revival of deities once important to popular religion.
54. See above, p. 11.
55. If we accept δέει, Casaubon's conjecture, in line 522. Cf. Thuc. 2.37.3.
56. For the "classic view" of Sophocles' piety and its relationship to interpretation of the plays see Whitman, *Sophocles,* 4–21. Cf. B. M. W. Knox, *The Heroic Temper,* 52–54.
57. The earliest explicit claim of Sophocles' exceptional piety is apparently the scholion to S. *El.* 831 = T107[R]. Two other such explicit claims are thought to be found in Satyrus' *Vita* of Sophocles (third century B.C.) but are based on misinterpretations of the passages. The most recent detailed study of Sophocles' piety is Lefkowitz's *Lives of the Greek Poets,* 76, 83–84, 86–87. I give her translations of the *Vita* here, with my reservations stated below.

Vita 12: "Sophocles was more pious than anyone else, according to what Hieronymus says (frag. 31, Wehrli) . . . about his golden crown. When this crown was stolen from the Acropolis, Heracles came to Sophocles in a dream and told him to go into the house on the right and it would be hidden there. Sophocles brought this information to the citizens and received a reward of a talent, as had been announced in advance. He used the talent to establish a shrine of Heracles Informer." The word translated as "pious" is, however, θεοφιλής, and that is not what it means in classical Greek. It means, rather, "god-loved," and the point of the story (whether it be true or not; see Lefkowitz, 84) is that Sophocles is god-loved because the gods helped him find the crown which he presumably had been awarded and had dedicated to an Acropolis deity. He is not here being labeled pious for founding a shrine. On θεοφιλής see Dirlmeier, "ΘΕΟΦΙΛΙΑ–ΦΙΛΟΘΕΙΑ."

Vita 16: "Lobon says that this epitaph was written on his tomb: In this tomb I hide Sophocles who won first prize with his tragic art, a most holy figure." Σχῆμα τὸ σεμνότατον means, it must be emphasized, a figure "most respected," "most revered." Lobon's Sophocles was the receiver of the σέβας, not the giver of it. The Greek says nothing of Sophocles' own εὐσέβεια.

We may correct one further small misunderstanding arising from mistranslation of the *Vita*. Ister (*FGrHist* 334 F37) and Neanthes (*FGrHist* 84 F18) say that Sophocles died not "at the festival of the Choes" (Lefkowitz, 86) but "about the time of the Choes" (περὶ τοὺς χόας). If we believe their account, we know only the date of his death (ca. 12 Anthesterion 406 B.C.), not that he died while celebrating a sacred festival.

58. On the cult of Dexion see Lefkowitz, *Lives of the Greek Poets*, 84; Ferguson, "The Attic Orgeones," 86–91. For a recent assessment of Sophocles' role in the founding of the Asclepios cult in Athens see Aleshire, *The Athenian Asklepieion*, 9–11.

59. See above, p. 39.

60. See above, pp. 39–41. See also B. M. W. Knox, *The Heroic Temper*, 54–58.

61. See above, pp. 162–164.

62. For the Christian assumptions lying behind such a view see Schlesier's comments on Euripidean criticism in "Götterdämmerung bei Euripides?" 39–40.

63. See above, p. 178.

64. See above, p. 48. Nestle (*Euripides*, 66) notes that from the traditional list Sophocles omits only divination, which of course he would have had to assign to the gods.

65. Even the sanctuary of a hero such as Proteus was exceptional as a place of asylum. See above, p. 259 n. 22.

66. See above, p. 121.

67. Cf. Fraenkel on A. *Ag.* 1602.

68. On this scene see Burian, "Supplication and Hero Cult."

69. On the "double burial" see Winnington-Ingram, *Sophocles*, 125 n. 31; Gellie, *Sophocles: A Reading*, 38–39; Kitto, *Form and Meaning*, 138–158: and, most recently, Rothaus, "The Single Burial of Polyneices."

70. On the ritual elements in the two burials see Bradshaw, "The Watchman Scenes."

71. See above, p. 85.

72. See above, p. 85.

73. For Sophocles' possible manipulation of the Athenian Oedipus cult to achieve unity in the *Oedipus at Colonus* see Pfister, *Der Reliquienkult*, 110–112. To the list of Sophocles' irregularities might be added the prayer (*Ant.* 1126–1152) to a Delphic/Theban/Athenian Dionysus to come and "purify" Thebes.

74. A fuller study of this topic appears in Mikalson, "Zeus the Father and Heracles the Son in Tragedy."

75. E.g., 126–128, 139–140, 251–280, 499–500, 1021–1022, 1278.

76. The praises of deities and Athens may be mixed (see Kamerbeek on 668–

670, 707–711), but the focus is usually on Colonus. In 668–719, e.g., the Panathenian deities are introduced through links with flowers and produce of Colonus.

77. Cf. 62–63.

78. According to the biographical tradition (T81–84[R]), the aged Sophocles, as his only defense against charges of senility and incompetence lodged by his son, read this ode to the jury. The charges were judged baseless. For a very skeptical account of this story see Lefkowitz, *Lives of the Greek Poets,* 84–85.

79. Poseidon Hippios and Athena Hippia: 707–719, 1070–1073. Pausanias saw at Colonus, near Oedipus' tomb, altars of these two deities (1.30.4). Cf. Thuc. 8.67; E. *Ph.* 1707. On the cult of these two deities see Farnell, *The Cults of the Greek States,* 1:270–272; Burkert, *GR,* 138, 221. Demeter Euchloös (1600) should be identified with Demeter Chloe ("Of Green Vegetation"). She had a sanctuary near the Acropolis in Pausanias' time (1.22.3), and her sanctuaries, sacrifices, festivals, and priestesses are attested throughout Attica from the fourth century B.C. to the second century A.D. (*IG* II² 1356, 1358, 1472, 4748, 4750, 5129). From *OC* 1600–1603 some have assigned her a shrine on a hill near Colonus. On her cult see Jacoby on *FGrHist* 328 F61; Nilsson, *Geschichte der griechischen Religion,* 1:151, 467; Farnell, *The Cults of the Greek States,* 3:33–48. Zeus Morios and Athena Moria: 694–706. On their cult see Nilsson, *Geschichte der griechischen Religion,* 1:442; K. Latte, "Moria," *RE* 16 (1933), cols. 302–303. Prometheus: 55–56. Cf. Paus. 1.30.2; schol. to S. *OC* 56. Aphrodite and the Muses: 691–693. On their joint cult in Athens, with one site perhaps near the Cephisus River, see above, pp. 63–64. Colonus: 58–61.

80. Dionysus, Demeter, and Kore: 683–684, 1050–1053.

81. Cf. 54–55, 707–719, 887–889, 1070–1073, 1156–1159, 1285–1287, 1491–1495.

82. On the cult see p. 246 n. 105 above.

83. Cf. 258–262, 275–283, 1006–1013, 1124–1127.

84. See B. M. W. Knox, *The Heroic Temper,* 109.

85. For summaries of nineteenth-century views of Euripides see Jenkyns, *The Victorians and Ancient Greece,* 92, 106–110; Henrichs, "The Last of the Detractors"; Calder, "Wilamowitz: *Sospitator Euripidis*"; Michelini, *Euripides and the Tragic Tradition,* 3–51. For more recent proponents see Nestle, *Euripides*; Verrall, *Euripides the Rationalist*; note esp. Zuntz, *The Political Plays of Euripides,* 52: "I for one, though, should very much hesitate . . . to credit Euripides with even a passing devotion to the 'popular religion.' " Cf. *Euripide,* 205, 215. See also Klotsche, *The Supernatural in Euripides,* 98; Page, *Euripides: Medea,* ix; Gamble, "Euripides' *Suppliant Women:* Decision and Ambivalence," 405. Such views are also shared by some scholars who specialize in religion, not Greek tragedy—e.g., Rose in *La notion du divin,* 229: "I had always thought of (Euripides) as a man interested in religion as a subject of study and criticism, on occasion of antiquarian research, but personally of a non-religious temperament." Cf. Nilsson, *Geschichte der griechischen Religion,* 1:771–779.

For helpful correctives to the tradition of Euripides as antireligious see Schmid and Staehlin, *Geschichte der griechischen Literatur*, 1.3:701–726; Chapouthier, "Euripide et l'accueil du divin"; Grube, *The Drama of Euripides*, 41–62; Dover, "The Freedom of the Intellectual," 42–46; Lloyd-Jones, *The Justice of Zeus*, 144–155; Schlesier, "Götterdämmerung bei Euripides?"; Lefkowitz, "Was Euripides an Atheist?" and "Impiety and Atheism in Euripides' Dramas"; Yunis, *A New Creed*, passim.

86. See above, pp. 8–9.
87. Yunis, *A New Creed*, passim, esp. 11–58.
88. See below, pp. 233–235.
89. Cf. B. M. W. Knox, *Word and Action*, 326.
90. *IG* II² 1362 and 1177, lines 17–21.
91. See above, p. 5.
92. On the life of Euripides see Lefkowitz, *Lives of the Greek Poets*, 88–104, 110, 163–169, and "Was Euripides an Atheist?"; Stevens, "Euripides and the Athenians."
93. Avery, "My Tongue Swore, but My Mind Is Unsworn," 22–25; Fairweather, "Fiction in the Biographies of Ancient Writers," 255; Arrighetti, *Satiro, Vita di Euripide*, 125; Winiarczyk, "Wer Galt im Altertum als Atheist?" 170–171; Lefkowitz, "Was Euripides an Atheist?" 159–160. For the likelihood that the whole incident is a late fiction see Dover, "The Freedom of the Intellectual," 29, 42–46.
94. See above, pp. 5, 85–86.
95. MacDowell, *The Law in Classical Athens*, 162–164.
96. Barrett, *Euripides: Hippolytos*, 13.
97. For the three allusions see Ar. *Thesm.* 275–276, *Ran.* 101–102, 1471.
98. For what evidence some might adduce—namely *IT* 570–575, *HF* 1341–1346, and *Tr.* 884–888—see Reinhardt, *Tradition und Geist*, 232–234. On these passages see pp. 107–110, 156, 233–234.
99. E.g., Schlesier, "Daimon und Daimones bei Euripides" and "Götterdämmerung bei Euripides?"; Lefkowitz, "Impiety and Atheism in Euripides' Dramas."
100. On the actual and potential misuse, ancient and modern, of fragments to demonstrate Euripides' impiety see Dover, "The Freedom of the Intellectual," 44–46.
101. Cf. Yunis, *A New Creed*, 14.
102. Collard (*Euripides: Supplices*, pp. 407–408) recognizes that having the *deus ex machina* found or ratify cults is a Euripidean innovation. On *dei ex machina* see above, pp. 64–68. On the relationship of these aetiologies to the actual cults at Brauron and Halae see Lloyd-Jones, "Artemis and Iphigeneia." On *Suppliants* and the Theban heroes see Pfister, *Der Reliquienkult*, 189–190.
103. Cults of Heracles: Pfister, *Der Reliquienkult*, 202 n. 746. Cult of Medea: Pfister, 313–314, 567.
104. For a fuller list of such αἴτια in Euripides, Sophocles, Aeschylus, and other tragedians see Schmid and Staehlin, *Geschichte der griechischen Literatur*, 1.3:705 n. 7. Cf. Barrett on E. *Hipp.* 1423–1430.

105. See Barrett on *Hipp.* 24–40 ("addicted"); Conacher, *Euripidean Drama*, 304 ("bonuses"). On all this see Grube, *The Drama of Euripides*, 78–79.
106. Webster, *The Tragedies of Euripides*, 27. Cf. B. M. W. Knox, *Word and Action*, 326–327.
107. Kamerbeek in *Euripide*, 11; Schmid and Staehlin, *Geschichte der griechischen Literatur*, 1.3:705 n. 7, 1.2:480; Pfister, *Der Reliquienkult*, 571–572. Cf. Dodds, "Euripides the Irrationalist," 101, on Euripides: "The state religion meant little or nothing to him."
108. Schmid and Staehlin, *Geschichte der griechischen Literatur*, 1.3:707–708.
109. Diller, "Umwelt und Masse."
110. But on the greater realism, compared to Aeschylus' *Eumenides*, of the place and cult at Delphi see Zeitlin, "The Argive Festival of Hera and Euripides' *Electra*," 645 n. 3.
111. On the deities depicted in the *Medea* and *Phoenissae* see Mikalson, "Unanswered Prayers."
112. See above, pp. 121–123.
113. Cf., e.g., general cult, *Tr.* 1060–1076; birth ritual, *El.* 1124–1133, *Ion* 24–26, and frag. 2[N]; marriage ritual, *IA* 716–723, 1110–1114; festivals, *El.* 171–180, *Ph.* 784–791, *HF* 687–690, *Hec.* 466–474, *IT* 947–960; purifications, *HF* 922–942; initiation rites, *Bacchae*, passim, frag. 472[N]; sacrifice, *IA* 433–438, *Hyps.* frag. I.IV[Bond], 29–32; rites for specific deities, *Hipp.* 1423–1430, *IT* 1449–1467, *Med.* 1378–1383.
114. Schlesier, "Daimon und Daimones bei Euripides," 271.
115. See above, pp. 130–131.
116. On the "unexpected orthodoxy" of the *Supplants* see Conacher, "Religious and Ethical Attitudes in Euripides' *Supplants*" and *Euripidean Drama*, 93–108. Cf. Schmid and Staehlin, *Geschichte der griechischen Literatur*, 1.3:723–724; Pohlenz, *Die Griechische Tragödie*, 358, 364.
117. E.g., Zuntz, *The Political Plays of Euripides*, 3–54. Cf. his comment on the *Heraclidae*: "The trust in divine succour which the Chorus bases upon the righteousness of his cause and upon the punctual observance of the national cult could confirm and purify the convictions of the faithful. The '$σοφοί$' among the audience might perhaps tend to enjoy the last antistrophos mainly as the piece of beautiful lyric which it is . . . ; they might also substitute their philosophical concepts for the personal deities to whom the Chorus refers" (48).
118. E.g., Greenwood, *Aspects of Euripidean Tragedy*, 92–120; Conacher, "Religious and Ethical Attitudes in Euripides' *Supplants*" and *Euripidean Drama*, 93–108. Athenians of the fourth century certainly did not view the events of the *Heraclidae* and *Supplants* ironically. In much the form in which Euripides presented them these stories became standard features of Athenian self-encomia (Lys. 2.7; Dem. 7.8, Pl. *Menex.* 239B; Isoc. 4.54–56, 12.168–171; cf. Hdt. 9.27.3), and even foreigners wishing to curry Athenian favor could refer to them (Xen. *Hell.* 6.5.46–47).
119. See above, pp. 62–64, 152–153.

120. Dodds, "Euripides the Irrationalist," 97: "While Sophocles is a dramatist, Euripides happens to be, like Bernard Shaw and Pirandello, a philosophical dramatist." For a skeptical account of the biographical tradition linking Euripides to Anaxagoras, Protagoras, and Prodicus see Lefkowitz, "Was Euripides an Atheist?"

121. Chapouthier, "Euripide et l' accueil du divin," 205–225.

122. Xenophanes, frags. A32, B11, B12[DK]; cf. B14–B16, B23–B26[DK]. On possible relationships of these lines to the meaning of the play see Mikalson, "Zeus the Father and Heracles the Son in Tragedy"; Yunis, *A New Creed,* 157–171.

123. On which see Dodds on E. *Ba.* 274–285, 292–294. On *Ba.* 274–285 see also Henrichs, "Two Doxographical Notes," 110 n. 64; Lefkowitz, "Impiety and Atheism in Euripides' Dramas," 74–75.

124. See above, p. 284 n. 122.

125. On the relationship of Hecuba's invocation to the meaning of the play see above, p. 156.

126. Nestle (*Euripides,* passim, and "Untersuchungen über die philosophischen Quellen des Euripides"), Schmid and Staehlin (*Geschichte der griechischen Literatur,* 1.3:315–317), and Webster (*The Tragedies of Euripides,* 295) list numerous references in Euripides' plays to theories of identifiable philosophers (as distinct from passages exhibiting arguments in a "sophistic style"). From the complete plays the likely or even possible ones, in addition to those discussed here, are *Hipp.* 385–387, *Hec.* 798–805, *Suppl.* 201–215, *HF* 757–759, *IT* 389–391, *Ph.* 538–545, *Or.* 982–983, *Ba.* 201–203. Fragments 189[N], 282[N], 638[N], 833[N], and 839[N] may also have a philosophical background.

127. This was a philosophical conception to which Euripides turned several times, sometimes identifying Aether with Zeus (frags. 839[N], 877[N], 941[N]), sometimes making Aether the destination of the souls of the dead (*Suppl.* 531–536, 1138–1141, on which see pp. 114–115 above; *Hel.* 1014–1016; frag. 839[N]). But in no surviving play except the *Helen* does he create a cult for Aether. Aristophanes mocks Euripides' frequent references to Aether (*Ran.* 100, 888–894, *Thesm.* 14–15, 43, 51, 272, 1067).

128. See, e.g., Conacher, *Euripidean Drama,* 50–53, 81–83, 312.

129. For defenses of these lines as closing the *Medea, Bacchae, Hippolytus, Andromache, Helen,* and *Alcestis* see Roberts, "Parting Words"; Lefkowitz, "Impiety and Atheism in Euripides' Dramas," 80–82.

Bibliography

Editions and Commentaries Cited

Austin, C. *Comicorum Graecorum Fragmenta.* Berlin, 1973.
———. *Nova Fragmenta Euripidea.* Berlin, 1968.
Barrett, W. S. *Euripides: Hippolytos.* Oxford, 1964.
Bond, G. W. *Euripides: Heracles.* Oxford, 1981.
———. *Euripides: Hypsipyle.* Oxford, 1963.
Broadhead, H. D. *The Persae of Aeschylus.* Cambridge, 1960.
Collard, C. *Euripides: Supplices.* 2 vols. Groningen, 1975.
Dale, A. M. *Euripides: Helen.* Oxford, 1967 (reprinted 1981).
Dawe, R. D. *Sophocles: Oedipus Rex.* Cambridge, 1982.
Denniston, J. D. *Euripides: Electra.* Oxford, 1939.
Diehls, H., and W. Kranz. *Die Fragmente der Vorsokratiker.* 3 vols. Zürich, 1934–1954 (reprinted 1964–1966).
Diggle, J. *Euripides: Phaethon.* Cambridge, 1970.
———. *Euripidis Fabulae.* Vols. 1 and 2. Oxford, 1984, 1981.
Dodds, E. R. *Euripides: Bacchae²*. Oxford, 1960.
Dover, K. J. *Aristophanes: Clouds.* Oxford, 1968.
Easterling, P. E. *Sophocles: Trachiniae.* Cambridge, 1982.
Fraenkel, E. *Aeschylus: Agamemnon.* 3 vols. Oxford, 1950.
Garvie, A. F. *Aeschylus: Choephori.* Oxford, 1986.
Hansen, P. A. *Carmina Epigraphica Graeca.* Berlin, 1983.
Hutchinson, G. O. *Aeschylus: Septem contra Thebas.* Oxford, 1985.
Jacoby, F. *Die Fragmente der griechischen Historiker.* 3 vols. Oxford, 1926–1957.
Jebb, R. C. *Sophocles: The Plays and Fragments.* 7 vols. Cambridge, 1893–1896.
Johansen, H. F., and E. W. Whittle. *Aeschylus: The Suppliants.* 3 vols. Copenhagen, 1980.
Kambitsis, J. *L'Antiope d'Euripide.* Athens, 1972.
Kamerbeek, J. C. *The Plays of Sophocles.* 7 vols. Leiden, 1963–1984.
Kannicht, R. *Euripides: Helena.* 2 vols. Heidelberg, 1969.
———, and B. Snell. *Tragicorum Graecorum Fragmenta.* Vol. 2. Göttingen, 1981.
Lee, K. H. *Euripides: Troades.* London, 1976.

Müller, A. C. *Fragmenta Oratorum Atticorum*. 2 vols. Paris, 1846–1858.
Murray, G. *Euripidis Fabulae*. 3 vols. Oxford, 1902–1909.
Nauck, A. *Tragicorum Graecorum Fragmenta*². Leipzig, 1889 (reprinted with supplement by B. Snell, Hildesheim, 1964).
Owen, A. S. *Euripides: Ion*. Oxford, 1939.
Page, D. L. *Aeschyli Tragoediae*. Oxford, 1972.
———. *Euripides: Medea*. Oxford, 1938.
———. *Greek Literary Papyri*. 2 vols. Cambridge, Mass., 1942.
———. *Poetae Melici Graeci*. Oxford, 1962.
———, and J. D. Denniston. *Aeschylus: Agamemnon*. Oxford, 1957.
Pearson, A. C. *The Fragments of Sophocles*. 3 vols. Cambridge, 1917.
Platnauer, M. *Euripides: Iphigenia in Tauris*. Oxford, 1938.
Radt, S. *Tragicorum Graecorum Fragmenta*. Vols. 3 (Aeschylus) and 4 (Sophocles). Göttingen, 1985, 1977.
Seaford, R. *Euripides: Cyclops*. Oxford, 1984.
Stanford, W. B. *Sophocles: Ajax*. London, 1963.
Stevens, P. T. *Euripides: Andromache*. Oxford, 1971.
Wilamowitz-Moellendorff, Ulrich von. *Herakles*. 2 vols. Berlin, 1895 (reprinted 1959).
Willink, C. W. *Euripides: Orestes*. Oxford, 1986.

General Bibliography

Adkins, A. W. H. *Merit and Responsibility*. Oxford, 1960.
Aleshire, S. B. *The Athenian Asklepieion*. Amsterdam, 1989.
Alexiou, M. *The Ritual Lament in Greek Tradition*. Cambridge, 1974.
Arrighetti, G. *Satiro, vita di Euripide*. Studi Classici e Orientali 13. Pisa, 1964.
Avery, H. C. "My Tongue Swore, but My Mind Is Unsworn." *TAPA* 99 (1968), 19–35.
Ax, W. "Die Parodos des Oidipus Tyrannos." *Hermes* 67 (1932), 413–437.
Bächli, E. *Die kunstlerische Funktion von Orakelsprüchen, Weissagen, Träumen, usw. in der griechischen Tragödie*. Winterthur, 1954.
Bain, D. *Actors and Audience*. Oxford, 1977.
Ballentine, F. G. "Some Phases of the Cult of the Nymphs." *HSCP* 15 (1904), 77–119.
Benveniste, E. *Le vocabulaire des institutions indo-européennes*. 2 vols. Paris, 1969.
Blundell, M. W. *Helping Friends and Harming Enemies*. Cambridge, 1989.
Bowra, C. M. *Sophoclean Tragedy*. Oxford, 1944.
Bradshaw, A. T. von S. "The Watchman Scenes in the *Antigone*." *CQ* 56 (1962), 200–211.

Braund, D. C. "Artemis Eukleia and Euripides' *Hippolytus*." *JHS* 100 (1980), 184–185.
Bremmer, J., ed. *Interpretations of Greek Mythology*. London, 1987.
Brown, A. L. "The Erinyes in the *Oresteia*: Real Life, the Supernatural, and the Stage." *JHS* 103 (1983), 13–34.
Brown, P. *The Cult of the Saints*. Chicago, 1981.
Bruns, I. "Die griechischen Tragödien als religionsgeschichtliche Quelle." In *Vorträge und Aufsätze*, 48–70. Munich, 1905.
Burian, P. "Suppliant and Saviour: Oedipus at Colonus." *Phoenix* 28 (1974), 408–429.
———. "Supplication and Hero Cult in Sophocles' *Ajax*." *GRBS* 13 (1972), 151–156.
Burkert, W. *Greek Religion*. Translated by J. Raffan from the German edition of 1977. Cambridge, Mass., 1985.
———. *Homo Necans*. Translated by P. Bing from the German edition of 1972. Berkeley, 1983.
Burnett, A. P. *Catastrophe Survived*. Oxford, 1971.
———. "Human Resistance and Divine Persuasion in Euripides' *Ion*." *CP* 57 (1962), 89–103.
———. "Pentheus and Dionysus: Host and Guest." *CP* 65 (1970), 15–29.
———. "The Virtues of Admetus." *CP* 60 (1965), 240–255 = Segal, *Greek Tragedy*, 254–271.
Calder, W. M. III. "Ulrich von Wilamowitz-Moellendorf: *Sospitator Euripidis*." *GRBS* 27 (1986), 409–430.
———. "*Vita Aeschyli* 9: Miscarriages in the Theatre of Dionysos." *CQ* 38 (1988), 554–555.
Carapanos, C. *Dodone et ses ruines*. Paris, 1878.
Chantraine, P. *Dictionnaire étymologique de la langue grecque*. Paris, 1983–1984.
Chapouthier, F. "Euripide et l'accueil du divin." In *La notion du divin*, 205-237.
Christensen, K. A. "The Theseion: A Slave Refuge at Athens." *AJAH* 9 (1984), 23–32.
Clay, J. S. *The Politics of Olympus*. Princeton, 1989.
———. *The Wrath of Athena*. Princeton, 1983.
Clinton, K. "Artemis and the Sacrifice of Iphigeneia in Aeschylus' *Agamemnon*." In Pucci, *Language and the Tragic Hero*, 2–24.
———. "The Author of the Homeric *Hymn to Demeter*." *Opuscula Atheniensia* 16 (1986), 43–49.
Cole, S. G. "The Social Function of Rituals of Maturation: The Koureion and the Arkteia." *ZPE* 55 (1984), 233–244.
Conacher, D. J. *Euripidean Drama*. Toronto, 1967.
———. "Religious and Ethical Attitudes in Euripides' *Suppliants*." *TAPA* 87 (1956), 8–26.
Connor, W. R. *The New Politicians of Fifth-Century Athens*. Princeton, 1971.

———. "Tribes, Festivals, and Processions: Civic Ceremonial and Political Manipulation in Archaic Greece." *JHS* 107 (1987), 40–50.
———. "Two Notes on Diopeithes the Seer." *CP* 58 (1963), 115–118.
Cook, A. B. *Zeus*. 3 vols. Cambridge, 1914–1940 (reprinted 1964).
Crux: Essays Presented to G. E. M. de Ste. Croix. Special issue, *History of Political Thought* 6, no. 1–2 (1985).
Dassmann, E., and K. S. Frank, eds. *Pietas*. Münster, 1980.
Daux, G. "La grande démarchie: un nouveau calendrier sacrificiel d'Attique (Erchia)." *BCH* 87 (1963), 603–634.
Deichgräber, K. "Die Kadmos-Teiresiasszene in Euripides' *Bakchen*." *Hermes* 70 (1935), 322–349.
Derenne, E. *Les procès d'impiété*. Liège, 1930 (reprinted 1976).
Detienne, M. *Les maîtres de vérité*. Paris, 1967.
Deubner, L. *Attische Feste*. Berlin, 1932 (reprinted 1966).
Dietrich, B. C. *Death, Fate, and the Gods*. London, 1965.
———. *Tradition in Greek Religion*. Berlin, 1986.
Diggle, J. "The Prophet of Bacchus: *Rhesus* 970–973." *SIFC* 5 (1987), 167–172.
Diller, H. "Euripides' Final Phase: The *Bacchae*." In Segal, *Greek Tragedy*, 357–369.
———. "Unwelt und Masse als dramatische Faktoren bei Euripides." In *Euripide*, 87–105.
Dirlmeier, F. "ΘΕΟΦΙΛΙΑ–ΦΙΛΟΘΕΙΑ." *Philologus* 90 (1935), 57–77, 176–193.
Dodds, E. R. *The Ancient Concept of Progress*. Oxford, 1973 (reprinted 1985).
———. "Euripides the Irrationalist." *CR* 43 (1929), 97–104.
———. *Greeks and the Irrational*. Berkeley, 1951.
———. "On Misunderstanding the *Oedipus Rex*." *GR* 13 (1966), 37–49 = *The Ancient Concept of Progress*, 64–77.
Dörrie, H. "Überlegungen zum Wesen antiker Frömmigkeit." In Dassmann and Frank, *Pietas*, 3–14.
Dover, K. J. *Aristophanic Comedy*. Berkeley, 1972.
———. "The Freedom of the Intellectual in Greek Society." *Talanta* 7 (1976), 24–54.
———. *Greek Popular Morality*. Berkeley, 1974.
———. *Lysias and the Corpus Lysiacum*. Berkeley, 1968.
———. "The Political Aspect of Aeschylus' *Eumenides*." *JHS* 77 (1957), 230–237.
Easterling, P. E. "Anachronism in Greek Tragedy." *JHS* 105 (1985), 1–10.
Easterling, P. E., and J. V. Muir. *Greek Religion and Society*. Cambridge, 1985.
Edelstein, E. J., and L. Edelstein. *Asclepius*. 2 vols. Baltimore, 1945 (reprinted 1975).
Edelstein, L. *The Idea of Progress in Classical Antiquity*. Baltimore, 1967.
Edmunds, L. "The Cults and the Legend of Oedipus." *HSCP* 85 (1981), 221–238.
Ehnmark, E. *Anthropomorphism and Miracle*. Universitets Arsskrift Uppsala 12. Uppsala, 1939.

Ehrenberg, V. *Sophocles and Pericles*. Oxford, 1954.
Euripide. Entretiens Hardt, 6. Geneva, 1960.
Fairweather, J. "Fiction in the Biographies of Ancient Writers." *Ancient Society* 5 (1974), 231–275.
Farnell, L. R. *Greek Hero Cults*. Oxford, 1921.
———. *The Cults of the Greek States*. 5 vols. Oxford, 1896–1909 (reprinted 1977).
Ferguson, W. S. "The Attic Orgeones." *HThR* 37 (1944), 61–140.
Festugière, A. J. *Personal Religion among the Greeks*. Berkeley, 1954.
Finley, M. I. *The World of Odysseus*². New York, 1965.
Fitton, J. W. "The *Supplicant Women* and the *Herakleidai* of Euripides." *Hermes* 89 (1961), 430–461.
Foley, H. P. *Ritual Irony*. Ithaca, 1985.
Fontenrose, J. *The Delphic Oracle*. Berkeley, 1978.
———. "Poseidon in the *Troades*." *Agon* 1 (1967), 135–141.
———. *Python*. Berkeley, 1959.
———. "A Response to Wilson's Reply on the *Troades*." *Agon* 2 (1968), 69–71.
Fox, R. L. *Pagans and Christians*. London, 1986.
François, G. *Le polythéisme et l'emploi au singulier des mots ΘΕΟΣ, ΔΑΙΜΩΝ*. Paris, 1957.
Frazer, J. G. *Pausanias*². 6 vols. London, 1913.
Gamble, R. B. "Euripides' *Suppliant Women*: Decision and Ambivalence." *Hermes* 98 (1970), 385–405.
Garland, R. S. J. "Γέρας Θανόντων: An Investigation into the Claims of the Homeric Dead." *Ancient Society* 15–17 (1984–1986), 5–22.
———. *The Greek Way of Death*. Ithaca, 1985.
Gauger, B. *Gott und Mensch im Ion des Euripides*. Bonn, 1977.
Gellie, G. H. *Sophocles: A Reading*. Melbourne, 1972.
Gernet, L., and A. Boulanger. *Le génie grec dans la religion*. Paris, 1932 (reprinted 1969).
Gomme, A. W., A. Andrewes, and K. J. Dover. *A Historical Commentary on Thucydides*. 5 vols. Oxford, 1950–1981.
Gould, J. "Hiketeia." *JHS* 93 (1973), 74–103.
———. "On Making Sense of Greek Religion." In Easterling and Muir, *Greek Religion and Society*, 1–33.
Gould, T. "The Innocence of Oedipus." *Arion* 4 (1965), 363–386, 582–611.
Graf, F. "Milch, Honig, und Wein." In *Perennitas*, 209–221.
Greenwood, L. H. G. *Aspects of Euripidean Tragedy*. Cambridge, 1953.
Grube, G. M. A. "Dionysus in the *Bacchae*." *TAPA* 66 (1935), 37–54.
———. *The Drama of Euripides*. London, 1941 (reprinted 1961).
Guthrie, W. K. C. *The Greeks and Their Gods*. Boston, 1950.
———. *A History of Greek Philosophy*. 6 vols. Cambridge, 1962–1981.
Habicht, C. *Gottmenschentum und griechische Städte*². Münich, 1970.
Hall, E. *Inventing the Barbarian*. Oxford, 1989.

Havelock, E. A. *The Liberal Temper in Greek Politics*. New Haven, 1957.
Henrichs, A. "The Eumenides and Wineless Libations in the Derveni Papyrus." In *Atti del XVII Congresso internazionale di Papirologia*, 255–268. Naples, 1984.
———. "Human Sacrifice in Greek Religion: Three Case Studies." In *Le sacrifice dans l'antiquité*, 195–235.
———. "The Last of the Detractors: Friedrich Nietzsche's Condemnation of Euripides." *GRBS* 27 (1986), 369–397.
———. "The 'Sobriety' of Oedipus: Sophocles *OC* 100 Misunderstood." *HSCP* 87 (1983), 87–100.
———. "Two Doxographical Notes: Democritus and Prodicus on Religion." *HSCP* 79 (1975), 93–123.
Herington, C. J. *Athena Parthenos and Athena Polias*. Manchester, 1955.
Herman, G. *Ritualized Friendship and the Greek City*. Cambridge, 1987.
Hester, D. A. "To Help One's Friends and Harm One's Enemies: A Study in the *Oedipus at Colonus*." *Antichthon* 11 (1977), 22–41.
Hoerber, R. G. "Plato's *Euthyphro*." *Phronesis* 3 (1958), 95–107.
Hommel, H. *Der Gott Achilleus*. Sitzungsberichte der Heidelberger Akademie, Abhand. 1. Heidelberg, 1980.
Hooker, J. T. "The Cults of Achilles." *RhM* 131 (1988), 1–7.
Humphreys, S. C. "Family Tombs and Tomb Cult in Athens." *JHS* 100 (1980), 96–126 = *The Family, Women, and Death*, 79–130.
———. *The Family, Women and Death*. London, 1983.
Hunter, R. L. *The New Comedy of Greece and Rome*. Cambridge, 1985.
Ireland, S., and F. L. D. Steel. "Φρένες as an Anatomical Organ in the Works of Homer." *Glotta* 53 (1975), 183–195.
Jaeger, W. *Paideia: The Ideals of Greek Culture*[2]. Translated by Gilbert Highet from the German edition of 1936. 3 vols. Oxford, 1939 (reprinted 1965).
Jameson, M. "The Hero Echetlaeus." *TAPA* 82 (1951), 49–61.
Jeffery, L. H. "The *Battle of Oinoe* in the Stoa Poikile: A Problem in Greek Art and History." *ASBA* 60 (1965), 41–57.
Jenkyns, R. *The Victorians and Ancient Greece*. Oxford, 1980.
Jones, D. M. "Euripides' *Alcestis*." *CR* 62 (1948), 50–55.
Jones, W. H. S. "A Note on the Vague Use of ΘΕΟΣ." *CR* 27 (1913), 252–255.
Kamerbeek, J. C. "On the Conception of ΘΕΟΜΑΧΟΣ in Relation with Greek Tragedy." *Mnemosyne* 4, no. 1 (1948), 271–283.
Kaufmann-Bühler, D. "Eusebeia." *Reallexikon für Antike und Christentum*, 6:cols. 985–1020.
Kearns, E. "Change and Continuity in Religious Structures after Cleisthenes." In *Crux*, 189–207.
Kessels, A. H. M. *Studies on the Dream in Greek Literature*. Utrecht, 1978.
Kiefner, W. *Der religiöse Allbegriff des Aeschylos*. Spudasmata, 5. Hildesheim, 1965.

Kip, A. M. van Erp Taalman. "Euripides and Melos." *Mnemosyne* 40 (1987), 414–417.
Kirk, G. S. "Some Methodological Pitfalls in the Study of Ancient Greek Sacrifice (in Particular)." In *Le sacrifice dans l'antiquité*, 41–80.
Kirkwood, G. M. *A Study of Sophoclean Drama.* Ithaca, 1958.
Kitto, H. D. F. *Form and Meaning in Drama.* London, 1956.
———. *Poiesis.* Berkeley, 1966.
Klotsche, E. H. *The Supernatural in the Tragedies of Euripides.* Chicago, 1919 (reprinted 1980).
Knapp, C. "A Point in the Interpretation of the *Antigone* of Sophocles." *AJP* 37 (1916), 300–316.
Knox, B. M. W. *The Heroic Temper.* Berkeley, 1964 (reprinted 1983).
———. "The *Medea* of Euripides." *YCS* 25 (1977), 193–225 = *Word and Action*, 295–322.
———. *Oedipus at Thebes.* New Haven, 1957.
———. *Word and Action.* Baltimore, 1979.
Knox, N. *The Word Irony and Its Context.* Durham, 1961.
Köhnken, A. "Götterrahmen und menschliches Handeln in Euripides' *Hippolytos*." *Hermes* 100 (1972), 179–190.
Kovacs, P. D. *The Andromache of Euripides.* Ann Arbor, 1980.
———. "Euripides, *Troades* 95–7: Is Sacking Cities Really Foolish?" *CQ* 33 (1983), 334–338.
———. *The Heroic Muse.* Baltimore, 1987.
———. "Treading the Circle Warily: Literary Criticism and the Text of Euripides." *TAPA* 117 (1987), 257–270.
Kroll, J. *Theognis-Interpretationen. Philologus,* suppl. 29 (1936).
Kron, U. *Die Zehn attischen Phylenheroen.* Berlin, 1976.
Kurtz, D. C., and J. Boardman. *Greek Burial Customs.* Ithaca, 1971.
Langholf, V. *Die Gebete bei Euripides und die zeitliche Folge der Tragödien.* Göttingen, 1971.
Lefkowitz, M. "Impiety and Atheism in Euripides' Dramas." *CQ* 39 (1989), 70–82.
———. *The Lives of the Greek Poets.* Baltimore, 1981.
———. "Was Euripides an Atheist?" *SIFC* 5, no. 2 (1987), 149–166.
Leo, F. *Plautinische Forschungen*². Berlin, 1912 (reprinted 1973).
Linforth, I. M. "Philoctetes, the Play and the Man." *University of California Publications in Classical Philology* 15 (1956), 95–156.
———. "Religion and Drama in *Oedipus at Colonus*." *University of California Publications in Classical Philology* 14, no. 4 (1951), 75–192.
Lloyd-Jones, H. "Artemis and Iphigeneia." *JHS* 103 (1983), 87–102.
———. "Ehre und Schande in der griechischen Kultur." *Antike und Abendland* 33 (1987), 1–28.
———. "Les Erinyes dans la tragédie grecque." *REG* 102 (1989), 1–9.

———. *The Eumenides by Aeschylus*. Englewood Cliffs, 1970.
———. *The Justice of Zeus*². Berkeley, 1983.
———. "Modern Interpretation of Pindar: The Second Pythian and Seventh Nemean Odes." *JHS* 93 (1973), 109–137.
———. "Zeus in Aeschylus." *JHS* 76 (1956), 55–67.
Loraux, N. *Tragic Ways of Killing a Woman*. Translated from the French edition of 1985 by Anthony Forster. Cambridge, Mass., 1987.
Lucas, D. W. "Hippolytus." *CQ* 40 (1946), 65–69.
MacDowell, D. M. "*Hybris* in Athens." *GR* 23 (1976), 14–31.
———. *The Law in Classical Athens*. Ithaca, 1978.
Macleod, C. W. "Politics and the *Oresteia*." *JHS* 102 (1982), 124–144.
Malkin, I. *Religion and Colonization in Ancient Greece*. Leiden, 1987.
Mason, P. G. "Kassandra." *JHS* 79 (1959), 80–93.
Matthiesen, K. "Zur Theonoeszene der Euripideischen *Helena*." *Hermes* 96 (1969), 685–704.
Meijer, P. A. "Philosophers, Intellectuals and Religion in Hellas." In Versnel, *Faith, Hope, and Worship*, 216–263.
Meridor, R. "The Function of Polymestor's Crime in the *Hecuba* of Euripides." *Eranos* 81 (1983), 13–20.
Merkelbach, R. "Die Heroen als Geber des Guten und Bösen." *ZPE* 1 (1967), 97–99.
Messer, W. S. *The Dream in Homer and Greek Tragedy*. New York, 1918.
Michelini, A. N. *Euripides and the Tragic Tradition*. Madison, 1987.
Mikalson, J. D. *Athenian Popular Religion*. Chapel Hill, 1983.
———. "Erechtheus and the Panathenaia." *AJP* 97 (1976), 141–153.
———. "The *Heorte* of Heortology." *GRBS* 23 (1982), 213–221.
———. "Religion and the Plague in Athens, 431–423 B.C." *GRBS* Monograph 10 (1984), 217–225.
———. "Unanswered Prayers in Greek Tragedy." *JHS* 109 (1989), 81–98.
———. "Zeus the Father and Heracles the Son in Tragedy." *TAPA* 116 (1986), 89–98.
Most, G. W. *The Measures of Praise*. Göttingen, 1985.
Musurillo, H. "Euripides and Dionysiac Piety." *TAPA* 97 (1966), 299–309.
Mylonas, G. E. *Eleusis and the Eleusinian Mysteries*. Princeton, 1962.
Nestle, W. *Euripides, der Dichter der griechischen Aufklärung*. Stuttgart, 1901 (reprinted 1969).
———. "Untersuchungen über die philosophischen Quellen des Euripides." *Philologus*, suppl. 8 (1901), 557–665.
———. *Vom Mythos zum Logos*². Stuttgart, 1941 (reprinted 1975).
Nilsson, M. P. *Geschichte der griechischen Religion*. Vol. 1^3. Munich, 1967.
———. *Greek Popular Religion*. New York, 1940 (reprinted as *Greek Folk Religion*, 1961).
———. "Die Griechengötter und die Gerechtigkeit." *HThR* 50 (1957), 193–210.

———. "Kultische Personifikationen." *Eranos* 50 (1952), 31–40 = *Opuscula Selecta*, 3:233–242. Lund, 1960.
Nock, A. D. "The Cult of Heroes." *HThR* 37 (1944), 141–174 = *Essays*, 2:575–602.
———. *Essays on Religion and the Ancient World*. Edited by Z. Stewart. 2 vols. Cambridge, Mass., 1972.
———. "Religious Attitudes of the Ancient Greeks." *Proceedings of the American Philosophical Society* 85 (1942), 472–482 = *Essays*, 534–550.
North, H. *Sophrosyne*. Ithaca, 1966.
Norwood, G. *Essays on Euripidean Drama*. Berkeley, 1954.
La notion du divin. Entretiens Hardt, 1. Geneva, 1954.
Ober, J. *Mass and Elite in Democratic Athens*. Princeton, 1989.
Oliver, J. *The Athenian Expounders of the Sacred and Ancestral Law*. Baltimore, 1950.
O'Neill, E. G. "The Prologue of the *Troades* of Euripides." *TAPA* 72 (1941), 288–320.
Osborne, M. I. "Honours for Sthorys (*IG* II² 17)." *ABSA* 65 (1970), 151–174.
Parke, H. W. *Festivals of the Athenians*. Ithaca, 1977.
———. *The Oracles of Zeus*. Cambridge, Mass., 1967.
Parker, R. "Greek States and Greek Oracles." In *Crux*, 298–326.
———. *Miasma: Pollution and Purification in Early Greek Religion*. Oxford, 1983.
———. "Myths of Early Athens." In Bremmer, *Interpretations of Greek Mythology*, 187–214.
Peek, W. *Kerameikos*. Vol. 3. Berlin, 1941.
Perennitas: studi in onore di Angelo Brelich. Rome, 1980.
Pfister, F. *Der Reliquienkult im Altertum*. Giessen, 1909 (reprinted 1974).
Plescia, J. *The Oath and Perjury in Ancient Greece*. Tallahassee, 1970.
Podlecki, A. J. *Aeschylus: Eumenides*. Warminster, 1989.
———. *The Political Background of Aeschylean Tragedy*. Ann Arbor, 1966.
Pohlenz, M. *Die Griechische Tragödie*². Göttingen, 1954.
Powell, C. A. "Religion and the Sicilian Expedition." *Historia* 28 (1979), 15–31.
Price, S. R. F. *Rituals and Power*. Cambridge, 1984.
Pritchett, W. K. *The Greek State at War*. 3 vols. Berkeley, 1971–1979.
Pucci, P., ed. *Language and the Tragic Hero*. Atlanta, 1988.
Quincey, J. H. "Greek Expressions of Thanks." *JHS* 86 (1966), 133–158.
Radermacher, L. "Euripides und die Mantik." *RhM* 53 (1898), 497–510.
Rawson, E. "Family and Fatherland in Euripides' *Phoenissae*." *GRBS* 11 (1970), 109–127.
Reinhardt, K. *Tradition und Geist*. Göttingen, 1960.
Richardson, N. J. *The Homeric Hymn to Demeter*. Oxford, 1974.
Ritchie, W. *The Authenticity of the Rhesus of Euripides*. Cambridge, 1964.
Rivier, A. "L'élément démonique chez Euripide jusqu'en 428." In *Euripide*, 43–86.

Roberts, D. H. *Apollo and His Oracle in the Oresteia.* Göttingen, 1984.
———. "Parting Words: Final Lines in Sophocles and Euripides." *CQ* 81 (1987), 51–64.
Robertson, M. "Greek Art and Religion." In Easterling and Muir, *Greek Religion and Society,* 155–190.
Robertson, N. "The Origin of the Panatheneia." *RhM* 128 (1985), 231–295.
Rohde, E. *Psyche*[8]. Translated by W. B. Hillis. London, 1925 (reprinted 1966).
Rose, H. J. "Theology and Mythology in Aeschylus." *HThR* 39 (1946), 1–24.
Rosenmeyer, T. G. "The Wrath of Oedipus." *Phoenix* 6 (1952), 92–112.
Roth, P. "Teiresias as *Mantis* and Intellectual in Euripides' *Bacchae.*" *TAPA* 114 (1984), 59–69.
Rothaus, R. M. "The Single Burial of Polyneices." *CJ* 85 (1990), 209–217.
Rudhardt, J. "La définition du délit d'impiété d'après la législation attique." *MH* 17 (1960), 87–105.
———. *Notions fondamentales de la pensée religieuse et actes constitutifs du culte dans la Grèce classique.* Geneva, 1958.
Rusten, J. "*ΓΕΙΤΩΝ ΗΡΩΣ*: Pindar's Prayer to Heracles (*N.* 7.86–101) and Greek Popular Religion." *HSCP* 87 (1983), 289–295.
Le sacrifice dans l'antiquité. Entretiens Hardt, 27. Geneva, 1981.
Sandys, J. E. *Aristotle's Constitution of Athens*[2]. London, 1912.
Sartre, J.-P. "Why the *Trojan Women*?" In Segal, *Euripides,* 128–131.
Schachter, A. *Cults of Boeotia. BICS,* suppl. 38 (1981).
Schadewaldt, W. *Monolog und Selbstgespräch.* Berlin, 1966.
Schein, S. L. "Electra, a Sophoclean Problem Play." *Antike und Abendland* 28 (1982), 69–80.
Schlesier, R. "Daimon und Daimones bei Euripides." *Saeculum* 34 (1983), 267–279.
———. "Götterdämmerung bei Euripides?" In Zinser, *Der Untergang von Religionen,* 35–50.
———. "Der Stachel der Götter." *Poetica* 17 (1985), 1–45.
Schmid, W., and O. Staehlin. *Geschichte der griechischen Literatur.* 5 vols. Munich, 1929–1948.
Scodel, R. *The Trojan Trilogy of Euripides.* Göttingen, 1980.
Segal, E., ed. *Euripides.* Englewood Cliffs, 1968.
———. *Greek Tragedy.* New York, 1983.
Siewert, P. "The Ephebic Oath in Fifth-Century Athens." *JHS* 97 (1977), 102–111.
Skutsch, O., and H. J. Rose. "*Mactare—Macula*?" *CQ* 32 (1938), 220-223.
Smith, N. D. "Diviners and Divination in Aristophanic Comedy." *Classical Antiquity* 8 (1989), 140–158.
Solders, S. *Die ausserstädtische Kulte und die Einigung Attikas.* Lund, 1931.
Solmsen, F. *Hesiod and Aeschylus.* Ithaca, 1949.
———. "Strata of Greek Religion in Aeschylus." *HThR* 40 (1947), 211–226.

Speyer, W. "Die Hilfe und Epiphanie einer Gottheit, eines Heroen und eines Heiligen in der Schlacht." In Dassmann and Frank, *Pietas*, 55-77.
Spira, A. *Untersuchungen zum Deus ex Machina bei Sophokles und Euripides*. Frankfurt, 1960.
Stengel, P. *Opferbräuche der Griechen*. Leipzig, 1910 (reprinted 1972).
Stevens, P. T. "Euripides and the Athenians." *JHS* 76 (1956), 87-94.
Strohm, H. *Euripides: Interpretationen zur dramatischen Form*. Munich, 1957.
Taplin, O. *The Stagecraft of Aeschylus*. Oxford, 1977.
Tod, M. N. *A Selection of Greek Historical Inscriptions*. Vol. 2. Oxford, 1948.
Usener, H. "Dreiheit." *RhM* 58 (1903), 1-47, 161-208, 321-362.
van Straten, F. T. "Gifts for the Gods." In Versnel, *Faith, Hope, and Worship*, 65-151.
Verrall, A. W. *Euripides the Rationalist*. Cambridge, 1895.
Versényi, L. *Holiness and Justice*. Lanham, 1982.
Versnel, H. S., ed. *Faith, Hope, and Worship*. Leiden, 1981.
Wachsmuth, D. Πόμπιμος ὁ Δαίμων. Berlin, 1967.
Webster, T. B. L. *The Tragedies of Euripides*. London, 1967.
Whitman, C. H. *Sophocles*. Cambridge, Mass., 1951.
Wilamowitz-Moellendorff, Ulrich von. *Aischylos: Interpretationen*. Berlin, 1914 (reprinted Dublin, 1966).
——. *Der Glaube der Hellenen*. 2 vols. Berlin, 1931-1932 (reprinted 1955).
Wilson, J. R. "Poseidon in the *Troades*: A Reply." *Agon* 2 (1968), 66-68.
Winiarczyk, M. *Diagorae Melii et Theodori Cyrenaei Reliquiae*. Leipzig, 1981.
——. "Wer Galt im Altertum als Atheist?" *Philologus* 128 (1984), 157-183.
Winnington-Ingram, R. P. *Euripides and Dionysus*. Cambridge, 1948.
——. "A Religious Function of Greek Tragedy." *JHS* 74 (1954), 16-24.
——. "The Role of Apollo in the *Oresteia*." *CR* 47 (1933), 97-104.
——. *Sophocles: An Interpretation*. Cambridge, 1980.
Witte, B. *Die Wissenschaft vom Guten und Bösen*. Berlin, 1970.
Woodbury, L. "The Date and Atheism of Diagoras of Melos." *Phoenix* 19 (1965), 178-211.
Wünsch, R. *Defixionum Tabellae*. In *IG* III.3. Berlin, 1897.
Wycherley, R. E. *The Athenian Agora*. Vol. 3, *Literary and Epigraphical Testimonia*. Princeton, 1957.
——. "The Olympieion at Athens." *GRBS* 5 (1964), 161-179.
——. *The Stones of Athens*. Princeton, 1978.
Yunis, H. *A New Creed: Fundamental Religious Beliefs in the Athenian Polis and Euripidean Drama*. Göttingen, 1988.
Zeitlin, F. I. "The Argive Festival of Hera and Euripides' *Electra*." *TAPA* 101 (1970), 645-669.
Zielinski, T. "L'évolution religieuse d'Euripide." *REG* 36 (1923), 459-479.
Zinser, H. ed. *Der Untergang von Religionen*. Berlin, 1986.
Zuntz, G. "On Euripides' *Helena*: Theology and Irony." In *Euripide*, 198-241.
——. *The Political Plays of Euripides*. Manchester, 1955.

Index of Passages Cited from Tragedy

Following the titles are page references to more general discussions of the plays. In line references, shorter passages are sometimes included in longer passages: for example, lines 124–129 might be included under lines 123–130, and line 127 might be included under 127–128.

Aeschylus
  Ag.: 61–62, 77, 167, 211
    11: 104
    42–44: 294 (n. 178)
    60–71: 260 (nn. 43, 44)
    86–91: 293 (n. 167), 294 (n. 169)
    109–157: 95, 266 (nn. 137, 139), 268 (nn. 183, 186)
    134–159: 253 (n. 220)
    146–150: 253 (n. 218)
    192–204: 253 (n. 218)
    198–204: 95
    206–211: 287 (n. 32)
    219–220: 287 (n. 32)
    245–247: 288 (n. 58)
    249: 95
    258: 260 (n. 36)
    261–263: 293 (n. 167)
    274–275: 104
    336: 241 (n. 23)
    338–347: 256 (n. 262), 288 (nn. 54, 56)
    338–339: 260 (n. 36)
    351: 104
    355–402: 260 (n. 43), 288 (n. 67)
    355–384: 260 (n. 44)
    362–402: 288 (n. 65), 289 (n. 74)
    362–366: 167
    377–383: 266 (n. 138), 291 (n. 113)
    381–384: 277 (n. 7)
    396–402: 167, 192, 277 (n. 10), 288 (n. 67)
    434–436: 274 (n. 275)
    437–444: 249 (n. 161)
    468–470: 250 (n. 168)
    506–507: 274 (n. 275)
    509–513: 56
    513: 259 (n. 27)
    515: 260 (n. 36)
    516–517: 243 (n. 58)
    524–528: 50, 256 (n. 262), 288 (n. 54)
    527: 288 (n. 54)
    534–537: 260 (n. 43)
    567–569: 115, 271 (n. 232)
    577–582: 248 (n. 140), 288 (n. 55), 293 (n. 163)
    581–582: 294 (n. 182)
    603: 248 (n. 144)
    634–635: 253 (n. 221)
    649: 253 (n. 221)
    661–663: 252 (n. 215)

699–716: 260 (n. 43)
699–705: 167, 192, 260 (n. 44)
704: 295 (n. 188)
710–713: 288 (n. 57)
744–749: 260 (n. 44)
758–781: 289 (n. 74), 290 (n. 111), 291 (nn. 112, 113, 115)
785: 260 (n. 36)
810–829: 288 (nn. 65, 67), 289 (n. 74)
810–812: 253 (n. 215)
833: 260 (n. 36)
852–853: 253 (n. 215)
912–913: 288 (nn. 65, 67)
913–915: 50
921–929: 180
922: 292 (n. 131), 293 (n. 163)
925: 260 (n. 36)
946–949: 60
961–965: 60
970–971: 211, 250 (n. 173)
1015–1017: 211, 250 (n. 173)
1019–1021: 251 (n. 196)
1022–1024: 251 (n. 192)
1072–1330: 266 (n. 142)
1074–1079: 243 (n. 51)
1130–1135: 99
1150–1154: 291 (n. 112)
1167–1171: 294 (n. 168)
1174–1175: 241 (n. 27)
1202: 270 (n. 211)
1275: 270 (n. 211)
1279–1280: 190, 294 (n. 179)
1335–1337: 50, 190, 213
1338–1342: 241 (nn. 23, 27)
1356: 295 (n. 197)
1385–1387: 300 (n. 34)
1390–1392: 250 (n. 168)
1415–1418: 295 (n. 187)
1417–1420: 287 (n. 32)
1431–1434: 262 (n. 68)
1451: 270 (n. 220)
1468–1482: 241 (n. 28)
1493: 287 (nn. 32, 43)
1509–1512: 249 (n. 161)
1517: 287 (n. 32)
1525–1529: 116, 271 (n. 235)
1555–1559: 271 (n. 233)
1563–1564: 288 (n. 67)
1568–1573: 241 (n. 28)
1577–1582: 288 (nn. 65, 67)
1602: 302 (n. 67)
1643–1646: 287 (nn. 32, 43)
1667: 241 (n. 27)
Ch.: 52, 116–118, 169, 214
  1–2: 52
  4–5: 272 (n. 238)
  7: 274 (n. 282)
  9: 274 (n. 272)
  14–15: 274 (n. 288)
  18–19: 52
  32–41: 266 (n. 137), 267 (nn. 169, 175)
  38–41: 117, 271 (n. 235)
  44–46: 267 (n. 178), 287 (nn. 32, 43)
  55–60: 260 (n. 36), 277 (n. 8)
  59–60: 277 (n. 7)
  87–99: 117
  94–95: 117
  96–99: 295 (n. 200)
  106–121: 245 (n. 92)
  117–121: 117
  122–123: 169
  127–128: 250 (n. 174)
  129–130: 117, 272 (n. 240)
  130–151: 245 (n. 92)
  130–139: 117
  139: 272 (n. 238)
  140–141: 117
  142–144: 117, 272 (n. 239), 294 (n. 179)
  147–148: 272 (nn. 240, 242)
  149: 117
  157: 272 (n. 238)
  164: 116

168–180: 274 (n. 282)
190–191: 173
193: 295 (n. 200)
197–200: 274 (n. 282)
200: 295 (nn. 200, 201)
215: 117
218–219: 117
226: 274 (n. 282)
244–245: 277 (n. 7), 288 (n. 67)
255–257: 292 (n. 144), 293 (n. 163)
306–314: 288 (n. 67)
315–371: 245 (n. 92)
315–318: 272 (n. 238)
318: 270 (n. 220)
320–322: 295 (n. 200)
324–331: 271 (n. 235), 272 (n. 239)
332–333: 272 (nn. 238, 240)
336–337: 259 (n. 22)
354–362: 116, 271 (n. 234)
382–409: 288 (n. 67)
382–385: 300 (n. 34)
399–489: 250 (n. 176)
400–404: 117
429–443: 273 (n. 269), 274 (n. 274), 295 (n. 198)
434–443: 295 (nn. 196, 201)
459: 272 (n. 238)
460: 117
461: 249 (n. 152)
462: 288 (n. 67)
479–509: 117, 245 (n. 92)
483–485: 122, 245 (n. 93), 271 (n. 235), 295 (nn. 200, 201), 296 (n. 202)
489: 249 (n. 152)
495: 270 (n. 220)
497–499: 117, 249 (n. 152)
502: 272 (n. 240)
508: 272 (n. 238)
509: 117
510–511: 295 (n. 200)
517–518: 245 (n. 92), 271 (nn. 228, 230, 231)

523–550: 267 (n. 178)
523–531: 267 (n. 169)
525: 287 (n. 32)
540–541: 117, 245 (n. 92)
551: 266 (n. 137), 267 (n. 175)
559: 270 (n. 211)
565–566: 241 (nn. 27, 28)
584: 249 (n. 152)
641–645: 260 (n. 36), 288 (n. 67)
704–706: 261 (n. 58)
729: 249 (n. 152)
788–789: 288 (n. 67)
900–903: 285 (n. 131)
909–911: 242 (n. 38)
926: 273 (n. 262)
928–929: 117, 267 (n. 169)
948–952: 288 (n. 66)
966–967: 287 (n. 32)
986: 287 (nn. 32, 43)
1005–1006: 59, 242 (n. 39)
1016–1017: 287 (nn. 32, 39)
1027–1028: 287 (n. 32)

Eum.: 13–14, 35, 53–54, 64, 76, 85–87, 120, 183–185, 214–217
1–4: 250 (n. 176)
7–8: 270 (n. 214)
12–13: 260 (n. 36)
15–16: 187
18: 270 (n. 211)
19: 264 (n. 117)
22: 260 (n. 36)
40: 287 (nn. 32, 39)
60–63: 251 (nn. 188, 191), 264 (n. 104), 270 (n. 211)
79: 254 (n. 229)
94–139: 267 (n. 169)
94–99: 174, 271 (n. 235), 296 (n. 202)
106–110: 294 (n. 168)
151–154: 76, 287 (nn. 32, 39)
162–172: 184
169–172: 184, 270 (n. 211), 291 (n. 118)

175–177: 273 (nn. 258, 259)
179–197: 291 (n. 124)
208–228: 183
208: 291 (n. 122)
209: 184
210–212: 173, 287 (nn. 32, 39)
213–216: 186, 188, 295 (n. 194)
227–228: 184
229: 184
230–275: 287 (nn. 32, 39)
232–234: 76, 259 (n. 26), 260 (nn. 35, 38)
267–275: 171, 273 (n. 259), 288 (n. 65), 289 (n. 74)
269–272: 120, 167, 212, 260 (n. 36)
273–275: 120, 212, 300 (n. 34)
280–283: 287 (nn. 32, 39)
323–327: 291 (n. 122)
334–340: 183, 273 (n. 259)
340: 273 (n. 258)
349–352: 291 (n. 121)
354–359: 183
385–388: 273 (n. 259), 291 (n. 121)
389–393: 183
393–396: 183, 291 (n. 121)
397–402: 248 (n. 140)
415–433: 184, 291 (nn. 118, 119)
416–417: 250 (n. 169), 291 (n. 121)
429–430: 85
435: 260 (n. 36)
471–472: 291 (n. 120)
476: 291 (n. 118)
482–486: 63, 81, 263 (n. 96), 286 (n. 11), 295 (n. 194)
511–548: 289 (n. 74)
517–565: 290 (n. 111)
517–543: 184
517–525: 217
520: 290 (n. 99)
522: 301 (n. 55)
532–548: 291 (n. 112)
532–537: 60, 290 (n. 110)
538–565: 288 (n. 65), 293 (n. 156)

538–548: 191, 288 (nn. 55, 56), 289 (n. 74)
545–548: 171, 260 (n. 36), 286 (n. 8)
552–565: 291 (n. 115)
558–565: 288 (n. 67), 291 (n. 113)
558–560: 136
570–573: 63
595: 270 (n. 211)
598: 214, 245 (n. 92), 272 (n. 240)
600–602: 287 (n. 32)
614–618: 264 (n. 117), 270 (n. 211)
621: 85
647–651: 243 (n. 49)
653–656: 287 (nn. 32, 39)
660–661: 59
667–668: 254 (n. 229)
679–680: 81, 263 (n. 91), 286 (n. 11), 295 (n. 194)
681–710: 63, 213, 217
690–703: 184
704–706: 270 (n. 220)
707–708: 254 (n. 229)
708–710: 81, 85, 263 (n. 96), 295 (n. 194)
711–716: 184
715–716: 270 (n. 211)
721–722: 291 (nn. 121, 124)
723–728: 260 (n. 36), 261 (n. 53), 291 (n. 123)
747: 184
762–774: 35, 81
767–771: 35
770: 268 (nn. 183, 188)
772–774: 245 (n. 86), 254 (n. 229)
778–792: 184
780–787: 54, 56, 59
791–792: 291 (n. 121)
794–807: 291 (n. 127)
794–796: 184
800–803: 54
804–807: 185
824: 291 (n. 127)

Index of Passages Cited

826–828: 250 (n. 168)
829–831: 54
833–836: 59, 185, 291 (n. 127), 293 (n. 161)
837–846: 291 (n. 126)
845–846: 291 (n. 118)
848: 291 (n. 127)
854–857: 292 (nn. 131, 132), 293 (n. 161)
858–862: 254 (n. 229)
862–865: 249 (nn. 159, 161)
868–869: 62, 185
870–880: 291 (n. 126)
890–891: 185
894–895: 184
897: 260 (n. 36)
903–987: 64
904–909: 54, 255 (n. 237)
909: 59
910: 260 (n. 36)
911–912: 288 (n. 65)
913–915: 63, 64, 190, 213, 254 (n. 231)
916–917: 190
917–920: 254 (n. 228)
921–987: 184–185
921–926: 54
927–937: 217
930–931: 216
938–945: 54
956–957: 242 (n. 38)
959–960: 252 (n. 204)
976–980: 53
992–995: 185, 217
996–1002: 63
1003–1047: 185
1003–1038: 293 (n. 161)
1014–1020: 63
1017–1018: 254 (n. 229)
1018–1020: 260 (n. 36)
1028–1031: 252 (n. 204), 293 (n. 166)
1033: 185

Pers.: 35–37, 181–182, 214
80: 245 (n. 96)
94: 50
157–158: 241 (n. 27), 245 (n. 96)
163–164: 60, 252 (n. 208)
176–230: 267 (n. 169)
201–230: 267 (n. 178)
201–211: 104, 267 (n. 177)
205–211: 268 (n. 186)
205–206: 267 (n. 179)
219–223: 36, 272 (n. 242)
224–227: 267 (n. 175)
293–294: 50, 213
344–347: 241 (nn. 23, 26, 27), 248 (n. 145)
347: 63, 248 (n. 146), 254 (n. 229)
353–354: 241 (n. 27)
454–455: 50, 213
472–473: 241 (n. 27), 243 (n. 145)
513–516: 50, 213, 241 (n. 26), 248 (n. 145)
517–526: 267 (nn. 169, 178)
601–602: 241 (n. 26)
607–622: 36
609–617: 123
620–622: 36, 194
628–630: 241 (nn. 24, 26)
631–632: 37
634–640: 272 (n. 238)
634: 36, 245 (n. 96)
640–643: 36, 245 (n. 96), 250 (n. 176)
651: 245 (n. 96)
655: 36
682–708: 116
685–688: 36, 38, 116
688–692: 36
691: 116
697: 38, 116
711: 245 (n. 96)
724–725: 241 (n. 27)
739–831: 37
739–741: 264 (n. 109)

745–772: 290 (n. 110)
745–751: 180, 291 (n. 115)
762–764: 294 (n. 178)
772: 290 (n. 99)
782: 181, 289 (n. 88)
807–831: 291 (nn. 112, 115)
807–814: 102, 288 (n. 54)
807–808: 289 (n. 88), 290 (n. 110)
811: 290 (n. 104)
820–831: 290 (n. 110)
820: 182, 289 (nn. 88, 89)
827–828: 289 (n. 91)
829–830: 182
845–846: 241 (n. 27)
856: 36, 245 (n. 96)
905–906: 50, 213
909–912: 241 (n. 27), 248 (n. 145)
915–917: 26, 242 (n. 38)
918–921: 241 (n. 27), 242 (n. 37), 248 (n. 145)
942–943: 241 (n. 27)
1005–1007: 241 (n. 27)

Pr.: 47–48, 94, 186
7–8: 292 (n. 142)
29–30: 186, 292 (n. 142)
38: 292 (n. 142)
48: 292 (n. 142)
82–83: 186, 291 (n. 112), 292 (n. 142)
107–108: 292 (n. 142)
170–171: 186
209–211: 250 (n. 176)
215–216: 292 (n. 136)
228–231: 186
248–254: 247 (n. 130)
358–359: 250 (n. 168)
442–506: 247 (n. 130)
454–458: 53
478–483: 57–58
484–499: 94, 104
484–486: 267 (n. 175)
542–543: 292 (n. 142)
640–672: 267 (n. 169)

658–672: 267 (n. 176)
661–662: 90
667–668: 250 (n. 168)
747–754: 271 (n. 232)
761: 258 (n. 16)
829–835: 264 (n. 104)
916–923: 250 (n. 168)
945–946: 186, 292 (n. 142)
992–994: 250 (n. 168)
1016–1018: 250 (n. 168)
1043–1046: 250 (n. 168), 253 (n. 216)
1080–1090: 250 (n. 168)
1084–1087: 253 (n. 216)

Suppl.: 52–53, 64, 71–72, 74–75, 120, 134, 166–167, 210–211
9–10: 174
24–26: 243 (n. 58)
33–36: 253 (n. 216)
36–38: 174
77: 288 (n. 65)
78: 288 (n. 67)
81: 290 (n. 111)
83–85: 257 (n. 9), 260 (n. 37)
104–110: 289 (n. 87), 290 (nn. 93, 97, 110), 291 (n. 115)
116: 295 (nn. 198, 201)
130–132: 253 (n. 221)
155–161: 266 (n. 138), 300 (n. 34)
188–189: 74, 259 (n. 27)
190: 76, 257 (n. 9)
192: 259 (n. 29)
206–223: 74
218–219: 252 (n. 215)
227–231: 120, 174, 212, 266 (n. 138), 300 (n. 34)
242: 259 (n. 27)
262–266: 286 (n. 19)
333: 259 (n. 27)
345–347: 167, 259 (n. 29)
355: 259 (n. 27)
359–360: 259 (n. 29)
365–369: 249 (n. 158), 258 (n. 11)

Index of Passages Cited 325

375: 258 (n. 11)
381–386: 74, 258 (n. 12), 259 (n. 29), 260 (n. 35)
395–396: 258 (n. 12), 289 (n. 72)
397–401: 249 (n. 158)
402–406: 258 (n. 12), 288 (n. 65)
404: 289 (n. 72)
407–419: 289 (n. 87)
413–416: 120, 212, 259 (n. 29)
416: 273 (n. 258)
423–424: 258 (n. 14)
426–427: 258 (n. 11), 259 (n. 29)
429–430: 258 (n. 12)
437: 258 (n. 12)
443–445: 252 (n. 210)
449–451: 248 (n. 140)
457–467: 73
472–473: 258 (n. 11)
478–479: 259 (n. 29)
482: 257 (n. 9)
483–489: 249 (n. 158)
583–585: 300 (n. 33)
610: 258 (n. 16)
615–620: 258 (n. 11), 259 (n. 29)
625–709: 64, 255 (n. 243)
627–629: 260 (nn. 43, 44), 293 (n. 163), 300 (n. 31)
633–638: 52
640–642: 259 (n. 29), 289 (n. 87)
651–655: 167, 258 (n. 11)
659–666: 52, 251 (n. 199)
659–660: 251 (n. 185)
670–673: 260 (nn. 43, 44)
674–677: 59–60, 252 (nn. 200, 206)
678–683: 53, 249 (n. 157), 251 (n. 199)
684–687: 251 (nn. 185, 191)
688–690: 211, 250 (n. 173)
691–693: 241 (n. 27)
701–709: 296 (n. 214)
701–703: 52
704–709: 171, 195, 289 (n. 74), 293 (n. 163)

732–733: 188, 258 (n. 11), 295 (n. 192)
750–759: 166–167, 180, 288 (n. 54)
750–752: 75, 134, 257 (n. 9), 259 (n. 30)
755–759: 134, 259 (n. 30)
762: 258 (n. 12)
802–803: 271 (n. 232)
811–816: 259 (n. 29)
812: 258 (n. 10)
815–816: 76
817–821: 258 (n. 11)
880–881: 258 (n. 11)
890–892: 250 (n. 176)
893–894: 134, 241 (n. 26), 258 (n. 12), 259 (n. 30)
900–902: 250 (n. 176)
921–923: 134, 241 (n. 26), 259 (n. 30)
927: 258 (nn. 13, 16)
934–937: 249 (n. 156)
980–982: 247 (n. 127)
991–1013: 249 (n. 158)
1024–1025: 288 (n. 57)
1034–1037: 186

Th.: 49–50, 159–160
14–16: 288 (nn. 51, 55)
16–20: 59
21–23: 50
24–29: 266 (nn. 137, 138)
35: 50
42–48: 81, 262 (n. 68)
69–77: 248 (n. 140)
76–77: 239 (n. 8), 292 (n. 144)
87–117: 248 (n. 140)
104: 260 (n. 38)
106: 22
109–180: 50
128–186: 248 (n. 140)
169: 260 (n. 38)
174–180: 294 (n. 168)
174: 241 (n. 24)
219–222: 283 (n. 105)

230–236: 49–50, 248 (n. 140), 293 (n. 163)
236: 288 (n. 57), 292 (n. 144)
251–255: 248 (n. 140)
251: 260 (n. 38)
265–281: 50, 248 (n. 140)
266: 50, 51
271–278: 50, 248 (n. 140)
276–278a: 248 (n. 141)
301–320: 50, 248 (n. 140)
301–303: 50
343–344: 240 (n. 20), 256 (n. 262)
375–396: 285 (n. 134)
377–383: 160, 266 (n. 137)
387: 290 (n. 101)
410: 290 (n. 101)
422–446: 189, 285 (n. 134), 291 (nn. 114, 115)
422–426: 290 (n. 110)
425–431: 159
425: 289 (n. 89), 290 (n. 101)
430–431: 250 (n. 168)
438–446: 285 (n. 139), 291 (n. 115)
438–439: 289 (n. 89), 290 (n. 101)
440–446: 159
444–446: 250 (n. 168)
457–471: 285 (n. 134)
465–469: 159, 291 (nn. 114, 115)
481–485: 248 (n. 140), 290 (n. 101)
486–520: 189, 285 (n. 134)
491–494: 159
497–498: 240 (n. 20), 290 (n. 101)
501–503: 290 (n. 111), 291 (n. 115)
512–513: 250 (n. 168)
526–549: 285 (n. 134)
529–532: 160, 262 (n. 68)
536–537: 290 (n. 101)
550–551: 285 (n. 139), 290 (n. 101)
563–567: 285 (n. 139), 291 (nn. 112, 114, 115)
568–596: 181
580–584: 160, 288 (n. 50)
593–594: 181
597–614: 288 (nn. 65, 67), 289 (n. 74)
597–598: 289 (n. 72)
602–608: 62, 288 (n. 67)
610: 181
617–618: 266 (n. 139)
626–630: 248 (n. 140), 250 (n. 168), 288 (n. 67)
661: 290 (n. 101)
662–663: 288 (n. 66)
671: 290 (n. 101)
679–682: 286 (n. 20), 287 (nn. 32, 42)
705–708: 241 (n. 27)
710–711: 267 (n. 172)
734–738: 287 (nn. 32, 42)
742–757: 90
785–791: 242 (n. 35)
794: 285 (n. 139)
812–813: 242 (n. 37)
829–831: 287 (nn. 32, 42)
852–860: 273 (n. 269)
857–860: 243 (n. 51)
885–886: 242 (n. 35)
975–977: 242 (n. 38)
986–988: 242 (n. 38)
1001: 241 (n. 27)
1002–1003: 193, 275 (n. 291), 296 (n. 203)
[1017–1025]: 160, 275 (n. 291), 288 (n. 50), 295 (n. 197)
[1017–1019]: 273 (n. 260), 288 (n. 51)
[1022–1024]: 295 (n. 198)
[1046]: 275 (n. 291), 295 (nn. 197, 201)
[1054–1056]: 242 (n. 35)
Fragments [R]
44: 250 (n. 174), 251 (n. 181)
55: 243 (n. 58)
70: 300 (n. 37)
95: 268 (nn. 183, 185)
100: 249 (n. 161)

Index of Passages Cited   327

154a: 291 (nn. 113, 114, 115)
161: 242 (n. 42), 294 (n. 169)
255: 242 (n. 44), 271 (n. 232)
266: 170, 271 (nn. 228, 230)
273a: 300 (n. 34)
300: 251 (n. 181)
301: 288 (n. 67)
350: 270 (n. 211)
353: 115
362: 242 (n. 38), 270 (n. 219)

Euripides
  Alc.: 26–28, 35, 78–80, 121–122
    1–14: 78
    3–6: 27, 250 (n. 168), 251 (n. 192)
    8: 261 (n. 54)
    11–13: 242 (n. 40)
    22–23: 27, 261 (n. 53)
    25: 242 (n. 43)
    28–76: 26
    29–31: 291 (n. 123)
    32–34: 242 (n. 40)
    41–42: 261 (n. 53)
    53–55: 293 (n. 150)
    68–69: 261 (n. 56)
    91–92: 243 (n. 53)
    98–103: 121
    103–104: 273 (n. 269)
    112–130: 27, 243 (n. 46)
    121–130: 27, 251 (n. 192)
    128–129: 250 (n. 168)
    132–135: 27, 243 (n. 53)
    146–147: 243 (nn. 46, 53)
    149: 275 (n. 290)
    158–161: 273 (n. 266), 275 (nn. 290, 291)
    162–169: 59
    202–203: 243 (n. 46)
    214: 242 (n. 40)
    218–225: 243 (n. 53)
    240: 242 (n. 40)
    251: 243 (n. 53)
    334–335: 59

357–362: 242 (n. 41), 243 (n. 46), 245 (n. 87)
363–364: 271 (n. 233)
381: 271 (n. 227)
384: 242 (nn. 37, 40)
393: 242 (n. 40)
404: 271 (n. 229), 272 (n. 248)
424: 274 (n. 270)
426–429: 273 (n. 268)
430–431: 274 (n. 270)
435–444: 245 (n. 87)
455–459: 243 (n. 46)
476: 261 (n. 54)
499–500: 242 (n. 29)
523: 242 (n. 40)
537–605: 261 (n. 54)
551–552: 261 (n. 55)
561: 241 (n. 27), 242 (n. 40)
566–567: 192
569–605: 78
579–587: 78
588–596: 78
600–601: 261 (n. 55)
604–605: 78, 261 (n. 57)
609–610: 122
612–613: 275 (nn. 290, 291)
618–619: 275 (nn. 290, 291), 295 (nn. 198, 201)
631: 275 (n. 290)
658–660: 294 (n. 183)
662–665: 122, 273 (n. 266)
695: 242 (n. 40)
726: 271 (n. 229)
741–746: 35, 120
747–772: 261 (nn. 54, 55)
767–769: 122
785: 242 (n. 40)
790–791: 187
795: 242 (n. 40)
809: 261 (nn. 54, 55)
822–823: 192, 261 (nn. 54, 55)
830: 261 (n. 54)
840–860: 79

843–851: 273 (n. 268), 287 (n. 30)
843–844: 273 (n. 268)
854–860: 261 (n. 54)
857: 192
859–860: 261 (n. 55)
889: 242 (n. 40)
913–914: 242 (n. 40)
935–936: 242 (nn. 29, 40)
937–938: 271 (n. 232)
962–990: 26, 243 (n. 46), 277 (n. 7)
969–972: 58, 251 (n. 191)
995–1005: 35
1000–1005: 35, 241 (n. 26), 272 (n. 242)
1012–1018: 261 (nn. 54, 55), 274 (n. 270)
1037–1040: 192, 242 (n. 40), 261 (nn. 54, 55)
1075–1076: 243 (n. 46)
1119–1120: 261 (n. 56)
1128: 261 (n. 56)
1135: 243 (n. 52)
1140: 242 (n. 40)
1143–1146: 275 (n. 294)
1147–1148: 261 (nn. 56, 57), 289 (nn. 72, 74)
1151: 261 (n. 54)
1154–1158: 293 (n. 167)
1159–1163: 263 (n. 82)
Andr.: 72–74, 136–139
42–44: 258 (n. 9)
50–55: 137
98–99: 242 (n. 29)
115: 72
117–140: 258 (n. 9)
161–167: 258 (n. 17)
161–162: 257 (n. 9), 258 (n. 9)
246–263: 258 (n. 17)
246: 72
253–260: 258 (n. 17)
253: 258 (n. 9)
258: 74
260: 73, 257 (n. 9)

262–263: 258 (n. 9)
269–272: 49, 251 (n. 195)
277: 241 (n. 24)
293–300: 266 (n. 142)
296: 266 (n. 136)
311: 72
314–315: 73
334–335: 168–169
357–358: 257 (n. 9)
380–383: 73, 258 (n. 9)
411–414: 73, 257 (n. 9)
425–432: 73
427: 257 (n. 9)
439: 73
491: 286 (n. 18)
523–525: 272 (n. 250)
565–567: 257 (n. 9), 258 (n. 18), 293 (n. 149)
614–615: 286 (n. 21)
775–776: 272 (n. 254)
859: 258 (n. 17)
900: 277 (n. 16)
973–974: 242 (n. 29)
1002–1006: 277 (n. 16)
1009–1027: 284 (n. 114)
1010–1036: 278 (n. 20)
1014–1018: 294 (n. 173)
1025–1027: 284 (n. 113)
1085–1157: 137
1092–1095: 277 (nn. 14, 18)
1106–1108: 137
1123–1138: 277 (n. 18)
1123: 278 (n. 19)
1135: 277 (n. 18)
1147–1149: 137
1156: 277 (n. 18)
1160: 275 (n. 290)
1161–1165: 138, 278 (n. 20)
1161: 266 (n. 136)
1182–1183: 242 (n. 37), 249 (n. 148)
1194–1196: 137
1197–1198: 273 (n. 269)

1202: 277 (n. 16)
1209–1212: 137, 273 (n. 269)
1226–1230: 241 (n. 24), 256 (nn. 248, 250)
1231–1272: 255–256 (n. 246)
1239–1242: 138, 256 (n. 256)
1243–1245: 258 (n. 17)
1247–1252: 66
1253–1258: 256 (nn. 256, 258)
1259–1262: 253 (n. 219), 256 (n. 256)
1263–1264: 246 (n. 107)
1268–1269: 256 (n. 253)
1270–1272: 68, 242 (n. 39)
1284–1288: 263 (n. 82)

Antiope (fragments)
48 [Kambitsis]: 256 (nn. 246, 252, 253, 256), 292 (n. 139)
189[N]: 306 (n. 126)

Ba.: 52, 95, 145, 147–152, 179, 187–188, 234
1: 281 (n. 67)
10–11: 147
20–22: 147
26–33: 147, 281 (n. 67)
39–42: 147, 281 (n. 67)
44–48: 147, 149, 159, 281 (nn. 67, 78), 285 (n. 132)
50–52: 147, 150
82: 200
90: 250 (n. 168)
170–369: 266 (n. 141)
170–209: 147
179: 147, 179, 265 (n. 134), 266 (n. 141), 281 (n. 70)
183: 188, 281 (n. 71)
186: 147, 179, 265 (n. 134), 266 (n. 141), 281 (n. 70)
191–192: 293 (n. 162)
199: 188
200–203: 283 (n. 98), 296 (n. 214), 297 (n. 216), 306 (n. 126)
204–205: 281 (n. 71)
206–209: 148, 281 (n. 71), 293 (nn. 151, 162, 163)
215–247: 148
220: 293 (n. 163)
226–232: 147
248–254: 151, 281 (n. 71)
250: 283 (n. 93)
255–262: 99, 149, 282 (n. 92)
263–265: 148, 281 (n. 74)
266–810: 148
268–271: 151, 179, 282 (n. 90)
272–327: 276 (n. 315)
272: 283 (n. 93)
273–274: 293 (n. 151)
274–285: 234, 306 (n. 123)
274–277: 251 (n. 181)
284–285: 293 (n. 166)
286–297: 234, 281 (n. 77)
286: 283 (n. 93)
292–294: 266 (n. 154), 306 (n. 123)
309: 293 (n. 151)
311–312: 289 (n. 86)
319–321: 187, 188
322: 283 (n. 93)
325: 149, 159, 281 (n. 78)
326: 289 (n. 84)
328–342: 149
328–329: 270 (n. 211), 290 (n. 100), 293 (n. 151)
332: 179, 282 (n. 90)
333–336: 149, 151, 282 (n. 79)
337–340: 285 (n. 139)
342: 187
345–351: 149, 176–177, 282 (n. 92)
345: 99
358–369: 149
358–359: 283 (n. 92), 289 (nn. 84, 85)
360–363: 282 (n. 81)
366: 298 (n. 233)
368–369: 179, 266 (n. 141), 281 (n. 70)
370–402: 149

370–378: 277 (n. 7), 282 (n. 82)
374–375: 291 (n. 112)
386–388: 285 (n. 139)
387–402: 283 (n. 98)
395: 289 (n. 84)
396: 179
399–402: 179
419–420: 277 (n. 7)
427–432: 149, 152
434–450: 149
439: 282 (n. 88)
453–459: 281 (n. 72)
466–468: 149, 281 (n. 67), 283 (n. 93)
471–476: 281 (n. 73)
476: 149
480–506: 282 (n. 90)
480: 179
483–484: 151, 282 (n. 92), 283 (n. 98)
485–488: 281 (n. 73)
489–490: 179, 283 (n. 98)
490–502: 149
500: 149
504: 290 (n. 100)
506: 179, 282 (n. 91)
516–518: 149, 290 (n. 111), 291 (nn. 112, 115)
519–575: 150
553–555: 291 (n. 112)
581: 281 (n. 67)
582: 298 (n. 233)
596–599: 250 (n. 168)
603: 281 (n. 67)
621–622: 282 (n. 88)
635–637: 150, 282 (n. 88)
640: 282 (n. 88)
642–659: 150
655–656: 282 (n. 90), 283 (n. 98)
666–667: 282 (n. 85)
670–671: 151, 282 (n. 92), 283 (nn. 92, 95)
677–774: 148

704–713: 282 (n. 85)
714–723: 240 (n. 11)
716: 282 (n. 85)
717–723: 240 (n. 14)
726–727: 282 (n. 85)
728–768: 150
755–758: 282 (n. 85)
760–764: 282 (n. 85)
769–774: 282 (n. 85)
770: 293 (n. 151)
780–786: 150
780: 151
785–786: 283 (n. 92)
787–808: 150
794–797: 281 (n. 78), 282 (n. 87)
809ff.: 150
810–861: 283 (n. 94)
811–816: 281 (n. 73)
820: 151
829: 281 (n. 73)
857–861: 150, 152, 275 (n. 290), 281 (n. 67), 282 (n. 86), 283 (n. 99)
877–880: 294 (n. 175)
882–896: 283 (n. 98)
882–887: 180, 188, 289 (n. 84), 290 (n. 97)
886–887: 188
890–896: 151, 296 (n. 214)
895–896: 297 (n. 216)
897–900: 294 (n. 175)
912–970: 283 (n. 94)
912–916: 281 (n. 73)
940: 148
947–948: 179, 282 (n. 90)
991–1001: 277 (n. 7), 283 (n. 95), 289 (nn. 72, 73)
1007–1010: 283 (n. 98), 292 (n. 144)
1011–1016: 277 (n. 7), 289 (nn. 72, 73)
1024–1152: 283 (n. 94)
1030–1031: 151, 293 (n. 151)

1061–1062: 281 (n. 73)
1080–1081: 283 (n. 93)
1117–1121: 152, 283 (n. 101)
1150–1152: 152, 181, 282 (n. 90)
1249–1250: 283 (n. 102)
1255–1257: 159, 281 (n. 78), 283 (n. 92)
1293: 283 (n. 93)
1296–1297: 291 (nn. 112, 115)
1301–1304: 283 (n. 98), 289 (n. 86)
1302–1329: 283 (n. 92)
1303–1305: 283 (n. 102)
1325–1326: 151, 283 (n. 102)
1330–1378: 255 (n. 246)
1330–1339: 66, 272 (n. 255)
1333: 256 (n. 253)
1338–1339: 115, 120
1340–1349: 283 (n. 102)
1340–1343: 52, 249 (n. 153), 256 (n. 253), 281 (n. 67), 283 (n. 100), 290 (n. 100)
1347: 291 (n. 112)
1349: 256 (n. 253), 281 (n. 67)
1361–1362: 115
1374–1378: 283 (n. 102)
1388–1392: 263 (n. 82)
Cycl.: 157–158
26: 284 (n. 126)
30–31: 284 (nn. 126, 128)
96: 157
102: 157
110: 241 (n. 27)
125–128: 157
231: 157
262–269: 263 (n. 88)
271–272: 263 (n. 88)
288–298: 158
288–289: 284 (n. 128)
299–303: 157, 260 (n. 42)
310–312: 158, 284 (nn. 126, 128)
316–346: 158
316–317: 158, 252 (n. 208)
320–323: 250 (n. 168)

334–339: 284 (n. 128)
342–344: 157
348–349: 157, 158, 284 (n. 126)
350–355: 158
377–378: 284 (nn. 126, 128)
396–397: 284 (nn. 126, 128)
438: 284 (n. 126)
524: 22
548–551: 157
578–580: 158
602: 284 (n. 126)
605: 157
693: 284 (n. 128)
696–700: 264 (n. 109)
709: 298 (n. 233)
El.: 35–37
6–7: 248 (n. 140)
58–59: 36, 271 (n. 225)
80–81: 250 (n. 165)
91–92: 36, 273 (n. 268), 274 (nn. 281, 282)
122–123: 271 (n. 225)
144–150: 36, 245 (n. 89), 273 (n. 269)
144: 271 (n. 225)
171–180: 305 (n. 113)
192–197: 36, 293 (n. 163)
323–328: 36, 193, 274 (n. 282), 275 (n. 291), 295 (n. 198)
399–400: 265 (n. 133)
415–416: 293 (n. 167)
479–484: 174, 287 (n. 32), 288 (nn. 65, 67)
511–515: 36, 274 (nn. 281, 282)
513: 245 (n. 88), 246 (n. 99)
583–584: 288 (n. 67), 289 (n. 70)
600: 287 (n. 46)
625–626: 252 (n. 200)
645: 287 (n. 43)
677: 287 (n. 43)
678: 272 (n. 251)
683: 287 (n. 43)
734–736: 250 (n. 168)

743–744: 200
761–764: 293 (n. 167)
781–843: 231–232
803–810: 136
826–833: 104, 105, 265 (n. 132)
831: 268 (n. 188)
894–904: 276 (n. 306)
926–927: 174
973–977: 287 (n. 39)
990–993: 186, 252 (n. 215), 292 (n. 137)
1000–1001: 248 (n. 140)
1124–1133: 305 (n. 113)
1143–1145: 271 (n. 233)
1168–1171: 287 (nn. 32, 43), 288 (nn. 65, 67)
1233–1237: 241 (n. 26), 256 (nn. 247, 248, 250)
1238–1356: 256 (n. 246)
1238: 256 (n. 252)
1241–1242: 252 (n. 215)
1245: 241 (n. 26)
1247–1248: 256 (n. 253)
1252–1276: 66
1258–1269: 254–255 (n. 232)
1260–1262: 288 (n. 48)
1264: 256 (n. 253)
1276–1277: 276 (n. 306)
1282–1283: 256 (n. 253)
1290–1292: 66, 256 (n. 253)
1298: 241 (n. 26)
1301: 256 (n. 253)
1319–1320: 254 (n. 229), 255 (n. 234)
1328: 241 (n. 26)
1329–1330: 68
1347–1356: 252 (n. 215), 254 (n. 225), 288 (n. 65), 289 (n. 74)
1354–1356: 62, 67, 82, 241 (n. 26)
Erech. (fragments): 32–34
  41[A]: 254 (n. 231)
  50[A]: 60, 188, 254 (n. 231), 288 (n. 55), 292 (n. 144), 293 (n. 163)
  65[A], 55–117: 32–33, 256 (n. 246)
  55–57: 254 (n. 229), 256 (n. 252)
  59–60: 246 (n. 107)
  68–74: 81, 114
  72: 256 (n. 258)
  77–80: 254 (n. 229), 293 (n. 163)
  99–100: 256 (n. 253)
  352[N]: 268 (n. 193)
  369[N]: 248 (n. 140)
Hec.: 37–38, 61–62, 79–80, 134
  1–58: 274 (n. 288)
  37–44: 38
  37–39: 253 (n. 218)
  40–43: 246 (n. 99), 253 (n. 220)
  43–44: 242 (n. 38), 270 (n. 219)
  47–52: 261 (n. 59)
  68–97: 267 (n. 171)
  70–71: 103
  79–82: 267 (n. 178)
  87–89: 265 (n. 134), 266 (n. 137), 267 (n. 175)
  94–95: 246 (n. 99)
  96–97: 267 (n. 178)
  107–115: 246 (n. 99), 253 (n. 218)
  113–115: 38, 253 (n. 220)
  124–126: 38
  136–140: 271 (n. 235)
  145: 257 (n. 2)
  163–164: 241 (n. 26)
  197–201: 241 (n. 27)
  232: 242 (n. 39)
  239–246: 257 (n. 2)
  258–331: 38
  273–278: 257 (n. 2)
  303–320: 253 (n. 220)
  304–310: 246 (n. 99)
  317–320: 193, 295 (n. 201), 296 (n. 203)
  328–331: 276 (n. 313)
  342–345: 257 (n. 2), 259 (n. 28)
  386: 245 (n. 88), 246 (n. 99)
  391–393: 38
  422–423: 116, 271 (n. 233)

Index of Passages Cited

430: 274 (n. 277)
466–474: 305 (n. 113)
466: 254 (n. 229)
474–475: 250 (n. 168)
527–542: 38
535: 274 (n. 283)
536–541: 38, 253 (n. 218)
551–552: 271 (n. 235)
578: 273 (n. 266), 275 (nn. 290, 291)
592–593: 250 (n. 167)
609–618: 273 (n. 266), 275 (n. 291)
615: 275 (n. 290)
650–656: 273 (n. 269)
702–707: 267 (n. 171)
714–716: 79, 261 (n. 59)
721–722: 242 (n. 29)
737–753: 257 (n. 2)
743–744: 266 (n. 139)
780: 273 (n. 266)
781–782: 261 (n. 59)
788–794: 79, 134, 167, 261 (n. 59)
796–797: 261 (n. 59)
798–805: 79, 261 (n. 59), 296 (n. 214), 306 (n. 126)
852–853: 79, 261 (n. 59)
897: 246 (n. 107)
900: 253 (n. 218)
956–960: 134
989–993: 261 (n. 59)
1004: 261 (n. 59)
1023–1034: 261 (n. 59)
1066–1068: 136
1071–1074: 261 (n. 59)
1086: 261 (n. 59)
1120–1121: 79
1125–1251: 261 (n. 59)
1289–1290: 38, 253 (n. 218)
Hel.: 5–36, 68, 77–78, 95–100
10–15: 96, 266 (n. 144), 292 (n. 140)
17–21: 226
31–36: 99

34: 98
61: 258 (n. 16)
69: 252 (n. 208)
140: 98
144–150: 96, 264 (n. 104), 266 (n. 136)
164–178: 273 (n. 269)
212–213: 241 (n. 27)
317–320: 96
367–368: 273 (n. 268)
370–374: 273 (n. 269)
449: 260 (n. 42), 261 (n. 51), 284 (n. 127)
455: 241 (n. 27)
479–480: 261 (n. 51)
515–539: 96
518–519: 246 (n. 107)
541–547: 257 (n. 8)
547: 36
560: 277 (n. 7)
582–586: 98, 99
605–619: 98, 99
669: 241 (n. 27)
744–760: 96, 98, 100, 129, 266 (nn. 136, 139, 148)
753–754: 293 (n. 166)
758–760: 97
797–801: 266 (n. 152)
800: 257 (n. 9), 259 (n. 22)
801: 260 (n. 35)
865–872: 78, 97, 98
878–891: 98
900–904: 78, 288 (n. 67)
914–916: 78, 288 (n. 67)
919–923: 266 (n. 145), 267 (n. 159)
954: 261 (n. 51)
962: 36
980–987: 73, 76, 295 (n. 192)
998–1001: 78
1002–1004: 266 (n. 145)
1005–1008: 98

1013–1016: 98, 114–115, 120, 267 (n. 155), 271 (n. 226), 306 (n. 127)
1013: 273 (n. 257)
1020–1021: 78
1024–1029: 78
1062: 275 (n. 290)
1068: 275 (n. 290)
1086: 260 (n. 35)
1087–1089: 273 (nn. 268, 269)
1095–1096: 99
1165–1168: 36, 245 (n. 94)
1186–1188: 273 (n. 268)
1224: 273 (n. 268)
1275: 273 (n. 266)
1277: 275 (n. 295)
1279: 275 (nn. 290, 291)
1301–1368: 56, 266 (n. 152)
1414: 275 (n. 290)
1421: 271 (n. 230), 274 (n. 285)
1465–1475: 230
1473–1475: 288 (n. 58)
1495–1511: 252 (n. 215)
1495–1500: 98
1581–1588: 253 (n. 221)
1632: 78
1638: 261 (n. 49)
1642–1679: 255 (n. 246)
1642–1643: 256 (n. 252)
1646: 256 (n. 253)
1647–1649: 78, 261 (n. 50)
1652–1655: 256 (n. 253)
1660–1661: 241 (n. 26), 256 (n. 253)
1662–1675: 66
1663–1665: 252 (n. 215)
1666–1669: 256 (nn. 253, 256)
1676–1679: 68, 120, 241 (n. 26), 256 (n. 253), 272 (n. 255)
1688–1692: 263 (n. 82)
Heraclid.: 34–35, 71, 232–233
33: 259 (n. 24)
61: 257 (n. 9)

69–72: 258 (nn. 10, 11), 259 (n. 24), 295 (n. 192)
78–79: 74, 258 (nn. 10, 11), 259 (n. 24), 295 (n. 192)
93–94: 260 (n. 42)
96–97: 71
97–98: 258 (n. 10), 259 (n. 24)
101–104: 258 (nn. 10, 12), 259 (n. 24), 289 (n. 74), 295 (n. 191)
107–108: 258 (n. 12), 260 (n. 42)
112–113: 258 (n. 10), 259 (n. 24), 260 (n. 42)
121–124: 257 (n. 9)
130–131: 258 (n. 12)
193–196: 71
196: 257 (n. 9)
220–222: 71, 258 (n. 10), 259 (n. 25)
236–246: 71
238–239: 71, 257 (n. 9)
243–244: 72, 257 (n. 9), 258 (nn. 10, 16)
249: 257 (n. 9), 258 (n. 10)
254: 258 (nn. 10, 12)
259: 257 (n. 6)
260: 76, 259 (n. 24)
264: 258 (n. 11), 259 (n. 24)
286: 258 (n. 10)
320–328: 116
329–330: 260 (n. 41)
340: 266 (n. 137)
347–352: 51
369–370: 258 (n. 12)
387–388: 180
399–409: 248 (n. 140), 266 (n. 137), 268 (n. 192)
403–405: 265 (n. 120)
416–418: 260 (n. 42)
488–490: 248 (n. 140), 265 (n. 120), 266 (n. 137)
591–596: 115–116, 271 (n. 232), 272 (n. 253)
597–599: 275 (n. 293), 295 (n. 201)

Index of Passages Cited 335

673: 268 (n. 192)
695–697: 248 (n. 140)
766–769: 51, 294 (n. 182)
770–783: 248 (n. 140), 249 (n. 149), 254 (n. 231)
770–773: 254 (nn. 229, 230)
777–783: 293 (n. 163)
786–787: 248 (n. 140)
819–822: 248 (n. 140), 266 (n. 137), 268 (n. 192)
901–908: 288 (n. 65), 289 (n. 72)
901–903: 259 (n. 24), 289 (n. 73), 292 (n. 144)
906–908: 288 (n. 67)
922–923: 254 (n. 229)
924–925: 258 (n. 11)
933–934: 254 (n. 229)
934–935: 241 (n. 27)
936–937: 248 (n. 140)
954–955: 71
961–966: 286 (n. 21)
1009–1011: 169
1026–1044: 34, 89, 230, 264 (n. 109)
1040–1043: 34, 41
HF: 221–223, 233–234
    48–50: 221–222, 248 (n. 140), 257 (n. 9)
    54: 221–222
    177: 250 (n. 168)
    209–212: 288 (n. 67), 289 (n. 68)
    242–246: 258 (n. 17)
    255: 258 (nn. 12, 17)
    260–262: 258 (nn. 11, 17)
    284–285: 258 (n. 17)
    329–335: 275 (nn. 290, 291)
    329: 273 (n. 266)
    342–343: 260 (n. 38)
    375–379: 293 (n. 163)
    440: 241 (n. 27)
    490–496: 272 (n. 237)
    521–522: 221–222
    523–550: 116

525–526: 273 (n. 266)
548: 275 (nn. 290, 291)
556–557: 277 (n. 7)
562: 273 (n. 266)
596–597: 105, 116, 268 (n. 186)
599: 252 (n. 204)
607–609: 293 (n. 163)
632–633: 298 (n. 231)
655–672: 49
687–690: 305 (n. 113)
702–703: 273 (n. 266), 275 (nn. 290, 291)
713–716: 134
723–724: 75, 134
757–759: 306 (n. 126)
772–773: 288 (nn. 65, 67)
813–814: 288 (n. 67)
820–821: 251 (nn. 186, 191)
840–842: 293 (nn. 152, 154)
884–885: 241 (n. 27)
922–942: 305 (n. 113)
922–927: 169
940: 169
974: 257 (n. 9)
1025–1027: 273 (n. 269)
1155–1156: 287 (n. 32)
1161–1162: 287 (n. 32)
1195: 241 (n. 27)
1219: 287 (n. 32)
1232–1233: 278 (n. 28), 287 (n. 32)
1233–1237: 287 (n. 38)
1242–1243: 241 (n. 26)
1281–1284: 286 (n. 23)
1302: 287 (n. 32)
1311–1312: 22
1314–1319: 233–234
1323: 254 (n. 229)
1324–1325: 287 (n. 32)
1331–1333: 186, 293 (n. 163)
1338–1339: 190
1341–1346: 226, 234, 304 (n. 98)
1360–1361: 273 (n. 266), 295 (nn. 198, 201)

1389–1390: 273 (nn. 268, 269)
Hipp.: 7, 42, 85–86, 144–147, 186–187, 228–229
5–8: 145, 180, 187, 188, 201
12–14: 145, 146
15–20: 145, 187
21–22: 145
24–40: 305 (n. 105)
43: 145
48–50: 145, 280 (n. 54)
55–56: 293 (n. 163)
79–81: 241 (n. 23), 280 (n. 47), 290 (n. 96)
82–83: 280 (n. 47)
89: 180
99–101: 145
105: 180
106: 145, 293 (n. 149)
107: 145, 292 (n. 144)
113: 145, 280 (n. 58)
114–120: 146, 282 (n. 81), 289 (n. 90)
141–169: 240 (n. 22)
145–150: 253 (n. 219)
161–169: 146
228–231: 253 (n. 219)
236–238: 266 (nn. 137, 139)
241: 241 (n. 27)
359–361: 280 (n. 61)
385–387: 306 (n. 126)
443–446: 280 (n. 59), 289 (n. 90)
473–476: 290 (n. 110), 291 (n. 115)
525–564: 146
537–540: 280 (n. 64)
601–612: 86
611–612: 167, 193, 280 (n. 48)
612: 7, 85, 228, 229, 238 (n. 15)
616–624: 48, 146
642–643: 146
654–658: 7, 86, 280 (nn. 47, 48)
675–677: 288 (nn. 65, 67)
683–684: 250 (n. 168)
689–731: 86

710–714: 81, 82
757–762: 268 (nn. 183, 187)
764–766: 174
771: 241 (n. 27)
772–775: 241 (n. 23)
885–886: 172–174, 192
952–954: 280 (n. 50), 293 (n. 163)
974: 255 (n. 234)
993–996: 181, 280 (n. 47)
996: 146
1025–1033: 86, 263 (n. 81)
1033: 86, 280 (n. 48)
1039–1040: 192
1055–1059: 105, 266 (n. 139), 268 (n. 186), 280 (n. 58)
1060–1064: 7, 86, 280 (nn. 47, 48)
1080–1081: 172, 192, 289 (nn. 72, 74)
1171–1172: 192
1201–1202: 250 (n. 168)
1257–1260: 286 (n. 8), 295 (n. 187)
1268–1281: 146, 186
1283–1439: 255 (n. 246)
1283–1284: 256 (n. 252)
1286–1287: 287 (n. 32)
1307–1309: 86, 280 (n. 48)
1320–1322: 266 (n. 139)
1331–1334: 256 (n. 253)
1339–1341: 67
1364–1369: 146, 280 (n. 47)
1370–1373: 271 (n. 232)
1373: 242 (n. 44)
1387–1388: 242 (n. 44)
1401: 22, 146
1402: 280 (n. 53), 293 (n. 155)
1406: 22
1419: 42
1423–1430: 42, 186, 256 (nn. 256, 258), 304 (n. 104), 305 (n. 113)
1433–1434: 68
1437–1439: 243 (n. 51)
1447–1453: 287 (n. 32)
1455: 59

Hyp. fragments [Bond]
 I.IV, 29–32: 305 (n. 113)
 22 + 60: 270 (n. 211), 276 (n. 305)
IA: 61–62
 10–11: 253 (n. 218)
 57–60: 81
 87–92: 253 (n. 218), 266 (nn. 137, 139)
 351–352: 253 (n. 218)
 358–359: 253 (n. 218)
 391–392: 81, 277 (n. 7)
 394a-395: 263 (n. 86)
 433–438: 305 (n. 113)
 444–445: 241 (n. 27)
 473–476: 81, 286 (n. 9)
 520: 267 (n. 157)
 607–610: 268 (nn. 183, 185, 186, 188)
 673–676: 288 (n. 57)
 716–723: 305 (n. 113)
 718: 280 (n. 63)
 864: 277 (n. 7)
 900–901: 257 (n. 2)
 911: 257 (nn. 2, 9)
 975–976: 241 (nn. 24, 26)
 987–989: 268 (nn. 183, 184)
 1034–1035: 288 (nn. 65, 67), 289 (nn. 69, 70)
 1104–1105: 287 (n. 32)
 1110–1114: 280 (n. 63), 305 (n. 113)
 1136–1137: 241 (n. 27), 242 (n. 29)
 1185–1190: 287 (n. 32)
 1250–1252: 271 (n. 227)
 1317–1318: 287 (n. 32)
 1323–1329: 250 (n. 168), 253 (nn. 216, 218)
 1408: 159, 281 (n. 78), 284–285 (n. 131)
 1437–1438: 273 (n. 268)
 1448: 273 (n. 268)
 1467–1483: 248 (n. 140)
 1491–1497: 253 (n. 218)
 [1521–1527]: 253 (n. 218)
 [1570–1576]: 248 (n. 140), 253 (n. 218)
Ion: 72–73, 75–76, 90–91, 105
 4: 241 (n. 26)
 5–7: 264 (n. 116)
 8–9: 254 (n. 229)
 12: 254 (n. 229)
 15–26: 230
 24–26: 305 (n. 113)
 30: 254 (n. 229)
 64–73: 59, 91
 69–73: 91
 82–237: 232
 94: 200
 109–111: 298 (nn. 231, 232)
 129–130: 293 (n. 163), 298 (n. 232)
 131–132: 298 (n. 232)
 151–152: 298 (n. 232)
 181–183: 298 (nn. 231, 232)
 187: 200
 211: 254 (n. 229)
 212–213: 250 (n. 168)
 267–273: 230
 281–282: 246 (n. 107)
 302–306: 59
 303: 264 (n. 104)
 309: 298 (n. 232)
 327: 298 (n. 232)
 337: 277 (n. 7)
 374–377: 266 (n. 147)
 387: 270 (n. 211)
 404–409: 59, 264 (n. 104)
 414–420: 232
 438: 260 (n. 38)
 442–443: 248 (n. 136)
 453–454: 254 (n. 229)
 534–537: 59, 91
 615: 295 (n. 187)
 681–685: 91
 682: 270 (n. 211)
 685: 266 (n. 136)
 729: 266 (n. 136)

338   Index of Passages Cited

755: 266 (n. 136)
779: 266 (n. 136)
827: 22
871: 254 (n. 229)
972–975: 176, 177, 282 (n. 80)
1045–1047: 282 (n. 80), 286 (n. 20)
1090–1095: 174
1182–1210: 105
1187–1193: 268 (nn. 185, 186)
1227: 59
1253–1255: 259 (n. 32)
1256: 73
1258: 245 (n. 88)
1259–1260: 73
1269–1270: 241 (n. 27)
1275: 259 (n. 32)
1279–1281: 259 (n. 32)
1285–1289: 73
1290–1295: 286 (n. 20)
1297: 254 (n. 229)
1309: 259 (n. 32)
1312–1319: 75
1334: 286 (n. 20)
1353: 22
1516–1517: 266 (n. 136)
1537–1538: 91
1549–1552: 256 (nn. 248, 250)
1553–1618: 256 (n. 246)
1555: 254 (n. 229)
1571–1594: 66
1574–1584: 254 (n. 229)
1601–1603: 91
1604–1605: 66
1609–1622: 289 (n. 68)
1615: 68
1619–1622: 284 (n. 121), 288 (n. 67)

IT: 19–21, 81–82, 104, 107–110, 235
15–24: 266 (nn. 137, 139)
26: 245 (n. 88)
35–36: 293 (n. 149)
42–63: 108, 267 (n. 171)
69–75: 20
71: 108
73–76: 267 (n. 173)
77–94: 108
90–97: 267 (n. 173)
105: 108, 292 (n. 134)
106–112: 20
120–121: 265 (n. 136), 269 (n. 203)
143–235: 108
148–156: 267 (n. 171)
157–159: 242 (n. 37)
159–166: 123, 274 (n. 273)
167–168: 287 (n. 30)
172–173: 273 (n. 268), 274 (n. 282)
201–207: 241 (n. 27), 242 (n. 29)
213: 252 (n. 200)
264–278: 19–20
273: 240 (n. 13)
348–350: 267 (n. 171), 269 (n. 202)
354: 250 (n. 168), 253 (n. 216)
381–383: 286 (n. 18)
384: 293 (n. 149)
386–391: 226, 306 (n. 126)
434–438: 253 (n. 219)
531–533: 267 (n. 160)
560: 289 (n. 68)
569–571: 108, 110, 267 (n. 171)
570–575: 108, 304 (n. 98)
627: 273 (n. 266)
632: 275 (nn. 290, 291)
634–635: 274 (n. 273)
662: 265 (n. 134)
703: 273 (n. 268), 274 (n. 282)
711–715: 108, 109
711: 270 (n. 211)
719–723: 109
725–899: 109
735–765: 81
748: 292 (n. 140)
749: 263 (n. 81)
774–776: 292 (n. 140)
867: 241 (n. 27)
870–872: 287 (nn. 32, 42)
934–957: 287 (nn. 32, 39)

Index of Passages Cited

937–982: 108
937: 265 (n. 136)
947–960: 230, 305 (n. 113)
958–960: 254 (n. 229), 288 (n. 58), 293 (n. 163)
1012–1015: 108, 254 (n. 229), 266 (n. 136)
1084–1085: 109
1128–1131: 109, 270 (n. 211)
1168–1178: 287 (nn. 32, 39)
1200: 287 (nn. 32, 39)
1209–1229: 287 (n. 32)
1234–1282: 109
1252–1269: 270 (n. 214)
1255: 266 (n. 136)
1259–1282: 103, 110, 129
1267–1269: 185, 250 (n. 176)
1279–1282: 109, 110, 185, 269 (n. 204)
1414–1419: 240 (n. 12), 252 (n. 215)
1435–1489: 109, 255 (n. 246)
1435–1436: 256 (n. 252)
1438: 266 (n. 136)
1441: 254 (n. 229)
1442–1445: 240 (n. 12), 252 (n. 215)
1446–1469: 240 (n. 20), 305 (n. 113)
1449: 255 (n. 234)
1450–1467: 66
1452: 254 (n. 229)
1458–1461: 293 (n. 163)
1469–1472: 255 (n. 232), 300 (n. 40)
1475–1476: 256 (n. 247)
1480–1481: 254 (n. 229)
1487–1489: 253 (n. 216)
1497–1499: 277 (n. 7)
Med.: 63–64, 82–84, 135–136
20–23: 262 (nn. 71, 72)
127–130: 241 (nn. 27, 28)
157: 263 (n. 83)

160–163: 83, 84, 262 (nn. 71, 72)
165: 262 (n. 72)
168–170: 83, 84, 262 (nn. 71, 72)
205–213: 82, 84, 262 (n. 72)
208–209: 262 (n. 72), 263 (n. 83)
332: 262 (n. 72)
410–414: 83, 262 (n. 71)
439–440: 83, 262 (n. 71)
467–468: 83, 262 (n. 75)
492–498: 83, 135–136, 262 (n. 71)
493: 262 (n. 73)
510–511: 262 (n. 71)
516–519: 48
577–578: 262 (n. 72)
667–681: 59, 90, 264 (n. 104)
671: 59, 241 (n. 27)
692: 262 (n. 72)
709–758: 262 (n. 76)
709–715: 257 (n. 2)
714–715: 59
728: 258 (n. 16)
735–755: 84
755: 83
764–767: 262 (n. 72), 263 (n. 83), 288 (n. 66)
771: 254 (n. 229)
796: 262 (n. 78), 287 (n. 32)
802: 262 (n. 72), 263 (n. 83), 288 (nn. 65, 67), 289 (n. 74)
824–845: 63
824–826: 255 (n. 234)
846–850: 287 (n. 32)
920–921: 252 (n. 205)
930: 252 (n. 205)
964: 190
966: 241 (nn. 26, 27)
1013–1014: 262 (n. 77)
1032–1036: 273 (n. 266), 274 (n. 277), 295 (nn. 198, 201), 296 (n. 203)
1035: 168, 275 (n. 291)
1109–1111: 242 (n. 37)
1207–1210: 242 (n. 39)

1228–1232: 241 (n. 27)
1268–1270: 262 (n. 78), 287 (n. 32)
1282–1289: 262 (n. 78), 287 (n. 32)
1323–1328: 287 (n. 32)
1327–1328: 262 (n. 78)
1340–1341: 82
1346: 287 (n. 32)
1347–1350: 241 (n. 27), 242 (n. 29)
1351–1353: 262 (n. 72)
1371–1373: 262 (n. 78), 287 (n. 32)
1378–1383: 305 (n. 113)
1383: 262 (n. 78), 287 (n. 32)
1389–1390: 277 (n. 7)
1391–1392: 83, 136, 241 (n. 26), 261 (n. 58), 262 (n. 71)
1405–1414: 83, 136
1406–1407: 287 (n. 32)
1410: 83
1415–1419: 263 (n. 82)
Or.: 17–18, 118
  4–10: 285 (n. 139)
  24–26: 287 (n. 32)
  39–40: 275 (n. 294)
  96: 274 (n. 282)
  112–113: 272 (n. 243), 274 (n. 282)
  128: 274 (n. 282)
  213–214: 277 (n. 7)
  215–238: 256 (n. 247)
  221–222: 298 (n. 229)
  255–279: 256 (n. 247)
  341–344: 241 (n. 27)
  374: 287 (nn. 32, 39)
  382–384: 257 (n. 2)
  394: 241 (n. 27)
  398–399: 277 (n. 7)
  418: 298 (n. 233)
  481: 286 (n. 17), 287 (nn. 32, 39)
  500–503: 286 (n. 17), 287 (n. 32)
  504: 241 (n. 27)
  515: 287 (n. 32)
  518–519: 287 (n. 32)
  546–547: 287 (nn. 32, 33, 39)
  562–563: 287 (nn. 32, 33, 39)
  611: 275 (n. 290)
  667–668: 241 (nn. 26, 27), 294 (n. 175)
  674–677: 118
  782: 277 (n. 7)
  796–797: 118
  827–830: 287 (nn. 32, 39)
  900: 286 (n. 17)
  903–945: 240 (n. 14)
  925: 287 (n. 32)
  935–937: 287 (n. 32)
  960–964: 194, 273 (n. 269), 287 (n. 30)
  982–983: 306 (n. 126)
  1066: 273 (n. 266)
  1084: 271 (n. 228)
  1086–1087: 114
  1137–1139: 293 (n. 167)
  1225–1242: 118
  1231–1234: 272 (n. 238)
  1241–1243: 272 (n. 238), 277 (n. 7)
  1321–1323: 272 (n. 243), 274 (n. 282)
  1361–1365: 288 (nn. 65, 67)
  1366–1502: 239 (n. 2)
  1431–1436: 272 (n. 243)
  1493–1498: 17–18
  1522: 271 (n. 232)
  1580: 18
  1602–1604: 248 (n. 140), 286 (n. 23)
  1624: 287 (nn. 32, 39)
  1625–1690: 255 (n. 246)
  1625–1665: 18
  1625: 256 (n. 252)
  1633–1634: 19, 256 (n. 253)
  1635–1637: 252 (n. 215), 256 (n. 256)
  1650–1652: 66, 288 (nn. 65, 67)
  1652–1656: 256 (n. 253)
  1666–1670: 256 (n. 247)
  1682–1683: 187, 277 (n. 7)

1683–1690: 256 (n. 256), 293 (n. 163)
1691–1693: 277 (n. 7)
Ph.: 22–25, 82, 105, 134–135
13–23: 23, 90, 242 (n. 31), 264 (n. 104)
33–37: 24, 264 (n. 104)
49–50: 24
66–70: 25, 173
154–155: 288 (nn. 65, 67)
156–157: 24
182–184: 250 (n. 168), 277 (n. 7)
253–255: 25
256–260: 288 (nn. 65, 67)
274–275: 257 (n. 9)
350–353: 25, 241 (n. 28)
379–382: 24, 25
408–425: 269 (n. 196)
424–425: 269 (n. 196)
467–468: 288 (n. 67)
481–483: 262 (n. 69)
491–493: 262 (n. 69), 289 (n. 74)
504–506: 135
524–525: 82, 135, 289 (n. 72)
528–585: 135
538–545: 306 (n. 126)
580–582: 269 (n. 196)
604–608: 277 (nn. 8, 12), 288 (n. 50)
609–610: 262 (n. 69)
638–648: 264 (n. 104)
676–689: 248 (n. 140)
766–773: 135, 266 (n. 137)
766–768: 265 (n. 136)
782–783: 135, 248 (n. 140)
784–791: 305 (n. 113)
798–811: 23, 24, 277 (n. 7)
834–959: 266 (n. 137)
852–857: 135
867–952: 95, 266 (n. 139)
868: 23
870–871: 242 (n. 34)
872–877: 25, 192

878–879: 135
888: 24, 241 (n. 27)
903–911: 265 (n. 136)
931–941: 266 (nn. 137, 139)
954–959: 99, 265 (n. 133), 270 (n. 211)
955: 266 (n. 136)
971: 265 (n. 136)
1019–1046: 24, 25
1060–1066: 252 (n. 200)
1111–1112: 290 (n. 110)
1172–1192: 105
1187–1192: 268 (nn. 183, 186)
1197–1199: 241 (nn. 26, 27), 248 (n. 148)
1250–1251: 248 (n. 140)
1255–1258: 266 (nn. 137, 138)
1265–1266: 241 (n. 27)
1318–1321: 170, 194, 275 (n. 291), 295 (nn. 198, 201)
1354–1355: 25
1359–1376: 136, 231, 248 (n. 140)
1372–1376: 277 (n. 8)
1426: 25
1472–1473: 248 (n. 140)
1524–1525: 273 (n. 268)
1548–1549: 298 (n. 231)
1556–1662: 23, 25, 127
1663: 276 (n. 306), 291 (n. 112)
1664–1670: 295 (n. 198)
1667–1669: 273 (n. 266)
1670: 295 (n. 201)
1686: 298 (n. 231)
1703–1707: 264 (n. 109)
1707: 303 (n. 79)
1744–1746: 127
1763: 25
1764–1766: 277 (n. 7)
Phaethon [Diggle]
227–244: 280 (n. 65)
Suppl.: 46–48, 71, 105–107, 126–128, 232–233
5–7: 107, 264 (n. 104)

16–19: 275 (n. 304), 276 (n. 305), 296 (n. 206)
28–31: 250 (n. 164)
39–40: 276 (n. 307)
62: 274 (n. 288)
65: 276 (n. 307)
71–86: 273 (n. 269)
78: 275 (nn. 290, 292), 276 (n. 308), 295 (n. 198), 296 (n. 203)
86: 271 (n. 232)
123: 276 (n. 307)
138–146: 90, 264 (n. 104)
138: 269 (n. 199)
139–141: 107
155–161: 106, 186, 266 (n. 137), 269 (n. 200)
195–215: 46–47, 105
201–215: 306 (n. 126)
205–207: 53
211–213: 105–106, 265 (n. 132), 266 (n. 136), 268 (n. 193)
219–225: 107, 264 (n. 104), 269 (n. 198)
221: 269 (n. 201)
229–231: 106, 265 (n. 136), 266 (n. 137), 268 (n. 193)
267–268: 257 (n. 9)
297–331: 276 (n. 313)
301–302: 276 (n. 305), 296 (n. 206)
306: 276 (n. 308)
308: 276 (n. 305)
311: 275 (n. 304), 296 (n. 207), 297 (n. 217)
315: 276 (n. 308)
328: 276 (n. 307)
367–368: 276 (nn. 307, 308)
373–374: 276 (nn. 307, 308)
377: 254 (n. 229)
463–464: 241 (n. 27)
494–505: 127, 268 (n. 193), 285 (n. 136)
511–512: 127, 276 (n. 306)

526–527: 128, 275 (n. 304), 276 (n. 307), 297 (n. 217)
531–536: 114, 128, 271 (n. 226), 306 (n. 127)
537–541: 128, 275 (n. 304), 297 (n. 217)
548: 128
550–555: 241 (n. 27)
559: 276 (n. 307)
561–563: 275 (n. 304), 276 (n. 313), 296 (n. 207)
564: 276 (n. 307)
575: 276 (n. 306)
589–593: 241 (n. 23), 242 (n. 29)
594–597: 249 (n. 148), 268 (n. 193), 288 (nn. 65, 67), 300 (n. 39)
608–616: 268 (n. 193), 288 (n. 67), 289 (n. 68)
628–631: 51, 248 (n. 140)
630–633: 276 (n. 306)
640: 250 (n. 168)
662–663: 292 (n. 139)
671–672: 275 (n. 304), 297 (n. 217)
721–723: 258 (n. 9)
728–730: 276 (n. 306)
743–744: 276 (n. 306)
762–763: 298 (n. 229)
772–775: 274 (n. 272)
802–804: 274 (n. 272)
831: 250 (n. 168)
832–833: 264 (n. 104)
834: 107
925–927: 290 (n. 102)
973–974: 273 (n. 268)
975–976: 243 (n. 51)
1000–1005: 271 (n. 232)
1006–1008: 242 (n. 37)
1138–1141: 271 (n. 225), 306 (n. 127)
1145–1146: 288 (nn. 65, 67)
1183–1226: 81, 255 (n. 246)
1183: 256 (n. 252)
1205–1209: 246 (n. 109)

Index of Passages Cited 343

1211–1212: 256 (n. 256), 275 (n. 294)
1213–1226: 66
1230–1231: 254 (n. 231)
Tr.: 118–119, 121–122, 153–157
  4–7: 153
  7: 283 (n. 106)
  9–12: 283 (n. 112)
  15–17: 154
  23–27: 154, 155
  26–27: 187–188, 284 (n. 113)
  41–44: 153, 288 (n. 48)
  45–47: 154, 284 (n. 112)
  49: 22
  56: 241 (n. 26)
  67–73: 155, 176, 291 (nn. 112, 115)
  68: 284 (n. 117)
  72: 284 (n. 112)
  77–81: 250 (n. 168), 253 (n. 216)
  82–84: 252 (n. 215)
  85–86: 155, 176, 290 (n. 105), 291 (nn. 112, 115)
  88–91: 252 (n. 215)
  95–97: 122, 180, 284 (n. 124), 288 (n. 54)
  98–104: 241 (n. 27), 284 (n. 119)
  148–152: 283 (n. 110)
  204: 241 (n. 27)
  207–219: 255 (n. 234)
  249–255: 288 (n. 48)
  271: 271 (n. 232)
  329–454: 153
  352–461: 266 (n. 142)
  377–378: 273 (n. 266)
  378–379: 274 (n. 275)
  381–382: 274 (n. 277)
  389: 274 (n. 275)
  390: 273 (n. 266)
  446: 122
  453: 284 (n. 116)
  459–461: 116, 271 (n. 233)
  469–471: 52, 156
  480–482: 273 (nn. 268, 269)
  483: 245 (n. 88), 283 (n. 108)
  525–541: 284 (n. 112)
  561: 283 (n. 112)
  573–576: 248 (n. 140)
  587–594: 118, 272 (n. 245)
  599–600: 154
  601–607: 119, 271 (n. 232)
  612–613: 155–156
  622–623: 246 (n. 102)
  632–638: 119, 271 (n. 227), 272 (n. 249)
  641–642: 119, 271 (n. 232)
  673–678: 118
  696: 155, 242 (n. 30)
  735–739: 126
  752–753: 119
  775–777: 155, 242 (n. 30)
  793–794: 273 (n. 269)
  801–803: 254 (n. 231)
  820–859: 153
  858–859: 155
  867–868: 260 (n. 43), 288 (nn. 65, 67)
  884–889: 156, 234, 284 (n. 122), 288 (n. 67), 304 (n. 98)
  948–949: 241 (n. 26)
  971–982: 226
  1060–1080: 154, 156, 260 (n. 38), 283 (n. 109), 305 (n. 113)
  1075–1076: 283 (n. 110)
  1081–1085: 118, 274 (n. 288)
  1132–1133: 118
  1143–1144: 273 (n. 266)
  1147: 275 (n. 290)
  1152: 273 (n. 266)
  1181–1184: 122
  1194–1199: 119
  1200–1208: 275 (nn. 290, 291)
  1221–1225: 119
  1232–1234: 116, 271 (n. 233), 273 (n. 266)
  1235–1236: 273 (n. 269)
  1240–1242: 156, 294 (n. 168)

1242–1245: 284 (n. 120)
1247: 273 (n. 266)
1248–1250: 274 (n. 285), 275 (n. 292)
1277–1279: 119, 154
1280–1281: 156
1287–1292: 156, 283 (n. 109)
1303–1316: 118, 119
1319–1322: 154
Rh.: 44–45
30: 248 (n. 140)
56–58: 241 (n. 27), 248–249 (n. 148)
63–69: 265 (nn. 134, 135), 266 (n. 137)
179–180: 248 (n. 140)
240–241: 22
301: 43
317–320: 241 (n. 27), 249 (n. 148)
355–359: 43
385–387: 43
469–470: 248 (n. 140)
637–638: 249 (n. 151)
665–667: 249 (n. 151)
728: 241 (n. 27), 242 (n. 37), 249 (n. 148)
780–788: 267 (n. 172)
816–819: 263 (n. 81)
882–889: 241 (n. 27), 249 (n. 148), 256 (n. 248)
886: 65
890–982: 256 (n. 246)
890–903: 43
895–914: 256 (n. 251)
941–942: 254 (n. 229), 255 (n. 240)
943–947: 44, 247 (n. 124)
952–961: 256 (n. 251)
962–973: 43
963–964: 43, 251 (n. 181)
965–966: 44
970–971: 241 (n. 26), 247 (n. 125)
972–973: 44, 247 (n. 126)
986–992: 256 (n. 251)
995–996: 241 (n. 27), 242 (n. 29), 249 (n. 148)

Fragments [N]
2: 305 (n. 113)
20: 252 (n. 208), 277 (n. 7)
37: 241 (n. 27)
140: 241 (n. 27)
151: 288 (n. 66)
176: 271 (nn. 229, 230), 295 (nn. 196, 201), 296 (n. 204)
189: 306 (n. 126)
248: 277 (n. 7)
256: 180, 237 (n. 11), 283 (n. 96), 289 (n. 80), 290 (n. 106), 292 (n. 144), 298 (n. 234)
273: 241 (n. 27)
282: 306 (n. 126)
286: 237 (n. 12), 292 (n. 144)
352: 268 (n. 193)
369: 248 (n. 140)
388: 290 (n. 102)
446: 41–42, 181, 237 (n. 11), 292 (n. 138)
449: 271 (n. 232)
450: 271 (n. 229)
453: 277 (n. 7)
472: 305 (n. 113)
491: 59
506: 288 (n. 67)
516: 250 (n. 164)
532: 271 (nn. 227, 229)
577: 289 (n. 70)
584: 288 (nn. 65, 67)
585: 288 (n. 67)
606: 288 (n. 67)
618: 60
638: 306 (n. 126)
640: 271 (n. 230), 274 (n. 285)
645: 84, 289 (n. 74)
667: 261 (n. 58)
781: 250 (n. 168)
794: 293 (n. 149)

Index of Passages Cited   345

795: 100, 237 (n. 12), 265 (n. 135), 266 (n. 139)
800: 237 (n. 11)
832: 288 (n. 67)
833: 271 (n. 232), 306 (n. 126)
835: 288 (n. 67)
839: 115, 250 (n. 174), 306 (nn. 126, 127)
852: 171, 191–192, 254 (n. 224)
853: 171, 191, 195, 296 (n. 214), 297 (n. 217)
877: 306 (n. 127)
892: 251 (n. 181)
912: 300 (n. 34)
916: 242 (n. 39), 270 (n. 219)
941: 306 (n. 127)
946: 237 (n. 11), 288 (n. 59)
948: 237 (n. 11)
971: 270 (n. 222)
972: 6
973: 6, 100
980: 6
991: 6
1018: 6, 277 (n. 7)
1023: 250 (n. 174)
1025: 237 (n. 11)
1032: 282 (n. 89)
1049: 257 (n. 9), 259 (nn. 26, 31, 33), 296 (n. 214)
Other fragments
2[A]: 59, 252 (n. 203), 264 (n. 104)
153[A]: 252 (n. 208), 277 (n. 7)
13[P]: 264 (n. 117)
16[P]: 259 (n. 28)

Sophocles
Aj.: 21–22, 51–52, 126–127, 142–144, 219–220
1–126: 279 (n. 45)
1–88: 21, 144
36: 279 (n. 43)
51–52: 143
86: 279 (n. 44)
89–93: 51, 143, 248 (n. 140)
112–113: 143
116–117: 143, 249 (n. 150)
118–133: 143–144
118: 159
121–126: 279 (n. 44)
127–133: 143, 159, 181, 290 (n. 110), 291 (nn. 113, 114, 115)
172–181: 21, 288 (n. 62)
172: 240 (n. 20)
176–178: 240 (n. 21), 248 (n. 140)
243–244: 21
457–458: 143
506–507: 294 (n. 183)
507–509: 59
534: 241 (n. 29)
581–582: 58
589–591: 279 (n. 42)
654–656: 168
666–677: 297 (n. 222)
743–744: 279 (n. 42)
756–779: 21, 143, 266 (n. 139), 279 (n. 40)
758–761: 100–101, 279 (n. 41), 289 (n. 89)
762–769: 51
763: 279 (n. 41), 289 (n. 89)
766–775: 240 (n. 20)
766: 279 (n. 41), 289 (n. 89)
777: 289 (n. 89)
783: 265 (n. 134)
865: 116
950: 21
952–953: 279 (n. 40)
955–960: 279 (n. 45)
970: 21
971: 279 (n. 45)
1057–1061: 21, 242 (n. 38)
1062–1068: 276 (n. 310)
1089–1092: 276 (nn. 306, 310)
1108–1110: 276 (nn. 307, 310)
1128–1132: 21, 275 (n. 304), 276 (nn. 305, 310), 296 (nn. 206, 214)

1132: 127
1133: 276 (n. 312)
1150–1155: 276 (n. 310), 290 (n. 110)
1151: 276 (n. 306)
1164–1167: 295 (n. 199)
1168–1184: 219
1173–1179: 220, 273 (n. 268)
1192–1196: 114, 270 (n. 221)
1214–1215: 242 (n. 37)
1221–1222: 255 (n. 234)
1316–1380: 144
1332–1345: 127, 128, 295 (n. 197)
1332–1335: 276 (nn. 305, 307, 310), 279 (n. 44)
1342–1345: 275 (n. 304), 276 (nn. 305, 310), 279 (n. 44), 295 (n. 201), 296 (nn. 207, 214)
1348–1349: 276 (n. 310)
1365: 127, 128, 279 (n. 44)
1374–1375: 279 (n. 45)
1381–1388: 279 (n. 45)
1383–1395: 276 (n. 310)
1384–1385: 276 (n. 306)
1386–1392: 170, 275 (n. 291), 277 (n. 7), 288 (n. 67), 289 (n. 74)
1394–1395: 116
1398–1399: 279 (n. 45)
1404–1406: 273 (n. 266)
Ant.: 48, 85, 124, 126–128, 139–142, 179, 180, 194, 219–221
21–25: 275 (n. 291), 295 (nn. 197, 201), 296 (n. 202)
25: 246 (n. 107)
29–30: 278 (n. 27)
37–38: 279 (n. 35)
45–46: 279 (n. 36)
58–99: 278 (n. 23)
65–67: 276 (n. 305)
71–72: 276 (n. 308), 279 (nn. 35, 37)
73–77: 271 (n. 233), 278 (n. 25), 279 (n. 35)
74: 276 (n. 307), 279 (n. 34)
76–77: 142, 275 (n. 304), 276 (n. 305), 279 (n. 34), 296 (n. 206)
80–81: 279 (n. 36)
89: 279 (n. 35)
96–97: 279 (n. 37)
128–137: 250 (n. 168), 285 (n. 139), 290 (n. 110), 291 (nn. 114, 115)
141–143: 248 (n. 140)
172: 287 (nn. 32, 42)
182–190: 276 (n. 312)
184: 263 (n. 81), 278 (n. 27)
192–214: 127, 140–141, 276 (n. 312)
196–197: 246 (n. 107), 274 (n. 287), 275 (n. 294)
198–201: 285 (n. 138), 288 (n. 50)
205–206: 278 (n. 27)
207–210: 275 (n. 291), 295 (nn. 197, 201)
245–258: 220
247: 275 (n. 294)
255–256: 124
257–258: 278 (n. 27)
259–275: 240 (n. 11)
264–267: 81, 263 (n. 87)
278–289: 140, 220, 278 (n. 25)
278–279: 278 (n. 32)
282–289: 191, 285 (n. 138), 288 (n. 50)
284–285: 246 (n. 107), 275 (nn. 291, 292), 295 (n. 197)
304–331: 85
304–314: 81, 263 (n. 81)
304–305: 278 (n. 27)
330–331: 293 (n. 167)
332–375: 48, 219
337–352: 54
337–341: 250 (n. 174)
361–362: 243 (n. 49)
363–364: 58
368–369: 263 (n. 97), 288 (n. 67)
384–436: 220

Index of Passages Cited 347

388–396: 85, 221
395–396: 275 (nn. 290, 291)
413–414: 240 (n. 11)
430–431: 274 (n. 273), 295 (n. 198)
441–460: 278 (n. 25)
449–460: 127, 275 (n. 304), 276 (n. 307), 279 (n. 34), 296 (n. 214)
449–455: 288 (n. 67)
450–470: 140, 142
450–455: 277 (n. 7), 296 (nn. 208, 215)
453–460: 140, 194
456–457: 195, 278 (n. 25), 297 (n. 216)
461–470: 279 (n. 37)
466–468: 279 (n. 36)
486–489: 278 (n. 27)
499ff.: 278 (n. 23)
502–504: 276 (n. 308), 279 (nn. 35, 36, 37)
504–509: 278 (n. 32)
511–517: 279 (n. 36)
511: 276 (n. 308), 279 (n. 37)
514–523: 140–141, 278 (n. 25)
514–516: 295 (nn. 197, 201)
519–522: 140, 275 (n. 304), 276 (n. 312)
535: 81
545: 275 (n. 294)
559–560: 279 (n. 35)
641–644: 59
658–659: 278 (n. 27)
683–765: 127, 141
692–700: 278 (n. 32), 279 (n. 37)
693–695: 276 (n. 308)
696–698: 278 (n. 27)
699: 276 (n. 308), 279 (n. 37)
710–733: 278 (nn. 22, 32)
744–745: 142, 278 (n. 23), 296 (n. 210)
753–755: 278 (n. 22)
775–776: 169
777: 243 (n. 45)

802–805: 278 (n. 32)
817–822: 279 (n. 37)
832–833: 242 (n. 37)
854–855: 242 (n. 44)
867–868: 271 (n. 233)
872–874: 278 (n. 23)
889: 286 (n. 19)
891–903: 271 (n. 233)
897–904: 279 (n. 35)
899: 279 (n. 36)
900–904: 273 (n. 266), 274 (n. 273), 275 (nn. 290, 291), 289 (n. 81), 295 (nn. 198, 201)
905–920: 279 (n. 36)
913–915: 295 (n. 197)
921–928: 275 (n. 304), 276 (n. 307), 288 (n. 67), 289 (nn. 68, 74)
921: 278 (n. 25)
923–924: 249 (n. 154), 279 (n. 34)
925–928: 279 (n. 37)
943: 279 (n. 34)
955–965: 281 (n. 68), 285 (n. 139), 290 (n. 110), 291 (nn. 112, 114, 115)
988–1090: 139, 141–142
991–995: 99
992: 289 (n. 78)
996: 289 (n. 77)
998–1032: 265 (n. 132), 266 (n. 137)
1015–1022: 124, 128, 141, 276 (n. 309), 278 (n. 27)
1015: 179, 278 (n. 22)
1023–1028: 101, 179, 278 (n. 22), 285 (n. 141)
1031–1032: 179
1033–1063: 99
1039–1044: 141, 278 (n. 27)
1039: 246 (n. 107)
1050–1052: 179, 278 (n. 22)
1054: 265 (n. 136)
1059: 99, 266 (n. 141)
1064–1075: 140, 278 (nn. 25, 26)

1070–1075: 275 (n. 304), 276 (n. 305)
1080–1083: 128, 275 (n. 294), 278 (n. 27)
1089–1090: 179, 278 (n. 22)
1091–1094: 265 (nn. 135, 136)
1095–1114: 139
1098: 278 (n. 22), 289 (n. 81)
1100–1104: 278 (nn. 22, 32), 289 (n. 79)
1105–1114: 278 (n. 33)
1113–1114: 139, 140, 275 (n. 304), 296 (n. 214)
1126–1152: 302 (n. 73)
1137–1145: 190
1165–1171: 278 (n. 31)
1201: 273 (n. 266)
1218: 239 (n. 4)
1240–1243: 278 (n. 22), 289 (n. 81)
1260–1262: 278 (n. 22)
1261–1353: 139
1261–1276: 179, 278 (nn. 22, 33)
1306–1311: 278 (n. 31)
1317–1325: 278 (n. 33)
1324–1332: 242 (n. 38), 270 (n. 219), 278 (n. 31)
1347–1353: 180, 285 (n. 139), 291 (nn. 112, 114, 115)

El.: 85, 117, 118, 172–173
47–48: 85, 221
51–53: 274 (n. 282)
124–126: 287 (nn. 32, 43)
137–139: 117, 245 (n. 92), 271 (n. 230)
179: 277 (n. 7)
209–210: 288 (n. 67)
237–243: 172, 275 (n. 295), 295 (n. 200)
245–250: 287 (n. 32), 289 (n. 68)
245–246: 117
278–281: 293 (n. 167)
307–309: 290 (n. 102)
355–356: 172

406–448: 274 (n. 283)
406–410: 267 (n. 178)
406: 274 (n. 282)
410–427: 267 (n. 170)
426–427: 267 (n. 178)
436: 117, 270 (n. 220)
439–446: 117, 274 (n. 282)
443–445: 295 (nn. 196, 200, 201)
448–451: 274 (n. 282)
453–460: 117, 245 (n. 92)
457–458: 274 (n. 282)
459–460: 103, 267 (n. 170)
461–464: 172
463: 117
464–465: 290 (n. 102)
482–487: 287 (n. 25)
498–502: 104, 267 (n. 170)
563–576: 253 (nn. 218, 220), 279 (n. 41), 285 (n. 139), 290 (n. 111), 291 (nn. 114, 115)
583–584: 289 (n. 68)
630–659: 136, 267 (nn. 178, 179)
644–647: 267 (n. 170)
648–649: 252 (n. 207)
658: 22
660–799: 85
707: 255 (n. 234)
759–760: 274 (n. 275)
792–794: 291 (n. 113)
823–825: 250 (n. 168)
837–841: 271 (n. 234)
870: 273 (n. 269)
893–895: 274 (n. 282)
900–901: 274 (n. 282)
908: 295 (n. 200)
916–919: 241 (n. 27)
967–969: 172, 287 (nn. 37, 40)
999–1000: 241 (n. 27)
1058–1062: 287 (n. 34)
1063–1065: 172, 173, 250 (n. 168)
1066–1069: 271 (n. 236)
1093–1097: 172, 173, 296 (nn. 214, 215)

Index of Passages Cited 349

1138–1142: 273 (n. 266)
1139: 275 (nn. 290, 291)
1156–1159: 241 (n. 27), 241–242 (n. 29)
1170: 117, 271 (n. 232)
1212–1214: 295 (n. 198)
1265–1270: 241 (n. 26)
1305–1306: 241 (n. 27)
1380–1383: 287 (nn. 32, 44)
1401: 275 (n. 290)
1417–1421: 169, 271 (n. 235)
1426–1427: 295 (n. 187)
1487–1490: 276 (n. 306)
OC: 32, 39–41, 224–225
   36–45: 40
   54–56: 303 (nn. 79, 81)
   58–63: 303 (nn. 77, 79)
   65: 243 (n. 58)
   72–74: 246 (n. 109)
   76: 241 (n. 27)
   84–105: 247 (n. 113)
   92–93: 246 (nn. 109, 110)
   95: 250 (n. 168)
   107–110: 254 (n. 229), 257 (n. 5)
   125–169: 40
   212: 40–41
   258–285: 257 (n. 5)
   258–265: 254 (n. 227), 260 (nn. 41, 42), 303 (n. 83)
   266–288: 41
   275–283: 258 (n. 12), 295 (n. 192), 303 (n. 83)
   275–278: 258 (n. 11), 286 (n. 4), 293 (n. 154)
   282–288: 257 (n. 5), 295 (n. 191)
   287–290: 246 (n. 109)
   387–420: 247 (n. 113)
   388: 265 (n. 136)
   390: 39
   399–411: 246 (n. 110)
   421–460: 246 (n. 110)
   450–454: 247 (n. 113)
   455–463: 257 (n. 5)
   492: 40
   576–582: 246 (n. 109)
   621–628: 247 (n. 113), 264 (n. 109)
   621–622: 39, 246 (n. 110), 270 (n. 220)
   626–628: 246 (n. 109)
   631–637: 257 (n. 5)
   632–633: 260 (n. 42)
   644–647: 246 (nn. 109, 110)
   650: 263 (n. 87)
   668–719: 224, 303 (n. 76)
   668–670: 302–303 (n. 76)
   675: 40
   681–693: 63–64
   683–693: 303 (nn. 79, 80)
   694–706: 254 (n. 231), 303 (n. 79)
   707–719: 63, 248 (n. 133), 303 (nn. 76, 79, 81)
   709: 22
   784–790: 246 (n. 110)
   787–788: 247 (n. 112)
   823–825: 289 (n. 72)
   854–855: 246 (n. 111)
   864–870: 246 (n. 110)
   864: 241 (n. 24)
   887–889: 303 (n. 81)
   902–928: 257 (n. 5)
   919–923: 257 (n. 5), 258 (nn. 10, 12, 14, 16)
   944–946: 174, 287 (n. 32, 36)
   954–955: 246 (n. 111), 271 (n. 232)
   960–1002: 41
   969–973: 264 (n. 109), 265 (n. 136)
   1003–1013: 257 (n. 5), 295 (n. 192), 303 (n. 83)
   1006–1007: 62, 166
   1050–1053: 303 (n. 80)
   1070–1073: 187, 303 (nn. 79, 81)
   1124–1127: 254 (n. 227), 303 (n. 83)
   1156–1159: 303 (n. 81)
   1158: 257 (n. 9)
   1173: 246 (n. 111)

350 Index of Passages Cited

1177: 246 (n. 111)
1179–1180: 257 (nn. 5, 7)
1197–1199: 246 (n. 111)
1220–1223: 274 (n. 270)
1273–1274: 246 (n. 111), 295 (nn. 187, 191)
1278: 295 (n. 191)
1285–1287: 260 (n. 35), 303 (n. 81)
1298–1300: 247 (n. 112), 266 (n. 139)
1328: 246 (n. 111)
1331–1332: 247 (n. 113)
1336–1337: 241 (n. 27)
1354: 246 (n. 111)
1370–1371: 241 (n. 27)
1375–1379: 172, 192
1381–1384: 246 (n. 111), 288 (nn. 66, 67)
1409–1410: 295 (nn. 197, 201)
1427–1428: 266 (n. 136)
1432–1434: 247 (n. 112)
1456–1504: 250 (n. 168)
1461: 39
1472–1473: 247 (n. 113), 265 (n. 136)
1480: 22
1486–1487: 246 (nn. 106, 108)
1489–1490: 246 (n. 109)
1491–1495: 303 (n. 81)
1500–1504: 250 (n. 168)
1509: 39
1518–1538: 246 (n. 109)
1521: 39
1522–1535: 41
1534–1538: 290 (nn. 93, 97, 110), 291 (nn. 112, 115)
1544–1552: 39
1552–1555: 246 (n. 109)
1555: 39
1556–1578: 29, 40, 242 (n. 44)
1578: 270 (n. 220)
1580–1583: 39

1597–1603: 273 (n. 266), 303 (n. 79)
1606: 300 (n. 34)
1612–1613: 39
1623–1628: 264 (n. 106)
1636–1637: 263 (n. 87)
1658–1682: 40
1689–1692: 39, 242 (n. 44)
1701: 39
1704–1708: 39, 270 (n. 220), 274 (n. 277)
1726: 41
1756–1767: 41
1764–1765: 246 (n. 109)
1767: 263 (nn. 81, 87)
1775: 39
OT: 28–29, 56–58, 99–100, 110–113, 168
19–21: 56
22–30: 54
34: 243 (n. 56)
35–39: 242 (n. 33)
40–43: 56
68–111: 56, 112
69–72: 113, 269 (n. 209), 270 (n. 214)
86–136: 110
95–111: 54, 56, 269 (n. 209)
96: 270 (n. 214)
97: 168
100–101: 168
132–136: 269 (n. 209)
133: 270 (n. 214)
149–150: 56, 58, 113, 269 (n. 209), 270 (n. 214)
151–215: 58
163: 270 (n. 214)
172–174: 59
190: 251 (n. 199)
200–203: 250 (n. 168)
236–275: 168
236–243: 286 (n. 16)
241–245: 110, 269 (n. 209)

Index of Passages Cited 351

244–245: 22, 243 (n. 56)
263: 242 (n. 38)
269–271: 54, 252 (n. 201)
274–275: 277 (n. 7)
278–281: 112, 270 (n. 214)
284–462: 266 (nn. 137, 139)
284–286: 270 (nn. 211, 214)
297–462: 111
297–299: 265 (nn. 134, 135)
305–309: 110, 269 (n. 209)
312–313: 113, 286 (n. 16)
334–403: 99
376–377: 270 (nn. 211, 215)
387–396: 99, 112
406–407: 111
410: 270 (n. 211)
455–464: 246 (n. 109)
469–470: 250 (n. 168)
483–486: 111, 265 (n. 134), 266 (n. 141)
498–501: 111, 112
558–573: 99, 112
603–604: 112
646–648: 167, 193
653: 286 (n. 11), 295 (n. 194)
705: 99
708–725: 111
711–714: 110, 112, 264 (n. 108)
712: 270 (n. 214)
720–722: 270 (n. 215)
723–725: 112
738: 270 (n. 215)
747: 268 (n. 188)
774–793: 264 (n. 104)
787–793: 24, 110, 190, 264 (nn. 108, 109)
788: 270 (n. 214)
815–816: 28
828–829: 28, 241 (n. 27)
852–854: 111, 264 (n. 108)
863–872: 195, 297 (n. 217)
870–872: 297 (n. 216)
873–879: 291 (n. 113)
883–896: 288 (nn. 56, 67), 289 (nn. 68, 70)
885–886: 241 (n. 26)
898–910: 111, 185, 188
911–921: 270 (n. 216)
912: 241 (n. 26)
946–953: 111
964–972: 105, 111, 112, 268 (n. 186)
965: 270 (n. 211)
967–968: 246 (n. 107)
994–996: 24, 110, 264 (nn. 108, 109)
1011–1013: 174, 270 (n. 214), 287 (n. 32)
1086–1095: 293 (nn. 151, 163)
1193–1196: 28, 29, 241 (n. 29)
1258–1260: 28
1287–1289: 174, 287 (n. 36)
1300–1302: 28, 29
1311: 29, 243 (n. 55)
1327–1328: 28
1329–1330: 29, 270 (n. 215)
1349–1355: 270 (n. 215)
1371–1373: 271 (n. 233)
1378–1379: 241 (n. 26)
1381–1383: 168
1438–1445: 112
1440–1441: 287 (n. 32)
1478–1479: 241 (n. 27), 243 (n. 57)
1518–1520: 112, 287 (n. 32)
Ph.: 67–68
79–85: 289 (n. 72)
331–335: 242 (n. 38)
391–402: 250 (n. 176)
436–437: 222
446–452: 241 (n. 26), 242 (n. 39)
462–463: 241 (n. 27)
484–485: 257 (n. 2), 259 (n. 28)
528–529: 253 (n. 221)
604–613: 95, 266 (nn. 137, 139)
610: 265 (n. 136)

797–798: 242 (n. 44)
841–843: 270 (n. 211)
856–861: 270 (n. 220)
1035–1042: 288 (nn. 65, 67)
1049–1051: 289 (n. 72)
1075–1077: 248 (n. 142), 253 (n. 221)
1095–1100: 241 (n. 27), 250 (n. 168)
1208–1212: 271 (n. 233)
1288–1289: 81, 263 (n. 81)
1324–1325: 81, 263 (n. 81)
1336–1342: 95, 266 (nn. 137, 139)
1347–1348: 57
1409–1451: 255 (n. 246)
1409–1410: 256 (n. 252)
1415: 256 (n. 253)
1423–1430: 66
1439–1440: 256 (n. 253)
1440–1444: 67–68, 176, 256 (n. 253), 272 (n. 254)
1443–1444: 120, 256 (n. 263)
1467–1468: 22
1469–1471: 248 (n. 142), 253 (n. 221)
Tr.: 81, 221–224
 26: 222
 76–81: 90, 264 (n. 109)
 126–128: 302 (n. 75)
 139–140: 302 (n. 75)
 164–172: 222, 264 (n. 109)
 182–183: 248 (n. 140)
 200–201: 222
 237–241: 222, 248 (n. 140)
 251–280: 302 (n. 75)
 254–257: 81
 260–283: 261 (n. 58)
 280–283: 285 (n. 139), 290 (n. 111), 291 (nn. 114, 115)
 287–288: 222, 248 (n. 140)
 303–306: 222
 378: 262 (n. 70)
 398–399: 262 (n. 70)
 427–428: 262 (n. 70)
 436–437: 222, 250 (n. 168), 262 (n. 70)
 476: 283 (n. 99)
 491–492: 284 (n. 131)
 499–500: 302 (n. 75)
 653–654: 240 (n. 20), 249 (n. 161)
 750–754: 222, 248 (n. 140)
 760–761: 248 (n. 140)
 772–784: 262 (n. 70)
 807–809: 174
 821–830: 90, 264 (n. 109)
 909–911: 241 (n. 29)
 993–1003: 222
 993–995: 294 (n. 168)
 1000–1002: 58
 1021–1022: 302 (n. 75)
 1037: 287 (nn. 32, 43)
 1040–1043: 242 (n. 44), 270 (n. 220)
 1085: 242 (n. 44)
 1086–1088: 222, 250 (n. 168)
 1159–1174: 90, 222, 264 (n. 109)
 1173: 271 (n. 232)
 1185–1224: 81
 1185–1190: 222, 263 (n. 81)
 1189–1191: 173
 1191–1216: 222
 1239–1240: 81
 1245–1251: 172, 174
 1278: 302 (n. 75)
Fragments [R]
 247: 294 (n. 181)
 472: 80, 167
 524: 250 (n. 168)
 646: 241 (nn. 26, 27)
 653: 241 (n. 27)
 698: 271 (n. 232)
 710: 57
 724: 249 (n. 161)

771: 264 (n. 111)
837: 272 (n. 256)
922: 277 (n. 7)
932: 263 (n. 85)

933: 263 (n. 89)
951: 242 (n. 38), 270 (n. 219)
Other fragments
    4[P]: 275 (n. 291), 288 (nn. 65, 67)

General Index

This index includes topics and the names of historical figures and of cult deities and heroes. The names of the characters (human and divine) of the tragedies are not included. For references to general discussions or passages of the individual tragedies, see the Index of Passages Cited.

Abstractions, personified as deities, 135, 158, 161, 262 (n. 68)
Acamas, 30
Achilles, as cult hero, 37–38, 61
Aeacidae, 30, 260 (n. 39)
Aeacus, 30
Aegeus, as cult hero, 30
Aether, 32–33, 97–99, 114–115, 120, 128, 195, 209, 231, 235
Aetiological myths, 4, 13–14, 216, 223, 226, 229–231
Afterlife, 98, 103, 114–121, 169–170, 193–194; rewards and punishments in, 74, 115, 119–121, 174–175, 209–213
Agriculture and animal husbandry, 46–48, 53–56, 63–64, 105, 152–153, 158, 184, 205–219 passim, 226
Ajax, as cult hero, 30
Amphiaraus, as cult hero, 101–102, 290 (n. 102)
Anaxagoras, 105, 234, 306 (n. 120)
Anaximenes, 234

Anthropomorphism, ix–xi, 3–5, 201, 203, 218–219, 226–227, 233–236
Antiochos, as cult hero, 30
Aphrodite, as cult deity, 4, 63–64, 146–147, 224
Apollo: as cult deity, 57, 84; of Delion, 125; Delios, 228; Pythios, 29–30, 88, 92, 101, 111, 113; of Zoster, 228
Ares, as cult deity, 21
Arrephoria, 230
Artemis: as cult deity, 61, 67, 146–147, 235; of Brauron, 230, 252 (n. 202); Eukleia, 58; of Halae, 230; Limenitis, 253 (n. 219); Neosoös, 253 (n. 219); Tauropolos, 21
Asclepios, 4, 31, 33, 39, 57, 101–102, 218
Aspasia, 174
Asylum, xi, 5, 30, 34, 36, 41, 62, 69–77, 120, 126, 134, 153, 155, 160–167 passim, 176, 178, 180, 191–196, 206, 209–227 passim, 232–233
Athena: as cult deity, 55, 60, 102; of Bronze House, 70; Hippia, 224; Hygieia, 4, 10, 102; Moria, 224; of Pallene, 34; Polias, 4, 10–11, 33–34, 70, 74; Skiras, 10
Athenians, piety of, 40, 62–64, 152–153, 156–157, 166, 216–217, 224, 233, 262 (n. 76)

Bacis, 92

Battle. *See* War
Brasidas, 292 (n. 141)

Cecrops, 30
Children, 59–60, 64, 146, 153, 171–175, 184–185, 205, 210, 216, 226; killing of, 62, 83–84, 124, 168, 171; oracles about, 59, 88–91, 207. *See also* Parents
Choes, 230
Chresmologues, 92, 97
Cimon, 30
Cleomenes, 70
Cleon, 228–229
Codrus, 215
Colonization, 30, 88–89, 92, 207
Colonus, 224
Curses, 23–25, 28, 40–41, 54–55, 59–60, 95, 172–173, 192, 214, 219–220; in oaths, 80–81, 167
Cychreus, 30
Cylon, 69–70, 74, 215

Daimones, 17–29, 35–36, 43–46, 50, 63, 65, 114, 134–136, 206, 209, 232
Death, 25–28, 47, 114–131, 141, 170, 183, 208–209; causes of, 24–28, 68, 114, 205–206, 208–209; prayers to dead, 12, 36, 115–119, 209. *See also* Afterlife; Funeral rites; Pollution; Tomb cult
Dedications, 4–5, 49–50, 60, 154, 162–163, 175–177, 188–191, 197, 213, 268 (n. 186)
Demeter: as cult deity, 4, 55–56, 84, 177, 224; Euchloös, 224
Deus ex machina, 64–68, 205; and new cults, 42–44, 66–67, 89, 230; and prophecy, 65–66, 106–107, 208
Dexion, 39, 218
Diagoras of Melos, 177–178, 254 (n. 226), 282 (n. 81)
Diogenes of Apollonia, 99, 234

Diogenes the Cynic, 254 (n. 226)
Dionysus, as cult deity, 55, 70, 224
Diopeithes, 265 (n. 125)
Dioscuroi, as cult deities, 33, 39, 61
Dreams, 94, 101–104, 107–110, 113, 117, 129, 208

Echetlos, 244 (n. 61), 292 (n. 141)
Eclipses, and divination, 93, 104, 163
Eirene, 53
Eleusinian Mysteries, 20, 55–56, 177, 224, 272 (n. 256), 282 (n. 81)
Enyalios, as cult deity, 21
Erechtheus, as cult hero, 30, 32–34, 67
Erinyes, in cult. *See* Semnai, as cult deities
Eucleides, 93
Eumenides, in cult. *See* Semnai, as cult deities
Euphron, 292 (n. 141)

Fate, 17–18, 22–29, 66, 114, 205–206, 209
First fruit offerings, 32–33, 35, 49, 54, 60, 185
Fortune, 17–18, 22–29, 45–46, 114, 163, 205–206, 209
Funeral rites, 5, 9, 36, 62, 69, 71, 116, 121–130, 134, 139–144, 153, 158–163, 170, 175–179, 182, 193–197, 206, 219–221, 227, 231–233

Gaia, as cult figure, 55, 84

Hades, as cult deity, 24, 26–27
Halon, 31, 39, 218
Health and healing, 31, 47–48, 56–58, 64, 153, 168, 184, 205, 210, 215–216, 219, 226; and divination, 56–57, 88–89, 94, 101–102, 110–113, 207–208; and pollution, 56–57, 110–113, 168
Hecate, 31, 83–84
Helios, 83–84

Hera, as cult deity, 70
Heracles: as cult deity, 33, 39; Menytes, 39, 218
Heraclitus, 6, 234
Hero cult, 29–46, 89, 118, 120, 123, 186, 207, 209, 213–214, 218, 224; and asylum, 74; and colonization, 30; and healing, 31, 57
Hierocles, 92
Hippolytus, as cult hero, 42
Hippothoön, 30
Homeric epic: afterlife in, 209; deities in, ix, 4, 18–22, 51–52, 56–58, 65, 143–144, 203–205, 214, 218, 225, 230–231, 233; divination in, 95, 208
Homicide, 5, 62–63, 110–113, 120, 124, 168–174, 183–184, 198–199, 201, 213–216; of children, 62, 83–84, 124, 168, 171; of suppliants, 70–71, 73; victim's wrath at, 116–117, 169–170; of *xenos*, 77, 79. See also Pollution
Hyacinthia, 230
Hyacinthus, 33
Hybris, 60, 72, 126–127, 136, 143–144, 149, 155, 159–160, 179–183, 197, 232
Hygiainon, 228–229
Hymns, 57, 177, 189–191, 197, 212

Iatros, 31

Justice of the gods, ix–x, 1, 3, 48, 51–53, 60, 63, 74–75, 82–84, 86–87, 120, 136–140, 155–156, 161, 178, 184, 203, 206–207, 211–218, 225–226, 229, 234–235; and piety, 82–84, 135–136, 178–179, 199–201, 206, 209

Lampon, 92
Leos, 30
Loyalty to country. *See* Treason
Lysander, 126

Musaeus, 92

Nicias, 20, 60, 93, 125, 162–164, 210, 218

Oaths, 5, 7, 32–35, 54–55, 60–69 passim, 80–87, 129–131, 135–136, 144, 153, 158–168 passim, 175, 178, 182, 191–193, 196, 206–216 passim, 221–222, 227–229, 233, 275 (nn. 299, 302); curses in, 80–81, 167
Oeneus, 30
Omens, 20–21, 35, 47, 66, 88, 92–96, 99, 102–106, 112, 129, 160, 163, 208, 213
Oracles, 20, 23–24, 29–37 passim, 41, 56–59, 66, 88–94, 103–114, 129, 137–138, 168, 176, 184–185, 190, 205–208, 222, 250 (n. 176)
Orpheus, 43–44, 92

Pandion, 30
Parents: religious responsibilities towards, 5, 64, 120, 122, 124, 130, 162, 169–175, 178, 191–192, 195–199, 206–209, 212, 227; responsibilities of, 124, 171, 173, 175
Pausanias of Sparta, 70
Peloponnesian War, religious incidents in, 20–21, 57, 69–70, 92–93, 97, 124–125, 156–157, 162–164, 210, 254 (n. 223), 262 (n. 62), 268 (n. 186), 269 (n. 210), 275 (n. 303)
Pericles, 18–19, 21, 46, 58, 69–70, 92, 102, 105, 174, 190, 194, 202
Perjury. *See* Oaths
Persian Wars, religious incidents in, 30–31, 125, 222, 250 (n. 171), 254 (n. 223), 275 (n. 299)
Philosophical theory, ix, xi, 1, 5–10 passim, 22, 48, 99, 105, 115, 120, 136, 141, 148, 156, 178–179, 195, 198, 203, 207, 209, 212, 219, 225–226, 233–236
Phrynichus, 124
Pisistratus, 21, 294 (n. 177)

Plague. *See* Health and healing
Plouton, 252 (n. 208)
Pollution, 175, 214; of adultery, 174; of death, 27, 73, 123–124, 128, 141, 170, 219; and divination, 88–89, 110–113, 141; and health, 56–57, 110–113, 168; of homicide, 54–57, 110–113, 168–171, 174; and human fertility, 59; of incest, 174; and sacrifice and prayers, 128, 141, 168–169; and sailing, 62; and violation of asylum, 69–73
Poseidon: as cult deity, 61; Erechtheus, 33–34; Hippios, 224
Prayer, 5, 22, 27, 37–38, 49–53, 56–61, 64, 76, 96–98, 102–103, 109, 113, 135, 147, 158, 162, 177, 189, 199, 213, 247 (n. 127); to dead, 12, 36, 115–119, 209; and pollution, 128, 141, 168–169; unanswered, 12, 83, 136, 155–156, 161, 282 (n. 81)
Prodicus, 234, 281 (n. 76), 306 (n. 120)
Prometheus, as cult figure, 48, 224
Prophets. *See* Seers
Protagoras, 254 (n. 226), 306 (n. 120)

Sacrifice, 5, 12, 22, 27, 30, 35, 54, 123, 136, 145, 150, 154, 158, 162–163, 169, 171, 175, 177, 183–192 passim, 197–201, 213, 215, 227–228, 231–232, 247 (n. 127); and divination, 47, 49–50, 88–89, 92–99, 102–106, 160; human, 62, 108, 235; and pollution, 128, 141, 168–169
Sailing and voyages, 37–38, 47–48, 61–63, 67, 105, 153, 171, 192, 205, 210, 219; and divination, 66, 94, 96, 104, 208
Seers, 6, 8, 11–12, 47, 60, 66–67, 92–114, 129, 135, 139–142, 147–150, 153, 159–163, 176, 180–181, 198, 205, 208
Semnai, as cult deities, 13–14, 70, 214–217, 235
Soothsayers. *See* Seers

Sophrosyne, 143, 179–182, 184, 209, 235
Sthorys, 92–93
Suppliants. *See* Asylum

Telamon, 30
Themistocles, 124
Theomachoi, 147–152, 158–162, 177–178, 182, 188–189, 206
Theseus, as cult hero, 30–31, 44, 207
Tomb cult, 5, 35–38, 115–124, 170–172, 193–194, 207
Treason, 5, 124, 126, 128, 140, 160, 175–176, 181, 190–191, 227

Unwritten laws, 127, 139–142, 161, 170–171, 191, 194–197, 209–210

Vows, 49–50, 60
Voyages. *See* Sailing and voyages

War, 21, 30–35, 40, 49–53, 63–64, 143–144, 152–153, 159–160, 163, 176–177, 180, 185, 189–190, 205, 210, 213, 216, 222, 224; burial of dead, 125–128, 194; and divination, 20–21, 30, 35, 49–50, 66, 88–89, 92–94, 102–106, 208, 213; killing of enemy, 169
Wealth, 60–61, 136, 163, 184, 205, 210, 216, 226; and divination, 60, 88, 93, 163, 208
Weather (lightning, rain, thunder, wind), 37–38, 46–47, 53–55, 61, 63, 88, 101–102, 104–105, 158–159, 186, 196, 211, 215, 222

Xenia, 5, 27, 35, 41, 62, 69, 77–80, 83, 120, 129–130, 134, 136, 139, 157–167 passim, 178, 191–192, 195–197, 206, 209, 211–212, 227
Xenophanes, 234
Xenophon, 93, 101–102, 218

Zeus, as cult deity, 61, 84, 101–102, 156, 170; Agonios, 222; Agoraios, 258 (n. 20); Basileus, 101–102; Boulaios, 204; Herkeios, 4, 154, 204, 278 (n. 27), 283 (n. 112); Hikesios, 74–75, 77, 167, 196, 211–212; Horios, 204; Horkios, 83–84, 196, 222; Kenaios, 222; Ktesios, 4, 60, 204, 252 (n. 210); Meilichios, 60, 93; Morios, 224; Naios, 88, 92, 204, 222; Oitaios, 222; Olympios, 204; Olympios of Syracuse, 163; Phratrios, 204; Soter, 204, 221–222, 231; Synaimos, 278 (n. 27); Teleios, 204; Tropaios, 222, Xenios, 77, 158, 167, 192, 196, 211–212